# The Structure of Social Stratification in the United States

## FOURTH EDITION

## Leonard Beeghley

*University of Florida*

Boston   New York   San Francisco
Mexico City   Montreal   Toronto   London   Madrid   Munich   Paris
Hong Kong   Singapore   Tokyo   Cape Town   Sydney

*For MAH*

**Senior Editor:**  *Jeff Lasser*
**Editorial Assistant:**  *Sära Owen*
**Marketing Manager:**  *Krista Groshong*
**Production Administrator:**  *Marissa Falco*
**Editorial Production Service:**  *Holly Crawford*
**Electronic Composition:**  *Peggy Cabot*
**Composition and Prepress Buyer:**  *Linda Cox*
**Manufacturing Buyer:**  *JoAnne Sweeney*
**Cover Administrator:**  *Kristina Mose-Libon*

For related titles and support materials, visit our online catalog at www.ablongman.com

Between the time Website information is gathered and then published, it is not unusual for some sites to have closed. Also, the transcription of URLs can result in unintended typographical errors. The publisher would appreciate notification where these occur so that they may be corrected in subsequent editions.

**Library of Congress Cataloging-in-Publication Data**

Beeghley, Leonard.
    The structure of social stratification in the United States / Leonard Beeghley.—4th ed.
       p.  cm.
    Includes bibliographical references and index.
    ISBN 0-205-37558-8 (pbk.)
      1. Social classes—United States.   2. Social stratification—United States.   3. Social structure—United States.  I. Title.
    HN90.S6B44 2005
    305.5'0973—dc22

                                          2003065961

Printed in the United States of America

10  9  8  7  6  5  4  3       RRD-VA  09  08  07  06  05

# Contents

## 8   *The Middle Class      183*

## 9   *The Working Class      211*

# *Preface*

In this book, I have tried to distill out of the rich vein of sociological research some of what is known about the *structure of stratification* in the United States. The term refers to the distribution of resources in society, such as income, prestige, and power. The structure of stratification affects every aspect of life: where (and whether) one lives, whom one marries, how (and whether) one earns a living, who one's friends are, and much more. In revising the book, my objective has been to make each chapter factually accurate, interesting to read, and relevant to readers' lives. In the process, the book has been completely reorganized, updated, and rewritten for this fourth edition.

In making these revisions, I have tried to keep in mind that science is the art of asking questions. But questions are always asked in light of an intellectual framework—which needs to be explicit. In Chapter 1, the ideas of the most important theorists of stratification are reviewed and a coherent strategy for studying stratification is developed and used throughout the book. This strategy has three elements: First, as often as possible, I place data in a historical and cross-national context. This information leads to important questions. For example, if the rate of poverty has fallen in all Western societies (and it has), one wants to know why. But if, even given the historical decline, the rate of poverty in the United States is much higher than the rate in Western Europe (and it is), one again wants to know why. Second, I distinguish between social psychological explanations of individual actions and structural explanations of rates of behavior. Just as one obtains different insight from examining a painting up close and afar, these two levels of analysis provide complementary but different insights into social life. For example, the reasons why individuals become poor (for example, they lack skills) have nothing whatsoever to do with why so many people are poor (for example, macroeconomic policy restricts the number of jobs that are available whenever it is necessary to control inflation). There is an enduring insight here: Regardless of the topic, the variables explaining why individuals act differ from those explaining why rates of behavior vary. This fact will be illustrated throughout the book. This distinction aids in understanding issues as diverse as poverty, mobility, voting, gender stratification, and racial/ethnic stratification. Third, I emphasize the importance of power for understanding the structure of stratification. The story of the last century is one of increasing control over human affairs. As just one example, nations now control how much inequality and poverty exist. Hence, the periodic use of macroeconomic policy to restrict the number of jobs provides one example (there are others) of how poverty is created and maintained in this country. More generally, I argue that the level of inequality in the United States reflects the power of the rich and middle class to protect their lifestyles. Again, there is an enduring insight here: *The higher the social class, the greater the influence over the distribution of resources in the society.*

This statement is introduced in Chapter 1 as the Political Power Hypothesis. It is just one of many hypotheses and findings presented in the book. The importance of hypothesis testing is emphasized throughout. This is, in part, a pedagogical device. It illustrates for students (rather than merely asserting) the possibilities of scientific sociology by showing both how much we know and, by implication, how much remains to be learned. Most hypotheses and empirical generalizations (stable findings) are phrased as statements of covariance. This tactic shows students how a change in one phenomenon is associated with change in another. This point is typically made in methods and (less often) theory courses, but neglected elsewhere. Too frequently, I think, text writers give the impression that sociological knowledge depends on the assumptions observers make. Nothing could be further from the truth. In part, however, the emphasis on hypothesis testing is also a statement about the nature of social science. If science is the art of asking questions, then our answers must reflect knowledge based on observation.

Yet how observations are to be interpreted remains a vexing issue. In the study of stratification, for example, the relationship among class, race, and gender as systems of ranking has become controversial in recent years. Throughout this book, I try to show how they are interrelated. Minorities remain unequal to Whites; women remain unequal to men. This inequality reflects the historical legacy and continuing impact of prejudice and discrimination. Yet these forms of inequality have declined in recent years. In considering these issues, the larger question is the degree to which people's location in the stratification structure is determined by birth or achievement. One of the paradoxes of modernity is that our very concern with gender and racial/ethnic stratification reflects a degree of movement (I would say progress) toward class-based stratification structures. When societies are stratified by class, unlike medieval estates, there is an increased emphasis on achievement. This historical transformation is one example of what I meant earlier in saying that people and, indeed, entire societies, now have greater control over how they organize themselves.

*The Structure of Social Stratification in the United States* is written primarily for students, but also for general readers who want to know more about how the distribution of resources occurs. I have tried to write simply and clearly. Although some jargon is unavoidable, I have kept it to a minimum. When technical terms are necessary, they are introduced, defined, and illustrated. Even so, most textbooks are boring. Having taught social stratification for over 25 years, I have found that the use of metaphors, vignettes, even nursery rhymes, can be useful pedagogical devices. So I sometimes invent people, families, and situations in order to introduce or describe sociological findings. Occasionally, these episodes are (I hope) mildly humorous. Underlying such efforts at relieving the tedium, however, is a serious issue: The great world trend has been movement in the direction of more democracy and less inequality (the two are connected). The United States is thus part of a great historical process. I am convinced that sociology can and should inform public debate about it.

*L. B.*

# Acknowledgments

No author works alone. I would like to take this opportunity to thank those individuals who helped in the process of revising this book. My most enduring debts are to George Wilson of the University of Miami and to Marion Willetts of Illinois State University.

Each took time out of their busy lives to read much of manuscript and make valuable suggestions. Their comments and criticisms were extremely useful, often at crucial times. In addition, my student Rachel Bird read the entire manuscript and helped me clarify the prose. My editor at Allyn & Bacon, Jeff Lasser, has been very helpful throughout the project. Finally, the support of colleagues and friends is one of the joys of academic life. This book is better as a result and probably would be better yet if I had just had the good sense to take more of the advice offered. The usual caveat applies: Any errors that remain are my responsibility.

# 1

# *Sociology and Stratification*

All societies display stratification. The term conveys an image of geological strata, of layers stacked one upon the other. Like geological strata, societies are also composed of interconnected layers that display a ranked structure. The **structure of social stratification** can be defined as the distribution of resources in society, such as income, wealth, occupational prestige, education, and power. Possession of these resources affects people's **life chances,** their ability to share in the available goods and services.[1] It also affects people's **lifestyle,** their consumption habits, use of leisure time, and fundamental values. Although geological strata may appear to be static and unchanging, this is misleading. In reality, dynamic processes shape the formation of the earth, which means that understanding the geological record requires looking at both stability and change. This orientation is also necessary when studying stratification.

One indicator of the dynamic processes shaping the stratification structure is the degree of inequality in the distribution of resources. Conflict over possession of resources is inherent to social life. People and groups struggle to keep and expand their share (of

---

[1]Weber (1968:843, 924). Weber wrote that the term *life chance* refers to members of a class who share a common "market situation," meaning that "similar economic exigencies . . . causally influence the material standards of their existence."

1

income and wealth, for example) and thereby enhance their life chances and lifestyles. Imagine that all the goods and services available in a society are like a pie. Everyone competes, both as individuals and as members of groups, for a piece of the pie. And no one wants to diet; everyone wants a bigger piece, at least so long as it is obtained fairly. The issue can be expressed by a simple question: Who gets what and why? The answer is reflected in the three systems of ranking that characterize modern societies.[2]

The first is by class. People in the same **class** tend to be equal to one another in terms of the distribution of resources. For example, those with similar levels of occupational prestige display roughly similar levels of income and education. People in different classes tend to be unequal in these same terms. Such variations affect people's life chances and lifestyles. For example, because they differ in income, they also differ in housing location and size, alcohol consumption, health, and even mate selection. As a system of ranking, class is rather new in history. It arose with economic development and democracy as these came into being over the last few centuries. Although birth, shown by the social class of one's family of origin, affects people's initial class placement and plays a role throughout their lives, educational and occupational achievement become more important in class systems. The latter makes class systems unique.

The second system of ranking is by race and ethnicity. Members of racial and ethnic groups are often unequal to one another in terms of income, occupational prestige, and other resources. For example, due to prejudice and discrimination, fewer minority group members are middle class than Whites. Even within the middle class, members of minority groups are often unequal to Whites. This is partly because they still endure prejudice and discrimination. Their life chances are restricted as a result. Even so, racial and ethnic inequality has declined over the last two centuries as achievement-related criteria have become more important.

The third system of ranking is by gender. Women and men are unequal to one another in terms of income, occupational prestige, and other resources. Historically, discrimination in the form of traditional gender norms meant that women have not only had less access to resources than men but also less autonomy in shaping their lives. Their life chances have differed and differ today as well. Gender inequality has declined over time, however, as both women and men are increasingly evaluated by their educational and occupational achievements.

Another indicator of the dynamic processes shaping the stratification structure is the degree of emphasis on ascription versus achievement, factors that are implicit in the three systems of ranking described above. **Ascription** refers to the use of non-performance-related criteria in evaluating a person, such as class of origin, race/ethnicity, or gender. This is a complicated way of saying that people obtain positions based on birth. For example, the extent to which certain types of people—say, white males—have advantages in seeking to become physicians indicates an emphasis on ascription. **Achievement** refers to the use of performance-related criteria that are equally applied to all persons when they are evaluated, such as grade point averages, college degrees, or skill requirements. This is a complicated way of saying that people obtain positions based on hard work and ability. The extent to which anyone—regardless of class of origin, race/ethnicity, or gender—

[2]The image of society as like a pie comes from Lieberson (1980). The simple question, as will become clear, comes from Lenski (1984).

can become a physician based on grades and other skills indicates an emphasis on achievement.

In no society, of course, does either ascription or achievement constitute the sole basis for evaluating people. Seen as two ends of a continuum, they are "pure types," to use a phrase of Max Weber's. But history reveals a pattern, at least in economically developed societies: On the one hand, ascription remains important. People's family background in the form of class of origin, race/ethnicity, and gender all affect access to resources and, hence, life chances, regardless of how much ability people have or how hard they work. As shall be emphasized, it makes a difference if one is born rich or poor, white or brown, male or female. On the other hand, achievement has become more important over the last few centuries, and it also affects life chances. Increased opportunity exists; people can now advance compared to their parents, occupationally and in other ways, based on their abilities. This change means that modern societies display a built-in tension that can never be fully resolved.

In sociology, the dynamic processes producing variation in both the level of inequality and the degree of emphasis on ascription or achievement in modern societies are called "structural changes." The term **social structure** refers to the way context affects action, leading to predictable rates of behavior. It is a sociological truism that understanding the context in which people choose is as (or more) important than understanding their specific choices. As will be explained later, an interrelated set of structural changes lead to the rise of class-based systems of stratification with their greater variability in the level of inequality and increased emphasis on achievement. This fact implies something new in history: Societies can now control how resources are distributed.

## Theoretical Perspectives on Stratification

The social sciences are relatively young disciplines. The first generation of sociologists did not appear until the nineteenth century. Although the scholars reviewed here made mistakes, some of which I will mention, they also confronted many of the key problems faced by any nascent science: developing a model of the stratification structure, learning to ask testable questions, obtaining objective empirical data, and forming tentative abstract hypotheses.[3]

## Karl Marx

The background for Marx's ideas lies in the huge increase in productivity that resulted from industrialization and the rise of capitalism. Marx emphasized that these two structural changes shaped the modern world—including the structure of stratification.

According to Marx, the combined impact of industrialization and capitalism led to a rapid and permanent increase in inequality. The key word here, as you will see, is his view

---

[3]The following sketches are necessarily brief and I have avoided citing the secondary sources. For more extended commentary on Marx and Weber, see Turner, Beeghley, and Powers (2002). On the modern theorists, see Turner (2003).

that this increase is "permanent." The result was a paradox in the middle of the nineteenth century: Although technological advance meant huge increases in productivity, only a few people actually benefited: the very rich who owned capital (income-producing assets). He observed that the capitalists were the most powerful class and that they exploited the masses, who lived in great misery and deprivation.

Marx was both a revolutionary and a sociologist. Marx the revolutionary sought to stimulate the masses to overthrow capitalism. The communists, he said, would substitute collective control of society by the people, who would act cooperatively to reduce the level of inequality so that everyone's needs could be met. In such a context, everyone would be free to develop their full potential as human beings. Marx the sociologist developed a theory that appeared to show such collective control is historically inevitable. The result, he wrote in the *Communist Manifesto,* would be a communist society in which "the free development of each is the condition for the free development of all."[4] In this new society, Marx believed, the powerful few would no longer exploit the many.

In developing his theory, Marx began with the idea that only human beings produce goods to satisfy their needs, which he called the "materialist conception of history." He meant that people's social relationships and values reflect productive activity. This insight has endured; it is one (although not the only) way of describing how the context affects action. But capitalist societies, Marx wrote in the *Manifesto,* were unique in history. Wherever capitalism and industrialization combine, huge bursts in productivity occurred. Their inherent dynamism led to the continuous creation of new modes of production (for example, computers). In the process, small tradespeople lost out as large companies undercut their prices (for example, when Wal-Mart enters a town). Moreover, capitalism was spreading around the world (today we call this process "globalization"), destroying traditional cultures wherever it appeared. In so doing, capitalism was also creating a homogeneous worldwide culture (a McDonald's in every city). Although Marx wrote the *Manifesto* in 1848, the parenthetical comments suggest that he had great insight into the nature of capitalism, even by today's standards.

In this new historical context, Marx continued, not only does inequality increase permanently but also the stratification structure becomes more rigid, without much opportunity for advancement. A small class of owners controls the distribution of resources. It follows that they have a stake in maintaining the status quo and protecting their wealth, which they do by dominating the government and affecting public policies. When he looked at social arrangements, Marx always asked a simple question, one that modern sociologists also ask: Who benefits? For example, in his greatest work, *Capital,* he showed how the capitalists' attempts at lengthening the working day and raising productivity in order to secure greater profit for themselves also increased workers' exploitation.[5] In every arena—at home, at work, in court, at church, and in the doctor's office—Marx argued, it is useful to ascertain who benefits from current social arrangements. The answer usually suggests which classes are the most powerful in a society.

The answer also suggests which classes are relatively powerless; that is, their members usually find it hard to overcome the disadvantages with which they are born. Because

---

[4]Marx and Engels (1848:112). Although both Marx and Engels's names are on the published version, Marx wrote the final draft of the *Manifesto* (see Turner, Beeghley, and Powers, 2002).
[5]Marx (1867).

they do not own capital, most people must sell their ability to work in order to survive. This necessity means they continually recreate their own exploitation. Because auto-workers, for example, need cars in which to get to work each day, they return their wages to the company and its stockholders (most of whom are rich and powerful). This is a generalized process: As they go about obtaining goods and services, working people return nearly all their income to the capitalists. The capitalists, in turn, reinvest their profits to make still more money. As Marx put it in *Capital,* "the circle in which simple reproduction moves alters its form and . . . changes into a spiral."[6] He meant that the exploitation of working people by capitalists is a self-perpetuating social structure.

Strangely, however, even though their interest lies in changing this social structure, most workers accept the status quo. According to Marx, this acceptance occurs because the schools, the media, government, and even religion teach them that their own exploitation is right and proper. For example, he argued that "religion is the sigh of the oppressed creature—the opium of the masses."[7] He meant that religion diverts people's attention from their exploitation in this world by promising an illusion: happiness in the next world. Thus, he asserted, the nonobvious impact of religious teaching is to make the masses blind to their interest in overthrowing capitalism, thereby benefiting those who desire to maintain it: the capitalists. In this context, Marx said, alienation is widespread. That is, most people see themselves as powerless, unable to control their own lives; and, most importantly, they do not understand that they are being exploited or how it is accomplished. The pervasiveness of alienation is a dominant theme in Marx's work. It constitutes the standard by which he judged societies. In a nonalienated world, inequality would be less and the stratification structure would be relatively open so that people could move up based on achievement. But such opportunities, Marx believed (incorrectly), could not occur in capitalist societies.

Marx divided the stratification structure into two parts: the bourgeoisie (capitalists) and proletarians (working class). This two-class division allowed him to emphasize that class conflict pervades all societies and constitutes the mechanism for historical change— the vehicle that would lead to a communist revolution. Thus, he believed, the transition from capitalism to communism was inevitable because capitalists created both the productive forces necessary for a communist society and the people capable of making a revolution: proletarians. He predicted their number would increase over time and they would become steadily poorer and more alienated as inequality increased. In the context of ever-worsening economic crises caused by overproduction, Marx claimed, proletarians would become class conscious: They would not only understand how they were being exploited but also be willing to act to change the situation. With help from the Communist Party, the proletarians would revolt against capitalism.

The proletarians, Marx said in the *Manifesto,* would begin by seizing control of the state, taking all capital from its owners, and centralizing the means of production. Although Marx's goal was human freedom, these measures lead inevitably to totalitarianism. Marx, in fact, forecast a temporary "dictatorship of the proletariat."[8] Nonetheless, Marx was an optimist. The *Manifesto* ends with some of the most famous lines ever

[6]Marx (1867:581).
[7]Marx (1843).
[8]Marx (1875).

written: "Let the ruling classes tremble at a Communist revolution. The Proletarians have nothing to lose but their chains. They have a world to win. WORKING MEN OF ALL COUNTRIES, UNITE!"[9]

Although Marx's apocalyptic vision did not come true, his writings contain important themes that remain relevant to sociological inquiry. The first is the emphasis on social structure. Marx was a structuralist, although he did not use that word. For example, his analysis in the *Manifesto* of the context under which proletarians transform themselves into a class-conscious revolutionary group does not deal with social psychological issues, such as the decision-making processes or cost-benefit calculations of individuals. Rather, he tried to show that urbanity, education, political sophistication, and other factors can lead large numbers of oppressed people to recognize their common condition and revolt. But they do not revolt, at least not in capitalist societies. While capitalism does generate greater inequality initially, Marx failed to see that this inequality is not permanent and usually declines over time. This process is one reason why mass movements of oppressed persons in capitalist societies (not just the working class, but women and minorities as well) have responded by seeking to get into the class system rather than overthrow it. Nonetheless, a structural approach is implicit; that is, he focused on showing how the historical context in which people act affects rates of behavior.

The second theme is the degree of opportunity built into the stratification structure. Marx believed that it was becoming more rigid and that as the masses became steadily poorer they would recognize their situation and overthrow capitalism. Implicit, here, is the idea that ascription would remain—as it always has throughout history—the most important determinant of people's access to valued resources. But he was wrong: The stratification structure in modern capitalist societies is much more open than in the past; it contains built-in opportunity. As it turns out, a relatively high rate of mobility based on achievement occurs in class-based societies. This mobility, both upward and (less often) downward, indicates that ability and hard work are becoming more important for people's life chances. As mentioned earlier, a tension exists between ascription and achievement. What should the proper balance be?

The third theme is the significance of class conflict. Marx believed that class conflict would be the historical mechanism by which a communist society would emerge. Although this grandiose view of history proved incorrect, he was right to emphasize that classes have different and often opposing interests. He was also right in noting that these differences are often hidden by a set of ideological beliefs that seem reasonable on the surface. A key question is thus how values lead to and sometimes veil exploitation. This is another way of recognizing that social facts are not always what they seem to be—an essential sociological orientation. This insight can be applied to the other dimensions of stratification as well: One might wonder, for example, how traditional gender norms hide (or justify) the exploitation of women by men.

The fourth theme is the emphasis on power. For Marx, power was redemptive; that is, when the people held power, they would use it for the common good, to liberate human beings from exploitation. But the people can never rule, at least directly. In every society, including the United States, a small aggregate exercises a great deal of power. This is

---

[9]Marx and Engels (1848:125).

called an **oligarchy.** In those societies that subsequently became communist, the necessity for representation meant total rule by the Communist Party, which justified its position by invoking the common good. This invocation was an ideological veil, however, as the Party functioned much like a feudal aristocracy.[10] The few exploited the many. Despite revolutionary rhetoric, the practical issue is not whether the ends justify the means. It is, rather, can the means produce the ends desired; that is, can power unfettered by accountability produce individual freedom? The answer is no. History shows that capitalist, not communist, societies display less exploitation and alienation, partly because those exercising power are held accountable for their decisions. Capitalist societies tend to be democratic, a fact that Marx did not recognize. Nonetheless, his emphasis on power constitutes an enduring legacy, one that Gerhard Lenski would build upon.

The final theme is the importance of alienation. If, as Marx suggested, alienation ought to be the criterion by which societies are judged, then he had it wrong: Modern capitalist societies display much less alienation than those in the past. But less, even much less, does not mean there is no alienation in capitalist societies. Parts of the population (for instance, the poor, some members of minority groups) are indeed relatively powerless and unable to control their lives. Yet their alienation is often hidden behind an ideological veil. Observers who ask Who benefits? can sometimes pierce the veil.

## *Max Weber*

During the early part of this century, Max Weber rejected Marx's apocalyptic vision of capitalism's demise. Even though he recognized and agreed with many of Marx's insights into the nature of capitalism and its transformative impact, Weber analyzed its significance rather differently. In so doing, he built on Marx's work in three areas.

First, he argued that the structure of stratification in capitalist societies can only be understood by distinguishing between *status* and *class,* terms he used in rather unique ways.[11] Implicit in their use, I argue, is an attempt at distinguishing between what sociologists now call *ascription* and *achievement.* Thus, like Marx, Weber wanted to account for the degree of opportunity built into the stratification structure in modern societies. But unlike Marx, Weber recognized that the rise of capitalism with its increasing emphasis on achievement meant more opportunity.

Some background is necessary before explaining what Weber meant by *class* and *status.* In the traditional societies that existed before capitalism appeared in the seventeenth century, behavior was based on custom, often sanctified by religious belief. In this context, inequality was great and the stratification structure was relatively rigid, with most people's life chances determined at birth. Today, sociologists would describe this situation in terms of a high level of ascription. Modern societies differ. They have been transformed. Just as dynamic forces shape geological strata, an interrelated set of structural changes lead to the rise of modern societies.[12] The factors leading to modernization are important and will be referred to in subsequent chapters.

---

[10]Djilas (1965), Voslenski (1985).
[11]Weber (1920:926).
[12]Weber (1905; 1923). see also Elias (1978), Berger (1986), Kuznets (1955), and Lenski (1984).

First, as Marx understood, with **industrialization** new forms of energy were substituted for muscle power, leading to huge advances in productivity—the indicator of economic development. Moreover, in order to take advantage of this new technology the occupational structure changed in fundamental ways. It led initially to the rise of blue-collar (working-class) jobs and eventually to the dominance of white-collar (middle-class) jobs. Second, as Marx also recognized, **capitalism** gradually became the dominant economic system. The term refers to the production of goods and services in an open market for the purpose of making a profit. Third, the application of science to solve practical problems turned into an organized source for knowledge about the environment, physical and social, leading to industrialization. Continuous technological change based on science has become characteristic of modernity. Fourth, democratic societies arose, with their emphasis on personal freedom and recognition of the innate dignity of every individual. Democracy has become one of the standards by which societies are judged. Fifth, rules of law came to regulate conflict between individuals and groups. One result has been a long-term decline in interpersonal violence as a mechanism for solving disputes; another has been an increase in predictability in human interaction that allows capitalism to flourish. And sixth, all these forces were buttressed by the development of the culture of capitalism as the dominant value orientation in modern societies. Taken together, these structural changes display what Weber called an "elective affinity" for one another; they came into being gradually over the long span of Western history and coalesced in the nineteenth century to produce an engine for change and prosperity never before seen in history. Furthermore, prosperity has a seductive quality that few who experience it can resist. This is why oppressed people do not rebel in economically developed societies.

Although Weber emphasized how these six dynamic processes combined to produce modern societies, he was especially interested in the significance of the last one: the culture of capitalism. He argued that all class-based societies display, in some form, a set of mutually reinforcing values. These values originated in the West and manifest themselves in extreme form in the United States. Some observers, in fact, refer to them as the "American Dream:"[13] (1) *Hard work:* People want to get ahead, to achieve occupational success. Failure to work hard to obtain (or at least strive for) occupational success implies that one does not make a contribution to the society. (2) *Individualism:* People want to "make it" on their own, as individuals. Americans are deeply committed to—obsessed with—notions of individual rights and individual autonomy. Although this emphasis distorts people's view of the world because it implies that individuals make decisions without regard to social context, it also stimulates them to compete with one another, emphasize personal self-reliance, and interpret governmental attempts at regulating their lives skeptically. (3) *Universalism:* In the quest for success, people want to be evaluated based on merit, on objective standards applied equally to all. This stress on merit may be one reason why democracy and capitalism are so closely linked. (4) *Wealth:* Above all, people want to make lots of money. Although he did not use this phrase, Weber argued

---

[13]Weber (1905). See also Turner, Beeghley, and Powers (2002). On these values, see Turner and Musick (1985). On the argument that the United States manifests these values in extreme and that they can be described as the "American Dream," see Messner and Rosenfeld (2001). For a critique of their work, see Beeghley (2003).

that a "fetishism of money" characterizes American society, not only because wealth comprises the standard by which each individual's level of achievement is evaluated but also because it has become a value in itself. (5) *Activism:* People want to master the situations in which they find themselves, ideally in the most efficient way possible. And (6) *Rationality:* In the process of "making it" on their own, Americans want to deal with problems they face methodically, ideally using science and technology to produce solutions. Weber argued that the culture of capitalism combined with the structural changes described above to transform history, ushering in modern societies with their increasing emphasis on achievement.

In this new context, class-based societies arose.[14] Now Weber used the concept *class* narrowly to refer to people's economic situation as indicated by their source and amount of income and other resources, but its implications are broader. The issue is how people are evaluated. People's "class," Weber said, reflects a market situation in which all the values just described apply. As he put it, "class oriented action" is "instrumentally rational" in that means and ends are objectively identified based on knowledge. Class considerations indicate the importance of achievement in modern societies as people strive for economic success.

Yet, birth (in the form of family background) continues to matter. Weber used the concept *status* to get at the continuing impact of ascription. By *status,* he meant the evaluations people make of others' **lifestyle,** as indicated by their consumption habits, use of leisure time, and fundamental choices and values. Some elements of status reflect moral stances while others constitute aesthetic judgments. For example, one's house and its furnishing as well as selection of wine or entertainment (the ballet versus professional wrestling) convey lifestyle. It is also expressed by the educational goals held for children (public school versus prep school, the state university versus Ivy League college). Finally, status is indicated by people's values and how they organize their lives—for example, such basic choices as gender roles in marriage and attitudes toward abortion. Such cases constitute what Weber called "status oriented action." They are "value rational" in the sense that they reflect people's standards of honorable behavior.

Weber's emphasis on status (lifestyle) is important because people understand their class location and actively maintain it. They do so by means of a simple mechanism: **discrimination,** the unequal treatment of individuals and groups based on their personal characteristics. In practice, discrimination results from the fact that lifestyle is rooted in family experience. Before individuals reach maturity, they participate in their family's claim to social prestige, its occupational subculture, and its educational level. They experience its religiosity, suffer its unemployment, and enjoy its leisure pursuits. Thus, even in the absence of formal organization, families in the same class share a style of life, attitudes, and many other characteristics. As a result, people from similar backgrounds need not communicate in order to identify those who are like themselves and discriminate against others who are different. They act in concert without being organized to do so. This fact has significant implications: Weber recognized that status considerations indicate the degree of ascription that occurs in modern, class-based societies.[15]

---

[14]Weber (1920:302,901). Some observers suggest that the United States is becoming a "classless society." See Kingston (2000), Grusky and Weeden (2001).

[15]Controversy exists over whether classes need to be organized in order to discriminate (see Grusky & Sørensen, 1998). Some of the wording in this paragraph comes from Bendix (1974).

For example, even though they are not organized groups, Weber showed that members of each class act to maintain their distinctive lifestyle—they discriminate—in specific ways:[16] (1) People extend hospitality only to social equals. Thus, they tend to invite into their homes, become friends with, eat with, and socialize with, others who are like themselves. (2) People restrict potential marriage partners to social equals. Thus, they tend to live in neighborhoods and send their children to school with youngsters of others who are like themselves, with the result that their offspring generally marry someone with a similar lifestyle. (3) People practice unique social conventions and activities. Thus, they tend to join organizations, such as churches and clubs, and spend their leisure time with others who share similar beliefs and ways of living. Most importantly, (4) people try to obtain and retain "privileged modes of acquisition" and pass them on to their children.

Although he did not use the term, these tactics constitute the mechanism of class conflict in modern societies. As the members of each class compete for their share of the available resources (such as income and wealth), they determine the structure of stratification. In every society, of course, life chances are inherited to some degree and the class structure is reproduced from one generation to another. Yet, as will be shown in Chapter 4, a great deal of mobility occurs in modern societies. To use Weber's language, these facts suggest that class and status are interrelated in that income makes lifestyle possible and lifestyle makes income possible. In today's language, ascription and achievement exist on a continuum, and the greater emphasis on ability and hard work characteristic of modern societies means that there is an inevitable tension between them.

Weber added to Marx's insights in a second way by outlining a model of the class structure in modern societies.[17] Like Marx, Weber began with the recognition that the most fundamental division occurs between those who own capital and those who do not. He continued, however, by identifying additional classes within these two rubrics. The middle class becomes especially significant as economic development occurs.

Among owners of capital, Weber sketched two classes, which he called "rentiers" and "entrepreneurs."[18] "Rentiers" comprise those who live off their investments and pursue a relatively nonacquisitive lifestyle, ranging from public service to indolence. They often inherit their wealth. "Entrepreneurs," in contrast, comprise those who own and operate businesses or pursue economic gain in other ways. They are often upwardly mobile persons, usually from the middle class. Members of both groups, of course, are very rich and comprise only a small proportion of the population. Thus, regardless of whether they work as an avocation or vocation, the possession of capital allows such persons to consume expensive amenities, influence public policy to benefit themselves, and thereby protect their life chances. So despite their differences, the possession of money allows the rich to exercise enormous power—especially in the United States.

Unlike Marx, Weber recognized that those who do not own capital also possess important resources in economically developed societies, mainly the worth of their services and skills. Weber divided these people, the great mass of the population, into two classes: the middle class and the working class.

---

[16]Weber (1920:306, 935).
[17]Weber (1920:305).
[18]Weber (1920:935).

The middle class comprises those who possess services and skills based on knowledge: public officials, managers of businesses, technicians, members of the professions, and other white-collar workers. Writing a half-century after Marx, Weber saw that industrialization based on scientific advance requires highly educated people and that the occupational structure was changing and becoming more complex as a result. Because their services and skills are in demand in modern societies, persons filling these newly created white-collar jobs usually have higher incomes and more political power than those who work with their hands. Like the rich, middle-class people use their resources to enhance their life chances, influence public policy, and affect others' opportunities—albeit at their level. For example, they try to insure their children attend "good" schools and end up with credentials that allow them to enter the professions (for instance, becoming a physician). More importantly, because they vote at such a high rate, elected decision-makers are responsive to middle-class interests. As a result, middle-class people protect their life chances, and the stratification structure remains stable.

Without explanation, Weber divided the working class—people who do manual labor—into three groups: skilled, semiskilled, and unskilled workers. It is unclear whether he saw these groups as separate classes or subdivisions within a single "working class." In any case, like the rich and middle class, working-class people also try to protect their life chances. Their share in the distribution of resources is less, however, and their lifestyles are more precarious as a result. Nonetheless, because hard work and ability can pay off in economically developed societies, some people from working-class origins are upwardly mobile into the middle class. Even so, the class structure is reproduced over time. As will be seen in later chapters, the class structure in the United States resembles the model originally sketched by Max Weber many years ago.

Weber added to Marx's contributions in a third way as well: He laid the ground work for objective social scientific research into the structure of stratification and other topics by arguing that sociology's goal ought to be to tell observers "what is," not "what ought to be." In this respect, the existence of sociology and the other social sciences reflects a historical process that Weber called **rationalization.** Because of the transformation to modernity described earlier, Weber said that social life is becoming more and more dominated by methodical calculation of means and ends based on scientific knowledge. Social scientific research constitutes one example of this tendency. In this context, Weber argued, analyses of the structure of stratification and life chances that result should strive to be "value free" in the sense that data should be categorized in terms of clear concepts, proper rules of evidence must be followed, and conclusions should be based on logical inferences.[19] In this way, the findings can be as objective as possible. Once the facts are clear, then it becomes possible to explain why they occur, discuss options, and (sometimes) suggest the implications of selecting one option over another—for example, reducing the level of inequality. Sociologists should not, however, as sociologists, tell people what to do. Weber believed that social scientific knowledge can help people make informed choices based on their values, economic interests, or some other criterion. With luck, such choices will be wiser.

---

[19]Weber (1904).

Now producing objective knowledge of the stratification structure is difficult; it is a goal pursued very imperfectly. One reason for this difficulty is that human beings possess will and volition. People often go their own way, with the result that findings are imprecise. Another reason is that sociologists are embedded in their subject matter. Those studying, say, gender inequality, bring to the topic their past experiences and values. Bias can follow. In order to reduce bias as much as possible, sociologists emphasize the norms characteristic of all sciences: skepticism and replication. Sociology is characterized by a debunking motif, an emphasis on seeing beyond common sense. The norm of skepticism simply applies this orientation to research reports (or textbooks): Do not believe everything you read. The norm of replication calls on researchers to do more than criticize; they must repeat the research to see if the finding remains stable. These norms mean that at its best and over the long term, science is self-correcting. Stable findings are called empirical generalizations.

Alas, because people change, the social sciences carry a special burden in that even empirical generalizations are subject to revision.[20] Such instability rarely happens in the natural sciences, which is why technology works. In the social sciences, however, findings vary over time and across societies because human beings rebel, subvert the established order, enact new laws, and in other ways change society. Thus, observers can never be sure that what they find today will be true tomorrow. But this burden carries with it an unexpected benefit: The social sciences are granted eternal youth, which is to say that findings must be revisited.[21]

### *Kingsley Davis and Wilbert Moore*

In the mid-1940s, Kingsley Davis and Wilbert Moore wrote an essay, titled "Some Principles of Stratification," that asked a simple question: What is the function of stratification for the society? They answered that its hidden impact is to "insure that the most important positions are conscientiously filled by the most qualified persons."[22] As a result, they argued, stratification functions to insure a society's survival. In so doing, they shifted the discussion away from the dynamic processes shaping the stratification structure. This was not a good move.

In all societies, Davis and Moore said, a division of labor exists in which positions are clustered in four areas necessary for a society's survival: economic, political, technological, and religious. In each sphere, people must be motivated to fill positions and enact roles; some, for example, must become carpenters and others physicians. Davis and Moore claimed that a few positions in each area are more important for societal survival than others and that they are also more difficult to fill because they require scarce talent, extensive training, or both. Hence, such positions must be more highly rewarded. Their example is from modern medicine. Medical training is so long, costly, and burdensome, they argued, that few persons would become physicians if the position did not carry very high rewards. They concluded that societies use unequal rewards (resources such as high

---

[20]Lieberson (1992).
[21]Weber (1904:104).
[22]Davis and Moore (1945:244).

income and occupational prestige) to motivate people to obtain functionally important and difficult to fill positions in each of the four areas.

Sociologists are often skeptical of others' ideas and, hence, the Davis-Moore analysis generated much debate. The conclusion is that the argument constitutes an illegitimate teleology and is untestable. A teleological statement imputes inherent purpose to a phenomenon. Thus, the purpose of an automobile is to provide transportation; it is designed and built with that goal in mind. The application of this notion to human societies, however, is dubious. Although a society must decide among priorities—such as cutting taxes or funding Head Start programs—these decisions reflect the outcome of political competition; the society was not designed for that purpose. Davis and Moore took an empirical generalization—the existence of stratification—and transformed it into a functional necessity. They thus avoided the dynamic issues in the study of inequality (such as variations in the level of inequality and the increasing emphasis on achievement) and the way these differences reflect the struggle of people and groups (such as physicians) for a greater share of the resources. Such a strategy cannot work. The thesis is untestable because the functionally necessary tasks and most important positions cannot be identified without invoking values. As a result, sociologists have rejected Davis and Moore's analysis.[23]

This same judgment applies to functionalism as a theoretical tradition. Davis and Moore were students of Talcott Parsons, the most well known functionalist in sociology, whose work reveals both of the outlined flaws.[24] Hence, functionalism is now passé, mainly for theoretical reasons but also for political ones. Indeed, it is easy to see how Davis and Moore's argument could be used to support the status quo in any society: Those obtaining the most resources (and, hence, enjoying the best life chances) would simply argue that their benefits are necessary for the survival of society. Physicians have made this argument very successfully in the United States.

Nonetheless, although functionalism has been rejected, the Davis-Moore essay and the theoretical tradition it illustrates contain two useful themes that remain relevant to the study of stratification structures.

One theme involves the simple act of looking for the functions of a social phenomenon. Although the term *functions* is too vague for detailed empirical analyses, attempting to uncover the functions of poverty, unemployment, and other social facts is sometimes a good way of piercing the veil justifying the status quo, which can be done without the problems afflicting Davis and Moore's analysis.[25] They tried to identify the nonobvious effects of stratification, which is good sociology, only to go wrong by imputing generic needs to society. In contrast, Robert K. Merton distinguished between the manifest and latent functions of social arrangements.[26] Like Marx, his point was that social facts are not always what they seem to be, that underlying interests and forces also exist, and that both aspects of reality must be understood. In this way, Merton argued (and I will show later

---

[23]International variations in mobility rates provide one context in which a quasi-functionalist hypothesis has been tested and refuted (see Chapter 4). See also the attempt at explaining occupational prestige hierarchies in functionalist terms in Chapter 5. For a recent critique of Davis and Moore, see Wallace (1997).

[24]Parsons (1951; 1954).

[25]Goode (1973).

[26]Merton (1968).

on), it is possible to see familiar issues in a new light, which can lead to greater under-standing of the stratification structure in modern societies.

In addition, functionalism provides a useful way of identifying the parts of the so-cial structure, a problem Marx and Weber also struggled with. Although Davis and Moore asserted that the tasks they identified—economic, political, technological, and religious—constituted functional necessities for survival, one need not make this assumption. Today, these tasks are termed **social institutions,** and they provide a model of the complex divi-sion of labor in modern societies. They are the parts of the social structure—seen horizon-tally. Thus, in studying the distribution of resources, observers typically look at how classes differ in terms similar to the institutions identified by Davis and Moore, Parsons, and others:

1. The occupation, amount of income, and source of income are identified, since they indicate people's economic and political interests.
2. The rate and type of political participation and power are examined, since they influ-ence the stratification structure.
3. The rate and type of crime are ascertained, since they are affected by class location.
4. The rate and type of religiosity are recognized, since they influence (and are influ-enced by) class location and values.
5. The level of educational attainment is investigated, since it is related to class location, political interests, and values.
6. Kinship characteristics are sketched, since they affect class location, economic and political interests, and values.

It is not hard to see that these basic tasks are interconnected. Thus, macroeconomic policies affect street crime (offenses some poor and working-class persons commit) by altering people's employment situation. In any science, it is essential to develop a model that identifies the structure of the phenomenon under investigation (for example, the parts of the body or the atom) and shows how they are interrelated. As noted earlier, Weber sketched a model of the class structure, one of the vertical dimensions of the stratification structure. The functionalists added to this analysis by identifying the social institutions that appear characteristic of each society—the horizontal dimension of the stratification structure.

## *Ralf Dahrendorf*

Functionalism constituted the dominant theoretical orientation in the United States from World War II until Ralf Dahrendorf's *Class and Class Conflict in Industrial Society* ap-peared in 1959. Responding to Marx, he argued that American sociologists had failed to realize the significance of class conflict in all modern societies. To rectify this problem, he observed, sociological study of stratification must become "an exact social science with precisely formulated postulates, theoretical models, and testable laws."[27] Alas, Dahrendorf's strategy was very flawed.

He began by developing a series of postulates, or assumptions, about the nature of society that contradicted those of Davis and Moore, Parsons, and other functionalists:

[27]Dahrendorf (1959:ix).

(1) "Every society is at every point subject to change; social change is ubiquitous." (2) "Every society displays at every point dissensus and conflict; social conflict is ubiquitous." (3) "Every element in a society renders a contribution to its disintegration and change." (4) "Every society is based on the coercion of some of its members by others."[28] The stratification structure is thus riven with class conflict.

Although Dahrendorf's conclusion is correct, these assumptions are unrealistic. After all, if a society were continually subject to change (item 1), then organized social life would be impossible. No science can assume relationships among the phenomena it is attempting to study. The scientific task is to test hypotheses, keeping assumptions to a minimum.

In the next step, Dahrendorf transformed his assumptions into a causal model that sketches how people move into and out of relationships of authority. Not a Marxist, he argued that possession of authority (rather than capital) identifies people's access to resources and their interest in keeping what they have and adding to it. The result is class conflict. Although this idea has merit, its correctness remains unknown because Dahrendorf asserted its truth by assumption. While his causal model displays other flaws, this one is the most serious.

Finally, Dahrendorf developed a testable theory that, he insisted, is derived from the model. This theory focuses on the conditions under which classes organize, the forms of class conflict, and the process of change.[29] While the theory comprises a large number of statements, I provide only one example here. In discussing the forms of class conflict, Dahrendorf proposed that "there is a close positive correlation between the degree of superimposition of [class] conflicts and their intensity." In plainer language:

*The more several class conflicts overlap with one another, the greater their intensity.*

In contrast to the assumptions outlined earlier, this hypothesis is useful. Because it is abstract (independent of time and space), it can be applied to many different empirical issues that divide social classes. Nonetheless, neither it nor the other elements of Dahrendorf's theory emerge from his model. Actually, his theory constitutes an extrapolation of work by Marx, Georg Simmel, Lewis Coser, and others.[30] This fact makes it less original than he asserts and calls his strategy for theory construction into question.

Although Dahrendorf's work is flawed, he contributed to the study of stratification in two essential ways. First, more than anyone else, he alerted sociologists in the United States to the fact that authority relationships and class conflict are built into the stratification structure in modern societies. American sociology (unlike European sociology) lacks a vibrant Marxist tradition, and, as a result, scholars were relatively insensitive to these issues. Thus, Dahrendorf observed that one need not be a Marxist to deal with the topics Marx raised. This point is important because, as indicated earlier, it is easy to show the continued relevance of his ideas. Second, in stating his propositions formally, Dahrendorf took theoretical analyses to a new level of sophistication. Theories could no longer be buried in discursive prose, a format that promotes vagueness and makes testing difficult.

---

[28]Dahrendorf (1959:162).
[29]Dahrendorf (1959:236–40).
[30]Simmel (1908), Coser (1956).

Dahrendorf is easy to criticize, mainly because he made his assumptions explicit, clearly identified his variables, defined them, and stated how they covary. Thus, while widely and appropriately criticized, his work redirected sociological research.


## Gerhard Lenski

Gerhard Lenski's book, *Power and Privilege,* constituted a decisive break with the past because he produced the first truly theoretical explanation of stratification processes.[31] His theory has two parts. First, he explained the basis for stratification in every society and, second, he explained why it has varied historically. In so doing, he tried to demonstrate "who gets what and why" in all societies over the course of history.

***The Basis of Stratification.***   In explaining the basis of stratification in all societies, Lenski focused on the distribution of power and privilege. Like Marx, he emphasized the importance of producing goods and services. He distinguished between societies in which people produce only the minimum necessary for subsistence and those in which a surplus exists and must be distributed. In the former, Lenski hypothesized, people "will share the product of their labor to the extent required to insure the survival and continued productivity of those others whose actions are necessary or beneficial to themselves."[32] In plainer language, the first hypothesis is:

> *The more dependent people are on each other for survival, the more they will share the products of their labor with one another.*

Lenski reasoned that individuals usually act out of self-interest. While familiar with Weber's writings, Lenski asserted that values are not primary determinants of the stratification structure, especially before industrialization. Thus, human groups capable of producing few goods are necessarily small, communal, hunting and gathering societies, in which each individual depends on all others. For this reason, people share what they produce.

When a surplus exists, the situation differs a great deal. "Power will determine the distribution of nearly all of the surplus possessed by a society," Lenski proposed.[33] In covariance form, the second hypothesis is:

> *The greater the surplus of goods and services in a society, the more power determines their distribution.*

In short, as Marx, Weber, and Dahrendorf all emphasized, albeit in quite different ways, Lenski argued that power is highly correlated with the distribution of resources—such as income, wealth, education, and occupational prestige—and the improved life chances that follow. In every society, he asserted, power leads to privilege, by which he meant improved life chances because people possess a greater share of the available resources.

---

[31]Lenski (1984).
[32]Lenski (1984:44).
[33]Lenski (1984:44).

***Historical Variation in Stratification.***     In order to explain why the stratification structure varies across societies over time, Lenski focused on two main factors: the level of technology and the nature of the state, ignoring the other transformative changes mentioned earlier. As Lenski phrased the hypothesis: "Variations in technology will be the most important single factor determining variations in distributive [or stratification] systems."[34] In covariance form, the third hypothesis is:

*The greater the level of technology, the greater the productivity and inequality.*

The term **technology** refers to scientifically verified knowledge about the environment. Improvements in technology, Lenski argued, are applied to the practical task of producing goods and services for people to enjoy. The result, following from the second hypothesis (and as Marx suggested), is that those with the greatest power acquire nearly all the surplus, which means they have access to most resources and better life chances. This process means that inequality is great and the stratification structure is rigid, without much mobility. As indicated earlier, this situation exists in all preindustrial (what Weber called "traditional") societies.

With industrialization, however, human history changed forever. Not only did the level of technology, and hence, productivity, increase exponentially, but also this process occurred at a time when democratic values and free societies were emerging. In this new context, Lenski said, where people vote and hold decision makers accountable, the many can combine against the few—leading to less inequality. Lenski's fourth hypothesis follows:

*The greater the level of industrialization and the more democratic the state, the less inequality.*

Lenski emphasized, however, that this statement only means that the rich possess a lower proportion of the total wealth. They remain, according to the second hypothesis, the most powerful class and they have greater access to valued resources.

In testing the theory, Lenski used archeological, anthropological, and historical data on all the world's known societies. He used evidence skillfully and demonstrated the accuracy of each element of the theory, except perhaps the last. Whether inequality must decline in industrial societies, and, if so, by how much, remains unclear. What is clear is that modern societies can control how much inequality exists.

Although their writings are flawed in various ways, the theorists reviewed here merit study, partly because they show how sociology has advanced over the years and partly because they contain enduring lessons. Stripped of its radical millenarianism (a belief in the coming of an ideal, communal society), Marx's work illustrates the usefulness of a structural approach focusing on how class location affects the choices people have. In addition, his emphasis on the significance of class conflict directs modern sociologists to look for the different levels of power, economic interests, and values displayed by various classes. Further, Marx's stress on alienation suggests the importance of ascertaining who benefits from public policies; sometimes the answer is not obvious. From Weber, modern sociologists take a recognition of the importance of class and achievement in modern societies, an understanding that people's lifestyle and values (what he

[34]Lenski (1984:90).

called "status") often influence behavior, a model of the class structure, an emphasis on power as a determining factor in social life, and a directive to do research that is as objective as possible. In addition, in their different ways, Marx and Weber both confronted how modern societies have been transformed by industrialization, capitalism, science, freedom and democracy, the rule of law, and the culture of capitalism. As a result, modern, class-based societies display an inherent tension between ascription and achievement. Davis and Moore, and functionalists generally, show that social arrangements frequently contain nonobvious dimensions—what Merton called "latent functions." In addition, the functionalists offer a model of the division of labor, the horizontal dimension of the stratification structure that remains useful. Dahrendorf reminded sociologists that issues related to class and class conflict can be analyzed outside a Marxist framework and that theories need to be stated formally. Finally, Lenski illustrated how a simple but powerful theory can be used to explain the basis of and historical variation in the structure of stratification.

## A Strategy for the Study of Stratification

The works reviewed above introduce many of the issues that must be confronted in the study of stratification. One way of taking advantage of them is to develop an overall theory, as in Jonathan H. Turner's *Societal Stratification*.[35] Turner translated the arguments made by Marx, Weber, Davis and Moore, Dahrendorf, and Lenski into a set of formal theoretical statements. He described this theory as a step toward a larger goal—the identification of the generic theoretical principles underlying all human behavior. Another approach, pursued in this book, involves using previous works as the basis for a middle-range analysis of the stratification structure.[36] Thus, I intend to build on the ideas of the theorists introduced above to explain the structure of stratification in the United States. This more modest goal requires a method, by which I mean a strategy for explanation rather than a statistical technique. The strategy used here is to (1) assess the historical and cross-national dimensions of stratification, (2) distinguish levels of analysis (individual and structural) for understanding stratification, and (3) describe how power affects the stratification process.

### Historical and Cross-National Dimensions of Stratification

Sociology at its best looks at the data along two dimensions: historical and cross-national.[37] Historical data reveal how much change in the level of inequality has occurred over time within one society, such as the United States. For example, in examining changes in racial and gender inequality, poverty, mobility, and other topics, I will usually extend the analysis back 100 to 200 years, or as far back as plausible data are available. This is a useful period to examine, since it marks the transition to modernity and the rise of class-based stratification structures. Cross-national data indicate the extent of inequality in several nations. Such information provides a way to place the U.S. experience in

---

[35]Turner (1984).
[36]Merton (1968).
[37]Kohn (1987).

perspective. I will usually restrict cross-national comparisons to Western societies. Since they share a common cultural heritage and display advanced economies, their similarities and differences regarding the issues dealt with in this book are especially revealing.

Max Weber pioneered use of such data in his studies of the relationship between religion and the origin of capitalism.[38] Weber wanted to understand why capitalism as an economic system arose in Western Europe and ushered in modern life. Thus, he performed a "logical experiment" by comparing the West in the seventeenth and eighteenth centuries with India and China at the same time. What distinguished Europe (and the United States) from these other nations was not the level of technology, a free labor force, or other factors. Rather, the West became unique due to the rise of the culture of capitalism as an unintended consequence of the Protestant Reformation. Recall that the term *culture of capitalism* refers to an interrelated set of values that emphasizes the importance of achievement and uses making money (legally) as a main indicator. What happened was that behaviors undertaken for purely religious reasons—such as hard work aimed at acquiring wealth—were transformed over time into secular cultural values. These ethical standards, in combination with the other dynamic changes summarized previously, helped to usher in a new kind of society, one never before seen in history—a society based on class with an increasing emphasis on achievement.

Weber's research strategy is significant because it can be used with any topic, not only stratification. As an aside, note that Weber's "logical experiment" differs from the approach usually presented in methodology courses. There, students are taught to form a hypothesis and gather data with which to test it. In contrast, Weber began by gathering data, which are then explained. This explanation is often multivariate in form, but the variables are related logically rather than mathematically. This strategy is often useful in dealing with structural issues.[39]

The use of historical and cross-national data leads to productive questions. For example, if the rate of poverty in the United States was high in the past (and it was), but is much lower now, one asks what has changed. Individual motives? Perhaps. But if the poverty rate in this country is much higher than in Western European nations, one wonders if structural barriers have been deliberately created that keep so many people impoverished. The strategy, once again, is to look for explanatory factors that differ historically and internationally, and appear logically related to poverty. Science, it seems to me, is simply the art of asking questions. The idea is that there are no secrets. The facts of nature, social life, even people's unconscious motives can be discovered if one asks the right questions. In sociology, historical and cross-national data provide an empirical basis for such queries. They lead to greater understanding. They also lead to a distinction between levels of analysis.

## *Levels of Analysis and Stratification*

In order to illustrate the importance of distinguishing levels of analysis, imagine you are enrolled in an art history course and must try to understand a painting by the Dutch impressionist Vincent van Gogh. Let us assume it is *The Café Terrace at Night* (finished in

---

[38]Weber (1905; 1913; 1917; 1920). For an overview, see Turner, Beeghley, and Powers (2002).
[39]Beeghley (1999; 2003).

1888). In looking at the painting, one sees a humble establishment where people eat, drink, and talk. Like much great art, *The Café Terrace at Night* can be understood on several levels, and each displays different properties. At one level, you might use a spectroscope to inspect the paint's chemical composition. Such an examination is useful because of the bright colors typical of van Gogh's works. At another level, you might use a magnifying glass to study his brush technique. This analysis would be useful because van Gogh used heavy, slashing strokes. At still another level, you might look at the painting from a short distance to see how the images fit together. At a final level, you might move several feet away to get an overall view. These last two levels are useful because distance alters what viewers see. What you should remember with this example is that each level of analysis not only provides different data, but also different explanatory variables. Yet, the explanation at each level is valid, and combining them leads to greater insight about the painting. So it is with the study of stratification.

The initial task is to understand why individuals act, which constitutes the first level of analysis. Only individuals vote or look for jobs. Only individuals justify their actions morally and live with the result. Only individuals give their lives meaning. The basis on which individuals make decisions is their personal experiences (which are not always conscious). Sociologists use the term **socialization** to describe these experiences. It refers to the lifelong process by which individuals learn norms and values, internalize motivations and (unconscious) needs, develop intellectual and social skills, and enact roles as they participate in the society.[40] In plainer language, *socialization* refers to the process of growing up, with the addendum that it continues throughout life. In effect, individuals' personal experiences form a template providing a basis for their behavior. The dimensions of this template can be formally stated:

1. Childhood interactions are usually more influential on individuals than later experiences.
2. Interaction in primary groups (such as family and religion) is usually more influential on individuals than interaction in secondary groups.
3. Interaction with people who are emotionally significant (such as parents, teachers, and friends) is usually more influential on individuals than interaction with more distant persons.
4. Long-term interaction is usually more influential on individuals than short-term interaction.[41]

Knowledge of these experiences helps observers understand how individuals' backgrounds lead them to act as they do. A person's biography is composed of family, friends, and enemies. It also comprises the schools attended, books read, television programs watched, the religious faith adhered to, the Scout troop joined, and the orgies participated in. Eventually it will include the gang joined, the occupational group entered, the political party identified with, and all other experiences. With this background, then, a person learns what is expected (norms and values), develops personality characteristics (motiva-

---

[40]Brim (1966).
[41]The elements of socialization theory are rarely stated formally, as here. To see how they can be useful, see Beeghley et al. (1990), Beeghley (2003).

tions and needs), and understands how to act (knowledge and skills). These are the elements of the socialization process defined above. Note the active verbs: Individuals attend, join, enter, and the like. Even when they are young, people choose. Socialization is an active (not a passive) process. It varies by class, race, and gender.

I mentioned that socialization continues throughout life. This means that the template through which individuals channel their behavior is not set in childhood and left that way forever. Rather, people periodically change their template—that is, they change their orientations in light of new experiences—as they move through life and adopt a variety of **reference groups** along the way.[42] The phrase refers to collectivities of people whose characteristics (values, norms, tastes, and patterns of action) are significant in the development of one's own attitudes and behavior.

Taken together, knowing how individuals are socialized and their choice of reference groups leads to understanding of their behavior. For example, poor people sometimes find that they have little control over what happens to them or their children. One's job disappears. A child witnesses a murder on the street. Savings stored under a mattress (because no banks are available) are stolen. As Marx would say, when such experiences cumulate, people become alienated. They lose hope and act out: with drugs. Or they become angry and act out: sexually or violently. Now these reactions do not happen as often as you might think, but they do happen. Although understanding does not excuse such behaviors, it does explain them.

Although the connection may surprise you, one can see alienation as a dominant theme in the *Star Wars* movies. Darth Vader represents all alienated people, acting out in extreme ways. Luke Skywalker represents the redeeming social values Darth has rejected. In the penultimate scene in the third movie (Episode 6), they are fighting to the death and, frankly, Darth is winning. Luke appeals to the goodness hidden inside Darth. Can he reject the seduction of the Emperor, who represents evil (or the devil, depending on your theology)? Ultimately, Darth overcomes his alienation, hurls the Emperor to his death, and, at the end of the movie, is reincarnated as Luke's father and reunited with Obiwan Kenobi and Yoda. The empire is defeated. One reason Americans feel so good after the movie is that it celebrates the triumph of individuals over great odds. Individuals, Americans believe, possess all the will and ability they need. Like Darth and Luke, they need only use it to achieve positive results. This belief may be why public policies in the United States often demand heroic action by exploited and alienated people. Such requirements are often shortsighted, as the following chapters show. Not many people possess either Darth's or Luke's fictional courage.

Understanding why individuals act, however, provides only one kind of information. Just as a painting can be understood at different levels, so can social life. The structure of stratification must be considered—the second level of analysis. As both Marx and Weber emphasized, the social structure provides the context in which people act and thereby affects rates of events, and rates of diverse events characterize a society and can only be explained at that level. Thus, in studying stratification, such issues as rates of occupational mobility, political participation, poverty, job perquisites, voting, gender inequality, and racial and ethnic inequality can be best understood structurally.

[42]Hyman (1942), Merton and Rossi (1968).

Yet this orientation seems backward to many people, primarily because the ethic of individual responsibility is so pervasive in the United States. The origins of this cultural value probably lie in the transformative effect of Puritanism, with its emphasis on each individual's personal relationship with God, along with the myth of the frontier, with its requirement that individuals be self-reliant in order to survive.[43] The long-term impact of these factors has produced in many Americans a preference for focusing on individuals when thinking about social issues. For example, if the rate of occupational mobility is high (and it is), then many people argue (incorrectly) that it reflects each individual's hard work. Similarly, if the rate of voting is low (and it is), then most people believe (again, incorrectly) that nonvoters must be satisfied with the status quo. The underlying assumption in both examples is that the whole, the rate of mobility or voting, is no more than the sum of its parts—the individual actions making up the rate. This assumption, however, is incorrect. Just as water is qualitatively different—in touch, taste, and many other characteristics—from its component parts (hydrogen and oxygen), so the rate of social events is qualitatively different from its component parts (individual behaviors). From this point of view, it makes sense to suggest, by analogy, that the rates of mobility, voting, and other issues reflect the structure of stratification.

Although Marx, Weber, and the other theorists reviewed before were all structuralists, another early sociologist, Emile Durkheim, explained this angle of vision most clearly when he said, that it is "in the nature of the society itself that we must seek the explanation of social life."[44] He meant that structural phenomena exist externally to individuals, guiding their behavior in predictable ways. But guidance is not force and not all individuals react in the same way. His example had to do with suicide. Although this is a solitary act, he showed that even in social contexts where the ties binding individuals to the society are strong—as among employed married people with children who regularly attend church—some suicides would occur. This fact is irrelevant to Durkheim's point, however, which was that the suicide rate would be lower in such contexts than in others, where the bonds tying individuals to the society are less.[45] Thus, if he was correct, it should be possible to show how the social structure produces varying rates of other events, such as the level of mobility or poverty, apart from individual acts.

The reason why social structure affects rates of events is that it determines the range of choices available to people.[46] Thus, people's location in the stratification structure (high to low) systematically influences their choices and their consequences. This argument can be formally stated as the *Class Structure Hypothesis:*

> *The lower the social class, the fewer choices people have and the less effective they are in solving personal problems.*

But the impact of social class is interrelated with the other dimensions of stratification. For example, the *Gender Hypothesis* is as follows:

> *Women at every class level have fewer and less effective choices than do men.*

---

[43]On Puritanism, see Weber (1905). On the significance of the frontier as myth, see F. J. Turner (1920).
[44]Durkheim (1895:128).
[45]Durkheim (1897).
[46]Merton (1968).

Similarly, the *Minority Group Hypothesis* is stated as follows:

*Minority groups at every class level have fewer and less effective choices than do Whites (non-Hispanic).*

Much of this book consists in demonstrating the usefulness of these hypotheses.

The rationale underlying these hypotheses is the same as Durkheim's: The structure of stratification is external to individuals; it provides the context that affects both people's choices and their effectiveness. Paradoxically, then, while the total number (or rate) of a phenomenon—such as the proportion of people in each class who vote—reflects the sum of individual actions, that information does not explain its level. For example, as I describe in Chapter 6, understanding the motives for voting does not explain why working-class and poor people go to the polls at lower rates than middle-class and rich persons. Only knowledge of how the social context influences the choices available to individuals in each class can explain these differences. For this reason, Durkheim said, "social facts are things"; they have a reality independent of individuals.

I want to focus for a few moments on the Class Structure Hypothesis. Although I have cited Durkheim and Merton as the primary sources underlying it, each of the theorists reviewed previously also influenced its formulation. Thus, I interpreted (some would say misinterpreted) Marx in terms consonant with it. Virtually every theme in his writings can be considered in light of this hypothesis, without recourse to his revolutionary millenarianism. Similarly, Weber's emphasis on the influence of values on behavior and his depiction of the class structure focuses attention on rates of events. The functionalists contributed by identifying key elements of the social structure that influence the level of poverty, voting, and many other phenomena. Although his work is flawed, Dahrendorf pointed out how class conflict is built into the social structure. Finally, Lenski's emphasis on the significance of power in the distribution of resources in society is obviously consonant with the theory presented here.

The Class Structure Hypothesis has many practical implications. For example, one can pick any behavior by individuals—finding a spouse, obtaining an education, getting a job, purchasing a car, recovering from mental stress, any behavior at all—and, if the hypothesis is correct, poor persons will usually have fewer choices and be less able to resolve their personal problems than the members of other social classes. This fact will be reflected in different rates of behavior by class. Moreover, these differences will exist no matter how hard poor individuals work or how much ability they have. Such insight helps observers to understand why impoverished people sometimes make decisions that appear unwise from a middle-class vantage point.

The Class Structure Hypothesis reflects a more general argument that I want to repeat: The social structure sets the context and affects rates of behavior. Yet, as also emphasized earlier, individuals choose. In sociological jargon, they have **agency.** The relationship between individuals and social structure has been a (in my view, needlessly) controversial topic in sociology. The issues are the degree to which individuals can act independently (do they have choices?) and whether the social structure can be changed. The answers are as follows: First, individuals have a great deal of independence, but in practical terms their choices are not unlimited. You can, for example, choose to use a typewriter rather than a word processor. You can also choose to have many spouses. Since the first is inefficient and the second illegal, only a few persons make such choices. In this sense, then, the social structure exists externally to individuals and sets boundaries (which are sometimes wide and sometimes narrow) on behavior. Second, people can and do change social structures. How this process might occur and the difficulty involved can be suggested by using college football as an example.

There is a sort of class and race structure to college football, and people choose within that context. In a game, for example, players operate within a set of rules that affects their behavior: Only ends and backs can catch forward passes, for example. In addition, players, many of whom are African American, often improvise during a play. But, while fans may not wish to recognize it, each game is part of a multimillion dollar industry that provides a context in which some people and organizations make a great deal of money at the expense of others.

The structural question, then, is who organizes the industry and to whose benefit, and how do these issues affect the players? Let us begin with the coaches. They are nearly always white and are relatively well paid (indeed, they make serious money at major universities). Coaches, of course, decide who gets to play and at what positions. They also have a lot of influence over rules adopted by the National Collegiate Athletic Association (NCAA), since its governing body is made up of coaches. So they have power. For example, at their behest, the NCAA decided that when Coach Charisma induces an 18-year-old football player to sign a contract to play at State University, he is bound to the school even if Mr. Charisma moves on to a (better paying) position at another institution. So the players are bound by contract but the coaches (usually) are not. In addition, along with coaches, athletic directors, university presidents, and NCAA administrators determine the rules under which games will be played and eligibility requirements for players, among other things. Like coaches, these people are nearly always white males, and they make lots of money.

In this context, if you happen to be an 18-year-old male with some football skill, your choices involve whether to take the right courses to become eligible, whether to play or not, and for whom to play. You cannot, however, negotiate about pay. You cannot even ask to be paid the minimum wage for all the hours put in practicing, attending meetings, lifting weights (often all summer), and playing in the games. In effect, you sign a contract to work long hours for room, board, and tuition. As one observer noted, this is an industry in which the employees are called "amateurs" and employee-employer contracts are called "scholarships."[47] As a result of this peculiar arrangement, the university obtains a certain degree of glory, and its athletic associations and others make lots of money. At the University of Florida, where I teach, the head football coach makes (via salary and other income-producing perquisites) more than a million dollars per year. Others do quite well also: announcers, television executives, and stockholders of firms that advertise on football telecasts, to name only a few. Yet most players and fans think this situation is proper. This is so even though many (if not most) players at major universities fail to graduate. So they do not even get an education for their labors. One might say that college football is the sigh of the oppressed creature—the opium of the players.

---

[47]Rhoden (2002).

Perhaps my sarcasm is unfair. But think about who has more choices and how effective they are. The players can choose to play or not. They can choose to attend (real) classes or not. But unless they organize themselves to strike before a big game or unless (until?) someone hires a lawyer to sue the NCAA, they will remain bound by contract even if a coach leaves and they will not be paid for their labors. So changing the structure of college football will be difficult for them. Coaches and administrators, on the other hand, make the rules. They can more easily change the structure of college football. But it would not be in their interests to do so, which means that paying the players (even minimum wage) is unlikely. My point: People at the top have greater ability to change the social structure than those at the bottom.

The structure of stratification is similar. Because of the six dynamic forces that created modernity (outlined earlier), the story of the past century or two has been one of increasing control over every aspect of the environment, social as well as physical. The implication is plain: In modern societies, the level of inequality—by class, gender, and race—is chosen. People with power use it to gain access to resources and the benefits that follow.

## Power and Stratification

Max Weber's definition of power as the ability of an individual or group to get things done, to achieve goals, even if opposition occurs, has become standard.[48] And, as Gerhard Lenski showed, power determines the distribution of resources in every society where a surplus exists. It follows that people have power when they can choose to spend or withhold money, prestige, or other resources from others. They have power when, faced with a divorce, lawsuit, or mental stress, they can find the right lawyer or therapist to help them deal with the problem. They have power when companies and governments pay attention to their needs and desires. But power is not confined to individuals. Because the ability to achieve goals is highly correlated with class, people with similar interests often act in concert and discriminate against others, even though they are not formally organized into groups. Hence, it is not possible to understand the structure of stratification without focusing on the class basis of power. In addition, however, as with college football, white males occupy most positions of power in this country. Hence, power is also race and gender based.

As you should recall, a class consists of those persons with similar occupational prestige, education, income, and other characteristics. In every society, power is class based and correlated with race and gender. This fact means that the very rich, both individually and as an aggregate, have more influence over access to valued resources than do middle-class people; that the middle class, in turn, has more influence over access to valued resources than do working-class people; and that the working class has more influence over access to valued resources than do poor people. This argument has many practical implications. It implies, for example, that rich people usually have a greater variety of choices and can be more effective in solving personal problems. This is, of course,

[48]Weber (1920).

another way of describing their better life chances. Similarly, as subsequent chapters will show, it suggests how to understand the distribution of wealth and poverty, the nature and level of benefits from income transfers, the level and kind of supervision on the job, the characteristics of housing occupied by different classes, the structure of political participation, and certain aspects of racial, ethnic, and gender inequality. In addition, this approach follows from theoretical analyses of stratification. This argument can be stated formally as the *Political Power Hypothesis:*

> *The higher the social class, the greater the influence over the distribution of resources in the society.*

Here is an example of the political power of the rich. One problem such persons face is retaining as much income as possible after taxes. As I will show in Chapters 6 and 7, over the past few years, the rich have persuaded Congress to transfer much of the tax burden from them to the rest of the population. As a result, despite what Lenski thought, income and wealth inequality have increased and are now at their highest point in U.S. history. Most of the time, tax breaks for the rich are justified by their benefits to "the economy" and to the majority of people through the so-called "trickle down effect." Such arguments are veils, of course, designed to hide the way in which the tax system channels income up rather than down. In reality, rich persons avoid contributing to the common good and retain most of their income because of their enormous political power. Put differently, the resources rich people have expand the range and effectiveness of their choices. Thus, instead of merely reacting to government policies, the rich decisively affect their formation. This fact provides them with enormous advantages over the members of other classes.

These advantages mean they can often affect how valued resources are distributed in society. Although it is true that every society displays stratification, the result of this dynamic process varies considerably. And this result affects people's life chances.

## *Summary*

Social stratification can be defined as the process by which resources are distributed in society. Possession of such resources as income, education, and occupational prestige affects people's life chances. One indicator of the dynamic processes shaping the stratification structure is the degree of inequality, which has three dimensions: class, race/ethnicity, and gender. People in the same class tend to be relatively equal to one another in terms of occupational category, income, source of income, education, and other resources. People in different classes tend to be unequal in these same terms. The impact of traditional gender roles means that women are often unequal to men. Because of prejudice and discrimination, members of different racial and ethnic groups are often unequal to one another. Although these differences have declined in recent years, they remain important. Another indicator of the processes shaping stratification is the emphasis on ascription versus achievement. All modern societies display a tension between these two bases of evaluation.

Karl Marx proposed that in all societies people produce goods and that a structure of stratification emerges based on private ownership of the means of production. Capitalist societies display two classes, Marx said, the bourgeoisie and the proletarians. He thought that class conflict was inevitable and would ultimately lead to a communist revolution. Although Marx was wrong, a number of sociological insights permeate his work: the emphasis on social structure, the degree of opportunity built into the stratification structure, the significance of class conflict, the emphasis on power, and the importance of alienation.

Max Weber added to Marx's sociological insights by emphasizing that people act in terms of both economic considerations (which he called "class") and lifestyle or value considerations (which he called "status"). By discriminating against others who are different, the members of each class use their power to maintain their positions. In addition, Weber filled out Marx's model of the stratification structure by recognizing that the rich constitute two different groups, rentiers and entrepreneurs, and that those without capital can also be divided into at least two groups: the middle and working classes. Finally, Weber emphasized the importance of striving for objectivity. The goal of social science, he believed, should be to identify "what is" not "what ought to be."

Kingsley Davis and Wilbert Moore argued that stratification is the means society uses to motivate people to fill difficult and functionally important positions. Their analysis, however, is an illegitimate teleology and untestable. Nonetheless, functionalism contributed to the study of stratification by emphasizing the importance of looking at nonobvious (or latent) aspects of social life and identifying the key elements of the division of labor.

Ralf Dahrendorf argued that sociology should develop a set of assumptions about the nature of society, a model in which variables are linked by assumption, and a set of testable hypotheses. This orientation is very flawed. Nonetheless, Dahrendorf's work remains useful because he taught U.S. sociologists that problems of class and class conflict can be dealt with in a non-Marxist framework. He illustrated the importance of formally stating hypotheses.

Gerhard Lenski developed a theory that explains why the distribution of power and privilege varies within and among societies, and tested his idea using historical and comparative data. He found that the more people are dependent on each other for survival, the more they will share the products of their labor. At the same time, however, the greater the surplus of goods and services, the more power determines their distribution. Among preindustrial societies, Lenski found that the greater the level of technology, the greater the productivity and the greater the inequality. Finally, Lenski proposed that the greater the industrialization and the more democratic the state, the less inequality. Empirically, the status of this last hypothesis remains unclear.

The initial step in developing a strategy for studying stratification is to assess its historical and cross-national dimensions. Historical data reveal how much change has occurred over time within one society, such as the United States. Cross-national data show the extent to which inequality in its various forms occurs at similar rates in other nations. This research strategy, which parallels Max Weber's, constitutes a "logical experiment" that facilitates identifying the structural variables affecting rates of behavior.

The second step is to distinguish levels of analysis. This procedure is important because the psychological variables explaining why individuals act differ from the structural variables explaining why rates of behavior vary.

People act in terms of their personal experiences, which can be described by the socialization process. The term refers to the lifelong process by which individuals learn norms and values, internalize motivations and (unconscious) needs, develop intellectual and social skills, and enact roles as they participate in society. Socialization is an active process. As people move through life, they adopt a variety of reference groups—collectivities whose characteristics are significant to the development of their own attitudes and behavior. Taken together, knowing how individuals are socialized and their choice of reference groups leads to understanding their behavior.

The social structure affects rates of events—such as poverty, occupational mobility, and the like—because it determines the choices available to people. The Class Structure Hypothesis follows:

> *The lower the social class, the fewer choices people have and the less effective they are in solving personal problems.*

This hypothesis, along with the Gender and Race Hypotheses, has practical implications. It means that regardless of the problem, poor persons will usually have fewer choices than members of other social classes, and this fact will be reflected in differences in behavior by class.

The third step is to look at how power affects access to valued resources. Power—the ability to achieve goals even if opposition occurs—is not confined to individuals; it is class based and correlated with race and gender. Again, this argument has practical implications. It implies *the higher the social class, the greater the influence over access to valued resources in society.*

# 2

# Race/Ethnicity and Stratification

This chapter tells the story of Jefferson's Dilemma. In the Declaration of Independence, written in 1776, Thomas Jefferson declared: "We hold these truths to be self-evident, that all men are created equal. They are endowed by their creator with certain unalienable rights, such as life, liberty, and the pursuit of happiness." A revolution was fought and a new nation established based on this value.[1] The statement "all men are created equal" implied that both African Americans and Whites should have the same rights and ability to succeed in light of their talent and skills. In a society that values personal freedom and democracy, it follows that achievement-oriented criteria should be applied to all. Thus, the Declaration established an altogether new moral standard for people—and nations— to live up to.

[1]Lipset (1963). The phrase, "Jefferson's Dilemma," comes from Shipler (1993). On the history of the Declaration, see Maier (1997).

But Jefferson did not live up to this standard. He was a slave owner. His only book, *Notes on the State of Virginia,* written in 1785, shows that he believed in the inferiority of those held in bondage.[2] So he and the other founders of the new nation excluded African slaves from its moral promise. He thus created a dilemma: freedom and equality for all versus freedom for some and slavery for others. Jefferson apparently recognized the difficulty this dilemma represented. The original draft of the Declaration contained an indictment of slavery that the Continental Congress deleted. In *Notes,* he forecast the long-term harm to the nation created by a division into free and unfree. Yet he fathered children by one of his slaves, Sally Hemings. He freed only two slaves during his lifetime and only five in his will. Jefferson never resolved his dilemma.[3]

Nor have we. Over time, the United States has become one of the most heterogeneous nations in the world. Immigrants from Cuba, India, Vietnam, Korea, and many other nations now enrich our communities and schools. Yet we remain preoccupied with race and ethnicity. The term **race** refers to groups identifiable in light of their physical traits, such as skin color. Thus, African Americans, Whites, and the various Asian minorities are typically defined as races. You should understand, however, that "race" is meaningless genetically; skin pigmentation merely reflects adaptations to climate.[4] Racial distinctions are only meaningful because we attach meaning to them. The term **ethnic group** refers to aggregates with distinctive social and psychological characteristics, as indicated by their nationality, religious heritage, and other unique elements of their background. Thus, the Irish and Italians are typically defined as ethnic groups. So are persons who came from or whose ancestors came from various Hispanic, Asian, and African nations. Note, however, that few "Hispanic" or "Asian" people see themselves as sharing a common culture. Rather, they identify with their ethnic group—for example, as Chinese Americans or Mexican Americans.[5] Thus, in one sense, the names serve as an arbitrary way of presenting data. As a convention, when I refer to "Whites," the reference excludes Hispanics, who can be of any race. The current U.S. population is about 281 million people. Of this number, about 69 percent are white American, 13 percent African American, 13 percent Hispanic American, 4 percent Asian American, and less than 1 percent Native American.[6] In another sense, though, these racial and ethnic categories are metaphors for this nation's dilemma.

These divisions have existed since the beginning. In 1790, just after the Constitution was adopted, 60 to 80 percent of the white population was of English origin.[7] Hence, all

---

[2]Jefferson (1999).

[3]On the DNA evidence, see Foster et al. (1998). Gordon-Reed makes the logical case for Jefferson's paternity (1997).

[4]Cavilli-Sforza et al. (1995).

[5]de la Garza (1992), Takaki (1989).

[6]U.S. Bureau of the Census (2001:8,17).

[7]The white population estimate comes from U.S. Bureau of the Census (1975:1168). Although the population was mostly English, they came from varying backgrounds. In *Albion's Seed: Four British Folkways in America,* David Hackett Fischer shows that English immigration occurred in four waves from different regions, and that people from each region differed in speech, courtship and marriage customs, religious rituals, attitudes toward education and freedom, and other ways (1989). These differences appeared where they settled—New England, Virginia, the Delaware Valley, and the Colonial backcountry—and the legacy of the original immigrants can still be found in these areas.

other groups have not only been forced to adapt to English norms and values but also to endure their prejudice and discrimination. **Prejudice** refers to people's hostile attitudes toward others in a different group or toward other groups as a whole. **Discrimination** refers to the unequal treatment of individuals and groups due to their personal characteristics, such as race or ethnicity.

The extent of prejudice and discrimination today remains controversial. Some observers argue that significant change has occurred. America, it is said, is becoming a "color blind" society such that members of nonwhite groups are increasingly integrated into the mainstream of American life.[8] Others, however, argue that hostile attitudes and unequal treatment continue to be pervasive. America, it is said, displays a huge, seemingly permanent chasm between Whites and other racial and ethnic groups.[9] In a way, both interpretations are correct. As a metaphor, consider a 16-ounce cup in which the level of the water has risen to 8 ounces. Should observers interpret the cup as now half-full or still half-empty? The data reflect this interpretive problem.

On the one hand, attitudinal surveys show a clear trend extending over more than half a century: Most people now embrace the value of equality, especially when phrased as equality of opportunity, and the level of prejudice has declined.[10] For example, in the 1940s about 68 percent of Whites thought that African American and white children should go to separate schools. Today, this question is not even asked because essentially no one argues for segregated schools. The pattern is similar with other topics, such as access to transportation, jobs, and housing. One of the best single indicators of prejudice lies in attitudes toward intermarriage. Jefferson (said he) opposed unions between Whites and African slaves, and most Whites opposed intermarriage until recently. In 1958, 96 percent of Whites disapproved of marriage between the races. By the turn of the century, however, only about 20 to 30 percent disapproved, depending on how the question was worded.

On the other hand, despite valuing equality, many Whites are like Jefferson so long ago in that they accept discrimination and oppose policies designed to provide equal opportunity for all.[11] For example, although only 3 percent of Whites object if their children's school has "a few" African American students, if "more than half" the children are African American, the proportion of Whites objecting rises to 59 percent. Moreover, 66 percent of Whites oppose busing children to achieve integration. Similar differences occur when Whites are questioned about access to housing, jobs, and other basic issues. Thus, even though equality has become a widespread value and the level of prejudice has declined, Whites remain like the founders of the new nation: willing to tolerate discrimination.

These contradictory data indicate that a gap exists between the experiences of minority groups and Whites in this country. Although attitudes have changed, we are not a color blind society; race and ethnicity comprise lenses through which all interaction is filtered. As a result, race and ethnicity still constitute a system of ranking based on birth

[8]See Thernstrom and Thernstrom (1997), Patterson (1997), Sniderman and Carmines (1997).
[9]On African Americans, see Hacker (1992), Sears et al. (1997). On Hispanics, see Delgado (1997).
[10]Bobo (2001). All the data in this paragraph come from this source.
[11]All the data in this paragraph are from the Gallup Poll (1997:17), General Social Survey (1996), and Bobo (2001).

that affects resource distribution and people's life chances. Jefferson's Dilemma is our dilemma.[12]

## *Dimensions of Racial and Ethnic Stratification*

### *Racial and Ethnic Stratification in the United States*

In order to assess the degree of change in the distribution of resources among various racial and ethnic groups, it is necessary to distinguish between its absolute and relative dimensions. "Absolute change" refers to difference over time. Thus, if the median income of African American households changed from about $1,900 per year in 1950 to about $29,500 per year in 2001 (and it did), then most are better off—even after taking inflation into account. "Relative change" refers to difference in relationship to some other group, such as Whites (recall that this term excludes Hispanics, unless indicated). Thus, if during the same period, the median income among white households changed from about $3,400 per year to about $46,300 per year (and it did), then the relative relationship between the two groups has changed. In 1950, African American households earned about 56 percent as much as white households. In 2001, African American households earned about 64 pecent as much as white households.[13] Over the last century, most minority groups have improved their situation absolutely and in some cases relatively as well.

*Civil Rights.*    The term **civil rights** refers to citizens' legally guaranteed opportunity to participate equally in the society. For example, those possessing civil rights can vote, eat where they choose, buy a house if they have the money, educate their children, obtain a job, and marry whomever they wish. Civil rights guarantee individual freedom. Without civil rights, entire groups are evaluated based on nonperformance criteria—ascription. For those without civil rights, the law itself can be and has been used as a mechanism for exploitation.[14]

When the Constitution was adopted in 1789, only property owners who paid taxes could vote, which meant only privileged English men enjoyed civil rights. Over time, accompanied by much protest and violence, those who did not own land and various white ethnic groups (German, Scandinavian, Irish, Italian, etc.) obtained a legal guarantee of equal participation.

Native Americans were much less successful.[15] The denial of civil rights occurred in a context of massive depopulation. The Native American population in what would become the continental United States was probably about five million souls, and possibly much more, at the time of contact with Whites in the fifteenth century. By 1900, it had fallen to about 375,000, mostly due to disease and systematic extermination. Although the population has rebounded since then, a 93 percent decline is a good definition of geno-

---

[12]This gap between American values and behavior was the theme of Gunnar Myrdal's classic book, *An American Dilemma,* originally published in 1944.
[13]U.S. Bureau of the Census (1975:297; 2002:17).
[14]Aguirre and Turner (1993).
[15]See Thornton (1987; 2001), Mann (2002).

cide. Initially, Whites agreed by treaty to treat Native American tribes as sovereign nations. In fact, however, the law was used to take tribal land and deprive Native Americans of their civil rights. This process culminated in 1871 when the Congress declared that no tribe shall be recognized as independent, thereby removing any basis for political sovereignty. For the next century, social life among many Native American tribes remained disorganized. The Bureau of Indian Affairs, run by Whites, regulated their civil rights. Since 1976, a new federal law has allowed some Native American tribes to regain legal recognition. This and other legal changes mean greater civil rights.

Those of Asian ancestry were also less successful.[16] By origin, the Asian population today is about 27 percent Chinese American, 23 percent Filipino American, 14 percent Japanese American, 13 percent Indian American, 13 percent Korean American, and 10 percent Vietnamese American. Much of this diversity has only developed over the last four decades. The few Chinese and Japanese immigrants who came to the United States in the nineteenth century faced very high levels of prejudice and discrimination, as indicated by their political disenfranchisement. For example, the passage of restrictive immigration laws along with court decisions kept the population of Asian heritage people small and prevented immigrants who were here from becoming citizens. Another indicator of the denial of civil rights was the seizure of property and confinement of U.S. citizens of Japanese descent to internment camps located east of the Rocky Mountains during World War II. Citizens of German descent neither lost their land nor were jailed. Thus, while nineteenth century European immigrants faced many obstacles, the barriers confronting Asian Americans were more significant. The huge influx of immigrants from Asian nations over the last 40 years reflects, in part, the impact of the Immigration Act of 1965 coupled with other legal changes that protect civil rights.

Hispanic people fared no better.[17] By origin, the Hispanic population is about 66 percent Mexican American, 9 percent Puerto Rican American, and 4 percent Cuban American, with the remainder coming from various Central and South American nations. Historically, the early settlers from Mexico displaced the Native Americans and regarded the Southwest as their homeland, until the Anglos (Whites) invaded in 1848 and made it part of the United States. Subsequently, Mexican Americans were treated as second-class citizens, segregated, and deprived of civil rights. Similarly, in the North, the small communities of Puerto Rican Americans were kept segregated and denied their rights, partly by custom and partly by law. Recent immigrants from Cuba and other Latin American nations have endured less discrimination due to passage of civil rights laws.

Finally, the Civil War's promise of freedom was empty as African Americans went from slavery to serfdom in the form of sharecropping.[18] After the war, the South began a campaign of terror against the former slaves that placed them in a system of segregation and debt peonage lasting for another century. The point was to keep African Americans poor and uneducated in order to insure the availability of a large and compliant labor force. These policies succeeded for a century; they hinged on the denial of civil rights.

---

[16]See Takaki (1989), Nakanishi (2001), U.S. Bureau of the Census (2001b). On the internment of Japanese American citizens, see Commission on Wartime Relocation and Internment of Civilians (1982).
[17]Camarillo and Bonilla (2001), U.S. Bureau of the Census (2001c).
[18]Foner (1988), Kennedy (1995), Oshinsky (1996).

In Mississippi in the 1950s, supposedly free African Americans still toiled for slave wages in the same fields where their forebears had picked cotton a century before. In some counties, African Americans outnumbered Whites by as much as four to one, yet it was common for not a single African American to be registered to vote and not a single African American to be found in jury pools. "The state kept it that way by sanctioning violence against black people who got above themselves by agitating for the vote, talking back to white folks, or failing to give way on the sidewalk."[19]

One of the symbols of oppression was the denial of access to public accommodations, which affected every aspect of daily life. In the spring of 1946, Jackie Robinson and his new wife, Rachel, boarded a plane in Los Angeles. A three sport All-American at UCLA and one of the rising stars of the Negro Baseball League, Robinson had recently signed a contract to play for the Brooklyn Dodger organization. The couple was bound for spring training: overnight from Los Angeles to New Orleans, with connections to Pensacola and Daytona Beach, Florida. After arriving in New Orleans, the Robinsons were "bumped" from their New Orleans-to-Pensacola connection, even though several seats were available. They went to the airport coffee shop for a snack and were refused service. The restrooms and drinking fountains in the airport were marked "White Only" and "Colored Only." After spending a night in one of the few hotels that accepted "Negro" guests, they went back to the airport for the next available flight. After boarding this plane, they were forced to give up their seats to a late arriving white couple. The Robinsons eventually took a 32-hour bus ride from New Orleans to Daytona Beach. (There was no interstate highway system in those days.) Of course, they rode in the back. This is the country ordinary African Americans lived in before the Civil Rights revolution. From today's vantage point, only a half century later, it is hard to believe that such a country existed.[20]

The structure of discrimination broke down in the 1950s and 1960s, as court decisions and legislative enactments made most forms of unequal treatment illegal. For example, in *Brown v. Board of Education,* the Supreme Court ruled in 1954 that segregated school systems violated the Constitution. This decision was but one, although a key one, in a series of acts by which the Court struck down the legal basis for the denial of civil rights. Furthermore, the struggle by minority groups for civil rights moved to the streets during this same period. Looking back, it is easy to see the battle over civil rights as a simple tale of morality in which a great wrong was made right by determined people led by Dr. Martin Luther King, Jr. But segregation had been maintained for a century or so by means of violence and terror; white southerners resisted. The bitter fight to overcome this system was chaotic, and the outcome uncertain.[21] Eventually, however, the Congress passed a series of acts designed to outlaw all forms of discrimination. As a result, all racial and ethnic groups obtained the right to vote, access to public accommodations, the right to equal educational opportunity, and the right to purchase housing, among many other changes.

---

[19]Staples (2003). The phrasing above the quotation parallels Staples's words.
[20]Simon (2002).
[21]See Garrow (1986), McWhorter (2001), Library of America (2003).

Although necessarily brief, this discussion shows that discrimination due to race or ethnicity is now illegal in the United States. African American, Hispanic, and Asian citizens improved their situation both absolutely and relatively. Although civil rights provide a legal basis for personal freedom and thus indicate a transition toward a class-based society, they do not mean equality of opportunity in other areas.

***Infant Mortality.*** The **infant mortality rate** refers to the number of live babies who die within the first year of life. It indicates life chances because it reflects people's level of nutrition, sanitation, housing, medical treatment (especially prenatal care), and access to other goods and services. As such, it provides a useful measure of overall health differences among racial and ethnic groups. Here are infant mortality rates in 1900 for various white ethnic groups and African Americans. The numbers refer to deaths per 1,000 live births.[22]

| | |
|---|---|
| Native Whites | 142 |
| English Immigrants | 149 |
| German Immigrants | 159 |
| Italian Immigrants | 189 |
| African Americans | 297 |

Thus, white ethnic groups who were immigrants displayed higher rates of infant mortality than did native Whites at the turn of the century. This means immigrants endured lower living standards than natives. Their life chances were unequal. In comparison, however, the African American infant mortality rate was far higher than that of immigrants and more than double that of native Whites. The magnitude of these differences suggests that while the living standards of white immigrants were low, they were far worse for African Americans, who confronted much greater discrimination.

This fact has not changed, even though infant mortality rates declined steadily over time. Here are data for 2000, in deaths per 1,000 live births:[23]

| | |
|---|---|
| Asian Americans | 5 |
| Hispanic Americans | 6 |
| White Americans | 6 |
| Native Americans | 7 |
| African Americans | 12 |

Not only does the mortality rate of African American babies remain twice that of Whites, but also it occurs at the same rate as that of some third world nations, such as Belarus. Thus, although much has changed in that everyone is healthier today; much remains the same in that African Americans have the poorest health of all racial and ethnic groups. But Whites, who live in different neighborhoods, rarely notice these differences in life chances.

---

[22]On the usefulness of infant mortality rates as a measure of inequality, see Collins and Thomasson (2002). The data below are from Lieberson (1980:46).

[23]National Center for Health Statistics (2002:4).

*Housing Segregation.*     Housing segregation also affects life chances.[24] Where people live influences the quality of education available, opportunities for employment, the probability of criminal victimization, access to community services (such as libraries and parks), and the degree of neighborhood disorganization (exposure to violence and drug markets). It affects every aspect of life. As people succeed, they usually move to better residential environments, which not only provide immediate benefits but also improve future prospects for wealth creation and occupational mobility due to greater access to neighborhood-determined resources. When such opportunities are blocked, however, so that a better job or increase in pay does not translate into better housing, the ability to maintain that success or pass it on to one's children declines.

In 1900, 90 percent of African Americans lived in the rural South.[25] But after two centuries of confinement to the land (on plantations or as sharecroppers), African Americans began moving north and found another trap—the urban ghetto, a context in which people were crowded together in impoverished conditions and unable to find work except in menial occupations. Throughout the twentieth century, African Americans have endured more housing segregation than any other racial or ethnic group, a situation that remains unchanged. The average white person living in an urban area today resides in a neighborhood that is 80 percent white and 7 percent African American. By contrast, the typical African American person resides in an area that is 51 percent African American and 33 percent white. These data understate the degree of residential segregation. Thirty metropolitan areas, in which about 40 percent of all African Americans live, are "hypersegregated" such that virtually everyone in their own and adjacent neighborhoods is also African American. "Hypersegregation" occurs in every large U.S. city, including New York; Chicago; Washington, DC; Philadelphia; Atlanta; and Los Angeles. It affects every facet of daily life and, hence, the ability to share in the distribution of goods and services that others (Whites) take for granted. Although the Fair Housing Act of 1968 was designed to prevent housing discrimination, it has no enforcement mechanism.

The consequences of housing discrimination are profound.[26] Many African Americans (poor and not poor) are forced to live in neighborhoods with concentrated poverty. Compared to other groups, they thus experience more educational failure, more unemployment, more unwed childbearing, more crime, higher rates of infant mortality, and other problems.

The level of residential isolation is less for other racial and ethnic groups, with the exception of Native Americans.[27] Thus, the average Hispanic person lives in a neighborhood in which 52 percent of the residents are also Hispanic. You should remember, however, that many Hispanics, such as those of Cuban ancestry, look white. So they endure much less segregation. Among Asian Americans, the average person lives in an area in

---

[24]Massey (2001).

[25]On the history of housing segregation, see Massey (2001), Massey and Denton (1993), and Lieberson (1980). Current data are from the Lewis Mumford Center (2001). On "hypersegregation," see Massey and Denton, pp. 76–77.

[26]Massey (2001).

[27]The data in this paragraph are from the Lewis Mumford Center (2001). About half of Native Americans live on reservations. Those in urban areas are relatively unsegregated because their population is so small. In some cities near reservations, however, segregation is high. On prejudice toward Asian and Hispanic Americans, see Massey (2001).

which 28 percent of the residents are also of Asian heritage. This lower level of housing segregation suggests that white prejudice toward these groups is less. Moreover, the level of housing segregation reflects the impact of immigration. Asian and Hispanic immigrants tend to cluster when they arrive in this country and disperse over time. As a result, their life chances improve. This is important because one way housing segregation limits life chances is through the restriction of access to jobs.

***Occupation and Income.*** Historically, the United States has been characterized by a rigid pattern of occupational segregation. Whites worked at higher prestige and higher paying jobs than other racial and ethnic groups. But this situation has altered somewhat over the past thirty years, as shown in Table 2.1. The table reveals that only 6 percent of African Americans worked in white-collar jobs in 1940, compared to 51 percent in 2000. Similarly, only 19 percent of Hispanics worked in white-collar jobs in 1960, compared to 38 percent in 2000. The lack of change between 1990 and 2000 reflects the huge increase in immigration among Hispanics. About 68 percent of Asian Americans now work in white-collar jobs. Although some of the data are more incomplete than I would like, the gap between Whites and others has become smaller over time, as members of nonwhite racial and ethnic groups have been upwardly mobile into white-collar jobs.[28] As a result of affirmative action policies, more employers have been more willing to hire people with potential, even when their credentials (such as education) are slightly less. Research shows that job performance is no worse and that workforce diversity pays off.[29]

This mobility has important implications, because more African Americans have the prestige and income to purchase homes in middle-class neighborhoods. As the occupational structure changes, more African Americans and members of other groups are becoming middle class. This relative change indicates less inequality.

Although the pattern of declining inequality can also be seen in the following table, when a few detailed occupations are considered, the change is not as great.[30] Begin by scanning across the rows for African Americans in 1970 and 2000: In most cases, their percentages have increased, which suggests less inequality. Temporal data for other groups are not available over this same time.

| | *African Americans* | | *Hispanic Americans* |
|---|---|---|---|
| *Job Category* | *1970* | *2000* | *2000* |
| Architects | 2% | 2% | 6% |
| Engineers | 1 | 6 | 4 |
| Physicians | 2 | 6 | 4 |
| Lawyers | 1 | 5 | 4 |
| Insurance agents | 3 | 7 | 4 |
| Electricians | 3 | 11 | 8 |
| Firefighters | 2 | 9 | 5 |
| Police | 6 | 13 | 10 |

[28]G. Wilson (1997), G. Wilson et al. (1999).
[29]Holzer and Neumark (2000).
[30]U.S. Bureau of the Census (1974:352; 2001:350).

**TABLE 2.1**  *Percentage of Racial and Ethnic Groups in White-Collar Jobs, Selected Years, 1940–2000*

|                     | 1940 | 1950 | 1960 | 1970 | 1980 | 1990 | 2000 |
|---------------------|------|------|------|------|------|------|------|
| White Americans     | 35%  |      | 44%  | 48%  | 54%  | 60%  | 64%  |
| African Americans   | 6    |      | 13   | 24   | 37   | 44   | 51   |
| Hispanic Americans  |      |      | 19   | 22   |      | 39   | 38   |
| Asian Americans     |      |      |      |      |      | 64   | 67   |

*Note:* The system of occupational classification changed between 1970 and 1980. Blank cells indicate that data are not available.

*Sources:* U.S. Bureau of the Census (2001:380; 2001d).

Despite these changes, job segregation remains. Now look down the columns for the year 2000. Although African Americans and Hispanics each comprise about 13 percent of the population, at the turn of the twenty-first century they included only 2 percent and 6 percent of architects, and 5 percent and 4 percent of lawyers, respectively. These data show continuing absolute inequality. They also suggest that non-Whites still have more difficulty obtaining high prestige and, hence, high-paying white-collar jobs.[31]

Data on income reveal continuing relative inequality. As shown below, the income of families varies by racial and ethnic group and the rank order looks like that displayed in Table 2.1.[32]

|                   | *Median Household Income, 2001* |
|-------------------|---------------------------------|
| Asian American    | $53,600                         |
| White American    | 46,300                          |
| Hispanic American | 33,600                          |
| African American  | 29,500                          |

Asian and white American households have the highest incomes, with African and Hispanic Americans significantly lower.

The United States is a heterogeneous society, comprising a variety of racial and ethnic groups who continue to be unequal to one another. The differences in access to valued resources portrayed here are not unique. Other nations show a similar pattern.

## *Racial and Ethnic Stratification in Cross-National Perspective*

In comparison to the United States, most European nations are relatively homogeneous by race and ethnicity. The United Kingdom is an exception, due mainly to its colonial legacy.

[31]G. Wilson (1997), G. Wilson et al. (1999).
[32]U.S. Bureau of the Census (2002:17).

**TABLE 2.2    *Unemployment by Racial and Ethnic Group, United Kingdom and United States***

| | Unemployment Rate | |
|---|---|---|
| *United States* | *2001* | |
| White Americans | 4% | |
| Hispanic Americans | 7 | |
| African Americans | 9 | |
| | | |
| *United Kingdom* | *2002* | |
| White | 5% | |
| Indian | 6 | |
| Black | 11 | |
| Pakistani | 12 | |
| Bangladeshi | 24 | |

*Note:* Data for Whites include Hispanic Americans.

*Sources:* U.S. Department of Labor (2002:168–69), Office for National Statistics (2002a:18).

Hence, I am going to present English data on racial and ethnic inequality, and compare it to the United States. I focus on a crucial issue: unemployment. This indicator of inequality is useful because, as will be shown in more detail in Chapter 9, those without jobs are economically deprived, display a lower self-concept, and are more likely to endure familial disruption, among other problems.

The United Kingdom has a population of about 60 million persons, of whom 2.3 percent are black from various Caribbean and African nations, 1.8 percent are of Indian origin, 1.6 percent are of Pakistani or Bangladeshi origin, and 1.4 percent are from other nations around the world. Thus, racial and ethnic minorities in the United Kingdom constitute about 7.1 percent of the total population.[33]

Table 2.2 displays unemployment rates in the United States and the United Kingdom by race and ethnicity. It reveals that Whites in both nations are significantly less likely to be out of work than members of racial and ethnic minorities. Other indicators of inequality, such as those used earlier in this section, show that racial and ethnic minorities in the United Kingdom suffer discrimination similar to that in the United States.[34]

The data presented in this section lead to three conclusions. First, racial and ethnic inequality has declined in certain areas, such as civil rights and occupation, in both absolute and relative terms. Second, even though a great deal of change has occurred, a great deal of inequality in life chances continues to exist, as indicated by infant mortality rates, residential segregation, and occupations and income. Finally, in certain respects racial and ethnic inequality in the United States today resembles that in the United Kingdom. These conclusions show that we have not become a color-blind society. Rather, the social divisions established when the new nation was formed have endured.

[33]Office for National Statistics (2002:30).
[34]Hiro (1991), Skellington (1992).

## Some Consequences of Racial and Ethnic Stratification

The passage of civil rights laws during the 1960s not only created opportunities for non-white racial and ethnic groups, but also committed the nation to using achievement-oriented criteria in evaluating people. This is one important consequence of the changes described above. As mentioned, this new context has allowed some people to become upwardly mobile, to move into the middle class and, in a few cases, to become rich. Another consequence, however, is that others have been left behind, leading to the formation of an **underclass:** people who are persistently poor, residentially concentrated, and relatively isolated from the rest of the population. More graphically, the term connotes people confined to a ghetto (an area inhabited by only one group). In the United States, the underclass comprises Whites residing in parts of Appalachia, Native Americans on reservations, Hispanics in some communities, and African Americans living in hypersegregated cities. The last make up about 60 percent of the underclass, so they are the focus here.[35] Today, large areas of the nation's central cities are composed of the most disadvantaged segments of the African American population. Many lack work experience. Indeed, Table 2.2 understates the problem of unemployment among African Americans.[36] Most manufacturing jobs used to be located in central cities, which meant that relatively uneducated people could find work. Over time, however, these jobs have moved to the suburbs, which are inaccessible to central city residents. Hence, many have learned to live without employment. All about them, they see others in similar circumstances.

An anomic setting exists. The term **anomie** refers to a lack of connection between dominant cultural values (such as occupational success) and the legitimate means to achieve them (such as hard work).[37] Thus, people living in hypersegregated environments still learn—at home, at school, and in the media—that hard work leads to success, but many find they cannot obtain it via employment. So the young mature without seeing stable families with parents leaving for work every day and children in school. The reaction of people forced to live in such contexts is predictable. Most work hard at legitimate but low-paying jobs and try to make the best lives they can, but many become disaffected, with predictable results: (1) violence and crime, (2) drug markets, and (3) sexual acting out.

### Violence and Crime

In an anomic context, crime and violence become common. Because of housing and other forms of racial discrimination, many African Americans reside in neighborhoods characterized by multiple and accumulated disadvantages and there emerges "a racially distinctive ecological niche of violence."[38] A "code of the street" develops, a set of informal but widely known norms governing interpersonal behavior in public places. In this environ-

---

[35]Ruggles (1990:112).
[36]W. J. Wilson (1996).
[37]Merton (1968).
[38]The phrase is Massey's (1995). See also Massey and Denton (1993), Massey and Fischer (2000). On the code of the street, see Anderson (1999; 1994). On residents' relationship to the police, see Anderson (1999:320); see also Simon (1991). For an explanation of high American homicide rates, see Beeghley (2003).

ment, residents see the police as abusing the people they are supposed to protect. Thus, inhabitants believe they must protect themselves. The code of the street constitutes an attempt at regulating the use of violence in a context where the law is viewed as irrelevant to daily life. Such contexts are inherently lethal because everyone is made hostage to the most violent among them.

The norms embodied in the code of the street dictate that people, especially males, should carry themselves in an assertive manner that communicates the willingness and ability to be violent. So they use gait, facial expression, and talk to promote "respect" and deter aggression. For example, people do not make eye contact; it can be taken as a challenge. Seeking "respect" (or honor) in these ways is more than mere vanity; it constitutes a form of social capital that is designed to help people keep themselves physically safe in public places. One way to protect oneself is to carry a gun because its display can intimidate others and thus provide a means of self-protection. Nationwide, about 5 percent of all high school students admit to carrying a gun at least once during the last 30 days, a figure that is probably higher in poor inner-city neighborhoods where violence is pervasive.[39] As a result of so many people going armed on the street, however, the violence takes on a life of its own. Some people use their guns.

This social context, then, is one in which the norms of civility with which middle-class people are familiar, based on mutual trust and the rule of law—buttressed by police protection—do not apply. It is, rather, a peculiar social niche in which honor can only be established and preserved by the strategic use of violence. From early childhood, individuals growing up in such environments are socialized to fight to protect themselves. In this social context, aggressive and violent behaviors are not aberrant; rather, they constitute a rational response to a hostile environment. Thus, poor African American neighborhoods are divided between "decent families" and "street families."[40] Even in the poorest areas, decent families comprise the majority of the population. They value hard work and self-reliance, employ strict child-rearing practices, ally themselves with churches and schools, and try to teach their children norms of civility. Street families, by contrast, lack jobs and education, seek "respect" as an indicator of self-esteem, and feel bitter about the pervasive discrimination (it is not rocket science to look around one's segregated neighborhood and see racism at work). At the extreme, the most alienated and embittered people show contempt for others, especially anyone representing "the system." They become predators. But this difference between "decent" and "street" oriented families turns out to be irrelevant in public places in inner-city neighborhoods, where everyone must live by the code of the street; everyone must fight. The carnage is very self-destructive. Murder is now the leading cause of death among African American men, aged 15 to 24, and a high percentage of young African American men live in jail.[41]

## Drug Markets

In an anomic context, drug markets develop to serve those who turn their anger inward. Like the psychotropic substances middle-class people obtain via prescription (ritalin, prozac), alcohol, crack cocaine, heroin, and other drugs help individuals cope with the

---

[39]Centers for Disease Control (2000:Table 6).
[40]Anderson (1999:35–65).
[41]National Center for Health Statistics (2001:31).

stress of life. An informal economy exists in every poor community, where people work off the books doing construction, cutting and styling hair, repairing automobiles, repairing appliances, driving cabs and jitneys, peddling goods, selling food from a cart—anything to make a few dollars.[42] This strategy turns an anomic setting to one's favor by combining work-oriented values with unconventional means. Selling drugs offers greater opportunity. In one study, for example, independent dealers—not gang affiliated—who worked about four hours each day earned an average of $24,000 per year.[43] Although this income seems modest, it is spectacular in neighborhoods bereft of opportunity, more than twice what one would earn at the minimum wage working full-time all year long. In some areas, however, gangs dominate the illegal drug market. In one study, gang leaders paid two fees to high-level suppliers, one for the right to distribute crack cocaine and the other for the product itself.[44] They profited a great deal, making between $50,000 and $130,000 annually, thus becoming the Bill Gates (or perhaps the Al Capones) of poor neighborhoods. They organized their employees into teams whose members' income ranged from the minimum wage and up, depending on the level of responsibility. Of course, these activities are not regulated by law but by violence, which is one reason why so many hypersegregated neighborhoods look like war zones.

### Sexual Acting Out

Finally, in an anomic context, some people use sex as an outlet for anger.[45] Men and boys make women and girls pregnant. Women and girls desire to become pregnant and give birth. After all, in an anomic setting, making babies is one of the few tasks at which people can be successful. It becomes a mark of one's existence in an environment that denies their significance. They fail to see the long-term negative consequences. The percentage of babies born to unmarried women by race and ethnicity indicate how extreme segregation, race and ethnicity, and the creation of an underclass lead to conduct. The data are for 2000.[46]

| | |
|---|---|
| African American | 69% |
| Puerto Rican American | 60 |
| Mexican American | 40 |
| Cuban American | 26 |
| White American | 22 |

African Americans display the highest rate of unmarried births. Among Hispanics, the rate of unmarried births corresponds to the degree of housing segregation and the proportion whose members look white.

These reactions to being placed in an anomic situation occur regardless of race or ethnicity. Whenever groups of people live in an upside-down world, they respond simi-

[42]Sassen-Koob (1989), Hagedorn (1998).
[43]Reuter et al. (1990).
[44]Levitt and Vankatesh (2000).
[45]Anderson (1999:142–78).
[46]National Center for Health Statistics (2002a:139; 2002b:46).

larly.[47] Thus, Liverpool, England, resembles many U.S. cities except that its population is almost completely white. As in the United States, manufacturing jobs have left and the rate of unemployment is very high. In fact, long-term unemployment has become normal for many persons, especially young adults. Poverty is rampant. Located outside the economic mainstream, poor people are concentrated together and isolated from the rest of the nation. They constitute a white underclass, and in this anomic setting, the same problems appear: crime and violence, drug markets, and sexual acting out.

Alas, the impact of an underclass, a result of three centuries of exploitation, cannot be easily fixed. Jobs would probably help. In any case, continuing racial and ethnic inequality and its consequences lead to several questions: (1) In what contexts does discrimination against individuals occur and what is its impact? The other questions are structural: (2) Why have members of some racial and ethnic groups succeeded at greater rates than others? (3) What factors maintain the level of racial and ethnic inequality shown here?

## *The Individual and Racial and Ethnic Stratification*

I have always liked nursery rhymes. "Humpty Dumpty sat on a wall. Humpty Dumpty had a great fall." Have you ever thought about why Humpty fell? He was just sitting there. Being an egg and, hence, oval, he probably took precautions to prevent falling. So it is unlikely that he fell accidentally. But maybe some of the other eggs were not used to seeing eggs like him on top of the wall. Maybe they thought eggs like him ought to remain at the bottom. Maybe they resented eggs like him appearing to be so high and mighty. So maybe someone pushed Humpty. The reason: He was a brown egg. "All the king's horses and all the king's men could not put Humpty together again." Disliking Humpty, maybe they did not try very hard. In fact, maybe they were glad to see him fall. After all, a white egg would replace him. This interpretation may be flawed (!), but it does make sense of the story. And it suits my purpose: People of color, regardless of race or ethnicity, have always been pushed off the wall of opportunity by prejudice and discrimination.

Moreover, the interpretation suggests some of the conditions under which prejudice and discrimination occur. The *Contact Hypothesis,* for example, emphasizes the importance of interaction and familiarity:

> *The less experience people from different groups have with one another, the more likely are members of the dominant group to display prejudice and discriminate.*

When you think about it, prejudice is simply a way of judging others without knowing anything about them (which is why I suggested the importance of being used to seeing someone who is different in an equal or superior position in the rhyme). Such hostility occurs because Whites make assumptions about the likely characteristics or behaviors of members of other racial or ethnic groups and develop negative stereotypes about them.[48] They then find it easier to discriminate (which is why I suggested that someone pushed

[47]Inniss (1992).
[48]Case et al. (1989), Forbes (1997), Bobo (2001:275).

Humpty). Two venues in which people might become familiar with others in different groups and have egalitarian and cooperative interaction are schools and neighborhoods, but these remain segregated.

Another situation in which prejudice and discrimination occur is when people from different groups seek the same jobs, land, or other resources (a spot on the wall). The *Resource Hypothesis* summarizes the argument:

> *The more people from different groups compete for scarce resources, the more likely are members of the dominant group to display prejudice and discriminate.*[49]

Population size often constitutes an intervening variable in this relationship. For example, as long as the population of a nonwhite group remains small, not much competition for jobs or other resources occurs and, hence, less hostility or unequal treatment. As the nonwhite population increases, however, Whites become threatened and act to protect their interests. They discriminate, which results in greater racial and ethnic inequality. In the process, Whites develop rationalizations about those at the bottom, which justify keeping them there. Such reasoning justifies practices, such as not hiring others of a different race (or gender), which would otherwise be seen as unjust. (This is why I suggested that "all the King's Horses" might stand by while Humpty lay broken.) Two contexts in which discrimination continues to exist are public places and organizations. Although the following discussion focuses on African Americans, the logic applies to all nonwhite racial and ethnic groups.

***Public Place Discrimination.***    Most Whites do not think about how the color of their skin affects their treatment by others.[50] This is a form of "white privilege"—ascriptive advantages simply because of skin color. Most African Americans, however, confront their color and its implications every day. This is because when they are away from family and friends, in public places, they have little protection from discriminatory behavior, regardless of civil rights laws.

One strategy for discrimination is avoidance.[51] Hailing a cab in a large city, for example, can be a difficult process for African Americans—especially men. It is a chance for drivers to discriminate, without being caught. Middle-class African Americans take this behavior as evidence of drivers' true feelings. More subtly, Whites may routinely cross the street to avoid African Americans and stop talking in elevators when they enter. I have seen Whites take their children away from play sites (a jungle gym, for example) when joined by dark-skinned children. So it becomes important to make Whites feel safe. Some African American males apparently whistle classical music while walking down the street as a sign they are not dangerous. Such actions make daily life more stressful for the victims.

Another strategy is rejection.[52] Providing poor quality service is one way. African Americans find that getting seated in restaurants often takes a long time. While waiting, they are sometimes handed coats to be checked. When they are seated, it is in the back by the kitchen door (even when other tables are available). Then the meal arrives cold. Harassment while going to work is another example: being frisked on suburban commuter trains and mistaken for a delivery boy when entering the building where one works. Finally, rejection occurs in the office. Clients wonder "why did I get the black lawyer" (or accountant, and so on); this concern is manifested in questions about qualifications ("where did you get your degree") that would not ordinarily be asked. Such experiences mean that ordinary interaction is often tinged with stress and anger.

A third strategy is verbal and nonverbal harassment.[53] Racial epithets occur—when it is safe: from passing cars, from across the street, in crowds during athletic events. The targets are both adults and children. The "hate stare" attempts intimidation without overt violence. When shopping, African Americans note that clerks and security guards follow them around the store. Such forms of psychological assault must usually be endured without reply. A response is often either impossible or dangerous. Then parents must explain hate to their children. Stress mounts.

The final strategy is violence in some form. Whites throw cans or bottles from moving cars. Occasionally, when middle-class African Americans find themselves in the wrong area, they are pulled from their cars or accosted on the street. Sometimes they are "merely" threatened. But murder happens, too. For example, here are three recent research findings: (1) The higher the African American population in a city, the higher the rate of White on Black interracial homicide. (2) The more unemployment levels of Whites resemble those of African Americans, the higher the rate of White on Black interracial homicide. (3) The greater the political influence of African Americans in cities, the higher the rate of White on Black interracial homicide.[54] Violence is a daily possibility that makes life more difficult.

The constant strain wears people down.[55] Assume for the moment that every person has 100 ergs of energy available each day. The average white person uses 50 percent of them coping with work-a-day issues and problems, leaving the other 50 percent for everything else. An average African American, also uses 50 percent of them coping with the same work-a-day issues and problems. In addition, however, each African American must also use 25 percent to deal with being black in a white society, leaving only 25 percent to do everything else. In my classes, white students sometimes say that small slights should be ignored, and they usually are. But the erg metaphor illustrates the cumulative impact of stress on the lives of African Americans. Occupational and other forms of success become harder.

***Discrimination by Organizations.***   Civil rights laws mean that discrimination by people in organizations is now illegal and those wishing to act on their prejudice must be covert.

One area in which unequal treatment occurs is in housing. Historically, the white public, real estate agents, and government acted overtly: As African Americans migrated to the North during the years after World War I, they were trapped in ghettos far more systematically than previous waves of European immigrants or Asian or Hispanic Ameri-

---

[53]Meeks (2000), Fifield (2001), Fountain (2002).
[54]Jacobs and Wood (1999). See also Beeghley (2003).
[55]Clark et al. (1999).

cans.[56] The strategies used to create and maintain African American ghettos were direct: (1) Whites used violence (riots, bombings, physical harassment, and threatening letters) to intimidate African American families purchasing a home in white areas. (2) Whites formed "neighborhood improvement associations" and placed restrictive covenants in deeds; thereby making the sale of a home to African Americans illegal. (3) White realtors guided African Americans to ghetto areas to increase demand; thereby increasing prices and profits. They controlled the size of the ghetto by "blockbusting." They would sell an African American family a home just outside the ghetto. They would then incite Whites to flee and sell the other houses on the block to them at low prices. The realtors then resold those homes at high prices to African Americans. (4) After World War II, Whites in the Federal Housing Administration and Veterans Administration established housing guidelines that promoted low-cost mortgages for Whites living in suburbs—leading to the largest increase in home ownership in U.S. history—by Whites. African Americans were left out.

Most Whites supported these actions, although the percentages have declined over time.[57] In 1942, 84 percent of all Whites agreed that "there should be separate sections in towns and cities for Negroes to live in." Similarly, in 1962, 61 percent of Whites agreed that "white people have a right to keep Blacks out of their neighborhoods if they want to and Blacks should respect that." In 1984, 28 percent agreed with this same assertion; in 1996, only 12 percent agreed. Yet, as I suggested at the beginning of the chapter, a gap often exists between attitudes and actions. Most cities remain segregated. Although Whites now seem accepting of open housing, they actually discriminate against African American neighbors, especially if there is more than one.

Banks and mortgage companies are aware of this gap between attitudes and behavior, and continue to discriminate (covertly) today. There is an old Eddie Murphy sketch (probably from "Saturday Night Live") that suggests the cruelty involved: A perfectly dressed Murphy is applying for a home loan. The lenders greet him with a smile, give him the application, and assure him it will be carefully considered. After Murphy leaves, the lenders dissolve in laughter and throw the application away. When a White person enters and asks for an application, the lenders open the vault and tell him to take what he needs. The skit is chilling in its accuracy. Regardless of income, African and Hispanic Americans are more likely to be denied home loans than Whites. And on receipt of them, African and Hispanic Americans often pay higher interest rates than do Whites with the same income and credit history.[58] This fact has important implications, because it means not only that African and Hispanic Americans spend more of their monthly income on housing—thus reducing their ability to share in other goods and services—but also that they acquire wealth more slowly than do Whites. (As an aside, African Americans also pay higher interest rates for automobile loans than do Whites with the same income and credit history.[59])

[56]Massey and Denton (1993).
[57]Massey and Denton (1993:49), General Social Survey (1996).
[58]Association of Community Organizations for Reform Now (1999), Center for Community Change (2002).
[59]M. Cohen (2001).

Realtors are also aware of the gap; they discriminate mainly because of the perceived prejudice of their white customers.[60] So they also smile and then deny African Americans and Hispanics the ability to rent or buy homes in white neighborhoods. In Worcester, Massachusetts, one outfit placed the word "Archie" next to houses not to be shown to African Americans or Hispanics. In Orange County, California, a realtor simply told minority applicants—falsely—that no apartments were available. These specific examples are generalizable. When housing audits are done, applicants with matched characteristics approach realtors seeking housing, either to rent or buy. The data below suggest that compared to Whites with similar family and economic characteristics, African and Hispanic American auditors are shown fewer units in white areas, steered to minority neighborhoods, and given fewer facts about units they are shown.[61]

|  | *Compared to White Auditors, Percent of Black and Hispanic Auditors who were:* | |
|  | *Denied Opportunity to See Houses* | *Denied Information about Houses* |
| --- | --- | --- |
| Black Renter | 46% | 15% |
| Black Buyer | 50 | 8 |
| Hispanic Renter | 43 | 12 |
| Hispanic Buyer | 46 | 8 |

The direct costs are significant; it is estimated that African and Hispanic American households pay a discrimination "tax" of almost $4,000, on average, each time they search for a house to buy.[62] In addition, of course, when cities remain segregated, people's life chances remain unequal.

Another area in which organizations discriminate is when employees must be hired. Since perfect job candidates rarely apply, imperfect candidates must be evaluated. Consider: The Aardvark Company advertises a job requiring a Master's degree and five years' experience. Imagine that the two best applicants are (1) a Hispanic male with a Bachelor's degree and ten years' experience and (2) a White male with a Master's degree and one year's experience. Aardvark hires the white male due to his educational qualifications. Now imagine that Aardvark has another opening and the two best applicants have reverse qualifications (the Hispanic with more education and less experience). This time Aardvark hires the white male due to his greater experience. After this process occurs many times, a workforce will remain white and male—but no discrimination has occurred because the "best" applicant was always selected. Again, the example is generalizable. Hiring audits are revealing. For example, when a young Hispanic with an accent applies for a job advertised in the newspaper, about 31 percent of the time he or she will be denied an application, refused an interview, or not hired.[63] A similar outcome takes place about 20

[60]On the motives of realtors, see Ondich et al. (2000). The anecdotes are from Herbert (1998).
[61]Fix and Struyk (1993:20). See also Ondich et al. (2000a).
[62]Yinger (1997).
[63]Fix and Struyk (1993:22).

percent of the time when a young African American applies. Names provide cues. In another study, researchers sent resumes in response to 1,300 help wanted ads placed in Chicago and Boston newspapers. Apart from their names, employers had no reason to distinguish between applicants. Given similar credentials, applicants with white names (such as Emily or Brendan) elicited 50 percent more callbacks than those with African American names (Lakisha or Jamal). Employers listing "equal opportunity employer" in their ads discriminate as much as do others.[64] People's life chances remain unequal as a result. Yet emphasizing individual experiences leaves the analysis incomplete.

## Social Structure and Racial and Ethnic Stratification

As a result of civil rights laws, the obvious manifestations of prejudice are gone now, like a bad dream. In this context, many Whites want to see the United States as becoming color-blind, as they say it should be. And movement in this direction has occurred; the cup has become half-full. Yet Whites accept discrimination, partly because many Whites harbor prejudice. This section focuses on the link between social structure and racial and ethnic stratification.

### Historical Variations in Racial and Ethnic Group Mobility

Whites often wonder why so few African Americans succeeded until recently. The numbers are revealing. In 1940, only 6 percent of all African Americans were white-collar workers. Although the gap has closed over the last 40 years (see Table 2.1), African Americans, Hispanics, and Native Americans lag behind Whites. Because this result seems odd, it sometimes leads to thoughtless conclusions. After all, many people can point to their own relatives (Germans, Irish, Italians, and others) who struggled and eventually succeeded in a new society. More recently, various Asian minorities have done relatively well, suggesting that the United States is a land of opportunity. At the risk of unduly simplifying a very complex historical process, I offer the following hypothesis:

> *Until recently, African Americans' relative lack of economic success compared to other immigrant groups reflects historical differences in (1) conditions of settlement, (2) prejudice and discrimination, and (3) affirmative action.*

***Conditions of Settlement.***    This factor refers to the situation in a group's homeland and the United States at the time of immigration. The first condition was the circumstances under which immigration occurred. That is, some groups came to these shores voluntarily while others arrived involuntarily and remained as slaves.[65] Voluntary immigrants responded to changing conditions in their homeland. For example, the German and Irish people who settled in the Midwest from 1820 to 1840 had been driven off land they had occupied for generations. This was a fairly typical experience. Other immigrants, already

---

[64]Bertrand and Mullainathan (2002).
[65]On the slave trade, see Harms (2001). On the "generations of captivity," see Berlin (2003).

urban, had skills or trades in demand in the United States. In fact, U.S. companies actively recruited immigrants. In all cases, the motive for leaving was the promise of a better life. With the passage of generations, many of these people became successful. In contrast, African people were taken from their homes to this continent involuntarily as forced (often skilled) labor. Slavery produced profit—for others. Plantation owners, of course, gained directly, but northern ship owners, bankers, and others also benefited from slavery. Forced labor was essential to the early development of capitalism. Generations passed during which enslaved people could not take advantage of the opportunities available to others.[66]

The second condition of settlement was the opportunity presented by the geographical size of the North American land mass. Europeans saw themselves as inheriting an open continent, mainly because the huge death rate of Native Americans from disease made it appear relatively uninhabited.[67] As a result, it seemed possible to accommodate many white groups as the frontier moved westward. Slaves could not take advantage of this situation.

The third condition of settlement was the opportunity presented by **industrialization** and the other dynamic processes that shaped modern societies. Recall that the term refers to the transformation of the economy by the substitution of new forms of energy for muscle power and the huge increase in productivity that followed. Early in the nineteenth century, people with basic skills were needed: stone masons, bricklayers, loggers, carpenters, and the like. Later on, the ability to operate (or learn to operate) machines became important. Moreover, throughout this period, opportunities for merchants and traders grew exponentially. In short, the expanding economy transformed the occupational structure, and millions of new arrivals benefited. Slaves did not.

In the years after the Civil War, immigrants from Russia, Scandinavia, Italy, and other places came here. The frontier was wide open, and many built farms on the prairie. Others settled in cities and found economic niches suitable for their skills. In the South, however, President Andrew Johnson pardoned ex-Confederate soldiers and allowed them to legally reclaim their land. They used the law to convert most of the former slaves into sharecroppers and trap them in a system of debt peonage. A few years later, white southerners imposed Jim Crow laws in order to institutionalize discrimination in the South, where most African Americans still lived.[68] This process effectively prevented freedom for another century.

As this brief description suggests, the conditions of settlement encountered by various white ethnic groups were relatively advantageous. Over time, these differences led to assimilation and group success for Whites. In comparison, African Americans were relatively disadvantaged.

---

[66]Many African slaves were imported precisely because they possessed needed expertise. They were multilingual, experienced in agricultural production, or had craft skills. For example, rice cultivation required a complex set of specialized techniques, technology, and processing skills, so Africans with this knowledge were brought to South Carolina for this specific purpose; see Vernon (1993), Carney (2001). Although unable to take advantage of economic opportunity, the enslaved people struggled, surprisingly successfully, to preserve both a degree of personal independence and the survival of their cultures; see Vernon (1993), Morgan (1998).
[67]Thornton (1987; 2001), Mann (2002).
[68]Woodward (1966), Smith (1987).

***Prejudice and Discrimination.***     People in every society tend to discriminate against those who are different. And the more different, the greater the discrimination. Feelings of prejudice often underlie such unequal treatment. The nineteenth-century United States, for example, was viciously anti-Catholic in outlook. There is little doubt that this prejudice led to discrimination. Yet a continuum of desirability clearly existed during this period.[69] Native Whites, the majority of the population, were of northern European ancestry and tended to rank immigrants from these nations as the most desirable. Next came central and southern Europeans, most of whom were Catholic. The Japanese and Chinese occupied a third rank. Deep-seated racial prejudice meant that the United States reacted against even small numbers of Asian immigrants. In 1924, after restrictions effectively cut off immigration, fewer than 150,000 persons of Japanese ancestry lived in this country. The Asian population of the United States remains low even today. Finally, African Americans fell into the last rank, suffering more prejudice and discrimination than any other group (except Native Americans). The data on residential segregation and infant mortality described earlier merely suggest the difficulties faced by the former slaves and their descendants.

The southern and central Europeans were not so different from those already here, mainly the English. They shared a common culture and often were not physically identifiable. As a result, they could melt into the new society, changing their name, dress, accent, and the like. Moreover, their immigration constituted a response to economic opportunity. Some returned to their homeland when their lives in this country proved too harsh. Their home governments could (and sometimes did) pressure the United States not to discriminate. These governments also encouraged immigration to the United States and provided assistance to migrants after their arrival. Despite anti-Catholic sentiment, such factors reduced prejudice and discrimination directed at southern and central European immigrants.

In contrast, newly "freed" African Americans remained concentrated in the South, especially in rural areas. They were visible due to their skin color and came from cultures that were devalued. Their "freedom" was not a response to economic opportunity and, given colonization of the African continent, no home government existed to protect them. While their "freedom" might have meant economic opportunity in the North, this possibility went unrealized due to discrimination.[70]

> Had it not been for racial discrimination, the North might well have recruited southern Negroes after the Civil War to provide labor for building the burgeoning urban-industrial economy. Instead, northern employers looked to Europe for their sources of unskilled labor. . . . European immigrants, too, suffered from discrimination, but never was it so pervasive. The prejudice against color in America has formed a bar to advancement unlike any other.

Finally, hostility toward and unequal treatment of African Americans also influenced the nature and quality of education made available to them.

In making this comparison between European immigrants and African Americans, I do not mean to imply that the former's assimilation was easy; it is never easy to start over

---

[69]Lieberson (1980).
[70]National Advisory Commission on Civil Disorders (1968:143–44).

in a new society. I do mean to suggest, however, that assimilation of southern and central European immigrants was easier because they endured less prejudice and discrimination. Until very recently, African Americans had to cope with pervasive hostility and unequal treatment that was built into both U.S. custom and law. These factors prevented freedom. It is very difficult for people to be occupationally successful when they are denied civil rights. Although manifestations of prejudice and discrimination tend to be covert today, they continue to inhibit mobility. Historically, the problems of prejudice and discrimination have been made worse by government policy.

*Affirmative Action.*    **Affirmative action** refers to public policies giving advantages to members of one group over others.[71] Such policies have become controversial in recent years, mainly because many Whites believe it is unfair to do more than guarantee civil rights to the entire population. Policies designed to ensure opportunity by requiring integrated education or the hiring of minority persons (and women) seem discriminatory. They are. It would be nice to have a color-blind society, but we do not. Although this problem can be seen in terms of fairness or morality, the underlying political issue is, as always, power. Racial and ethnic relations always involve obtaining *A Piece of the Pie,* as Stanley Lieberson titled his study of the topic.[72] When society is seen as like a pie to be consumed, the referent is a metaphor for the distribution of resources: jobs, land, education, wealth, prestige, and power. People will fight, discriminate, and use the law in order to obtain (or retain) their "fair" share. Most groups do not diet; they desire a bigger rather than smaller piece of the pie. So the question becomes who is going to divide it up.

One piece of the pie is land. As mentioned earlier, German immigrants settled in the Midwest. This location was not accidental. The Land Act of 1820 provided them some pieces of the pie. Immigrants could obtain 80 acres of land on credit, with payoffs at $1.25 to $2.00 per acre. Such prices made the land essentially free. After the Civil War, the federal government wished to open up the area west of the Mississippi River. Accordingly, it subsidized railroad expansion and passed the Homestead Act of 1862, among other policies. Scandinavian immigrants, like many others, settled throughout the Plains States under terms that allowed anyone who farmed 160 acres for five years to purchase them for $10. Again, such prices meant that the land was given away. Coupled with access to eastern markets via the railroads, the Scandinavians worked hard for a piece of the pie. This is another way of describing affirmative action, of course, the provision of opportunity for white immigrants.

In comparison, newly freed African Americans were promised 40 acres and a mule in the aftermath of the Civil War. In fact, under an executive order by General William Tecumseh Sherman, nearly a half-million acres were divided into 40-acre plots and, along with mules, horses, and food, were turned over to former slaves. In 1869, however, President Andrew Johnson rescinded the order and pardoned former Confederate officers. Reconstruction meant that freedom was short-lived. But if this commitment of land and the means to farm it had been kept, millions of second and third generation freed African

---

[71]I have chosen a deliberately provocative definition. See Swain (2001) for alternatives. She showed that Whites support affirmative action programs that are compensatory in nature such that people can achieve based on their hard work.

[72]Lieberson (1980).

Americans would have been upwardly mobile.[73] Like the Germans and Scandinavians, they would have worked hard to possess part of the pie. Instead, former Confederates reclaimed their lands and kept "freed" slaves in their place. Denied opportunity, African Americans found success difficult.

Another piece of the pie is access to education. In 1862, Congress passed the Morrill Act, which funded land grant colleges in every state. The federal government spent more than $250 million (in the nineteenth century!) under the principle that "every citizen is entitled to receive educational aid from the government."[74] The idea was that the children of farmers should be able to go to college. Yet this massive outlay of money did not go to "every citizen." In fact, it was directed at Whites, especially in the South. The University of Florida, where I teach, did not admit a single African American student until 1969. Instead, a few African American colleges were established, largely due to the efforts of private philanthropic organizations. Donated by Whites, receipt of the little money available depended on accepting a philosophy of "racial adjustment." (This was a euphemism for knowing one's place.) In 1890, the second Morrill Act led to the creation of separate land grant institutions in the South, such as Florida A & M. Poorly funded, these institutions kept southern states eligible for federal support while providing poor quality college education to very small numbers of African American youths.

This last statement also summarizes the educational opportunities available to African American children of all ages from the time of the Civil War until recently. There were simply few schools African Americans could attend.[75] In 1911, for example, only 64 high schools were available to African American students in the 18 southern states. There were none in Atlanta and other major cities. In most places, schooling for African American children stopped in the seventh grade. And elementary schools were underfunded, teachers poorly trained, supplies minimal, and the length of the school year short. For example, in Augusta, Georgia, in the 1940s, the African American elementary school had 1,600 students and 30 teachers. In one first grade class, there were 63 students but only 40 desks. The elementary school dropout rate was very high: from 400 pupils in the first grade to only 100 by the seventh. These examples illustrate the broader pattern of denial of educational opportunity to African Americans. For about a century after the Civil War, then, the United States practiced affirmative action—White children were provide educational opportunity, Black children were not.

A third piece of the pie is access to a job. Even without access to land or education, it is plausible to argue that the absence of job discrimination would have made upward mobility easier for African Americans, but discrimination was rampant. As noted previously, prejudice led northern employers to recruit European immigrants for factory work after the Civil War. But these industrialists soon found African Americans to be useful as strikebreakers.[76] Although European immigrants also served as strikebreakers, in due time they joined the union movement. African Americans were excluded.

---

[73]Smith (1987), Foner (1988:70–71). For a particularly good example of the impact of President Johnson's order, see Butterfield (1996:35–37).
[74]Smith (1987:115).
[75]These examples come from Lieberson (1980) and Butterfield (1996:72–81).
[76]Grossman (1989).

Partly as a result, when Congress passed a series of bills in the 1930s designed to allow workers to organize, African Americans were again excluded. The most important of these bills was the National Labor Relations Act (NLRA) of 1935. This initiative placed wages, hiring policies, layoffs, and other issues under the rule of law rather than the "goodwill" of an employer. In addition, worker organization under the NLRA facilitated other benefits: good credit rating, group insurance, group discounts, easier qualification for home loans, and the like. Working people were thus issued pieces of the pie. Although African American leaders lobbied for an antidiscrimination clause to be included in the NLRA, the New Deal coalition of President Franklin Roosevelt depended on the support of southern legislators. In addition, northern members of Congress did not care about discrimination. After all, few African Americans were allowed to vote. As a result, the NLRA left unions free to discriminate, which they did. Over the years, Whites parceled out jobs to kin, friends, and others like themselves.[77] For example, the National Apprenticeship Act of 1937 established government training programs under union control for skilled workers. This program not only covered blue-collar jobs but also training as occupational and physical therapists, librarians, medical technicians, and many others. In 1964, the same year as the Civil Rights Act was passed, the federal government paid $4 million in job subsidies. Over nearly 40 years, virtually all the participants in this program were white. Once again, the historical pattern reveals affirmative action for Whites. African Americans were left at the starting gate, as they had been a century before.

In sum, the answer to the question with which this section began is that more African Americans have not succeeded because structural impediments of U.S. society stacked the odds against them. Whites placed these limitations there. The few African Americans who succeeded overcame great obstacles in order to do so.

In describing affirmative action, Stanley Lieberson's metaphor of a piece of the pie has been used to illustrate how power affects which groups get a bigger share of the distribution of valued resources. Over time, Whites have used public policy to provide opportunity for Whites, at the expense of African Americans. During the 1960s, however, and continuing for the last 30 years or so, the federal government developed policies designed (very imperfectly) to provide some opportunity for minority groups to increase their share of the pie, especially in terms of access to jobs and education. Such policies have been mildly effective; one example is the increase in the proportion of African, Hispanic, and Asian Americans in white-collar jobs. During the past few years, however, many Whites have begun protesting that such policies are unfair. And this assertion is true. The protest reflects an underlying (albeit inchoate) goal: Whites want to retain their share of the pie.

## Racial and Ethnic Stratification Today

In Chapter 1, I observed that racial and ethnic stratification constitutes one of three interrelated systems of ranking. In that context, however, I gave class a certain priority, arguing that *minority groups at every class level have fewer and less effective choices than do Whites.* Although this argument cannot be tested here, it provides a way to understand racial and ethnic stratification today:

---

[77]Smith (1987).

*Racial and ethnic stratification today reflects (1) the reproduction of the class
structure and (2) institutionalized discrimination.*

***Reproduction of the Class Structure.***    A great deal of racial and ethnic inequality occurs as the unwitting result of individuals acting normally to raise a family and seek economic success. As they do these things, people from each class use their resources in order
to protect their lifestyle and pass it on to their children. This process can occur without
anyone discriminating. The result, however, is the reproduction of the class structure—
that is, its stability across generations.

Consider the following vignette: A large group of runners enter a race for economic
success in the form of jobs and income that began, let us say, in 1865. Some of the runners
are white, while others are African American, Hispanic American, and Asian American.
All the Whites run in the normal way. Minority group runners, however, must wear back-
packs carrying varying amounts of weight: 50 or 100 pounds, depending on the level of
discrimination. In this context, of course, it is easy to predict the outcome of the race:
Whites will be more successful, and so will their children and their children's children.
Their income, for example, will be significantly higher, which means their life chances
will be better, with disparities that will increase over time. In the 1950s and 1960s, however, the courts ruled that discriminatory laws were unconstitutional and Congress passed
civil rights acts. Although the runners then become more or less equal, the legacy of past
discrimination means that they are at different spots on the course: Even if no more discrimination occurs, Whites' head start means they will continue to be able to pass their
advantages on to their children. This is how the class structure reproduces itself.

Although a great deal of mobility occurs in this country, the mode is for occupational continuity across generations. For example, as will be shown in detail in Chapter 3,
parents employed in blue-collar jobs tend to have children who work in blue-collar jobs,
while parents employed in white-collar jobs tend to have children who work in white-
collar jobs.[78] This continuity reflects class-related differences in opportunity. Think about
the data presented earlier in terms of the vignette. At every class level, different levels of
infant mortality not only mean that fewer minority children survive, but also that those
that do, have inferior life chances. At every class level, housing segregation not only
means that minority children are isolated from whites, but also that they have less ability
to share in the available goods and services. Occupational and income differences have a
similar impact. Precisely because members of minority groups have always had less opportunity to succeed due to structural barriers, the odds of occupational mobility are still
stacked against them and their children—simply by their class of origin.

***Institutionalized Discrimination.***    A great deal of inequality results from **institutionalized discrimination**—the unequal treatment of people with different physical or social
characteristics that is embedded in the social structure. In many cases, such unequal treatment occurs without awareness or intention; no individual or organization is necessarily
trying to discriminate. My example involves the process of finding a job. Most people
learn about jobs informally, by word of mouth. They rely on relatives and friends in their

---

[78]Blau and Duncan (1967), Featherman and Hauser (1978), G. Wilson (1997), G. Wilson et al. (1999).

social networks as the primary source of information.[79] This pattern is most characteristic of blue-collar work openings, which tend to require fewer educational credentials as a condition of employment.

This manner of learning about jobs has enormous implications, mainly because Whites, African Americans, Hispanics, Asians, and Native Americans usually participate in different social networks. Segregation means that members of each group work at different jobs. Their children go to different schools. They live in different neighborhoods. They also attend different churches.[80] These variations identify the boundaries of the social networks in which people participate. The presence of such boundaries indicates how the social structure affects interaction patterns: contact, friendship formation, and the like. Although daily life may appear integrated, members of each group lead separate lives. As a result, individual Whites, African Americans, Hispanics, Asians, and Native Americans tell their relatives and friends about different job opportunities. Hence, even in the absence of prejudice, this process produces a high level of occupational segregation—and, hence, inequality.

Here is a hypothesis that follows from the fact that most people hear about jobs through word of mouth:

> *At each skill level, the more members of a minority group currently employed in an organization, then the greater the number of their job applicants and the greater the rate at which they will be hired.*

Assuming for a moment this hypothesis is correct (it should be tested), part of the reason lies in whom one knows. As indicated, people helping a relative or a friend obtain a job are not trying to discriminate. An additional reason why the hypothesis may be accurate is that other factors also influence whether people obtain jobs. For example, having heard about a job, people must then actually apply for it, undergo some type of screening by a potential employer, and get hired. These procedures allow ample opportunity for prejudice to lead to discrimination. They suggest why the workforce in many organizations remains segregated.

In addition, people must be physically able to get to a job. This is not always easy, especially for members of minority groups. In the past, cities were centers for the manufacture and distribution of goods. Hence, people without much formal education could find work. These opportunities have declined, however, as suggested by the *Spatial Mismatch Hypothesis:*

> *The more employment opportunities move from central cities to the suburbs and the greater the housing segregation, then the greater the unemployment among minority workers.*[81]

Since about 1970, cities have lost hundreds of thousands of manufacturing jobs. Many are now located in suburban areas. Housing segregation means fewer job opportu-

[79]Corcoran et al. (1980), Grieco (1987), Morris (1992).
[80]Beeghley et al. (1981), Gallup Poll (1997:13).
[81]On the spatial mismatch hypothesis, see Kain (1968), Mouw (2000). On the movement of jobs to the suburbs, see Kasarda (1995), Brennan and Hill (1999). On the impact, see W. J. Wilson (1996).

nities for African Americans and other minority groups because getting to these jobs requires a long and expensive commute by car or, in a more complex way, by public transportation. One study, for example, looked at what happened to the employees of a single company when it relocated from the central business district of Detroit to suburban Dearborn.[82] Detroit is one of the most segregated cities in the United States, with nearly all African Americans living in the metropolitan area residing in just a few neighborhoods. Suburbs like Dearborn are nearly all white. As in other metropolitan areas, evidence suggests that this result reflects discrimination. In this context, when the company moved, many of its white employees had shorter commutes and others were more easily able to relocate to keep their jobs. Many of its African American employees, by contrast, had longer commutes and were unable to relocate; hence, they were more likely to quit their jobs. Observers can only speculate about why these jobs have moved out of central cities. One reason is probably cheaper land and easier access to transportation (interstate highways and airports). Another reason is corporate aversion to African American workers.[83] Regardless of the reason, the result is massive unemployment in central cities, concentrated among minority people.

The continuation of racial and ethnic inequality in the United States today is not accidental, as shown by the reproduction of the class structure and institutionalized discrimination. And these factors, in turn, reflect the conditions of settlement of various groups, the degree of prejudice and discrimination they endured over time, and the history of affirmative action directed toward white ethnic groups.

It can be argued recently that the struggle for civil rights during the 1960s is really the story of how the United States moved toward becoming a modern—which is to say, class-based—nation. For example, as one observer pointed out, Dr. Martin Luther King, Jr. "had to overcome the determined resistance of terrorists without conscience, politicians without backbone, rivals without foresight, and an F.B.I. Director so malicious that he would stop at nothing to destroy a man who believed in justice."[84] Put more sociologically (but less evocatively), Dr. King and others strove to replace ascription with achievement as the basis for people's position in society. The task has begun but remains far from complete. We still live with Jefferson's Dilemma.

## Summary

The United States has always confronted a dilemma: freedom and equality for all versus freedom for some and slavery or discrimination for others. The historical dimensions of racial and ethnic inequality must be assessed in both absolute and relative terms. African Americans, Hispanics, Asians, and Native Americans were systematically denied civil rights throughout U.S. history until passage of civil rights laws in the 1960s. In other arenas, however, change has not been so great. Although significant absolute improvement has occurred, infant mortality rates of African Americans have always been about

---

[82]Zax and Kain (1996).
[83]Williams (1987); Zax and Kain (1996).
[84]Wolfe (1998:12).

double that of Whites. African American housing segregation has increased over the course of this century. Although data for Hispanics and Asians does not go back very far, these two groups are much less segregated. Although occupational segregation has been the norm in the United States historically, increasing proportions of African Americans, Hispanics, Asians, and Native Americans are employed in white-collar jobs (Table 2.1). In the highest prestige positions, however, far less change has occurred.

Most Western Industrial nations are relatively homogeneous compared to the United States. The United Kingdom, however, displays a significant minority population. Comparison of unemployment rates in the two nations shows that minority groups fare less well in both (Table 2.2).

The major consequence of racial and ethnic inequality was the creation of an underclass comprised of a large proportion of African Americans. This was as an unintended result of passage of civil rights laws in the 1960s. Such persons typically live in anomic settings, and crime, drug abuse, and sexual acting out are common results. This is so regardless of race.

Most discrimination against individuals occurs when people lack familiarity with others who are different and when members of different groups compete for scarce resources. Whites who have not had much contact with members of minority groups tend to avoid them in public places, reject them, harass and intimidate them, and subject them to violence. Although discrimination in and by organizations is illegal, it is also easy. Some examples involve housing and hiring.

In order to understand why more African Americans have not succeeded, it is useful to examine historical variations in racial and ethnic group mobility. The key issues involve the conditions of settlement, patterns of prejudice and discrimination, and affirmative action. The conditions of settlement refer to voluntary versus involuntary migration, and the opportunities presented by the geographical size of the United States and industrialization. Prejudice and discrimination have always affected African Americans, Hispanics, Asians, and Native Americans more than Whites. And affirmative action has always benefited Whites more than any other group. At the structural level, the most important factors producing racial and ethnic inequality today are the reproduction of the class structure and institutionalized discrimination. The latter is not always intended, as illustrated by the process of finding out about and getting to jobs.

# 3

# *Gender and Stratification*

Historically, men were supposed to focus their lives on producing an income and participating in the community. This emphasis meant that the value placed on achievement has been applied to men, especially white men, and that women were evaluated based on ascriptive criteria. Thus, it is no accident that a woman would be asked, "What does your husband do?" at social gatherings. Men's status in the community depended on what they did for a living, on their productive activity outside the home. It indicated their place in the stratification hierarchy, their ability to share in the distribution of resources. Men were breadwinners. Women, by contrast, were supposed to reproduce, raise children, and care for the home. This emphasis meant that educational and occupational opportunity was restricted, no matter how much ability they had or how hard they worked. Women's position was set by birth; as wives, they were attached to men, accompanied men, and helped men succeed. They did not, at least publicly, lead or dominate men. It would have been odd to ask a man, "What does your wife do?" Women were breadservers. This rather rigid gender-based ranking system meant that women at every class level have had more restricted life chances. But the issue for women goes beyond sharing in the distribution of goods and services to more basic issues: They have had less autonomy, less freedom to make life choices. The name for these expectations is **traditional gender norms.**[1]

Until recently, these different rules based on birth seemed right and proper. When I was growing up in the 1950s, a popular television series called *Father Knows Best* epitomized traditional gender norms. The main character was Jim Anderson. He left each day in the family's only car to sell insurance. His wife, Margaret, stayed home—isolated and dependent. She watched the children, cleaned house, ordered groceries, prepared dinner, and provided any other support services Jim needed. Minor problems occurred in each episode that Jim would resolve, since, of course, "Father knows best." Looking back, the popularity of this series suggests women's enormous ability to take a (bad) joke. After all, it was pretty clear that one sex was supposed to be the domestic servant of the other. These television characters mirrored social life at that time.

Despite traditional gender norms, some women worked for pay. But so-called "protective laws" and discrimination forced most of them into dead-end jobs. Such practices enjoyed overwhelming support. A 1945 Gallup Poll asked the following question: "Do you approve or disapprove of a married woman earning money in business or industry if she has a husband capable of supporting her?" Only 20 percent of women and 16 percent of men approved. Most people thought women should remain at home, like the fictional Margaret Anderson, regardless of talent.[2]

This fact can be illustrated by looking at the economic dependence of married women in the past.[3] As the middle class expanded between 1870 and 1930 or so, wives usually did not work for pay and husbands controlled the family's money. Wives often did not even know how much their husbands earned. Household funds were either given to wives on an as-needed basis or by allowance. But many men opposed allowances because they gave wives too much independence. Thus, middle-class women developed various strategies to acquire more money. They went through their husband's pockets for change, had shopkeepers put fake items on bills and took cash instead, kept money from goods and services produced at home (for example, by renting rooms and sewing), and saved money from housekeeping expenses. Because working-class families had lower and more unstable incomes (see Chapter 9), their situation differed. These husbands often held back some money for their own use and gave the remainder to their wives, who were also generally ignorant of their husbands' earnings. For both middle- and working-class women, this ignorance reflected a legal fact: Family income to belonged to husbands. They earned it; they had the right to spend it. Thus, although many men resembled the fictional Jim Anderson and had many fine traits, they kept their wives economically dependent.

Today, gender norms are changing, becoming more egalitarian, and both men and women are increasingly evaluated based on achievement. One indicator is that it has become more common for husbands to be asked, "What does your wife do?" The query

[1]Beeghley (1996).
[2]Niemi (1989:225).
[3]Zelizer (1994).

implies that norms about earning money have changed—a fact reflected in survey data. When a random sample of people was recently asked the same question about married women working for pay: 83 percent of women and 84 percent of men approved a wife's employment.[4] But these high percentages mislead: What people say and what they do often differs. Hence, most analyses of gender inequality find that while much has changed, much remains the same. People's gender still comprises a lens through which all interaction is filtered. This duality—the decline of gender stratification coexisting with its continuation—constitutes the theme of this chapter.

## Dimensions of Gender Stratification

Although traditional gender norms are slowly giving way to egalitarian gender norms, this process is not inevitable (nothing in history is) and is fraught with uncertainty (change always is). **Egalitarian gender norms** refer to expectations that women and men should balance their reproductive and productive tasks, and that when women engage in productive tasks they should be evaluated in terms of performance-related criteria that are equally applied to all.

### Gender Stratification in the United States

***Gender Differences in Labor Force Participation.***   When women are not employed, they may have access to resources (such as husband's income) but rarely control over them, which makes them unequal to men and makes their life chances inferior to those of men. For this reason, the most important change in women's roles over time has been the steadily increasing proportion who participates in the paid labor force. Not only is employment the key to improving life chances, but also paid work outside the home constitutes a rejection of traditional gender norms. This is so even among those women who state (sometimes passionately) that they are not feminists; employment carries the potential for economic independence. In 1890, about 75 to 80 percent of all men were in the labor force, a figure that has remained relatively stable over time. In comparison, in 1890, only 17 percent of all women were employed. This latter percentage rose steadily, however, to 71 percent in 2001.[5] Thus, a majority of women now work outside the home. These data, however, include unmarried women who usually must support themselves. Hence, traditional gender norms apply with less vigor.

The labor force participation rate of married women, especially those with children, is of greater significance in light of traditional gender norms. These data are presented in Figure 3.1. It shows that in 1890 only 5 percent of all married women participated in the labor force. These persons were mainly poor, members of minority groups, and immigrant women who could not—because they were impoverished and discriminated against—live according to traditional gender norms. For most women, if they ever worked for pay, they did so only before marriage. But this pattern has changed. As Figure 3.1 shows, the per-

---

[4]General Social Survey (1996).
[5]U.S. Bureau of the Census (1975), Organization for Economic Cooperation and Development (2002).

**Percentage**

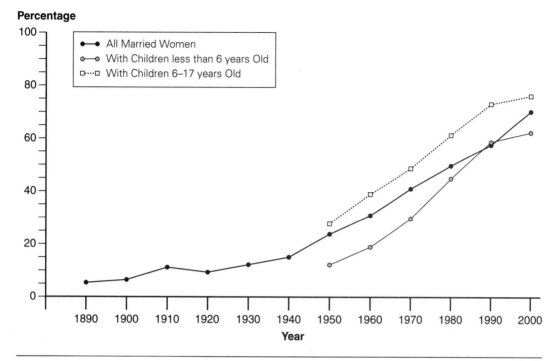

**FIGURE 3.1**   *Labor Force Participation of All Married Women and of Those with Children, 1890–2000*

*Sources:* U.S. Bureau of the Census (1975:133; 2001:373).

centage of married women participating in the labor force increased steadily until, in 2000, 60 percent worked outside the home. Although the data do not go back so far in time, the figure also reveals that married women with children have increased their employment rate over the years. While only 12 percent of those with preschool-aged children worked for pay in 1950, this proportion climbed to 63 percent in 2000. Similarly, among married women with school-age children, the labor force participation rate rose from 28 percent in 1950 to 77 percent in 2000. Thus, most women in the prime earning years are now employed, and this is so regardless of race or ethnicity.

The fundamental change in people's life chances that results from employment can be illustrated by juxtaposing it with the changing divorce rate. Please look back at Figure 3.1, noting the overall pattern of increasing labor force participation. Now imagine a line depicting the divorce rate that rises in a way roughly parallel to the lines in the figure. The divorce rate rose steadily over the last century until about 1970 when it leveled off at around 50 percent. In covariance form, the finding is:

> *The higher the rate of women's labor force participation, the higher the rate of divorce.*[6]

[6]Beeghley (1996), Sayer and Bianchi (2000).

In considering this finding, recall Marx's point that the context in which people make decisions is fundamental to understanding rates of behavior. In a social context in which few women are employed, as existed at the turn of the century, a relatively small proportion of them sought a divorce, simply because they could not be economically independent (since they had no job skills or their skills had eroded during their years as mothers and homemakers) and they did not have much opportunity to meet other adults. Similarly, only a small proportion of men sought a divorce because they were obligated to continue supporting, more or less indefinitely, both their former family and any new family they formed. Furthermore, legal and religious sanctions along with the fact that most people lived in rural areas created additional barriers to divorce. In this situation, most people had to maintain their marriages even if they had broken down.

The social context, however, has changed in several ways. Because of industrialization, advances in medical technology, and other factors to be explained later, women have entered the labor force. This historical process means that a higher proportion of women will end their marriages, simply because they enjoy a modicum of economic independence and take advantage of opportunity. Similarly, a higher proportion of men will seek a divorce, simply because they have fewer economic obligations to their wives. The recent leveling off of the divorce rate suggests that it may have reached its natural limit—at least under current conditions.

Paradoxically, however, the changes described here do not indicate gender equality. (Recall: Much has changed; much remains the same.) One reason is that nearly one-third of all married women are still homemakers and those employed still earn, on the average, far less than do men. Another reason is that women have difficulty obtaining equitable divorce settlements.[7] Hence, differences in earnings mean they usually endure a loss of living standards, with many ending up poor (see Chapter 10). Finally, child custody is nearly always given to women, many of whom manage without help from their former spouses. While child support laws exist in every state, they are not well enforced. Men becoming independent more easily, while wives and children are worse off does not reflect gender equality.

***Occupational Segregation.***     Although women have joined the labor force in increasing numbers over time, women and men still work at different jobs. Table 3.1 illustrates this fact by displaying both the current level of occupational segregation by gender and changes that occurred between 1970 and 2000.

Look first at the current level of occupational segregation. The table depicts the percentage of women in the major occupational categories established by the Census Bureau as well as selected detailed occupations. Looking down column (3) shows that women are bunched in specific major occupational categories. For example, 79 percent of all administrative support workers are female, compared to 45 percent of all executives and administrators. Similarly, 60 percent of all service workers are female, compared to 9 percent of all precision production employees.

This same pattern occurs when the detailed occupations are examined, as looking down column (5) reveals. For instance, 28 percent of physicians are women, compared to

---

[7]Peterson (1996), Smock et al. (1999). See also McManus and DiPrete (2001).

**TABLE 3.1** *Women as a Percentage of All Workers in Major Occupational Categories and Selected Detailed Occupations, 1970 and 2000*

| | Major Occupational Category, % | | Detailed Occupational Category, % | |
|---|---|---|---|---|
| *(1)* *Occupational Category* | *(2)* *1970* | *(3)* *2000* | *(4)* *1970* | *(5)* *2000* |
| *White Collar* | | | | |
| Executive, Administrative and Managerial | 19 | 45 | | |
|   Marketing Manager | | | 8 | 38 |
|   Financial Manager | | | 19 | 50 |
| Professional Specialty | 44 | 54 | | |
|   Architect | | | 4 | 24 |
|   Engineer | | | 2 | 10 |
|   Teacher | | | 71 | 75 |
|   Registered Nurse | | | 97 | 93 |
|   Physician | | | 10 | 28 |
| Technician | 34 | 52 | | |
|   Engineering Technologist | | | 9 | 20 |
|   Computer Programmer | | | 24 | 27 |
| Sales | 41 | 50 | | |
|   Sales Representative—Finance and Business | | | 17 | 45 |
|   Retail Sales | | | 62 | 64 |
| Administrative Support | 73 | 79 | | |
|   Supervisor | | | 56 | 60 |
|   Secretary | | | 98 | 98 |
|   Bank Teller | | | 87 | 90 |
| *Blue Collar* | | | | |
| Precision Production | 7 | 9 | | |
|   Mechanic | | | 3 | 5 |
|   Extractive | | | 2 | 2 |
|   Construction | | | 2 | 3 |
| Machine Operator | 40 | 25 | | |
|   Textile Machine | | | 79 | 78 |
|   Truck Drivers | | | 2 | 5 |
| Handler and Laborer | 17 | 20 | | |
|   Stock and Freight Handlers | | | 13 | 22 |
| Service | 69 | 60 | | |
|   Bartender | | | 21 | 52 |
|   Private Household | | | 96 | 95 |
|   Protective Service | | | 7 | 19 |
| Farming, Forestry, Fishing | 9 | 21 | | |
|   Farm Operator and Manager | | | 5 | 25 |

*Sources:* Rytina and Bianchi (1984), U.S. Bureau of the Census (2001:380).

93 percent of nurses. Similarly, 75 percent of teachers are women, compared to 10 percent of engineers. This pattern of occupational segregation also holds with regard to specialization within fields. For example, women physicians mainly specialize in fields such as pediatrics, psychiatry, and obstetrics, rather than, say, neurosurgery. The last is a much higher paying specialty. A similar situation occurs among teachers (data not shown in Table 3.1). For example, 83 percent of elementary school teachers are women, compared to 59 percent of secondary school teachers, and 43 percent of college professors.[8]

Column (5) also shows that occupational segregation occurs in nonprofessional jobs as well. For example, 64 percent of all retail sales clerks are women, compared to 45 percent of all sales representatives, who earn more. Similarly, 19 percent of all protective service workers, who are primarily police officers and firefighters, are women, compared to 95 percent of all private household workers, who are primarily maids. These data mean that occupational segregation by gender is pervasive in the United States. Much remains the same.

Nonetheless, much has changed: Occupational segregation has declined. Thus, comparing columns (4) and (5) shows that over a 30-year period the proportion of female physicians climbed from 10 percent to 28 percent, computer programmers rose slightly from 24 percent to 27 percent, sales representatives increased from 17 percent to 44 percent, and bartenders expanded from 21 percent to 52 percent. Although these data only refer to selected occupations and the format does not control for outside influences, they illustrate the decline in occupational segregation since 1970.[9]

One other major change in occupational segregation by gender, not shown in Table 3.1, has occurred among African American and Hispanic women. In 1940, three-quarters of African American women were doing private household and farming work. Today, although still overrepresented in service and private household jobs, their occupational distribution resembles that of white women; that is, it resembles that shown in column (5) of Table 3.1. This pattern is especially true of young Hispanic and African American women.[10]

Even though much change has occurred in recent years, these data understate the level of occupational segregation still existing in the United States.[11] For example, women and men in the same job category often work for different companies, with significant economic consequences. Thus, high-priced restaurants employ waiters (men) whose income is relatively high, while low-priced restaurants employ waitresses (women) whose income is relatively low. Moreover, men and women in the same job category work in different industries, again with significant economic consequences. Thus, women are often employed in the textile industry where the pay is low, while men work in the petroleum industry where the pay is high. Finally, even when men and women appear to have similar jobs within a company, the former often has more and the latter less income and authority. Just because a person has the title Manager does not mean she controls resources or makes fundamental decisions.

---

[8]U.S. Bureau of Labor Statistics (2002).
[9]Jacobs (1990); Goldin (1990), Baunach (2002). Weedon shows that gender-based occupational segregation also declined between 1930–1940, during the Depression (1998).
[10]King (1992), U.S. Bureau of Labor Statistics (2002), DiNatale and Boraas (2002).
[11]Padavic and Reskin (2002).

In general, job segregation means lower prestige in the community (see Chapter 5). Nurses have a lower level of occupational prestige than physicians. Elementary school teachers enjoy less honor in the community than do college professors. Administrative support workers constitute the lowest prestige white-collar category. Similarly, service workers usually enjoy less prestige than do precision production workers. Textile workers have less prestige than truck drivers. And private household workers endure lower standing than protective service workers. This pattern can be expressed as an empirical generalization:

> *The higher the proportion of women in an occupation, the lower its occupational prestige.*

Part of the reason for this finding is that, as shown in Table 3.1, employed women tend to be clustered in jobs that resemble traditional roles—assistings men, raising children, and picking up after others—caring tasks that are devalued in U.S. society. Nurses, after all, appear to assist doctors. Elementary school teachers not only impart knowledge, but they also (and just as importantly) socialize the very young, a task traditionally assigned to women who remain at home. Finally, private household workers pick up and clean other people's houses, while police officers and firefighters protect them. This last example provides an excellent image of how traditional gender norms reappear in the workplace.

In this context, occupational segregation also affects life chances because women earn less money and are less able to be economically independent. For instance, in the male-dominated occupations shown in Table 3.1, men are more likely to obtain promotions while women are more likely to leave their jobs.[12] Such outcomes have obvious implications for earnings.

***Income Differences.*** In the past many people accepted the idea that women should earn less then men. Today, survey data show that nearly everyone agrees that women working at the same jobs as men should receive equal pay.[13] This support means that achievement values are currently viewed as applicable to women, at least with regard to income on the job. Unfortunately, however, this ideal has never been realized in practice. It has been estimated, for example, that the median income of women working full-time was about 54 percent of men's in 1890.[14] Panel A of Table 3.2 shows that women still earned only 54 percent of men's income in 1950. Since then, the earnings of women employed full-time increased slowly and fitfully. As of 2001, women's median income is still only 76 percent of men's, indicating that a wage gap continues to exist.

The extent of the wage gap can be seen by examining gender differences in income by skill level, as displayed in Panel B of Table 3.2. Educational attainment is the indicator of skill. Panel B shows that at each higher level of education, women earn more; at the same time, however, at each level of education, women earn only 64 to 74 percent as much as do men. These data can be summarized by two empirical generalizations.

---

[12]Maume (1999), Cobb-Clark and Dunlop (1999).
[13]Gallup Poll (1994:187). Since agreement is so high, this question is no longer asked in sample surveys.
[14]Goldin (1990:60).

**TABLE 3.2**    *Women's and Men's Income*

**Panel A: Women's Median Income as a Percentage of Men's, 1950–2001**
*(Year-round, full-time workers, 18 years of age and older)*

| Year | Women's Income as % of Men's |
|------|-------------------------------|
| 1950 | 54% |
| 1960 | 61 |
| 1970 | 59 |
| 1980 | 60 |
| 1990 | 70 |
| 2000 | 73 |
| 2001 | 76 |

**Panel B: Mean Income by Gender and Education, 2001**
*(Year-round, full-time workers, 18 years of age and older)*

| Education | Men's Mean Income | Women's Mean Income | Women's Income as % of Men's |
|-----------|-------------------|---------------------|------------------------------|
| Elementary (< 9 years) | $24,300 | $18,000 | 74% |
| High School Degree | $37,400 | $26,700 | 71% |
| College Degree (or more) | $70,300 | $45,300 | 64% |

*Sources:* U.S. Bureau of the Census (2001a:9; 2002:7; 2002a).

*For both genders, the greater the skill level, the higher the income.*

This fact means that achievement pays off. However: *At every skill level, men earn significantly more than women.* This fact means that ascription remains a powerful force.

But less inequality exists among young men and women. The data below are median incomes of two age ranges of women and men employed full-time in 2001.[15]

| Age | Women | Men | Women's Percentage |
|-----|-------|-----|--------------------|
| 25–44 | $29,900 | $37,500 | 80% |
| 45–54 | $31,300 | $45,100 | 69% |

These ages identify people starting their work lives and in their peak earning years. As shown, older women earn only a little more than younger women on average; this is be-

---

[15]The data are from U.S. Bureau of the Census (2002a). See also Blau and Kahn (2000), DiNatale and Boraas (2002).

cause the former have often left the labor force for extended periods of time and suffered more from discrimination (issues discussed later). Younger women, however, have incomes closer to those of younger men, which may mean they suffer less discrimination. Racial and ethnic variations exist, of course, as white women earn more, on average, than do Hispanic and African American women. These differences between groups, however, are smaller than among men.[16]

## *Gender Stratification in Cross-National Perspective*

Women are also stratified along these same dimensions—labor force participation, occupational segregation, and income—in other Western industrial nations. Shown below are cross-national comparisons of women's labor force participation in 2001.[17]

| | |
|---|---|
| Sweden | 77% |
| United States | 71 |
| Canada | 71 |
| United Kingdom | 68 |
| Netherlands | 67 |
| Germany | 64 |
| France | 62 |

Thus, American women display a relatively high level of employment compared to some other Western nations. But these data hide significant variations.[18] Employed German women, for example, are more likely to work part-time. In all these nations, women display a high level of occupational segregation, with Canada and the United States having the lowest. Finally, income inequality by gender varies by country. In Sweden, for example, in 1996, women earned about 84 percent as much as men when they were employed full-time and were among the highest paid in the Western world. By contrast, in the United States, women earned about 76 percent as much as men when employed full-time.

The information presented in this section suggests the duality mentioned earlier: (1) Gender inequality has declined significantly in recent years and (2) a great deal still exists. The continuity of gender inequality is shown by the many women who remain out of the labor force and the high level of occupational segregation and income inequality. The reduction in gender inequality is revealed by rising female labor force participation along with declining occupational and income inequality. I will offer hypotheses to account for these patterns later in the chapter. Now, however, it is important to recognize that the difficulty most women have becoming economically independent, regardless of skill, indicates not only the continued salience of traditional gender norms but also how few women exercise authority and how many are victimized.

---

[16]Bowler (1999).
[17]Organization for Economic Cooperation & Development (2002). See also van der Lippe and van Dijk (2002).
[18]Hakim (1994), Blossfeld and Rohwer (1997), Anker (1998:176), Blau and Kahn (2000).

## *Some Consequences of Gender Stratification*

### *Authority and Gender*

The term **authority** refers to the legitimate exercise of power. As Max Weber observed, those with authority assert a right to make decisions affecting others, who believe they have a duty to obey.[19] This shared definition of right and obligation usually means that force does not have to be used. Thus, from the point of view of traditional gender norms, men have the right to exercise authority in the United States. Women's acceptance of male authority is reflected in traditional marriage vows: They pledge to love, honor, and obey. Although this prerogative has been challenged in recent years (marriage vows are changing), men dominate public life.

In economic matters, men, not women, set policy. Internationally, U.S. companies apparently have the highest proportion of women in management jobs in the world.[20] That is, however, not saying much. Of the top five most well paid corporate officers in each Fortune 500 company, only 5 percent are women.[21] Moreover, in these large companies, only 12 percent of all corporate officers at any level are women. Thus, men decide the height of assembly lines and the size of airplane cockpits, which affects women's ability to work in better paying blue-collar jobs (recall the distribution in Table 3.1). Men decide how occupations are to be evaluated, which may be part of the reason engineering is seen as more important than teaching. Pay levels follow.

This same pattern occurs in government. Men, not women, make laws and dictate how they will be enforced.[22] Only 13 percent of all Senators and 14 percent of all members of the House of Representatives are women. It is not accidental that until just a few years ago women were denied many basic civil rights. These included the ability to own property, obtain credit, and sue in court. Men made these laws. They still do. When bills about day care, or Head Start, or domestic violence (wife or child abuse) come before Congress, women have little impact.

Religion is no different. Men, not women, talk to God. Only 15 percent of all members of the clergy are women.[23] Those religious groups excluding women from leadership roles, do so for varying reasons. Most, however, appear to assert that although men and women are equal in the eyes of God, however known, scripture says men ought to be in positions of formal leadership. It should be no surprise, then, that God is defined as masculine and those interpreting His intentions have always justified men striking and chastising women and children.[24] It should be no surprise that, in His name, they chose to defend developing embryos over the needs of women. It should be no surprise that some Protestant faiths still assert that every woman should "submit herself graciously" to her husband's leadership.[25] "Father knows best."

---

[19]Weber (1920).
[20]Wirth (2001).
[21]Catalyst (1999).
[22]U.S. Bureau of the Census (2001:245).
[23]U.S. Bureau of Labor Statistics (2002).
[24]Greven (1991).
[25]Neibuhr (1998).

The situation is similar in court. Men dominate; they decide how laws are interpreted and enforced. It is not accidental that child support payments in the United States are set very low and are poorly enforced.[26]

When people seek medical treatment, men dominate. Men decide who should enter the field and its priorities. So men define who is sick and how they will be treated. In fact, organized medicine drove women from the field during the nineteenth century.[27] It is not accidental that this process began just when abortion became a safe medical procedure and increasing numbers of women sought to regulate their fertility.[28]

Finally, men dominate higher education. Walk down the hallway where administrators and faculty are housed; nearly all are men. The secretaries, of course, are women. This pattern also includes sociology.[29] It is not accidental that just 30 years ago, women's studies courses and departments were almost unheard of. It was assumed that analyses of women's experiences would yield little new insight. This assumption was, of course, buttressed by sociological theory.[30]

Although much change has occurred, women in authority remain rare. And deviant. Imagine women in jobs of real authority: as the chief executive officer of General Motors, as the majority leader of the United States Senate, as the parish priest. Think about how women in positions of dominance are described: "lady policemen" and "lady doctors." The diminutive term, "lady," relegates those performing such roles to unequal status. It implies they should not be there. This situation also occurs on campus, where the expression "lady" designates many women's athletic programs—as in "Lady Gators" and "Lady Bruins." Women's sports are, of course, always unequal compared to men's. Thus, the term *lady* still implies, as it always has, that women belong in the home, where men can protect them. Unfortunately, the paradoxical result of traditional gender norms is that women are not protected, either at home or at work.

### Victimization and Gender

Although often unrecognized, traditional gender norms and the inequality that follows lead to female victimization. Sexual harassment, rape, wife abuse, and child sexual abuse all involve the assertion of power by men over women. **Power** refers to people's ability to achieve their goals, whether legitimate or not, even if opposition occurs. Power often requires force or coercion. I mentioned earlier that authority relies on a shared acceptance of the right to dominate. In this case, traditional gender norms imply agreement that men belong on the job and women at home, dependent. Nonetheless, anyone approached by an armed police officer knows that the threat of force always underlies authority. Relations between men and women are similar. The combination of differences in physical size and men's dominance of public life means that the threat of force always exists and sometimes occurs. Women become victims. They are the only exploited people I know of who have been idealized into powerlessness.

---

[26]U.S. Bureau of the Census (2000).
[27]Starr (1982).
[28]Luker (1984), Reagan (1997).
[29]Beeghley and Van Ausdale (1990).
[30]Acker (1973).

**Sexual harassment** is a form of discrimination that occurs under one of two conditions.[31] First, a person pressures another for sexual cooperation as a condition of employment (such as hiring or promotion). Second, an intimidating or hostile environment is created in the workplace or educational institution. The latter takes place via repeated hazing or put-downs, repeated phone calls or letters, repeated pressure for dates, repeated physical touching, and repeated sexual remarks. Nearly all sexual harassment is directed by men toward women. Millions of women experience insults and assaults merely by choosing to work for pay rather than remain at home.

Sexual harassment is widespread. Various studies show that a significant proportion of employed women are sexually harassed.[32] For example, 37 to 48 percent of female physicians report they have been harassed—in medical school, during their internship, and in medical practice. Yet many, if not most, women find that sexual harassment is a crime without a remedy. In *Measure for Measure,* written around 1603, Shakespeare shows why.[33] In Act II, scene iv, Isabella tells Angelo:

> *With an outstretch'd throat I'll tell the world aloud*
> *What man thou art.*

Angelo responds:

> *Who will believe thee, Isabel?*
> *My unsoil'd name, th'austereness of my life,*
> *My vouch against you, and my place i' th'state,*
> *Will so your accusation overweigh,*
> *That you shall stifle in your own report*
> *And smell of calumny.*

Like Angelo, harassers often try to make the victim into the victimizer by accusing her of making untrue assertions harming his reputation (calumny). Like Angelo, they then move on with their careers, becoming chairs of academic departments (including sociology), administrators in Fortune 500 corporations, and judges and politicians.[34]

The consequences of sexual harassment are adverse.[35] Victims sometimes lose their jobs, either by being fired or quitting. Sometimes their lives are transformed: They lose self-confidence, become anxious, and suffer from headaches, ulcers, and other physical ailments. Some become clinically depressed; this term does not mean they merely feel bad. Everyone feels bad sometimes. Rather, **depression** occurs when people become psychologically incapacitated; they lose interest in daily activities for an extended period; they have little energy, feel worthless, and find it difficult to concentrate; they sometimes contemplate suicide; they often use and abuse drugs. As should be clear, harassers use sex as a means to express power.[36] As women enter traditional male occupations, men often

---

[31]Welsh (1999).
[32]Welsh (1999). For women physicians, see Frank (1998).
[33]Shakespeare (1991).
[34]Engelberg and Sontag (1994), Welsh (1999).
[35]Wagner (1992), Laband and Lentz (1998), Wolfe et al. (1998), Welsh (1999).
[36]Wilson and Thompson (2001).

become insecure; they believe women are invading their territory. Hence, they try to put women "in their place" by telling them they are not welcome and not respected. The resulting trauma inhibits occupational and economic success for many women.

So does rape. Studies consistently show that about 15 to 20 percent of women are raped at some point in their lives, most while young, often as children.[37] Some variation occurs by race and ethnicity, with Native American women more likely to be victimized than either white or African American women. Asian American women are least victimized. Rape keeps women unequal in two ways. First, fear of rape leads many women to alter their behavior. At an early age, women learn to avoid placing themselves in situations where they may be vulnerable, such as working at night. Yet, many high prestige and well-paying jobs require such extra hours. Thus, women who have not been raped are victims to the extent they change their behavior, act cautiously, do not take a job, or avoid an opportunity out of fear. Most rape victims know the assailant, who is a father, husband, boyfriend, or friend.[38] Second, actual victims display many problems.[39] About 30 percent become clinically depressed at some point in their lives, while another 31 percent develop **post-traumatic stress disorder.** The term refers to reactions to trauma: intense anxiety, inability to concentrate, becoming easily startled, nightmares, flashbacks, and insomnia. Physical symptoms are common: stomachaches, ulcers, and bulimia, among others. In addition, rape victims are more likely to use and abuse drugs of all sorts. Finally, about 33 percent of rape victims contemplate suicide, and 13 percent eventually try it. So the impact of rape is long-lasting and inhibits occupational success. Like sexual harassment, rape is an assertion of power by men, a means of controlling women and keeping them in their place: at home and out of the labor force.[40]

So is **wife abuse:** threatening or harming one's wife or companion. Men initiate most violence in families, which is why I use this term rather than the more common "spouse abuse."

About 25 percent of women say they have been physically assaulted or raped by a spouse or companion.[41] Native American and African American women have higher rates of victimization than do Whites, with Asian American women lower. Most injuries are scratches and welts (as when someone is hit), but broken bones occur about 11 percent of the time and even more serious results less often. In addition to physical injuries, abused women suffer in other ways as well. Although numbers are hard to obtain, battered women are at greater risk for post-traumatic stress disorder, depression, and suicide. Emotionally abusive and controlling behavior often accompanies violence against women. Once again, the issue is power: keeping women dependent. Abused women have less occupational or economic success over time.

[37]Koss et al. (1987), Merrill et al. (1998), Fisher et al. (1998), Brenner et al. (1999), National Institute of Justice (2000; 2000a), Russell and Bolen (2000), Silverman et al. (2001), Wordes and Nunez (2002). Rates by race/ethnicity are from National Institute of Justice (2000).

[38]National Center for Victims of Crime (1992), Saunders et al. (1999), National Institute of Justice (2000; 2000a).

[39]National Center for Victims of Crime (1992), Dansky (1997), Saunders et al. (1999), National Institute of Justice (2000; 2000a).

[40]Searles and Berger (1995).

[41]National Institute of Justice (2000b). All the data in this paragraph are from this same source. On the psychological and economic consequences, see Herman (1989; 1992), Lloyd (1998).

**Child sexual abuse** has the same impact. It refers to molestation or sexual penetration of children by adults. Official data indicate that about 87,000 cases occur per year, a rate of about two per 1,000 girls and less than one per 1,000 boys.[42] These are events reported to state authorities and, hence, significantly underestimate the true incidence. Self-report studies show rates ranging between 6 to 38 percent of girls, depending on the nature of the sample and question wording. As a reasonable guess, about 20 percent of girls and 10 percent of boys are sexually abused as children, nearly always by adult males. As with the other behaviors described here, child sexual abuse is about power rather than sex.[43] Thus, male adults engage in sexual behavior with young persons in order to feel powerful and in control. And the victims frequently react by feeling powerless. Men who are victimized tend to have inconsistent responses, some become depressed and others aggressive (often toward women). Women who are victimized also tend to become depressed and to see themselves as dependent on men. Such women often become sexually active at younger ages and endure early pregnancy (and abortion or birth), early marriage, and early divorce. Victims of both sexes frequently use and abuse drugs, and think about suicide.[44] These results limit their employment and income as adults.

This discussion suggests that women need to be protected from men rather than by men. If a few men assert power via sex, all men benefit to the extent that women stay home, stay dependent, and provide domestic service. Thus, while it may never occur to men who resemble the fictional Jim Anderson to threaten women like the fictional Margaret, family life is buttressed by the victimization of women. In *Trauma and Recovery,* Judith Lewis Herman emphasized that the most common location of trauma for women is the family and workplace.[45] Such locations continue to be regulated by traditional gender norms. Because these norms dictate that men ought to dominate women, they lead to silence when trauma occurs. In fact, Herman argued that it is the silence that haunts women even more than the crimes themselves: bystanders' denial that crimes have been committed. She said that the study of trauma endured by women depends on a political movement for equality: **feminism.** The term refers to an ideology and a social movement emphasizing that women and men should be equal. It seeks the generation of egalitarian norms for women and men. It argues that the roles women play as adults cannot be like those of men until women are no longer victimized, until sex is no longer a means of power by men over women.

## The Individual and Gender Stratification

Think about certain events in the life of Carol Hanson. She enrolls at State College with excellent test scores and good grades. Nearly any major is available to her. She initially considers engineering and takes a couple of courses, but ultimately she selects education.

---

[42]U.S. Department of Health and Human Services (2002). The self-report studies are summarized in Russell and Bolen (2000), who consider the "reasonable guess" in the text as far too low.
[43]Herman (1981).
[44]Boyer and Fine (1992), Jacobs (1994), Stock (1997), Rodriguez et al. (1997), Molnar et al. (2001), Strathlee (2001), Pillay and Schoubben-Hesk (2001).
[45]Herman (1992).

Carol graduates at age 23 and begins teaching in an elementary school. She marries Bertram ("Bertie") Robinson, who is still working on his engineering degree, so Carol supports them for two years. After Bertie graduates, he gets a job and they settle in Dawson Creek (well, why not?). She teaches fourth grade for five years and also does nearly all the housework. Then Bertie is offered a job in Chicago. Carol opposes the move; they argue and at one point Bertie throws the phone at Carol, giving her a black eye. They move. After relocating in a big new house, they decide to start a family (a common pattern). After the birth, which took place at Chicago Hope (of course), Carol, now 30, quits her job and focuses on childrearing, housework, and taking care of Bertie. After three years, she begins teaching again but starts near the bottom of the salary scale because her previous tenure only partially transfers. Thus, Carol's income is less than both Bertie's and others who obtained their teaching certificates at the same time but re- mained in the labor force. Carol continues, of course, to be responsible for childcare and housekeeping. After two years, Bertie gets another job offer. Carol again opposes the move, but to no avail. They move to a new zip code: 90210. A second child is born, and Carol quits working. She returns to teaching after two years. But once again she starts near the bottom of the salary scale. Five years pass, and Bertie is now making serious money but hating his rat race. He begins seeing his (much younger) secretary, Ms. Bimbo. After the divorce, he takes his engineering degree (remember, Carol supported him), his pen- sion (Carol provided support services while this was building), Ms. Bimbo, and the dog Toto back to Kansas. Because Carol has a good job, she receives no income support. What she gets is child custody and child support. After a short time, however, the latter stops. Carol now takes care of her children on her teacher's salary of $30,000 per year.

Though stereotypical, the vignette reflects the experiences of many women. Carol decided on a teaching career instead of, for example, building highways. Women often select occupations that require helping others.[46] One reason for this choice lies in her so- cialization at home (more on this in the next section). Another reason is that she became serious about Bertie and married him right out of college. Such women may lower their aspirations or choose a major (and career) that appears congruent with traditional gender norms. In either case, like many other women, Carol quit her job each time the family relocated and she gave birth.[47] What Carol probably did not realize is that the wage pen- alty for motherhood is about a 7 percent loss in income for each child. Finally, she went through a divorce and found child support to be unreliable. Again, this is common.[48] Note that, except for the breakup of her marriage and its consequences, each of these choices was Carol's. Women often make such decisions. Why?

## Women's Choices

When people enter the labor force, they make decisions about what skills to acquire and the relative priority their job will have compared to leisure time, child care, housework, and the like. Economists postulate an "efficient" job market in which these choices affect income variations independent of gender, race/ethnicity, or any other ascribed character-

---

[46]Bridges (1989), Valian (1998).
[47]Kaufman and Uhlenberg (2000), Boyle et al. (2001), Budig and England (2001).
[48]U.S. Bureau of the Census (2000).

istic. From this point of view, Carol earns less than Bertie because she is less productive. Productivity is assessed by people's **human capital:** their skills (education, work experience, and tenure on current job) and employment priorities (labor force continuity, choosing part-time employment, absenteeism due to a child's illness, and leaving a job due to a spouse's mobility). This argument can be phrased as the *Human Capital Hypothesis:*

> *The less valuable the skills people acquire and the lower the priority employment has versus other activities, the lower their income.*

Education and work experience reveal the job skills individuals like Carol and Bertie have chosen to develop, their employment priorities, and, hence, income. So Carol's selection of education over engineering produced skills (presumably) worth less than Bertie's. In addition, she chose to stop working for pay on two occasions, which also made her "less productive." This argument is generalizable beyond the vignette. Many women make similar decisions, which make them less productive—albeit in the narrow sense of producing goods and services. This angle of vision suggests, then, that such women deserve lower incomes because they are less skilled and less devoted to paid work. They value (economists would say they have a "taste for") housework, child care, and following their husbands. Earnings inequality follows.

Well, okay. But three observations suggest there is more going on here than gender-related differences in "taste."[49] First, if I understand the logic of the Human Capital Hypothesis correctly, it implies that women emphasizing family obligations would pick jobs that fit with these activities. But many of the occupations in which women cluster (shown in Table 3.1) do not fit with caring for children and husbands because, for example, the required hours are usually less flexible. Secretaries and private household help must typically keep rather rigid schedules. Nurses must often work nights and weekends. In fact, men's jobs often have more flexible hours, more unsupervised leave time, and more sick leave and vacation, which means that their jobs are more compatible with family responsibilities. Second, the hypothesis implies that single women (whose family responsibilities are less) would cluster in higher-prestige, higher-paying occupations. But this does not occur; such women's jobs are no different than those of married women.[50] These observations imply that "productivity" is not the only source of gender-related differences in income, that the job market is not "efficient." Third, tests of the hypothesis suggest just how inefficient.[51] Only about one-third of the variation in men and women's income results from so-called human capital factors, with another one-third reflecting the industry, union status, and other job-related factors. This finding means that the Human Capital Hypothesis only partly explains why women like Carol make less than men. More is going on here.

### Discrimination against Women

The "more" that is going on is **discrimination.** The term, you may recall from Chapter 1, refers to the unequal treatment of people or groups because of their personal characteris-

---

[49]England (1982), still the best critique of human capital theory.
[50]Padavic and Reskin (2002).
[51]Blau and Kahn (2000).

tics. Today, such behavior is often illegal. But not at home, and I would like to argue that the unequal treatment of women and men begins there.

First, the victimization of women constitutes discrimination. When Carol objected to moving to Chicago, Bertie threw the telephone at her. From that moment on, Carol was aware that force might be directed either at her or the children. More generally, the threat of wife abuse, rape, and child sexual abuse makes all women careful and impedes occupational success.

Second, discrimination occurs during divorce when the tangible assets (a house) and the intangible assets (a pension) are divided.[52] Although Carol's relationship with Bertie was intimate, in callous economic terms they were business partners for many years: She provided support services while he obtained a degree and made a career. She followed him from place to place, always providing services in the expectation that she would gain economic security in return. Then he walked away with Ms. Bimbo. It is a common tale, but true: Wives are treated unequally, especially when they have their own (less remunerative) careers and pensions.

Third, discrimination at home goes beyond these acts of power to the more subtle issue of socializing women and men to accept traditional gender norms. Economists in the human capital tradition will argue that when women like Carol choose elementary school teaching, they are selecting a job with flexible hours and slow skill deterioration precisely so they can easily relocate with their husbands and leave the labor force to bear and raise children. But this choice reflects socialization.[53] Even when children are infants, parents project their gender expectations onto children. As children grow up, data show that girls and boys perform different chores: Girls cook and clean, boys remove garbage and mow the grass. In play, children learn "appropriate" adult roles. Playing with dolls and dollhouses constitutes practice for adult responsibilities; girls learn to enjoy and to want to do what they will have to do as adults. Why do you suppose Carol, who was career oriented, so readily accepted her responsibilities at home? Boys' play, by contrast, turns into men's play. Few boys become cops or robbers, or major league baseball stars; many men practice target shooting and play softball and watch sports on television. These behaviors do not teach them to enjoy caring for others. Children actively try to make sense of their environment. They see their parents' division of household labor and learn expectations for their own behavior. Now there are many who would disagree with this third point, mainly, it seems to me, because they do not want to face the implications of their values. I will return to this issue when dealing with social structure and gender stratification.

Discrimination starts at home, but continues at work. The Equal Pay Act of 1963 and the Civil Rights Act of 1964 prohibit discrimination against women in earnings and occupation. Other federal legislation forbids discrimination in education, housing, and credit. Despite these laws, a great deal of covert discrimination occurs in the workplace. The methods used to prevent individual women from obtaining a job and earning a living are straightforward: recruitment and screening practices.

[52]Peterson (1996), Smock et al. (1999).
[53]Valian (1998).

When employers decide to hire people, they must recruit candidates. One relatively efficient way of doing this is by word-of-mouth, since this is how most people find jobs. This process disadvantages women, however, because of occupational segregation.[54] Since most women work in jobs that are dominated by women, they obtain information about other women-dominated jobs. Another approach is to place advertisements in the media. Hiring audits show the extent of discrimination. For example, when "job seekers" with similar résumés were sent to high-priced restaurants, the female "applicant" was interviewed for the job 40 percent less often, and was only half as likely to get a job offer.[55] A final approach is to fit a job for an "inside" candidate. My suspicion is that this happens more in government and academia, where the law requires advertising job openings, than in private industry where such pretenses are not necessary.

After recruiting job candidates, they must be evaluated, eliminating those who are ineligible or inappropriate. In so doing, it is legal to use subjective evaluations of job candidates. Thus, an interviewer's judgments about an applicant's "appearance," "self-confidence," "emotional make-up," and many other characteristics constitute appropriate criteria for hiring or not hiring someone. In this context, an employer's gender role stereotypes about women can easily enter the decision-making process. For example, the difference between a man who has "self-confidence" and a woman who is "too pushy" is very subtle. But the result can be very discriminating. Another evaluation device is the selective waiver of educational and experience requirements, a tactic that occurs most often in white-collar jobs. For example, let us say that a job is advertised requiring a Master's degree and five years' experience. Let us say further that the two best applicants are a woman with a Bachelor's degree and ten years' experience and a man with a Master's degree and one year of experience. Which person is hired depends upon how one evaluates the trade-off between experience and education, and the kind of person an employer is most comfortable with on the job. Now consider the way minority persons fit into this process. Imagine comparing Hispanic or African American women and men to white men when the mix of education and experience must be weighed. Experimental data suggest the implications of such evaluation processes.[56] When a screen was used to conceal the identities of candidates for positions with symphony orchestras, the proportion of female players who were hired rose from less than 5 percent to between 25 to 46 percent. The result, then, of the hiring process can be very discriminating, especially over the long run as employers consistently juggle criteria in favor of white males.

In sum, when the choices women make and the possibility of discrimination are combined, then the reason so many individuals achieve less than their skills suggest they should becomes clear. Yet this form of analysis remains incomplete. As I have argued previously, it cannot reveal why the overall rate of female accomplishment is so low. It remains unclear why women make the choices they do. After all, if it is not economically smart to become a housewife, why have so many normally intelligent women chosen this lifestyle over the years? In order to answer this question, it is necessary to look at the way the social structure influences people's options.

---

[54]Mencken and Winfield (2000).
[55]Neumark et al. (1996).
[56]Goldin and Rouse (2000).

## Social Structure and Gender Stratification

In George Bernard Shaw's play, *Pygmalion,* originally produced in 1914, the main character, Henry Higgins, wonders why women cannot be more like men.[57] Well, they can. The data presented earlier show that much change is occurring in precisely that direction: Women have entered the labor force and now increasingly obtain resources: prestige, education, income, and power. Women are more equal to (or like) men today than in the past. Even the data on female victimization reflect this fact because such events are now controversial. Yet, much remains the same: The data continue to show that—in every area—women remain unequal to men. It is useful to pause and think about this problem more abstractly.

In Chapter 1, I noted that the forces shaping the stratification structure, with its three systems of ranking (class, gender, and race/ethnicity), can be conceptualized by the degree of emphasis on achievement versus ascription. To the extent that performance-related criteria equally applied to all are used to evaluate people and to the extent these evaluations affect the distribution of resources, a society emphasizes achievement. The data suggest that the United States is moving in this direction and, in this sense, women and men are becoming more alike. Conversely, to the extent that non-performance-related criteria based on birth are used to evaluate people and to the extent such evaluations affect the distribution of resources, a society emphasizes ascription. The importance of gender as a system of ranking indicates a continuing emphasis on ascription, as suggested by the *Gender Hypothesis:*

> *Women at every class level have fewer and less effective choices than do men.*

Although this is not the place to test this hypothesis, the data presented earlier are consonant with it: At every class level, women's life chances—their ability to share in the available goods and services—still reflect their dependence on men rather than their own achievement.

As this duality reveals, societies are not monolithic entities. Historical change usually means that contradictory tendencies coexist. The decline of gender stratification coupled with its continuation illustrates this phenomenon.

### The Decline of Gender Stratification

The ideal of equality of opportunity for both men and women has become more widespread. As indicated, this is another way of talking about the applicability of achievement-oriented values to both genders. My hypothesis that accounts for this change is as follows:

> *The decline of gender inequality reflects (1) industrialization, (2) increasing female labor force participation, (3) advances in medical technology, (4) legal changes, and (5) the rise of feminism.*

***Industrialization.***    In the past, most people lived on farms, scratching a living from the soil. Husbands and wives did this together, using a simple division of labor to produce

---

[57]Shaw (1957). *Pygmalion* later became a Broadway musical and then a movie under the title *My Fair Lady.*

what they needed to survive. There was little surplus and, as Gerhard Lenski suggested, in such contexts people tend to share what is produced. Women were indeed like men: They worked at backbreaking productive tasks. Since modern labor-saving devices did not exist, the work required of women—baking, making soap, brewing beer, harvesting garden crops, managing barn animals, and much more—was very difficult. It is absurd to think that women were incapable of heavy work.[58] In addition, bearing children was a constant burden. The average woman became pregnant 10 to 12 times and bore 6 to 8 children.[59] But in this context, childbirth was a productive act because in just a few years children produced more than they cost.

The situation remained similar in the cities when capitalism emerged. In his *Autobiography,* published in 1795, Benjamin Franklin described how his wife, Deborah, assisted "cheerfully in my [printing] business, folding and stitching pamphlets, tending shop, purchasing old linen rags for the papermakers, etc."[60] Note that Franklin specifies that it is "my business." In the nascent market economy in which men were formally in charge, women's work constituted unpaid labor. Typically, the goods produced at home by unpaid female workers were partly consumed and partly sold or traded.[61] But no matter how such products were used, my point is the same as above: Productive activity occurred at home, where both women and men worked.

**Industrialization** changed this situation. As noted previously, the term refers to the transformation of the economy when new forms of energy substituted for muscle power, leading to advances in productivity. The application of technology based on fossil, steam, and other forms of energy requires a more complex division of labor than that found at home. It also requires workers to gather at one site in order to minimize the cost of energy, raw materials, transportation, and distribution. So production shifted away from the home. In a context where controlling pregnancy and birth remained difficult, most women remained at home. Men left; they worked to earn an income and support their families.

Industrialization did more, however, than separate home and work: It led to a decline in gender inequality by creating opportunities for women as well as men, mainly because the organization and type of work changed. As productivity increased, jobs requiring professional and technical expertise, administrative skills, sales ability, and record-keeping training became more plentiful. Put simply: More white-collar workers were required. As will be shown in Chapter 5, the percentage of white-collar workers rose from 18 percent in 1900 to 60 percent in 2000. Brainpower supplanted muscle power, which meant that women could compete on equal terms with men. So, they have entered the paid labor force in increasing proportions over time.

***Increasing Female Labor Force Participation.***    In her autobiography, written around 1905, Dorothy Richardson described her life as a working girl in the late nineteenth century.[62] She left home at age 18 and moved to New York City. There she worked for a variety of companies in entry-level positions. She titled her book *The Long Day* to empha-

[58]Easton (1976).
[59]Cherlin (1992).
[60]Franklin (1961:92).
[61]Goldin (1990).
[62]O'Neill (1972:267).

size the length of the working day, the hard labor, and the low wages. During the latter part of the nineteenth century, the average employed person worked 10 hours per day, 6 days per week. Despite such requirements, Richardson eventually enrolled in night school, acquiring education and some commercial skills. She then became a stenographer and, to use her word, "prosperous" and economically independent. In those days, women like her were rare. They have become more common over time.

Women's increased labor force participation lead to a decline in gender inequality because an income, even a low one, means that women need not be economically dependent on men. It changes women's options and changes family life. Some, like Dorothy Richardson, could be like men: They could support themselves. Such women sometimes never married, especially those with college degrees.[63] They simply remained employed.[64] Most women, of course, married. During the early years of the last century, marriage usually meant that women quit their jobs. As time passed, however, this pattern changed as married women increasingly entered the labor force. They did so mainly in response to expanding economic opportunities, such as those produced by industrialization, rather than to declining opportunities for their husbands.[65] This fact, however, has important implications—on the divorce rate, for example. People with jobs do not have to endure a marriage filled with sorrow. Thus, female employment has an insidious implication: A rejection of traditional gender norms. The demand for equality follows, as day the night, from economic independence. This is why I said earlier that all employed women are feminists, in fact if not ideology, since their jobs give them both a source of prestige and the potential to live on their own.

Although industrialization provides opportunity and labor force participation an income, these two factors will not lead to gender equality unless women can control fertility. This ability required advances in medical technology.

***Advances in Medical Technology.*** Advanced technology creates new choices. It allows behaviors that were impossible or considered immoral a few years ago and thereby creates social problems.[66] The invention of the rubber condom, the intrauterine device, and the birth control pill contributed to rising rates of premarital sexual intercourse.[67] Similarly, the development of tools and techniques for performing safe abortions raised moral issues that continue to divide the nation.[68] The nonobvious issue underlying both these problems, however, is women's roles. Specifically, should women's reproductive roles take precedence over their productive roles?

The answer to this question is now clear. Advances in medical technology lead to a decline in gender inequality by providing women the opportunity to regulate whether and when to give birth. Although significant limits on the ability to control fertility still exist, women can increasingly balance their various roles. Without this opportunity, they cannot take advantage of the transformation of the economy. Without this opportunity, employed

---

[63]Rothman (1984).
[64]Goldin (1990).
[65]Chinhui and Murphy (1997).
[66]Beeghley (1999).
[67]Beeghley (1996).
[68]Luker (1984).

women would be shunted into dead-end jobs they can easily enter and leave. When pregnancy and birth can occur without warning, without planning, women must be dependent on men for economic security. This fact can be suggested by a simple mental experiment. Imagine that industrialization has occurred but neither birth control nor abortions are possible. In such a context, a bright woman wants to go into civil engineering. But is it wise for an engineering school to admit her? One can argue that, like most women, she will marry and become pregnant many times. In such a situation, one can argue that most women will not be able to use their training. Moreover, even if she obtains a degree, who would (or should) hire her? After companies invested time and money in her, she would have to quit due to pregnancy or childbirth. Now there were exceptional women who succeeded under these circumstances, but they were few. For most of history, sexual differences between men and women meant that the latter had to bear children whenever pregnancy occurred.

Yet the opportunity created by advances in medical technology was not immediately available because the law restricted women's ability to take advantage of applied medical knowledge. They enjoyed neither civil nor reproductive rights. This fact had to change in order to increase women's (and men's) choices.

***Legal Changes.***    In democratic societies, laws not only regulate behavior, but also serve as codified norms. They represent people's collective judgment about right and wrong. They identify, preserve, and protect ways of thinking and acting that citizens believe are important. As such, people with different characteristics are often treated differently under the law. Children, for example, have both special rights and special restrictions. Their unique treatment is justified because children are viewed as relatively powerless against adults. Until recently, women have been treated differently as well. I shall describe women's unequal treatment under the law along two dimensions: civil rights and fertility rights.

The denial of civil rights to women was justified as "protective legislation." One category of laws imposed maximum working hours for women. Interestingly, no state had enforceable laws limiting women's hours of work prior to the 1880s. By 1919, however, 40 states had enacted such statutes.[69] Another category allowed discrimination against women in hiring and job retention. Thus, married women could not be hired as teachers in 61 percent of all school districts in 1928; they could not be retained after marriage in 52 percent of all school districts.[70] These laws constitute one reason women quit their jobs at marriage: They were forced to do so. Still another category of laws made occupational segregation legal. As a result, women were typically tracked into jobs without promotion ladders while men were tracked into jobs with promotion ladders. Thus, in 1940, a sample of 260 companies with more than 19 employees revealed that 74 percent explicitly restricted some jobs to women, and 70 percent restricted some jobs to men.[71] Gender was so important that employers and newspapers published separate listings for men and women.

---

[69]Goldin (1990:190).
[70]Goldin (1990:161).
[71]Goldin (1990:112).

Here are some examples from the "Help Wanted—Women" section of a Washington, DC, newspaper in 1956.[72]

- Airline Hostesses for TransWorld Airlines: High school graduate, age 20–27, height 5'2"–5'8", weight 100–135, attractive, unmarried. Apply in person.
- Cashier-Food Checker: White, middle-aged woman, honest, alert, intelligent. Experience in cashiering or food checking.
- Fountain Girl: White, for downtown drugstore; references.
- G.H.W. [general house work]: Colored girl to live in; good with children. Age 18–30. Off Sun. and half day Thurs. $20 wk.

It was perfectly legal to specify the gender and race of potential employees. Companies were proud of such policies. In addition to restrictions on hours of work, hiring and retention, and job type, many other limits on women's rights existed—again, by law. These constraints meant that women were unable to act as fully endowed citizens, as adults. They were denied the right to choose the kind of work they did, to strive for economic success, and to obtain power and prestige apart from men. They were denied the right to achieve—simply because they were women.

Two contradictory interpretations of protective legislation exist.[73] One is that young, single, employed women were prone to exploitation, so they had to be protected, like children. Moreover, it is argued, such laws ultimately benefited all workers, male and female. Hours of work per week, for example, dropped from about 60 in the nineteenth century to about 40 by 1930. Another interpretation, however, is that these laws were designed to restrict opportunities available to women. Note that many protective statutes were passed during the period 1880 to 1930 when the economy changed and women began entering the labor force. It can be argued that they were not designed to protect women at all. They were, rather, reactions by men and their representatives (male legislators) to increased competition and an attempt at retaining their power and privilege—within both the family and society. Conveniently, such statutes were justified in terms of traditional gender norms. It is my impression that while many of those seeking to protect women were well-intentioned, their efforts were short-sighted.

The drive to protect women did not occur without conflict. Some feminists proposed equality. For example, shortly after women obtained the right to vote in 1919, the National Woman's Party was organized and, under the leadership of Alice Paul, introduced the Equal Rights Amendment. But while equality is a morally powerful stance, such efforts were relatively ineffective for many years. From about 1890 until 1960, the law emphasized women's "protection." This constituted a collective normative judgment about right and wrong behavior. It expressed a simple value: Women should not be equal to men; they should remain dependent, like children; their access to valued resources should be determined by ascription.

This collective judgment changed, like so much else, during the 1960s, when women gained full civil rights. The legislative history of the Civil Rights Act of 1964 is

---

[72]Taken from Padavic and Reskin (2002:ix).
[73]Goldin (1990:192).

interesting, however, because the inclusion of women occurred by accident. The Act did not mention equal rights for women until the day before its passage when a southern congressman introduced an amendment to include sex along with race. Reportedly, some male members of Congress laughed, seeing it as a joke.[74] The southern strategy, it appears, was to load the bill with a variety of "absurd" amendments in order to defeat it. They miscalculated. As a result, women are now supposed to be treated equally in seeking and keeping jobs. Coupled with the Equal Pay Act of 1963, which requires that men and women be paid equally for equal work, Title IX of the Educational Amendments Act of 1972, and other statutes, the legal basis for gender discrimination ended. Thus, the trend in law has been transformed. Norms, codified into law, dictate that women and men should now be evaluated by performance-related criteria applied equally to all.

This is a clear instance of the change from ascription to achievement in orientation. As I emphasized in Chapter 2, when Thomas Jefferson wrote that "all men are created equal," the concept of equality was initially applied very narrowly: to white men who owned property. Historically, however, the trend toward greater inclusiveness has proven to be inexorable: Immigrants, religious minorities, racial and ethnic groups, and women have sought to be treated as full citizens. The logic is that human beings should not be treated unequally based on their personal characteristics. (It is not much of an extension to include sexual orientation. By what logic should homosexual men and women be treated unequally?) Women, however, find themselves in a peculiar situation because only they can bear children. It is hard to imagine gender equality without the ability to regulate pregnancy and birth.

The second dimension of unequal treatment under the law was the denial of fertility rights, including both preventing and terminating pregnancy. Such rights have been restricted by law until recently. Thus, beginning about 1870 and continuing in various states until the 1960s, the distribution of contraceptive information and devices was illegal under obscenity statutes.[75] Similarly, every state made abortion illegal between 1860 and 1890.[76] Now there are two ways of interpreting restrictions on birth control and abortions. One is that they were statements of moral principles: Sex outside of marriage is wrong, and abortion is murder. But as mentioned earlier, the underlying issue is the roles women can play, both in the family and in the larger society. These laws made women's reproductive ability the center of their lives. Barring celibacy, women's ability to obtain an education, have a career, enter politics, and participate equally in all spheres of life could be undermined at any time by pregnancy and birth. Hence, these laws kept women at home, like children, unequal to men. It is not accidental that these laws were passed during the same period as so-called "protective" legislation. As opportunities increased with industrialization, men (and some women) sought to keep women at home. It did not work.

As with civil rights, the denial of reproductive rights began to end during the 1960s. In a series of decisions, the Supreme Court declared that women and men had a right to obtain birth control regardless of their age or marital status. Legislative enactments facilitated this right. Various states, led by California in 1967, began changing their abortion

[74]Bird (1968).
[75]Reed (1978).
[76]Luker (1984), Reagan (1997).

laws. Ultimately, however, the Court's 1973 decision in *Roe v. Wade* invalidated all state laws proscribing abortions. Hence, the collective judgment of society is now different. The law guarantees women's ability to work for pay and, indeed, to participate fully in every area of society. Underlying these legal changes was the rise of feminism.

***The Rise of Feminism.*** The drive for equality by oppressed people usually requires both an ideology and a social movement. Feminism provides them. Ideologically, it emphasizes that men and women should be equal. Most feminists support the development of egalitarian gender norms. Without this orientation, the traumas experienced by women—the arbitrary denial of a job, rape, abuse—remain personal tragedies, and the process of bearing witness becomes meaningless.[77] Traumatic acts are not acknowledged; they are forgotten. But placed in the context of a movement for equality, these same acts are understood as examples of oppression, of tyranny. They allow victims to find a transcendent meaning in their experiences. They galvanize others and translate a personal tragedy into a social problem.

Feminism leads women to see themselves as individuals capable of doing more than bearing children. The Protestant Reformation, the Enlightenment, the abolitionist movement, the development of capitalism, and the French Revolution, among other factors, all contributed to a recognition by some women that they could fill productive roles in the society. A feminist movement followed.[78]

The history of the feminist movement is usually described in two waves.[79] The First Wave took place between the years 1848 and 1920 or so. Beginning with the Seneca Falls Convention of 1848, women began pressing for the removal of barriers to education and political participation. The mobilizing issue was the right to vote. This goal served as a symbol of women's status as full-fledged citizens: Women voters are adults, like men, who can and should participate in societal decision making. Apart from this issue, not all feminists of the period shared the same goals. Some argued for equality while others emphasized the uniqueness of women. Many of the latter supported "protective" legislation of the sort described earlier. After passage of the Nineteenth Amendment to the Constitution, which secured the right to vote, the movement became quiescent. Protection seemed like enough, with the result that the many traumas women experienced went unnoticed, at least publicly. The Second Wave emerged during the 1960s and continues to the present. Responding to a newfound ability to prevent pregnancy, to ideological manifestos, to the Civil Rights movement, and other factors, women began organizing again.[80] The National Organization for Women was founded in 1967 to press for full equality. As before, however, the feminist movement has various branches, each of which pushes a somewhat different agenda.[81] In all of them, however, the mobilizing issues have been birth control, the right to an abortion, and ending violence against women. These goals serve as symbols of women's ability to control their lives. Without this ability, equality remains an illusion.

[77]Herman (1992).
[78]Degler (1980).
[79]Cott (1987).
[80]For example, Friedan (1963).
[81]Ferree and Hess (2000).

Notice how a variety of historical events coalesced. Feminism arose just as capitalism combined with industrialization to transform the economy. The ideology of equality buttressed expanded opportunity. In this context, women joined the labor force in steadily increasing numbers. Advances in medical technology, the fruits of scientific progress that originated several centuries ago, made it possible for women to regulate and control pregnancy and birth. Even though legal changes were delayed and continue to be contentious, they finally allowed women to regulate fertility. These changes, of course, were stimulated not only by the existence of technology but by the overarching value of equality. One of the dominant trends in Western history has been the freeing of individuals from dependence on others, another way of placing an emphasis on achievement. Increasingly, when men and women join together, they do so out of desire, not need; and they remain together as a (truly) free choice rather than out of dependence. The historical trend is clear: increasing equality between men and women.

## *The Continuation of Gender Stratification*

Despite the changes described above, gender inequality continues. Why is this so? The answer must be structural. My hypothesis follows:

> *The continuation of gender inequality reflects (1) the salience of traditional gender norms and (2) institutionalized discrimination.*

***The Salience of Traditional Gender Norms.***    As noted earlier, traditional gender norms direct women and men into different spheres. According to this convention, then, the choices men and women make ought to be different. Even though they may be smart or creative, or both, and even though they may desire to become artists or scientists, women should focus their energy on family obligations. Most followed this dictum until recently. They became housewives, dependent on their husbands. Those who were employed worked at menial jobs, for low pay, or both, enduring discrimination. In a historical context where their choices were highly restricted, these ordinary women found whatever satisfaction they could. In certain respects, this situation has not changed. I have selected four indicators of the continuing salience of traditional gender norms:

**1.** A significant minority of women does not work for pay. Thus, Figure 3.1 reveals that 71 percent of all married women are in the labor force, an all-time high. This datum means, of course, that the remaining 29 percent of all women do not have an income. Excluding the aged and disabled, they are housewives, dependent on their husbands for economic support. Whether they like it (or admit it), they adhere to traditional gender norms.

**2.** Voluntary part-time employment is common among women: Among adults over age 20, 25 percent of employed women have part-time jobs, most by choice.[82] In comparison, only 9 percent of men work part-time. Women choose part-time employment to re-

---

[82]U.S. Bureau of Labor Statistics (2002).

duce the role conflict arising from job and family obligations. This priority is another way of adhering to traditional gender norms, of remaining dependent on their husbands.

**3.** Most employed wives have lower incomes than their husbands. Even though spouses usually have similar levels of education, wives earn only 69 percent as much as husbands.[83] So wives are more dependent on husbands than husbands on wives. This economic relationship usually occurs by choice, as indicated by family decisions to relocate for husbands' jobs—even when wives are opposed, even when wives' incomes suffer as a result. Income differences are important because they translate into power within a marriage: When a man earns the most, he can impose his desires on his wife. Moreover, wife abuse is more common and harder to stop when women are more economically dependent on men.[84] The fact that many women remain dependent reflects and reinforces traditional gender norms.

**4.** Finally, the home is contested terrain. The division of labor remains unequal, although differences are declining.[85] For example, employed women still spend thirteen hours per week on household tasks, compared to ten for men. Women spend four hours per week preparing meals, compared to two for men. Women spend almost two hours each week doing laundry and ironing, compared to about one-half hour for men. And men are often blissfully ignorant of what these differences in household tasks mean: "I just never knew, until my wife made me look, that dust gathered under a bed." The only areas in which men spend more time are outdoor tasks and auto maintenance. Even when household jobs are shared, women usually organize and supervise them. Thus, men "help" women do "their" work. This orientation means that women labor for much longer hours than their husbands. It means that employed wives often have two jobs: at home and at work. I always thought the comic's assertion that "a man around the house is an inanimate object" was too extreme, but it describes the division of labor in many marriages and reflects traditional gender norms. (Note that the total amount of housework done has declined a lot compared to forty years ago, when the number of hours was much higher.[86] In addition, the difference between men and women in hours spent on housework is also at the lowest level since the 1960s.)

These four indicators reveal the degree to which many people believe that women ought to focus on breadserving and men on breadwinning, and that everyone will be happier as a result. Although such beliefs are changing, their continued salience perpetuates gender inequality.

***Institutionalized Discrimination.***     The inequality of women and men is also buttressed by **institutionalized discrimination:** the unequal treatment of individuals or groups based on their personal characteristics that is embedded in the social structure. I have selected two indicators of institutionalized discrimination against women.

---

[83]Winkler (1998).
[84]Herman (1992).
[85]Padavic and Reskin (2002:160). The quotation below is from Horsfield (1998).
[86]Bianchi et al. (2000).

**1.** A skewed gender ratio in competitive contexts can lead to discrimination and affect women's ability to succeed.[87] Please look back at Table 3.1, which shows that women remain rare in many competitive jobs, like engineering and medicine. Such work settings often display a skewed gender ratio: a large proportion of men and a small proportion of women. Most of the latter occupy entry-level positions. In such a context, women constitute tokens—representatives of their kind—subject to performance pressures and social isolation.

Because there are so few of them, women are highly visible to peers and supervisors, which creates performance pressures: One's mistakes cannot be hidden. Furthermore, women are often expected to avoid making men look bad on the job, even though the situation is competitive. Also, women in high visibility jobs sometimes respond inconsistently, which makes their behavior unpredictable and social relations difficult. A self-fulfilling prophecy can occur in that women are expected to fail and do, often with a little help from male colleagues and supervisors. Women in such contexts have few choices. They can try to overachieve, a difficult tactic. Alternatively, they can seek success more covertly, thereby limiting their visibility but also reducing the chance for success via promotion.

Women in skewed gender ratio settings also suffer discrimination due to their isolation. Boundaries are established that isolate the "female intruder." Such contexts allow more opportunity for sexual harassment and other forms of unequal treatment. As a trite example, one innocuous strategy is to deliberately interrupt the flow of group events in some fashion in order to emphasize the presence of a woman. One might ask if it is okay to swear or apologize for doing so. The question emphasizes to a woman that she is different, that she disrupts normal behavior merely by being there: She is trespassing on a male domain. Other forms of harassment are much more serious, of course, and they inhibit success. In addition, such a context also makes it more difficult for women to secure mentoring, whether formally via on-the-job training or (just as importantly) informally. When male supervisors and colleagues meet informally—whether at exclusive clubs or just for drinks after work—they share sources of information, knowledge of shortcuts, and other factors vital to advancement. Sometimes these processes occur without (much) malice; rather, the female intruder is simply different, threatening, and left out as a result. Success, via promotion, becomes more difficult. Such processes may be one reason why women, even professional women, sometimes leave the labor force.

**2.** Occupational segregation also builds unequal treatment into the social structure. Recall that men decide how jobs are evaluated and paid. As new occupations developed over the last century, (male) employers "gendered" them, setting wages and organized tasks with either men or women in mind. This process still occurs.[88] So women usually have lower paid jobs involving helping and nurturing others, and higher paid jobs with authority go to men. In addition, the skills involved in building highways and bridges are judged as worth more than those involved in building children. I use the phrase "building children" to stress that, like the structures (male) engineers design, children are constructed; someone must teach them to be adults. In his book, *Childhood,* Melvin Konner

---

[87]Kanter (1978).
[88]Acker (1990), Maume (1999).

concluded that "children are living messages we send into the future, a future we will not see. . . . In effect we are building the house of tomorrow day by day, not out of bricks or steel, but out of the stuff of children's bodies, hearts, and minds."[89] Yet engineers are paid very high wages compared to teachers and childcare workers because men have determined that constructing highways is more difficult and more significant than children. This decision is, of course, political not economic. In my view, it would be more correct to see men and women with different skills. In any case, institutionalized occupational discrimination has two parts. Employers first segregate men and women, then pay the latter lower wages even if their jobs are of comparable worth. Once this fact is recognized, the data presented earlier make sense.

Taken together, traditional gender norms and institutionalized discrimination constitute inertial forces, preserving inequality between men and women. Much remains the same.

But think back: In October 1781, George Washington defeated Lord Cornwallis at the Battle of Yorktown. This win over the British forces, I would suggest, did not end the American Revolution. Nor did the signing of the Treaty of Paris two years later. Nor did the Constitution's adoption in 1789. Despite their importance, these events only marked the end of Part I of the struggle for freedom. They secured for white men certain fundamental rights: to vote, to be represented, and to obtain an education and a job based on hard work and ability. They reflected a long-term process by which white men are increasingly evaluated based on their achievements.

Women had none of these rights. They were still evaluated based on ascriptive criteria. Part II of the American Revolution began in a chapel in Seneca Falls, New York, in July 1848, where 240 people gathered and issued a declaration of the rights of women against men's oppression. It asserted that "we hold these truths to be self-evident: that all men and women are created equal; that they are endowed by their Creator with certain inalienable rights; that among these are life, liberty, and the pursuit of happiness." It went on to outline most of the elements necessary for the freedom and equality of women: the right to vote, to obtain an education, and to secure a job and income, among others. The Seneca Falls Declaration had little impact at the time, and, as the existence of this chapter, indicates, gender still constitutes a system of ranking separate from class. But the moral force of ideas is strong. The Declaration began a fundamental transformation not only in the way men and women relate to one another but also in stratification processes generally. Much has changed. Perhaps in the future, class—with its greater emphasis on achievement—will supercede gender as a basis for stratification.

## *Summary*

Married women's labor force participation rate rose steadily through this century. In addition, married women with children also increased their rate of employment (Figure 3.1). One implication of these changes is a higher divorce rate, which does not necessarily

[89]Konner (1991:428).

benefit women. Although some changes have occurred in recent years, men and women are still occupationally segregated (Table 3.1). This fact means they are unequal in both prestige and income. Among full-time employed workers, women earn about 76 percent as much as men (Table 3.2). There appears to be less difference, however, among recent entrants to the labor force.

Nonetheless, men still exercise authority in the United States, and women are still victimized, as indicated by sexual harassment, rape, spouse abuse, and child sexual abuse. Underlying all these differences are traditional gender norms. Quantitative research shows that women's own choices, skills, and labor force attachment only account for about one-third of the income difference between the genders. Thus, another cause of the inequality experienced by individual women must be discrimination.

The history of this century reveals a duality: the decline and perpetuation of gender stratification. It is hypothesized that five variables have led to a decline in gender stratification: industrialization, gender differences in labor force participation, advances in medical technology, legal changes, and the rise of feminism. In contrast, two variables are hypothesized to continue gender stratification: the salience of traditional gender norms and institutionalized discrimination. The former is indicated by the high proportion of women not working for pay, voluntary part-time employment by women, the economic dependence of women on men, and men's opposition to housework. The latter is indicated by the gender ratio common in competitive groups and occupational segregation.

# 4

# Social Class and Stratification

## Occupational Prestige and Class Identification

"What do you do for a living?" It is a simple question, usually asked shortly after strangers are introduced. Except for the rich (an important exception), occupations provide the focus for people's lives, both psychologically and materially. The answer, then, is like a calling card—a shorthand summary of a person's share in the distribution of resources, their ability to solve problems, their claim to be someone with standing in the community. "I'm a lawyer." This answer tells you that the respondent has high prestige, possibly high income, and possibly some degree of power and influence. "I work at the hospital." This answer tells you that the respondent is not a physician, but has some lower prestige job. "I am unemployed at the moment." This answer tells you that the respondent not only does not earn an income but also, at least for now, has little social standing. Losing one's job is a major assault on a person's self-identity and increases the odds of a family ending up poor.

Students ask similar questions, and for the same reason: "Where do you go to school?" "What is your major?" The answers locate the respondent in the collegiate class structure. The need to obtain such information early in a relationship reveals an underlying characteristic of modern class-based societies: People's self-identity, income, and power stem from their most important and time-consuming activity, their jobs.[1] This fact means that what people do each day and how it is evaluated constitute central issues in the study of stratification. One need not be a world-class (or even a good) lawyer or auto mechanic. The issue is how these tasks are evaluated.

The question "What do you do for a living?" carries another implication as well, since people often identify with a class based on their jobs. That is, they see themselves as, say, middle class, and this subjective sense of their location in the class structure guides their interaction with others. Lawyers, for example, want to live in neighborhoods with others like themselves, who are also middle class. They share interests, ranging from who gets elected to whom their children marry. And, as both Weber and Marx observed, they act on these interests. This chapter focuses on people's sense of occupational prestige and class identification as indicators of class location.

## Occupational Prestige

### Occupational Prestige in the United States

The study of **occupational prestige** assesses the social standing of the jobs people have. It is measured by giving a set of cards to a random sample of people and asking them to rate the occupations listed therein according to their standing in the society. For example, among the jobs listed would be electrician. Respondents are asked to place this card on a ladder with 9 boxes on it, signifying a range from the highest to lowest standing. The ratings for each job by each member of the sample are averaged to obtain a prestige score and all the occupations in the study are then placed in rank order. In the case of electricians, the score is 51, which is about in the middle of the hierarchy. Listed below are a few of the hundreds of occupations that are ranked, along with their scores.[2]

| | |
|---|---|
| Physician | 86 |
| Lawyer | 75 |
| Registered Nurse | 66 |
| Public Grade School Teacher | 64 |
| Police Officer | 61 |
| Business Person | 59 |
| Electrician | 51 |
| Secretary | 46 |
| Automobile Mechanic | 39 |
| Real Estate Manager | 38 |
| Cosmetologist | 36 |
| Assembly Line Worker | 35 |
| Garbage Collector | 28 |
| Sales Clerk | 28 |
| Bartender | 25 |
| Janitor | 22 |

[1]Glick (1995).
[2]Nakao and Treas (1994), General Social Survey (2003).

As this short list shows, physicians and lawyers are among the highest-rated people in the United States; that is, they carry the most social standing. Most (but not all) of the high-prestige occupations are white collar; that is, the jobs do not involve manual labor. On the other hand, garbage collectors and janitors are among the lowest-rated jobs in the United States; that is, they carry the least social standing. Most (but not all) of the low-prestige occupations are blue collar; that is, the jobs usually require manual labor. Note, however, that the dividing line between white- and blue-collar workers is not precise: Some blue-collar jobs, such as electrician, rank above some white-collar jobs, such as real estate manager.

## *The Meaning of Occupational Prestige*

The meaning of occupational prestige is significant because, along with ownership or control of capital, jobs are the major roles through which people obtain access to resources in modern societies. In *Occupational Prestige in Comparative Perspective,* Donald Treiman proposed an interpretation of what prestige scores mean.[3] As it turns out, I disagree with him; but this fact is useful because it provides a way of showing how sociologists question and evaluate one another's work.

Treiman argued that occupational prestige hierarchies result from the functional necessities faced by each society. Thus, he began by outlining a set of functional necessities that must be met if societies are to survive. Like all such lists, however, Treiman's is arbitrary and slightly different from that of previous scholars, such as Davis and Moore or Parsons.[4] His argument is that the functional necessity to obtain food and other commodities, exchange goods, develop shared values, and coordinate activities produces a division of labor. The task specialization inherent to any division of labor leads, in turn, to differences in power and privilege. These differences cause, finally, variations in prestige as people use the resources available to them. Unfortunately, however, this analysis reveals the flaws characteristic of all functionalist analyses. That is, it poses an illegitimate teleology (that every society has needs), and its presupposition (that the needs of society produce a division of labor) cannot be tested.

In contrast to Treiman, my preference is to explain the meaning of occupational prestige in terms of a simple hypothesis that can be tested:

*The greater the skills required, the higher the prestige of an occupation.*

Education provides a good (although not the only) indicator of the amount of skill required for a job.[5] As the list above implies, nearly all the jobs with higher prestige also require either a high level of formal education or considerable training.[6]

If I am correct, this argument suggests a different way of interpreting prestige rankings. That is, people symbolically reward those whose jobs indicate their skill, ability, and hard work by recognizing their authority. As a result, the hierarchy of occupational prestige carries important practical implications. People defer to their superiors, as

---

[3]Treiman (1977:1–25).
[4]Davis and Moore (1945), Parsons (1951).
[5]MacKinnon and Langford (1994).
[6]Nakao and Treas (1994).

indicated by their different occupations. They accept as equals those with roughly similar jobs. This fact affects people's lifestyle and life chances, since those considered equals comprise the population with whom one typically entertains, marries, shares meals, and engages in other forms of intimate social interaction. Finally, people denigrate their inferiors by making them acknowledge in some way their own inferiority and by avoiding intimate social relationships with them. For example, the use of titles such as "sir" and "Doctor" during interaction is often a tacit way for one person to recognize the prestige (and income) of another. Thus, prestige rankings embody society-wide patterns of domination and subordination, of power.

In everyday life, people do not think about prestige scores. They represent quantitative summaries of people's subjective judgments of others' standing in the society. Consider for a moment some of the differences between white- and blue-collar work. The image, white collar, suggests people who wear suits and ties on the job, and it is a fairly accurate symbol. As mentioned, white-collar jobs involve nonmanual labor. A college degree or professional training is often required of those in top-level jobs. People employed in these occupations usually sit behind desks, stay physically clean while working, and often have high income. They are usually paid at a fixed yearly salary rather than by the hour. In addition, a relatively high proportion of white-collar jobs entail supervisory responsibility, and many involve the risks of entrepreneurial (or business) activity. White-collar people usually direct blue-collar people and often run or manage businesses. This combination of characteristics, not all of which occur in every job, means that white-collar workers typically have higher occupational prestige and more political power (the two go together) than do blue-collar employees. These characteristics, along with income differences, indicate why white-collar people usually have more and better options available when confronted with personal crises, such as a divorce or a drug problem.

In contrast, the image, blue collar, suggests people who wear work clothes on the job and, as before, it is a fairly accurate symbol. As mentioned, blue-collar jobs often involve manual labor of some sort. People employed in these occupations frequently work with their hands, often become physically dirty while doing their jobs, and usually have less income and education than do white-collar workers. Most of the time, their occupations do not involve either supervising others or the risks of entrepreneurship. They are usually paid by the hour rather than at a fixed salary. This combination of characteristics means blue-collar workers generally have lower occupational prestige and less political power than do white-collar employees. They also have fewer choices when faced with personal crises.

Although these characteristics mean that blue-collar jobs often have lower prestige, they involve a wide range of skills. Service occupations—such as police officer (prestige score 61), cosmetologist (36), and bartender (25)—provide a good example. In a way, people in these jobs are special cases because they often stay clean. Moreover, some jobs require college education and carry great responsibility. Superior police officers, for example, must be both psychologists and crime fighters, a tough combination. The amount and difficulty of physical effort varies a lot in blue-collar occupations: In some automated industries, such as oil and chemical industries, the jobs are interesting but not physically arduous; in other industries, such as auto and steel, automation means boring and strenuous work. These variations mean that social scientific systems of classification are often imprecise.

Nonetheless, people make discriminatory judgments in everyday life (without hesitation) based on the answer to the question "What do you do?" Sometimes these appraisals are straightforward: "She and her husband are teachers and, hence, like us." Often, however, they are subtle. An auto mechanic I know, William Meadows, is a good example (prestige score 39). Although he becomes rather dirty on the job, he charges me $40 per hour to repair my car. Moreover, he owns the business, so he is also a business person (score 59) with all the risks that entails. Mr. Meadows usually has two or three employees who also work on cars. He pays them (much) less than $40 per hour (with no benefits) and pockets the rest for himself. The business does well and Mr. Meadows makes a good living; his home is on a lake in an exclusive development. He happens to be African American and so are most of his employees.

## Racial/Ethnic and Gender Differences in Occupational Prestige

As implied, prestige rankings affect interaction between members of different racial and ethnic groups, and between men and women as well. "What do you do?" On average, African Americans and Hispanic Americans will state a lower-prestige job than people from other groups. For example, average prestige scores in one study were 51 for Asian Americans (the scale is 1–90), 49 for white Americans, 41 for Hispanic Americans, and 41 for African Americans.[7] These scores have practical implications. When I drop off or pick up my car, Mr. Meadows's employees sometimes greet me with "sir" (he never does). The tacit recognition of differences (and similarity) in prestige and power also occurs between men and women. This is so even though average prestige scores by gender are rather similar: Men's average is about 49 and women's 47.[8] But this similarity is misleading. First, significant differences exist among women in various racial and ethnic groups. Second, many women are not in the labor force and, hence, do not obtain the social standing (and potential for economic independence) that follows from earning a living. "I am just a housewife." Third, as shown in Chapter 3, the occupational distribution of employed women and men differs; women work at lower-ranking jobs (for example, men as physicians and women as nurses). Thus, people's judgment of others' standing also reflects nonclass patterns of domination and subordination.

## The Stability of Occupational Prestige over Time

The literature on occupational prestige is very long and has resulted in an empirical generalization:

> *Hierarchies of occupational prestige are similar over time within the same society.*

Thus, the correlation in prestige rankings from one study to another are well above .90 in the United States.[9] This finding means that the rankings of, for example, physicians and

[7]Xu and Leffler (1992).
[8]Xu and Leffler (1992).
[9]Nakao and Treas (1994).

nurses have been essentially identical over time. This same result occurs in other nations as well. For example, in the Netherlands the correlation between 1953 and 1982 was .97.[10] In Japan the correlation between 1952 and 1964 was .96.[11] When correlations approach 1.0, as these do, it means almost perfect agreement exists.

This same finding also occurs in less economically developed nations, such as Brazil, India, Nigeria, and the Philippines.[12] For example, in Poland the ratings correlated .93 from 1957 to 1975, and .94 from 1975 to 1987.[13] There are problems with the samples for many of these studies, however. The data tend to come from urban areas, and respondents are often college students. Hence, they do not represent the entire population but, rather, its most Westernized segments. This problem becomes more significant with the next finding.

### *The Stability of Occupational Prestige across Societies?*

Another empirical generalization is

> *Hierarchies of occupational prestige are similar across societies.*

I have placed a question mark after the last heading to indicate that even though this finding is stable, it may not be correct.

Donald Treiman assessed the hypothesis with data for 52 countries from all regions of the world.[14] He reported that "all the available evidence points to the same conclusion: There is high agreement throughout the world regarding the relative prestige of occupations." He found a correlation of about .80 among all these studies. Although lower than the temporal correlation previously reported, this figure still means that substantial agreement exists from one society to another about which jobs carry the most and least standing. According to Treiman, whose book *Occupational Prestige in Comparative Perspective* remains the best analysis of this topic, this finding holds even when problems of terminology, weaknesses in the samples used, and disparities in the type of society are resolved. But his conclusion is probably too strong. Findings are labeled empirical generalizations because, as in this case, a large number of studies have been done and the results are uniform. Nonetheless, it turns out that criticisms of this finding are serious enough to call it into question.

The first problem is with the samples. Treiman argued that it makes no difference whether the samples are composed of rural or urban people, college students or nonstudents, that the judgments of occupational prestige in Ghana, Mexico, Turkey, and other societies are essentially the same as in the Netherlands or the United States. Other researchers, however, recalculated (that is, tried to repeat) Treiman's findings and showed that rural and urban people in various societies disagree regarding the evaluation of occu-

---

[10]Sixma and Ultee (1984).
[11]Treiman (1977).
[12]Treiman (1977).
[13]Sawinski and Domanski (1991).
[14]Treiman (1977:96).

pations.[15] This issue is important because many studies in less industrialized nations use samples of the population that are most influenced by Western values—college students and urban people, for example. Treiman argued that use of such samples does not matter. He may be wrong.

The second problem is the comparability of job titles across societies. Treiman went to extraordinary lengths to resolve this issue, but probably did not succeed. Many studies, especially of less-developed societies, use very few occupational titles (only ten in some cases) that are comparable to those in the United States and other industrialized nations. This situation means the occupational structure itself is not comparable, since the vast majority of the jobs people do are so different.

Surprisingly, then, despite the number of studies that have been done, the only way to resolve the issues mentioned here is with more data. Subsequent attempts at replication should be designed so as to address these two problems. Until that time, a less-sweeping empirical generalization is more appropriate:

> *Hierarchies of occupational prestige are similar across all western industrialized nations.*

As a caveat, it is possible that what Treiman found reflects a worldwide process of convergence: Thus, as less-developed nations become more economically developed, they may come to resemble the West in certain respects, such as their occupational structure, even though their own cultural values remain unique. If true, then similar occupational prestige hierarchies may emerge in these societies over time.

One last note before considering class identification. It is important for you to recognize that Treiman's book constitutes brilliant and enormously difficult work, representing years of thought. It remains an excellent example of high-quality social science. As Max Weber once suggested, over the long run, all good scientific research is superseded as subsequent scholars address the same issues and bring more knowledge to bear on them.[16]

## Class Identification

Occupational prestige scores are assessments respondents make of others' social standing, based on their jobs. **Class identification** is an assessment respondents make of their own social class. Sociological concern with this topic stems from Karl Marx's work. He was interested in understanding the conditions under which exploited groups would become class conscious and rebel against their oppressors. This concern, however, has proven to be less relevant in Western industrial nations because classes (at all levels) may act cohesively without revolutionary intent. For this reason, studies of class identification simply analyze people's ability to locate themselves in the class structure and assess the impact this fact has for their lifestyles and life chances.

---

[15]Treiman (1977).
[16]Weber (1904).

**TABLE 4.1**  *Class Identification among Men and Women, 1945, 1972, 2000*

| Class Identification | 1945 | 1972 | 2000 |
|---|---|---|---|
| | *Men* | | |
| Lower Class | 1% | 4% | 5% |
| Working Class | 51 | 45 | 44 |
| Middle Class | 43 | 47 | 45 |
| Upper Class | 3 | 3 | 6 |
| | 98% | 100% | 100% |
| | *Women* | | |
| Lower Class | | 5% | 7% |
| Working Class | | 45 | 46 |
| Middle Class | | 48 | 43 |
| Upper Class | | 2 | 4 |
| | | 100% | 100% |

*Note:* 2% of the sample did not answer the question in 1945.

*Sources:* Centers (1949), General Social Survey (2000).

## Patterns of Class Identification

Class identification was first measured by Richard Centers in his seminal book, *The Psychology of Social Classes.*[17] He asked this question: "If you were to use one of these four names for your social class, which would you say you belonged in: the middle class, lower class, working class, or upper class?" Subsequent research still uses essentially the same question, with results as shown in Table 4.1. The data show that most people have little difficulty placing themselves into a class and that most see themselves as either working or middle class. In 1945, just as World War II ended, Centers found that 51 percent of men identified as working class and 43 percent as middle class. Since then, the percentages have become more even, with about 43 to 46 percent of both genders identifying with each class. Only about 5 to 7 percent identify with the lower class, probably because people perceive the term as invidious and do not wish to see themselves in this way. Even fewer people identify with the upper class, in part because research samples typically do not include rich persons (who are most likely to view themselves at the top) and in part because many of those who are well-off do not see themselves as such.[18]

Patterns of class identification are highly correlated with occupation, such that blue- and white-collar men usually identify with different classes.[19] The result says a great deal about their lifestyle. White male workers in blue-collar occupations with the lowest pres-

[17]Centers (1949:233).
[18]Jackman and Jackman (1983).
[19]Vanneman and Pampel (1977).

**TABLE 4.2    *Class Identification by Racial and Ethnic Group, 2000***

|  | *White* | *African* | *Hispanic* | *Asian* | *Native American* |
|---|---|---|---|---|---|
| Lower Class | 5% | 13% | 10% | 7% | 7% |
| Working Class | 42 | 58 | 61 | 35 | 59 |
| Middle Class | 48 | 26 | 27 | 57 | 32 |
| Upper Class | 5 | 3 | 2 | 1 | 2 |
|  | 100% | 100% | 100% | 100% | 100% |

*Source:* General Social Survey (2000).

tige scores nearly all see themselves as working class. White male workers in white-collar occupations with the highest prestige scores nearly all see themselves as middle class. White male workers in the middle section of the prestige hierarchy divide themselves based on their occupations; thus, given similar prestige scores, those in blue-collar jobs usually see themselves as working class and those in white-collar jobs usually see themselves as middle class. These findings remain after controlling for education and income. I will discuss the issue of employed women's class identification later on.

Patterns of class identification vary by race and ethnicity, as shown in Table 4.2. About half of Whites (non-Hispanic) and a majority of Asian Americans see themselves as middle class. The order is reversed, however, among African Americans, Hispanic Americans, and Native Americans, with a majority saying they are working class. As seen in Chapter 2, this pattern correlates with the occupational distribution of these groups.

These data imply the existence of discrete and identifiable classes in the United States, not just as statistical constructs but as subjectively relevant categories in people's minds. It appears that working-class and middle-class labels reflect a class division between those who do manual and nonmanual labor; they are not merely prestige judgments.[20] Thus, people see their jobs as an indicator of their location in the class structure: Those with similar occupational characteristics generally see themselves as belonging to the same class. This argument is consonant with studies of social mobility to be presented in Chapter 5, where it will be shown that the division between blue- and white-collar work constitutes a semipermeable barrier to upward and downward mobility.

## The Meaning of Class Identification

In his analysis of the stratification structure in modern societies, Max Weber argued that people who share common lifestyles and values tend to discriminate against others who are different. He said that this process occurs naturally, without classes being formally organized, as people enjoy each others' hospitality and friendship, marry, select houses and neighborhoods in which to live, and practice social conventions with others who are like themselves. These social conventions are often revealed in subtle ways. For example,

---

[20]Vanneman and Pampel (1977:435).

my impression is that the location of the television and the amount of time spent watching it are class related. If true, in working-class houses, the television is often the center of attention in the living room and it is nearly always turned on.[21] In middle-class houses, however, the television is often in a room other than the living room and is not turned on so much. Assuming for a moment that I am correct, the issue is not whether this rather innocuous social convention is better or worse, good or bad. Rather, the issue is that such differences, which are correlated with class, express people's lifestyles and values. And they affect life chances.

Weber, in short, was right. When people identify with a class, they are saying something, in a symbolic way, about their experiences and their lifestyle preferences: They are identifying those with whom they prefer to interact in intimate ways, and they are commenting on their taste in entertainment and other leisure time activities. This fact is clearly shown in the best analysis since that by Centers, Jackman and Jackman's *Class Awareness in the United States*.[22] In this study, nearly 80 percent of the respondents reported they feel strongly about their class identification, which suggests it is important to them.

Just how important can be seen when the notion of class identification is linked to other arenas of life. Thus, the Jackmans found that people expressed "a marked tendency toward preference for [social] contact with one's own class," especially with regard to friendship choice, neighborhood preference, and marriage partners. For example, more than half of those people who identify themselves as working class say they prefer living in working-class neighborhoods and a similar proportion of those who identify as middle class assert a desire to live in middle-class neighborhoods. As it turns out, these preferences are realized in practice, since class, racial, and ethnic segregation characterizes most U.S. cities.[23] Such segregation means that informal interaction, friendship ties, and other forms of relatively intimate social relationships are usually class based. Since most people find jobs via word-of-mouth, this fact has important implications for life chances.

With regard to marriage, Jackman and Jackman reported that people who identify themselves as poor or working class usually prefer that their children "marry up." That is, they want their children to marry someone from a higher class. This preference reflects the fact that marriage can be a vehicle for upward mobility in terms of standing in the community. In contrast, people who see themselves as middle and upper class generally want their children to marry someone from the same class. It turns out, however, the spouses in most marriages come from similar class backgrounds. Hence, this most intimate form of interaction is typically class based. In sum, the evidence suggests that patterns of class identification reflect a fundamental division in U.S. society. People from different classes have different lifestyles and these variations affect life chances.

## A Note on Employed Married Women

I observed earlier that all good scientific research is superseded as subsequent scholars address an issue. The problem of class identification among employed married women

---

[21]Television Bureau of Advertising (1991).
[22]Centers (1949), Jackman and Jackman (1983:21 and 195).
[23]Massey (2001).

illustrates this process. Historically, women who were housewives assumed the class of their husbands. This process is called "status borrowing." It made sense in a context in which most women had no other source of standing in the community. But the situation is not as clear-cut today when so many married women have entered the labor force. Employed married women have a source of prestige and income independently of their husbands. Hence, over the last two decades researchers have become interested in this issue and found support for two different hypotheses.

The first is the *Status-Borrowing Hypothesis:*

> *Employed married women ignore their own jobs and education, and consider only their husbands' characteristics in deciding with which class to identify.*

This argument implies, for example, that a secretary or an elementary school teacher married to an electrician would see herself as working class, since her husband's job involves manual labor. The logic behind the hypothesis lies in traditional gender norms. From this point of view, women's primary adult roles should revolve around the household: bearing children, rearing them, and caring for their husbands. Hence, their major interest should be in the home—even if they are employed. By extrapolation, then, such women should see their position in the community as resulting from their husband's job. Solid, technically sound research supports this hypothesis.[24]

The second argument is called the *Status-Sharing Hypothesis:*

> *Employed married women take both their own and their husbands' characteristics into account in deciding with which class to identify.*

This argument implies rather different patterns of class identification among employed married women. For example, on the one hand, a secretary married to an electrician might see herself as working class because, even though she has a white-collar job and has many of the fringe benefits connected to such occupations, it is nonetheless the lowest-prestige white-collar work. On the other hand, the same person might emphasize the fact that her job is white collar regardless of its relatively low income, assess her husband's job as a highly skilled and relatively prestigious occupation, and identify herself as middle class. (Recall that the occupational prestige score for electricians is higher than that of many white-collar jobs.) In each case, respondents evaluate both spouses' positions in the community when determining their overall social standing. Hence, status-sharing occurs. The logic behind the status sharing hypothesis lies in egalitarian gender norms. From this point of view, women and men should be equal; that is, equally obligated to support the family, rear children, and care for one another. By extrapolation, then, employed married women should see their position in the community as resulting from a combination of their own and their husband's characteristics. Again, technically sound evidence supports this hypothesis.[25]

Obviously, both the hypotheses and the empirical findings cited above flatly contradict each other. Both cannot be right. Or can they?

---

[24]Felson and Knoke (1974), Jackman and Jackman (1983).
[25]Ritter and Hargens (1975), Van Velsor and Beeghley (1979).

Beeghley and Cochran examined this issue and showed that the research results just cited may be correct, even though the findings are contradictory.[26] Rather, the inability to confirm one or the other hypothesis may reflect the historical process of changing gender norms. Thus, over the past few years, U.S. society has been moving, in fits and starts, from an emphasis on traditional gender norms to an acceptance of egalitarian gender norms. Such changes do not come easily or quickly because they involve drastic alterations in the way people view themselves, the world in which they live, and the way they organize their lives. Previous research may simply reveal this confusion: At one time respondents display a status-borrowing pattern and at another a status-sharing orientation.

Yet there must be some method of sorting these differences out, and Beeghley and Cochran suggested that married women's orientation to gender norms might provide a way. They argue that such normative orientations set the context in which married women adopt either a status-borrowing or a status-sharing stance. Hence, they tested the following hypotheses:

1. *Employed married women who believe in traditional gender norms will consider only their husbands' characteristics in deciding with which class to identify.*

2. *Employed married women who believe in egalitarian gender norms will take both their own and their husbands' characteristics into account in deciding with which class to identify.*

In testing these hypotheses, Beeghley and Cochran used married women's support for the Equal Rights Amendment (ERA) and attitudes toward married women working outside the home as indicators of gender norms. They found that those supporting the ERA and favoring women's employment use a status-sharing approach in identifying with a class. In contrast, those opposing the ERA and opposing married women's employment, even though they have a job themselves, use a status-borrowing approach in identifying with a class. Beeghley and Cochran concluded by predicting that as an increasing proportion of women work outside the home and more people of both genders accept egalitarian gender norms, then the status-sharing hypothesis will be supported by an increasing proportion of employed married women.

One last observation: It is important for you to recognize that neither the findings reported by Beeghley and Cochran nor their prediction ends the matter. Recent data, for example, show that the class identification of employed wives continues to be in flux.[27] Gender norms remain in flux, and further research on this and related topics will show the direction in which they move. It is in this sense that Max Weber described the social sciences as blessed with eternal youth.

"What do you do for a living?" It is a question that has become meaningful only recently. In William Shakespeare's play, *Romeo and Juliet,* for example, set in the sixteenth century, one's job was less important than one's name.[28] Being a Capulet or a

[26]Beeghley and Cochran (1988). See also Zipp and Plutzer (2000).
[27]Yamaguchi and Wang (2002).
[28]Shakespeare (1989).

Montague—or being associated with one of these families—clearly indicated high status in Verona. Such persons were due respect. With industrialization, the rise of capitalism, and other historical changes, however, the criterion by which people evaluate each other has changed. One's name remains important, of course, but what people do and the class with which they identify provide an initial guide to their place in the community and the respect they should be given.

## *Summary*

This chapter describes the implications people's jobs have for their class location and suggests the meaning such views have for their lifestyle. Studies of occupational prestige assess the social standing of occupations. The basis for prestige assignments appears to be the level of education required in various jobs. Prestige hierarchies indicate patterns of domination and subordination characteristic of the class structure. These hierarchies vary by race/ethnicity and by gender. There are two main empirical generalizations: The hierarchy of occupational prestige is stable over time within and across societies. The second, however, probably needs to be modified. It is more likely that hierarchies of occupational prestige are similar in all Western industrial nations.

Class identification assesses the extent to which people see themselves as belonging to different classes and the implications this fact has for their lifestyles. In the United States, people find it easy to identify with a class, mainly the working and middle classes (see Table 4.1). Class identification is highly correlated with occupation and says a great deal about people's lifestyle: for example, whom they live near, who their friends are, and who are potential marriage partners. Patterns of class identification among employed married women are unclear, mainly because of changing gender norms. When this factor is controlled for, however, the finding becomes intelligible. It appears that employed married women who accept egalitarian gender norms use a status-sharing orientation, while those who accept traditional gender norms use a status-borrowing orientation in selecting a class with which to identify.

# 5

## Social Class and Stratification

### Mobility and Status Attainment

William H. Gates II was a prominent lawyer in Seattle in the 1950s. As such he would probably have seen himself as middle or upper-middle class. From this class of origin, his son, William H. Gates III, was born on October 28, 1955. As he grew up, young Bill developed an abiding, indeed compulsive interest in computer programming. Eventually, he founded the Microsoft Corporation, bought DOS, and in 1981 persuaded IBM to use a revised version of it as the operating system for its line of personal computers. When Microsoft became a publicly traded stock corporation in 1986, its Chief Executive Officer, Bill Gates, became an instant multimillionaire and eventually a multibillionaire.[1] The third Mr. Gates's experience implies important questions. Can you and I become billionaires? More prosaically, how much opportunity is there—really? What factors determine people's occupational location and, hence, their income, prestige, and ultimately

[1]Wallace (1993).

their life chances? In a relatively rigid society, people usually obtain jobs based on their birth—ascription. By contrast, in a relatively fluid society, people are more likely to get positions based on their ability and hard work—achievement. As described in Chapter 1, while modern class-based societies display greater emphasis on obtaining positions based on hard work, birth still matters, which means they display a built-in tension between achievement and ascription.

Sociologists assess the degree of opportunity in a society in two ways: by examining mobility rates and the status attainment of individuals. **Mobility** refers to changes in the occupational distribution, either intra- or intergenerationally. Intragenerational mobility occurs during people's own careers, beginning from their first main job. Intergenerational mobility compares parents' occupations to children's. In both cases, the question being asked is this: How many people move and how far? The answer, of course, must be in terms of rates of movement and the explanation must be structural. In presenting the data in the next section, I shall focus on intergenerational mobility when looking at the United States and intragenerational mobility when comparing this country with others. As you will see, the findings are parallel. **Status attainment** refers to the study of how individuals enter specific occupations. The question here is this: What combination of ascribed and achieved factors leads individuals into one occupation rather than another and why? The answer, of course, must be social psychological—either directly or indirectly. As an aside, because mobility and status attainment reflect people's occupations, such analyses say nothing about how ownership of capital (such as stock in the Microsoft Corporation) leads to opportunity and power—a topic considered later.

## Social Mobility

### Social Mobility in the United States

In order to describe long-term rates of intergenerational mobility, the flow of people out of and into occupations must be shown. This task requires an understanding of how the occupational structure changed over time. In the past, it did not display much variability; most people were farmers, just as their parents had been. In 1800, for example, 74 percent of the labor force was engaged in farming occupations, a figure that was probably an all-time low at that time.[2] It fell steadily over the century, to 55 percent in 1850 and 38 percent in 1900. People left farming jobs, moved to cities, and took newly available jobs. By 1900, as Table 5.1 shows, a sizeable working class had developed, defined as people doing nonfarm blue-collar work: about 45 percent of the population. Most of these jobs involved very hard, physically arduous tasks. Little mechanization existed, at least by today's standards. In addition, a small middle class had formed, about 18 percent of the population (at most). These people worked inside and many of them did not do manual labor.

As displayed in Table 5.1, the occupational structure continued changing. Today, only 2 percent of the population works on farms and about 38 percent in blue-collar jobs.

---

[2]U.S. Bureau of the Census (1975:139).

**TABLE 5.1**   *Occupational Distribution 1900, 1950, and 2001*

|  | *1900* | *1950* |  | *2001* |
|---|---|---|---|---|
| *White Collar* |  |  | *White Collar* |  |
| Professionals | 4% | 9% | Professional Specialty | 16% |
| Managers | 6 | 9 | Executives and Managers | 15 |
|  |  |  | Technicians | 3 |
| Sales | 5 | 7 | Sales | 12 |
| Clerical | 3 | 12 | Administrative Support | 14 |
|  | 18% | 37% |  | 60% |
| *Blue Collar* |  |  | *Blue Collar* |  |
| Crafts | 11% | 14% | Precision Production | 11% |
| Operators | 13 | 20 | Operators | 9 |
| Laborers | 12 | 7 | Handlers and Laborers | 4 |
| Service | 9 | 10 | Service | 14 |
|  | 45% | 51% |  | 38% |
| Farmers | 38% | 12% | Farmers, Foresters, Fishers | 2% |
| Total | 101% | 100% | Total | 100% |

*Note:* Percentages do not add to 100 because of rounding. As implied by the name changes, the occupational categories are not exactly comparable between 1950 and 2001.

*Sources:* U.S. Bureau of the Census (1975:139), U.S. Bureau of Labor Statistics (2002: Table 9).

Although such work remains arduous and, often, physically dirty, mechanization has transformed it. Tractors (sometimes with air conditioning) substitute for horse-drawn plows. Powered equipment makes blue-collar jobs easier and increases productivity—which is to say people get more done in less time. Nonetheless, as described in Chapter 4, most of these people would be seen and would see themselves as working class. Finally, the table shows that the majority of employed persons, 60 percent, now work in white-collar jobs. Most see themselves and would be seen by others as middle class.

Table 5.1 illustrates the long-term pattern: People have moved off the farm and into working- and middle-class jobs, often in historically new occupations generated by economic development. It is probable that Emily Perrin produced the first quantitative study of mobility in 1904. She compared the occupations of fathers and sons in order "to determine how far ancestral bent and how far environmental conditions influence a man in his choice of occupation in life."[3] Put differently, she wanted to understand how family background and achievement affect a person's occupation. As mentioned earlier, subsequent scholars have divided Perrin's questions in two: the study of mobility rates and status attainment by individuals.

[3]Perrin (1904:967).

The best early analysis of mobility was Pitirim Sorokin's *Social and Cultural Mobility,* originally published in 1927.[4] Sorokin, like all subsequent observers, recognized that a job is most people's main source of income and prestige in modern societies. Thus, he focused on how fathers' occupations were linked with their sons' occupations and thereby charted the rate of mobility across generations. The emphasis on the nexus between fathers and sons made sense at the time because few women were employed and most people believed that women should remain at home (recall Chapter 3). Sorokin analyzed the data then available, including Perrin's, and concluded as follows: First, much intergenerational occupational inheritance occurs. For example, he noted that "the hereditary transmission of occupation still exists. . . . The fathers' occupation is still entered by the children in a greater proportion than any other." Second, a lot of intergenerational mobility takes place such that a significant proportion of children move into different (usually higher prestige) occupations than their fathers. This fact, he noted, makes modern societies unique when compared to the past. Third, intergenerational mobility is usually short distance. In his words, "the closer the affinity between occupations, the more intensive among them is mutual interchange of their members." Although Sorokin's data were not very good, his findings anticipate later research.

Such research has developed reasonably accurate data for the late nineteenth and twentieth centuries. The result is three major findings about mobility rates among men. The mobility rates of women will be considered later.

**1.** *There is a great deal of occupational inheritance in the United States.* The dominant intergenerational pattern is for fathers in white-collar occupations to have sons who also work in white-collar occupations, while fathers in blue-collar jobs generally have sons who also work in blue-collar jobs. The extent of occupational inheritance means that the class structure is reproduced from one generation to another as people with a certain level of access to resources pass them on to their children. Unlike Sorokin, by the term *inheritance* I do not mean that sons take the same job as their fathers or even enter the same occupational category. Rather, they end up in the same social class—as white-collar or blue-collar workers, respectively. Panel A of Table 5.2 illustrates this finding. It shows, for example, that even during the nineteenth century, most sons of professional workers ended up in the white-collar workforce. Similarly, most sons of blue-collar workers and farmers followed in their fathers' footsteps. Thus, most sons (and daughters, see below) inherit the class of their parents. This finding shows that ascription was important in the nineteenth century and remains important today.

The sons of farmers, however, constitute an anomaly. Although they displayed high levels of occupational inheritance during the nineteenth century, the historical pattern (shown in Table 5.1) has been for them to move into blue-collar occupations (usually in cities) where farm-related skills could be used. This trend means that there are now two occupational classes in the United States: white-collar workers and blue-collar workers, with farm workers constituting a recessive class. The boundary between these two classes forms a semipermeable barrier to social mobility.

---

[4]Sorokin (1927).

**TABLE 5.2** *Occupational Mobility among Men, 1880–1900, 1963, 1973, and 1982–1985*

*Panel A: Illustrations of Intergenerational Occupational Inheritance among Men*

| Year | Percent | Result |
|---|---|---|
| 1880–1900 | 56% | of the sons of professionals became white-collar workers |
| " | 78% | of the sons of service/laborers became blue-collar workers |
| " | 60% | of the sons of farmers became farmers |
| 1963 | 68% | of the sons of salaried professionals became white-collar workers |
| " | 72% | of the sons of laborers became blue-collar workers |
| 1973 | 68% | of the sons of salaried professionals became white-collar workers |
| " | 71% | of the sons of laborers became blue-collar workers |
| 1982–1985 | 72% | of the sons of salaried professionals became white-collar workers |
| " | 60% | of the sons of laborers became blue-collar workers |

*Panel B: Illustrations of Intergenerational Occupational Mobility among Men*

| Year | Percent | Result |
|---|---|---|
| 1880–1900 | 26% | of the sons of crafts workers became white-collar workers |
| 1963 | 41% | of the sons of crafts workers became white-collar workers |
| 1973 | 45% | of the sons of crafts workers became white-collar workers |
| 1982–1985 | 45% | of the sons of crafts workers became white-collar workers |

*Panel C: Illustrations of the Difficulties of Long-Distance Intergenerational Occupational Mobility among Men*

| Year | Percent | Result |
|---|---|---|
| 1880–1900 | 3% | of the sons of farmers became professional workers |
| 1963 | <1% | of the sons of farmers became professional workers |
| 1973 | <1% | of the sons of farmers became professional workers |
| 1982–1985 | 0% | of the sons of farmers became professional workers |

*Note:* Occupational categories vary from one study to another.

*Sources:* Guest, Landale, and McCann (1989:359); Blau and Duncan (1967:28); Featherman and Hauser (1978:535); Hout (1988:1396).

The usual interpretation of this barrier is that the need for the prestige of being "white collar" together with the lack of saleable manual skills prevents a great deal of downward mobility among the sons of white-collar workers. Similarly, much upward mobility into white-collar jobs is prevented by lack of necessary skills and, often, lack of respect for those sorts of jobs. Many blue-collar people do not believe that "pencil push-ers" really work. After all, they do not sweat or get dirty or become physically tired from their jobs. The result is the reproduction of the class structure.

**2.** *Social mobility is widespread in the United States.* This empirical generalization means that, despite the first finding reported above, the occupational structure in modern societies is relatively fluid. Panel B of Table 5.2 provides illustrations. I am using craft occupations in the table because they comprise the highest prestige blue-collar jobs (see Table 5.1 and Chapter 4) and constitute a sort of jumping-off place for upward mobility. Thus, about 26 percent of the sons of crafts workers became white-collar workers during the years 1880 to 1900. This rate increased significantly during the twentieth century. By 1963, it had risen to about 41 percent and by 1973 to about 45 percent. Beginning in the 1890s (and probably earlier), each generation of men has been upwardly mobile com-pared to their fathers.[5] All this movement suggests that there has been lots of opportunity in the United States over the last two centuries and that the importance of achievement has increased.

Although historical data are unsystematic, intergenerational inheritance coupled with relatively high rates of upward mobility describe the occupational structure in the United States since Colonial times. The ability of white immigrants to improve their eco-nomic and social positions by acquiring land or entering business was one of the most important attractions of the colonies. After winning independence, America became the "first new nation," meaning one organized by different principles compared to the past.[6]

Widespread mobility is one of the markers of modernity. As described in Chapter 1, this process has a twin impact. On the one hand, it signifies the rise of class as a system of stratification, with its emphasis on achievement (rather than birth) as a basis of location. Most people interpret the increase in intergenerational upward mobility as liberating. On the other hand, as the occupational structure has changed over time (Table 5.1), the his-torical pattern has been for some occupations to be destroyed, especially those requiring manual labor, and others to be created, especially those involving nonmanual labor. You should understand—and this is an important point, so pay attention—that the people in occupations that have been destroyed are usually not the same ones as those in occupa-tions that have been created. Thus, some people lose their jobs, livelihood, self-concept, houses, even their marriages and children (see Chapter 9). When coupled with the other factors producing modernization, capitalism revolutionizes the economy and thereby lib-erates people; but it is also vicious.

In order to see how vicious, look back at Table 5.1, noting the rise in the number of people in sales and service jobs coupled with the decline of those in precision production and operative jobs between 1950 and 2001. Most of these changes occurred in the last 20 years, and they indicate fundamental dislocations in the labor market.[7] High-skilled and relatively high-paying blue-collar jobs in industry have declined, replaced by lower-skilled and significantly lower-paying jobs, mostly in sales and service sectors. Moreover,

---

[5]Biblarz et al. (1996).
[6]Lipset (1963), Main (1965), Pessen (1971), Williamson and Lindert (1980).
[7]DiPrete and Nonnemaker (1997).

this change does not reflect purely economic forces; it also indicates political decisions. Governments today can, if they wish, affect the rate of change and the degree of job protection ordinary working people have. Two results, at least in this country, are greater inequality and an increase in the number of working poor.

**3.** *Short distance movements exceed long distance ones.* In their now classic work, *The American Occupational Structure,* Peter Blau and O. D. Duncan mimicked Sorokin's words: "The closer two occupations are to one another in the status hierarchy, the greater is the flow of manpower between them."[8] Panel C of Table 5.2 illustrates the pattern by showing how few people move long distances. Thus, in 1880–1900 only 3 percent of the sons of farmers moved to the top of the prestige ladder by becoming professional workers. More recently, such mobility has occurred less than 1 percent of the time. Do not be misled by the 0 percent for 1982–1985; it reflects the small sample size. A little (very little) long distance mobility takes place.

These three findings are very stable. Although tentative evidence suggests that the pattern remains the same today, some observers have wondered if the mobility rates shown in Panel B of Table 5.2 have been declining in recent years.[9] More data are needed. It is now time for a new analysis of the American occupational structure—one that includes women and minority groups in addition to African Americans.

The available data on women's intergenerational mobility show patterns similar to those of men.[10] First, a great deal of occupational inheritance takes place. For example, 95 percent of the daughters of salaried professional fathers become white-collar workers, usually above the level of clerks. Second, much mobility occurs. For example, 74 percent of the daughters of craft worker fathers become white-collar workers. This figure falls to 37 percent, however, if administrative support workers are excluded. As described in Chapter 3, when women work for pay, they are often guided into "support jobs," such as clerks; that is, they take jobs that involve assisting men. Finally, most movement is short distance. For example, less than 1 percent of daughters of farmers become professional workers. As shown in Chapter 3, however, these similarities understate the differences in mobility rates of men and women over time.[11] "Gender-based occupational discrimination" (another way of talking about the importance of ascription) has always inhibited daughters' occupational mobility and continues to do so.

Mobility data on minority groups are limited to African Americans, and their historical pattern is much different than that for Whites. As recently as 1962, only 5 percent of African American men had professional or managerial jobs.[12] Unlike Whites, however, little occupational inheritance occurred for men in these categories. Rather, the sons of African American professionals usually displayed downward mobility: 63 percent of them had service, operative, and laborer jobs. More generally, the vast majority of African American men—68 percent—were employed in these three occupational categories as

[8]Blau and Duncan (1967:36).
[9]Sobel et al. (1998), Birdsall and Graham (2000), Treiman (2000), Rytina (2000).
[10]Hout (1988:1395), Biblarz et al. (1996).
[11]Biblarz et al. (1996).
[12]Featherman and Hauser (1978:326).

recently as 1962. Nearly all of them displayed great occupational inheritance from one generation to another. Thus, unlike Whites, who have often advanced intergenerationally, the debilitating effects of discrimination kept most African American men confined to menial jobs regardless of their parents' status. The year in which these data were collected is significant, as it was just prior to passage of the Civil Rights Act of 1963 and other measures. This fact suggests that between the end of the Civil War and the mid-1960s, little opportunity existed for African Americans, regardless of their family resources, ability, or hard work. As I argue in Chapter 2, the Civil War freed African Americans in name but not in fact.

Since the 1960s, however, the situation has changed considerably. The class structure among African Americans elongated, as it also has, it is reasonable to suspect, among Hispanics and other minorities. Table 5.3 suggests how much change has occurred. Today, more than half of all African Americans are white collar and 22 percent are in either professional or managerial jobs. Moreover, although this conclusion is tentative, it appears that the pattern of mobility is beginning to resemble that of Whites: occupational inheritance (in particular, a greater rate of inheritance at the upper occupational levels) and an increasingly high rate of upward mobility compared to the past.[13] As mentioned, these changes reflect the impact of civil rights and affirmative action. When African Americans became free and were provided with some opportunity, they began displaying upward mobility. Table 5.3 also shows the occupational distribution of Hispanics, revealing that a smaller proportion, 38 percent, are white collar compared to both African Americans and Whites (non-Hispanics). My guess is that the figures in the top half of the distribution are all-time highs for Hispanics. Thus, these data suggest that greater equality now exists among racial and ethnic groups. Remember, however, that Table 5.3 shows that a much higher proportion of Whites still work in the higher-prestige and higher-paying jobs. Moreover, the children of African Americans still display significantly higher rates of downward mobility than do Whites.[14] So a great deal of inequality remains. This double finding—greater equality along with continued inequality (and discrimination)—mirrors the theme in Chapter 2.

For now, however, it is important to examine cross-national mobility data. After all, you should wonder if this country is unique. For example, if the rate of mobility in the United States is higher (or lower) than in other nations, then it is useful to ask why this difference exists.

## *Social Mobility in Cross-National Perspective*

Cross-national studies show, however, that mobility rates in the United States are neither much higher nor lower than in similar nations. The American pattern is not unique.[15] This fact is illustrated by intragenerational mobility. You should recall that the issue here is how many people are mobile over the course of their careers. Presented below are the chances of men who begin their careers as skilled blue-collar workers (roughly equivalent

[13]Featherman and Hauser (1978), Davis (1997), Fosu (1997), G. Wilson et al. (1999).
[14]Davis (1997).
[15]Erikson and Goldthorpe (1993). The data that follow are from p. 333.

**TABLE 5.3**  *Occupational Distribution among Whites, African Americans, and Hispanics, 2001*

|  | *Whites* | *African Americans* | *Hispanics* |
|---|---|---|---|
| Professional Specialty | 16% | 12% | 8% |
| Executives and Managers | 15 | 10 | 7 |
| Technicians | 3 | 3 | 2 |
| Sales | 13 | 9 | 9 |
| Administrative Support | 14 | 17 | 12 |
| **Total White Collar** | **61%** | **51%** | **38%** |
| Precision Production | 12% | 8% | 15% |
| Operators | 9 | 15 | 14 |
| Handlers and Laborers | 4 | 5 | 8 |
| Service | 12 | 22 | 20 |
| **Total Blue Collar** | **37%** | **48%** | **57%** |
| Farmers, Foresters, Fishers | 3% | 1% | 5% |
| **Total** | **101%** | **100%** | **100%** |

*Note:* Totals do not add to 100% due to rounding.

*Source:* U.S. Bureau of Labor Statistics (2002:Tables 9 and 11).

to precision production workers in Table 5.1) ending up as professionals, managers, and technicians:

| | |
|---|---|
| Sweden | 22% |
| United States | 20% |
| England | 16% |
| France | 15% |
| Ireland | 8% |

These data lead to two conclusions. First, with regard to the United States, the intragenerational finding presented here parallels the intergenerational finding presented earlier: Most people are occupationally stable while a significant (although smaller) proportion are mobile. Second, although U.S. mobility rates are not unique, there is considerable international variation. Thus, in the United States and Sweden the odds of a man who begins his career as an electrician ending up as an engineer are about one in five. In England and France, however, they are about one in six, and in Ireland one in ten. So, these three nations display less mobility than does the United States.

Social structures in modern societies display three tendencies, all of which are illustrated by the study of mobility. First, they are stable over time. This is why so much occupational inheritance occurs. Comprising networks of relationships and values that tie people together, social structures set the range of opportunities and limitations that are available. People grow up within a context that provides specific skills and experiences:

schools, role models, and the like. Hence, the class structure is reproduced as the children of farmers learn to appreciate the land, children of blue-collar families learn how to work with their hands, and children of white-collar families learn how to succeed in school. I am being stereotypical, of course, simply to point out that there is a great deal of inter-generational occupational inheritance. Second, social structures in modern societies change over time, and deliberately so in light of political decisions. This is one reason why so much mobility occurs. For example, productivity increased when people invented machines to take advantage of fossil fuels. Not only was more food produced, but also problems of coordination arose and more white-collar jobs were created. The plausible range of opportunities expanded. Hence, mobility became widespread as people took advantages of new choices. Third, social structures vary internationally. This is why differences in mobility occur from one nation to another. In the next section, I offer an explanation for each of these tendencies.

## Social Structure and Mobility

### The Reproduction of the Class Structure

Recall that the first finding reported above is that most of the sons of blue-collar workers end up as blue-collar workers. And when their daughters are employed, most of them end up either in white-collar support jobs or as blue-collar workers. The result is that they are always economically insecure, regardless of how hard they work (see Chapter 9). Similarly, most of the sons of white-collar workers end up as white-collar workers. And when their daughters are employed, they too end up as white-collar workers, typically in jobs above the level of administrative support. What I am interested in, then, in this section, is the reproduction of the class structure over time—in other words, the continuing impact of ascription.

*A Vignette.*     In order to suggest how this process occurs, I have constructed a vignette about a game of Monopoly as it might appear if it were organized to reflect reality. The purpose of this little fantasy is to provide you with a subjective sense of what the data mean as well as to describe, at least metaphorically, some essential characteristics of American social structure.[16]

The game of Monopoly embodies the values characteristic of the culture of capitalism summarized in Chapter 1, especially in their extreme form as manifested in the United States. These values, you should recall, emphasize working hard to get ahead, individualism, universalism, obtaining wealth, actively mastering situations, and doing so in a methodical way. These values embody what some observers have called the American Dream: a context in which people compete (economically, politically, and in other ways) for material success.[17] Thus, in the game of Monopoly as it is actually played, each participant starts with an equal amount of money, $1,500. By combining luck (symbolized by

---

[16]The name of the game, Monopoly, is the trademark of Parker Brothers for its Real Estate Trading Game (Beverly, MA: Parker Brothers Division of General Mills Fun Group, Inc., 1935, 1946, 1961). An earlier version of this vignette appeared in my *Living Poorly in America* (Beeghley, 1983).

[17]Messner and Rosenfeld (2001), Beeghley (2003).

the roll of the dice) and shrewdness (symbolized by purchase and auction decisions), competitors seek economic success. The point to remember about the game is that everyone begins with the same chance of winning. After all, a game is only fair under such conditions and no one wants to participate in a contest in which some of the players have an unfair advantage at the beginning. Although many people believe that life is like a game of Monopoly and that their occupational achievement represents their reward for hard work, this attitude is self-deceptive; the real world is rather different in that some people are born with more advantages than others and the result of their hard work varies accordingly.

Here is a fictional version of Monopoly, one that is more analogous to the real world than the actual game. Begin by imagining that four groups of people are participating and that they compete both as individuals against all other individuals and, in certain situations, as members of their respective groups. Also, imagine that the game board is much larger than usual because there are so many contestants.

Group One is very small; in fact, its members are statistically insignificant. They are almost never included in sample surveys. But they are relatively advantaged at the start of the game, for they own some property and possess lots of Monopoly money, say, $5,000 each. In addition, the members of this group take care of the bank and, because of their enormous responsibility, get two rolls of the dice each turn. They view this benefit as justified because they see themselves as living according to dominant cultural values. They believe they embody the American Dream. Thus, while these people are statistically insignificant, they are of great substantive importance.

Group Two is very large but its members have considerably fewer advantages with which to begin the game. They have no property and about $2,000 each. Nonetheless, they believe in the cultural values characteristic of all capitalist societies and think that everyone else playing the game can be like Bill Gates and move into Group One if they work hard enough.

Group Three is also very large but its members are even more disadvantaged at the beginning of the game. They have no property and only about $1,000 each. Nonetheless, they also believe in hard work, individualism, and all the other elements of the culture of capitalism.

Group Four is smaller but still significant in size. Its members, however, are the most disadvantaged of all. They not only own no property and have very little money—about $500 each—but they also do not know all the rules of the game. Perhaps as a result, they often (more or less randomly) lose a turn and frequently pay more than list price for properties and fines. Even so, they also aspire to the American Dream.

One final point about this game. No one can stop competing; no one can quit striving for success. Any players who run out of money or go to jail are required to beg for more cash, pay their penalties, and continue playing—indefinitely.

In this context, then, the competition begins. Now Monopoly is a game played by individuals and it would be easy to measure the process by which each participant acquired income and property, and thereby found a place in the game. This would be the Monopoly equivalent of status attainment, of course. While such an analysis would be useful in order to understand precisely how individuals in the various groups behave, it would be misleading to extrapolate an explanation of the game as a whole based only on the analysis of the experiences of individuals. This is because the players were divided into groups with unequal advantages when the game began. An interpretation that does not recognize this fact—which does not ascertain the structure of the game—has to be misleading.

If, however, one takes a more holistic (or structural) view, it becomes possible to sketch the results of the game in a plausible way. The members of Group One, the rich, will generally remain well off unless they are very unlucky or unwise (in fact, downright stupid). This is because they began competing with many built-in advantages and share some of them; for example, they pool their "get out of jail free" cards. Furthermore, given their responsibility for taking care of the bank, a few of them illegally "borrow" money occasionally while other players are not looking. When caught, of course, they are (sometimes) forced to pay back what they stole.

Similarly, the members of Group Two will, with some variation, maintain their positions. Although upward mobility into Group One and downward mobility into Group Three will occasionally occur, most movement will be within Group Two itself and of relatively short distance. These people generally ignore the fact that few of them actually move into Group One and take satisfaction in being better off than less advantaged persons. They attribute this fact to their hard work and ability rather than the advantages with which they began. They live in nice neighborhoods (the Monopoly equivalent of, say, Marvin Gardens) and think they have obtained the American Dream.

The members of Groups Three and Four are obviously in the most precarious positions. While some upward mobility into Group Two does take place, most movement will be short distance, usually within or between the lower-level groups. Security is always uncertain for these participants in the game, mainly because the resources available to them are so minimal that it is difficult, on their own, to make much headway. Nonetheless, nearly everyone in these two groups works hard and learns to live with their precarious position in the game.

Some members of Groups Three and Four, however, become **alienated;** that is, their personal experiences lead them to believe they are powerless to influence their own lives. Alienated people find that the American Dream is hopelessly remote, even meaningless. Adhering to these values does not (indeed, cannot) lead to success. They recognize, albeit in an inchoate way, that the social structure in modern societies is **anomic;** that is, a disconnect exists between the values people believe in (the culture of capitalism) and legitimate means to success.[18] As a result, some readjust their goals and only play by going through the motions. Others, however, get high and just sit at the game board passively while their tokens are moved for them. Still others (surprisingly few) pull out guns and use them to alter their economic situation. But given spatial arrangements separating the various groups, their victims are usually other members of Groups Three and Four. When caught, these people are sent to jail for long periods.

With apologies to the many dedicated scholars working in the field, this fictional vignette reflects the major findings in the study of social mobility: While a great deal of mobility occurs—most of it short distance—the class structure is reproduced over time because occupational inheritance predominates.

---

[18]Merton (1968a). See also Beeghley (2003).

***The Inheritance of Social Class.***     The vignette is useful because it highlights the fact that the rewards of hard work go mostly to those who start life with some advantages. This result is why the mode is occupational inheritance—from blue collar to blue collar and from white collar to white collar. It is also why, as explained later, ascribed factors systematically influence status attainment at every stage. Thus, even though people do not inherit class position in modern societies and even though they must get and keep jobs based on achievement, ascription remains fundamental to understanding the stratification structure. People's family background is significant not only because it allows them to obtain educational credentials that qualify them for better jobs, but also because it provides them with knowledge, interpersonal skills, social contacts, values, psychological traits, and other less obvious characteristics that enable them to obtain and keep better jobs. I shall return to this issue in a few moments.

In addition, the vignette is useful because it suggests how the rate of mobility is affected by the social structure. As the fictional Monopoly game is constructed, no amount of individual effort will change the fact that most people will not cross class boundaries and those who do will go only a short way. This fact is inevitable in anomic social structures. This is why I set up the vignette to mirror the research reported previously.

Finally, the vignette is useful because it highlights a fundamental omission in both the mobility and status attainment literatures: The findings do not reflect the existence of an upper class, the rich—people like Bill Gates. Despite the use of "random samples," survey research cannot account for either the characteristics of this small class or the impact it has on the structure of stratification. This is because the rich do not make themselves accessible to survey researchers. One does not simply walk up to the doors of rich persons and hand them questionnaires. Yet, despite their statistical insignificance, the substantive importance of this small aggregate is enormous because they possess capital and wield enormous political power as a result. These factors, the importance of which Marx and Weber emphasized, make their occupations relatively unimportant as determinants of class. In effect, researchers have examined mobility and status attainment only for the vast majority of people, for whom occupation determines their class, and ignored the group for which it is not important. The omission of the property-owning class leads to an emphasis on individual achievement as the mechanism for mobility. It also leads to an image of the United States as without classes and class conflict. In this sense, mobility research is a throwback to a pre-1950s orientation, prior to the time Ralf Dahrendorf alerted U.S. sociologists to the importance of class conflict. Yet there remains the reality of mobility.

### *The Long-Term Pattern of Mobility*

Even though most people are occupationally stable, the data show that the United States has displayed a relatively high rate of upward mobility over time. Common sense, American style, suggests that individuals are upwardly mobile because they work hard and have ability; in so doing, they live by dominant cultural values. And this sequence often occurs. But a focus on individuals does not explain why the rate of mobility has been so high over the last century. In reality, the explanation for this fact has little to do with individuals' skills, motivation, or values. Rather, the social structure changed over time such that a great deal of upward mobility became possible for certain kinds of people. The factors causing the high rate of mobility can be stated formally, as in the following hypothesis:

*The rate of mobility in the United States reflects the impact of: (1) economic development, (2) class differences in fertility rates, (3) immigration rates, and (4) affirmative action for white males.*

In terms of the vignette used earlier, this hypothesis suggests that while the game may be rigged, at least everyone now gets to participate—a new phenomenon in history.

***Economic Development.***    Industrialization meant that new forms of energy—such as steam, fossil fuels, and (later on) nuclear energy—allowed the substitution of machines for human and animal muscle power. This fundamental change was based, of course, on scientific advance. It combined with capitalism, democracy, notions of individual dignity, and other dynamic factors, and the result was a radical increase in productivity. Put simply, such changes mean that machines increasingly performed many tasks that animals and people used to do, a process that continues to occur today. As a result, the number of farming and blue-collar jobs declined and the number of white-collar jobs expanded. More specifically, the three occupational categories that expanded most over the last 150 years were professional, executive and managerial, and administrative support jobs. In the past, who needed accountants, computer programmers, corporate financial officers, and more? For most of you reading this book, the jobs your parents have simply did not exist a century and a half ago. By contrast, the two occupational categories that declined the most during this period were farming and laboring jobs.[19] These changes meant increased opportunity for everyone. Put simply, without the tremendous increase in white-collar jobs over the last century, most people would still be farmers today and the rate of social mobility would have been very low. Hard work would not have produced mobility, no matter how much ability people possessed. In sum, "changes in the occupational structure are the only source of systematic variation in rates of intergenerational occupational mobility."[20]

What happened is that as economic development occurred vacant job slots were created in the top categories, which served as a "pull" factor stimulating upward mobility. Thus, while no individual was forced to be upwardly mobile, these jobs existed; they were attractive in terms of pay, perquisites (or privileges), and other characteristics (such as the ability to remain physically clean and avoid manual labor); and many individuals strove to attain them. It is important to understand, however, that the motives or abilities or any personal characteristic of those who filled them cannot explain the existence of these jobs. They reflect changes "in the nature of the society itself" that produced a high rate of mobility over time.[21] People's opportunities expanded.

***Class Differences in Fertility Rates.***    The term **fertility rate** refers to the average number of children each woman has. With the exception of the post-World War II "baby

---

[19]Blau and Duncan (1967).
[20]Hauser (1975:585), Sawhill (2000).
[21]The phrase is Durkheim's (1895:28).

boom," the long-term trend in fertility rates has been downward. The average woman born in the early 1800s had about eight children, while the average woman born since 1935 has had about two.[22] But the fertility of women from different classes has probably always varied such that lower-class women had more and upper-class women had less than average. Scattered data from throughout the nineteenth century show this tendency clearly.[23] Data from 1910, when the process of economic development was in full swing, also display this pattern: Rural and farm women had around five children on average, urban women married to blue-collar workers had around four children, and urban women married to white-collar workers had about three.[24] These differences are significant, since large families in farming and lower-level blue-collar occupations provided most of the people to fill the jobs opening up above them in the stratification hierarchy. In effect, class differences in fertility constituted a historical "push" factor, stimulating upward mobility in the United States.

*Immigration Rates.*    The United States is a nation of immigrants, and the years from 1870 to 1920 saw the highest level of immigration in U.S. history. In the decade from 1900 to 1910, for example, the immigration rate was 10 persons per 1,000 U.S. citizens, an all-time high.[25] These new residents typically entered the society at the lowest rungs. Nonetheless, immigration laws during this period required that new arrivals come equipped with skills.[26] The sheer force of numbers combined with education, literacy, and other vocational abilities constituted another "push" factor, stimulating upward mobility.[27] Thus, "the pressure of displaced manpower at the bottom and the vacuum created by new opportunities at the top [started] a chain reaction of short distance movements throughout the occupational structure. This push of supply at the bottom and pull of demand at the top [created] opportunities for upward mobility from most origins, as the vacancies left by sons moving up [were] filled by sons from lower strata."[28]

The significance of class differences in fertility rates and immigration rates has declined in recent years. Since about 1920, for example, the level of immigration into the United States has been kept at one or two persons per 1,000 citizens. Similarly, although class differences in fertility continue to exist, they have declined over the years.

*Affirmative Action for White Males.*    The term **affirmative action** refers to public policies giving advantages to members of one group over others. Historically, such benefits have gone to white males. They could achieve. Women and members of minority groups have been held back by ascribed barriers.

Unequal treatment has been built into the social structure in the form of **traditional gender norms.** These rules emphasize that men and women ought to have separate spheres: Women should bear and raise children and take care of their husbands. Men

---

[22]Cherlin (1992).
[23]Whelpton (1928), Jaffe (1940).
[24]Graybill et al. (1958).
[25]U.S. Bureau of the Census (2001:10).
[26]Lieberson (1980).
[27]Sibley (1942).
[28]Blau and Duncan (1967:66).

should provide for the family economically and dominate public life. In the past, such norms were implemented by denying women the right to vote, despite the fact that they were productive citizens. Such norms were also used to justify driving women out or keeping them out of high-prestige and high-paying jobs in medicine, education, business, and the like. Although these norms are changing, as indicated by the fact that many forms of unequal treatment have become illegal in recent years, they continue to influence behavior (see Chapter 3). They inhibit women's occupational success.

Affirmative action has also benefited white males at the expense of African Americans and other racial and ethnic groups. In Chapter 2, I argued that three factors inhibited mobility by nonwhites. First, variations in the conditions of settlement—free versus slave and citizen versus debt peonage—placed people of color at a disadvantage. Second, patterns of prejudice and discrimination (especially institutionalized discrimination) inhibited occupational success. And third, affirmative action aimed at Whites, mainly males, promoted their occupational success. The impact of such policies can be seen in the nineteenth century land acts and the development of land grant colleges, which provided conduits of mobility that were unavailable to African Americans. Although discrimination has become illegal today, some of the mechanisms by which it continues were described in Chapter 2. The result has been greater upward mobility by white males.

These elements of social structure—economic development, class differences in fertility rates, immigration, and affirmative action for white males—existed independently of individuals and influenced them, affecting their range of choices. People's behavior was directed in certain ways rather than others by factors over which they had little control. Thus, the structure of stratification developed a large number of open channels for achievement by some white males but considerably fewer and shorter channels for those individuals with the greatest inherited disadvantages. This is why women, African Americans, Hispanics, and others display lower rates of mobility: They were born to the wrong parents, worked in the wrong industry, or lived in the wrong region of the country. It is a grim fact that people with disadvantaged parents can be paragons of hard work and morality but most will remain poor or live on the edge of poverty.

### *Cross-National Variations in Mobility*

Attempts at showing the relationship between social structure and cross-national variations in mobility rates have a long history. The basic finding is this: *Economic development leads to higher rates of occupational mobility.* This relationship constitutes a basic characteristic of all modern societies, but considerable variation occurs from one nation to another. Thus, for example, data show that the occupational structure in Western nations did not change at the same time, the same rate, or to the same degree.[29] This fact was illustrated earlier with data on intragenerational mobility, which varies greatly from one nation to another. Modernity means that nations can now choose; they can regulate the degree of mobility and the inequality that follows.

If economic development and occupational mobility rates are related but can be regulated by public policies, then interest focuses on the decisions various nations make.

---

[29]Erikson and Goldthorpe (1993:102).

In this context, please recall my earlier discussion of how highly skilled and (relatively) high-paying blue-collar jobs in industry have declined; replaced by lower skilled and (significantly) lower-paying jobs mostly in sales and service. This mobility occurred in response to economic and technological developments as they were mediated by political decisions. Public policy, for example, can affect workers' job security when industries are contracting. It can also affect their ability to obtain support (welfare) when jobs are lost, the ease with which they can move from an industry that is contracting to (new, perhaps different jobs in) an industry that is expanding, and the ease with which persons in, say, their 50s or 60s can exit from the labor force altogether. For example, research shows tentative support for the following hypothesis:

> *When jobs decline in an industry: The less job security and the fewer the labor market boundaries, then the greater the emphasis on individual resources in determining occupational mobility.*[30]

The researchers looked at four nations and found that the United States protects worker job security less and places the fewest barriers between jobs in different industries, which means more emphasis on individual resources. It follows, as mentioned earlier, that a lot of mobility into sales and service occupations has occurred in recent years. This statement, however, does not do justice to the impact such changes have on people's lives (see Chapter 9). Sweden was next, displaying somewhat greater job security and labor market boundaries. The Netherlands and Germany were rather similar and better yet at protecting individuals from the impact of economic and technological change.

A lot of controversy exists about the wisdom of these policies. In this country, the dominant view (held by those with the power to make decisions) is that "the market" ought to determine where the jobs are. Whether this opinion serves as a veil for protecting economic and political interests of the rich and powerful is something you need to decide. In any case, remember that "the market" operates in a political context; jobs are created and destroyed in light of political as well as economic decisions.

Who makes these decisions? I will consider this issue in Chapters 6 and 7. For now, I want to shift the level of analysis from mobility rates to status attainment by individuals.

## *Status Attainment*

Individuals make decisions in the context in which they find themselves. There are about 135 million employed persons in the United States, which means that about the same number of jobs exist.[31] These are paid positions held by individuals. People enter one of them based on the way their parents' status produces advantages and disadvantages, their own efforts and abilities, and a degree of luck. Peter Blau and O. D. Duncan showed that this process can be studied as a causal sequence that identifies the factors in individuals' lives that influence attainment and how much each factor affects subsequent ones:[32]

---

[30]DiPrete et al. (1997).
[31]U.S. Bureau of the Census (2001:367).
[32]Blau and Duncan (1967:63).

We think of the individual's life-cycle as a sequence in time that can be described, however partially and crudely, by a set of classificatory or quantitative measurements taken at successive stages. . . . Given this scheme, the questions we are continually raising in one form or another are: How and to what degree do the circumstances of birth condition subsequent status? And how does status attained (whether by ascription or achievement) at one stage of the life-cycle affect the prospects for a subsequent stage?

## Status Attainment in the United States

The major variables in the status attainment process are shown in Figure 5.1, which depicts a sequence of ascribed and achieved factors.[33] A person's family background influences one's occupational status attainment, both indirectly because of its strong relationship to one's educational accomplishments, but also directly. Thus, while the importance of ascribed factors is greatest when a child is young, one's family influences a child's accomplishments throughout life. At the same time, however, achievement at each stage of life decisively affects prospects at subsequent stages. This fact means that issues over which individuals have more control assume greater importance with age. The boxes in the figure are numbered to correspond with the order of findings reported below. As before, the initial studies of status attainment dealt with men.

**1.** *The social class of a person's family of origin, as indicated by such variables as father's education, father's occupation, mother's education, and family income are all highly correlated and influences status attainment at all subsequent stages of a child's life.* Put simply, birth matters. It directly affects each stage of status attainment: the development of ability, academic performance, encouragement from significant others (such as teachers and friends), educational and occupational aspirations, educational attainment, and eventual occupational attainment. Thus, the overall impact of a person's family on eventual occupational success fits with most people's intuitive observation. This is a case where research shows that "common sense" is correct.

**2.** *Ability influences every subsequent stage of the status attainment process.* People of high ability usually do better than those with less. "Ability" is usually measured by either an achievement or intelligence test and, hence, refers to academic aptitude rather than other kinds of skills. Thus, ability most strongly affects academic performance (for example, grade point average) and educational attainment. But ability also influences the other intervening variables as well: educational and occupational aspirations and the encouragement a child receives from significant others. Finally, in addition to education, ability also affects the job a person ultimately gets. As an aside, you should remember that while ability has a biological basis, its development is socially determined.[34] Thus, middle-class children often possess advantages over others who have the same ability but

[33]The figure is intended as a summary of many studies. See, for example, Blau and Duncan (1967), Sewell et al. (1970), Hout and Morgan (1975), Alexander et al. (1975), Featherman and Hauser (1978), Jencks et al. (1979), Krymkowski (1991), England (1992), Duncan et al. (1998), Lin (1999), Treiman (2000), Mayer (2001), Warren et al. (2002).
[34]Duncan et al. (1998).

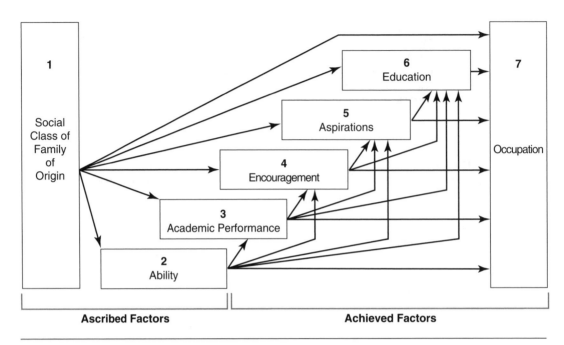

FIGURE 5.1 *The Process of Status Attainment*

come from working-class and poor backgrounds. This is because, for example, middle-class children often enter school better prepared and, hence, display better performance. The long-term impact increases the odds of occupational success for middle-class children.

**3.** *Academic performance directly influences subsequent status attainment: the level and kind of encouragement received from others, aspirations, and eventual educational and occupational attainment.* The dual impact of the schools becomes apparent early in people's lives. On the one hand, the schools facilitate achievement. Ambitious parents encourage and prepare their children, who enter the schools ready to use their abilities. As a result, they receive encouragement from teachers, develop aspirations, and get tracked into a college preparatory curriculum. They become less likely to drop out of school and more likely to attend college.[35] And a college degree is often what separates those in the middle class from those in the working class. On the other hand, school personnel often use ascriptive (nonperformance) criteria in evaluating and placing children. Teachers expect, and get, better performance from middle-class students.[36] Just as important, however, track placement typically reflects class background. Tracking is how the public schools prepare some students for college and others with vocational skills.[37] My guess is

[35]Haveman and Wolfe (1995).
[36]Rosenthal and Jacobson (1968).
[37]Jencks (1972), Oakes (1985).

that this practice constitutes a reaction to large class size: Heterogeneous groups of 25 (or more) are much harder to teach than 15 or so. Tracking makes teaching large groups easier. Class size is a function of funding, of course, much of which is dictated by middle-class voters (see Chapter 6). In this context, then, the schools provide some children with a vehicle for upward mobility. For many, however, they lock people in place.

**4.** *Encouragement by significant others affects aspirations and educational and occupational attainment.* The term **significant other** was coined by the psychiatrist Harry Stack Sullivan, who used it to refer to people who are emotionally important to individuals and, hence, especially influential on them.[38] Sullivan emphasized that the impact is strongest when individuals are young. Thus, parents, teachers, and peers constitute significant others who affect children's aspirations and their ultimate educational and occupational attainment. This influence occurs in combination with the effect of academic performance and other previously mentioned variables. Thus, children develop aspirations according to the evaluations they receive from others and their own self-assessment based on their academic performance, familial obligations, and the like. Further, children's peers are also significant others who influence the development of aspirations and educational and occupational attainment.

**5.** *Educational and occupational aspirations influence educational and occupational attainment.* **Educational aspirations** refer to children's plans and expectations about their ultimate level of schooling, such as going to college. **Occupational aspirations** refer to the kind of jobs children expect or would like when they become adults. Aspirations are the filter through which significant others influence children. Thus, parents who have college degrees provide role models and encouragement for their children to attend college. In addition, when people's friends comprise children of parents with college degrees, a collective expectation about college attendance develops. The result is higher educational attainment. In contrast, children raised in different contexts often develop lower aspirations, which result in lower educational attainment.

**6.** *Educational attainment strongly influences occupational attainment.* College attendance is crucial to getting many white-collar jobs. The best predictor of college attendance remains family background, with all the other variables shown in Figure 5.1 serving as filters for this factor. It has been known for a long time that middle-class children are much more likely to attend college than working-class or poor children, even if the latter have high ability.[39] What happens, of course, is that parents at the top of the class structure are more likely to encourage higher education and more capable of making it happen. This is so even if their children do not have as much ability as others, at least when measured by standardized tests. At the same time, however, a smaller but significant proportion of working-class parents whose children display high ability also get their children into college. Interestingly, class of family of origin does not predict either performance once a person enters college or graduating from college. And graduating is important. Those with a college degree have a significant occupational advantage over those without one. This

---

[38]Sullivan (1940), Sewell and Shah (1968a; 1968b).
[39]Coleman (1966), McPherson and Schapiro (1998).

means that in the race for prestige (and income), it is not attendance but the credential that counts. In this regard, the dual impact of education becomes clear once again. On the one hand, an educational credential constitutes a vehicle for preserving class boundaries. Middle-class parents ensure that their children reap the rewards of prestige and income associated with white-collar jobs. On the other hand, a significant minority of working-class children get into and complete college, and their achievement translates into white-collar prestige and income. To repeat: The status attainment process constitutes an interrelated chain of ascribed and achieved factors. This is also true for African Americans (and probably other minority groups) and women.

The status attainment process shown in Figure 5.1 describes African Americans' experiences as well as Whites'.[40] Yet this fact masks significant change that has occurred. During the 1960s, African Americans were less able than Whites to pass on whatever status advantages they achieved. Over time, however, more intergenerational continuity is occurring among African Americans, and racial differences in educational and occupational attainment have declined.[41] Nonetheless, it remains true that, on average, African Americans and Whites begin at different status levels and end up at different status levels. This is, of course, also true for other minority groups. Put bluntly, while everyone benefits from increased schooling, white males still benefit more. This variation reflects discrimination. Alas, models of the status attainment process, such as Figure 5.1, do not include this factor as a variable. So they do not get at a key issue.

The situation is similar with regard to gender differences.[42] The status attainment process is similar for women and men, but significant variations exist: Mothers' characteristics affect daughters' status attainment more than fathers' do. Women's first job tends to be higher in prestige then men's, but men's main job increases their prestige more. This difference occurs because women get locked into jobs (as clerks, for example) without a promotion ladder. Ultimately, however, while the status attainment model shown in Figure 5.1 describes both women's and men's experiences, it reveals little about the impact of discrimination.

### Status Attainment in Cross-National Perspective

The process of status attainment appears to be similar in all economically developed Western nations, although the models include fewer variables than shown in Figure 5.1:

> *1. Family background exerts a weak but significant and direct impact on one's occupation.*

> *2. A child's education exerts a strong and direct impact on one's occupation.*[43]

But while the pattern is similar across Western societies, significant variation exists. For example, one study compared the United States, West Germany, Great Britain, the

---

[40]Blau and Duncan (1967), Winship (1992).
[41]Jaynes and Williams (1989).
[42]England (1992).
[43]Treiman and Ganzeboom (1990), Krymkowski (1991).

Netherlands, and Sweden. Researchers found that the relationship between father's occupation and son's job is much lower in Sweden compared to the United States and other nations, while that between son's education and his job is much higher.[44] This finding suggests that ascription is less important than achievement in Swedish society. The Netherlands, by contrast, displayed the highest relationship between father's and son's jobs, and the lowest relationship between son's education and job. This finding suggests that ascription has a greater impact in the Netherlands, compared to the United States and other nations.

The process of status attainment illustrates how ascription and achievement combine in modern societies to affect where people end up in the class structure. Children participate in their family's social network, developing contacts and connections as a result; they enjoy their family's economic benefits; and in the family they develop skills, knowledge, and other abilities. So the class of a person's family of origin indicates the opportunities with which they begin seeking a place in society. At the same time, what individuals accomplish makes a difference.

## The Individual and Status Attainment

Recall for a moment the Class Structure Hypothesis presented in Chapter 1:

> *The lower the social class, the fewer choices people have and the less effective they are in solving personal problems.*

The number of choices people have and their effectiveness is important because status attainment begins from a specific class context, one in which some people (and families) have fewer advantages than others.

This fact was shown earlier by Figure 5.1. The arrows in the figure represent quantitative measures of the status attainment process. In this section, I want to humanize the relationships shown in the figure by sketching a vignette about two fictional families: the Smith's, a working-class family on the edge of poverty, and the Jones, a middle-class family. Be warned: The differences between the two families are portrayed in ways that emphasize the disadvantages of growing up near poverty and the advantages of growing up middle class. Hence, this sketch does not do justice to the full range of familial experiences children in different classes have. There is some danger of caricature, of assuming that the family background of poor and working-class children is always inferior to that of middle-class children. Nothing could be further from the truth. Nonetheless, the types of events depicted here are class related: poor and working-class families are more likely to display characteristics like the Smiths while middle-class families are more likely to resemble the Jones. This difference is reflected in the socialization process and, as a result, in status attainment. As a last point, problems of prejudice and discrimination are not considered here, either by race/ethnicity or gender, as they have been dealt with in previous chapters.

---

[44]Treiman and Yip (1989).

## A Vignette

Jane and Edward Smith are married and live in Cedar Key, Florida, a town on the Gulf Coast of about 1,000 people. Jane's mother and father both have high school degrees. Her mother works as a waitress and her father earns an uncertain living fishing in the Gulf. Edward's mother graduated from high school and works as a retail clerk. Although his father did not finish high school, he works steadily as a self-employed electrician.

They married when they were both 17 years of age. Jane was pregnant at the time with her first child, who was named Mary. At age 19, they had a second child, Emma, and at 20 a third, Sam. Initially, they tried to establish their own household, but they moved back into Jane's parents' home on two occasions. Living conditions were crowded, which added stress.[45] For several years, they had spells of unemployment and part-time employment. They were poor for several years and received public assistance twice, totaling about a year and a half. They are now 30 and work full-time in, respectively, a textile mill and food-processing plant. Jane operates a machine and earns about $18,000 yearly. Edward is a nonunion electrician, earning about $25,000 yearly. Today, their total income of $43,000 places them well above the poverty line (to be discussed in Chapter 10).

This income level is relatively recent. The financial hardships the Smith's experienced early in their marriage mean that the children lived in an environment of economic want without satisfaction. In this context, they learned that their parents could not control what happens to the family: how much there is to eat, what kind of house they live in, and other fundamental aspects of life. Although Jane and Edward stayed together and eventually achieved a stable living standard, their lifestyle remains precarious. Children internalize this knowledge, it becomes part of their interior vision of the world and their place within it, and it affects their behavior throughout life. They may learn, for example, to live for the moment, since waiting for future rewards is likely to bring disappointment. What such orientations mean in terms of the socialization process is that children learn to believe they are vulnerable and not in control of what happens to them. This lesson affects future behavior in school, making it more difficult to succeed occupationally later.

In addition to the financial limitations, the Smiths married and started a family while still young themselves. Hence, the children were raised by parents who were still, in years and experience, children themselves. Because Jane and Edward passed from girl and boy to wife and husband to mother and father so swiftly, they had less time to integrate and assimilate the psychological orientations and behaviors necessary for their new roles. So, at least initially, they lacked both marriage and parenting skills. As before, this fact means that their children's early years were spent in an environment in which want without satisfaction was everywhere, only in this case the thing wanted was psychological security. To be raised by people who are unsure of their own adulthood can mean that children are responded to in very inconsistent ways. In this case, Edward and Jane have always been loving parents. There were, nonetheless, periods of neglect in which their own needs (they were young adults, remember, 18 to 22 years of age) took precedence over their children's needs. Moreover, they struggled economically and lived in a crowded environment. Inevitably, they fought sometimes. So there were some occasions when Edward and Jane took out their frustrations on the children: They hit them. The

---

[45]Beeghley and Donnelly (1989).

long-term effects of such lack of predictability are straightforward: Children become angry and frustrated and, as a result, display inconsistent and inappropriate behavior. For example, they may be aggressive in the wrong way or passive at the wrong time. Such characteristics have important negative implications for success in school and for occupational attainment later.

Finally, the Smith children grew up with some other limitations. Neither Jane nor Edward was read to when they were little and, hence, did not recognize the importance of reading to their own children. Moreover, other forms of stimuli were unavailable either because of the cost or the Smiths' rural location: piano lessons, trips to museums, computer camps, and the like. Such experiences help prepare children for school and expose them to the dominant culture. These activities are important when the children enter school and throughout the school years. Teachers identify which children are going to have difficulty in the first grades. Those who have not learned certain skills—naming colors, counting, the alphabet, among others—enter the school at a disadvantage. The Smiths' oldest child, Mary, is a good example. Mary was enrolled in Cedar Key Elementary School at age five and was a low achiever from the beginning. Jane Smith had meetings at the school and tried to respond to the teachers' suggestions, but she was not forceful in dealing with educators. By the beginning of third grade, Mary was placed in a special education class even though she tested at normal intelligence. Mary is now in middle school, reading at an elementary school level. Last summer, as every summer, Mary and her siblings stayed with their grandmother and spent much of the day watching television. One suspects that her educational and occupational future is dim.

Yet children have different experiences. Recall that schools have a dual impact, facilitating high achievement that is independent of family background for some. The Smiths' minister, as luck would have it, was an undergraduate music major and saw that Emma (the middle child) had unusual musical ability for a little girl. He encouraged the child, even buying her a violin. With the Smiths' support, he taught Emma for several years, and she did well. He also paid for her to attend a music camp each summer. As a result of this attention, teachers have now taken an interest in her, both academically and musically. Although prediction is difficult, Emma's long-term educational future seems brighter, as does her occupational future.

In the jargon sociologists use, the Smiths lack financial capital (money), human capital (employment-related skills), and social capital (friendship and family networks, and knowledge of the larger culture) that lead to occupational success.[46] But neither the terminology nor the arrows in Figure 5.1 get at the many practical problems they faced. The vignette suggests these problems. It also suggests their underlying courage. Against the odds, they have grown up, stayed together, worked hard, and raised their children in as stable an environment as possible. (As an aside, you may have noted that I did not mention the Smiths' youngest child, Sam. If you want to know what happens to him, look ahead to Chapter 10. The Smiths' lives take a turn for the worse because Edward loses his job when the company moves the fish plant to Mexico where labor is cheaper.)

Harriet and Peter Jones live in Evanston, Illinois, an upper-middle-class suburb of Chicago. Harriet's parents both have advanced degrees. Her father is an engineer and her

---

[46]Granovetter (1995), Portes (1998).

mother a computer programmer. Peter's parents also have advanced degrees. His father is an accountant and his mother an elementary school teacher. Thus, as with the Smiths, both Harriet and Peter come from similar class backgrounds. Unlike the Smiths, however, Harriet and Peter remained in school and started their careers before thinking about marriage. The met at age 26 and married at 28. Their child, Everett, was born two years later. Harriet works as a reporter, and Peter is a college professor. Their combined income is over $100,000 per year. Not only is their income relatively high, but also Harriet's parents gave them the money for the down payment on their house in an exclusive area with good schools.

Being raised in a relatively affluent environment, produces many advantages. It has never occurred to Everett to wonder about whether there will be enough food to eat. Moreover, their home is large and, hence, it has been easier to separate when people became frustrated with one another. So compared to the Smiths' children, Everett experienced a more stable and predictable lifestyle from a very young age. He learned that life is not precarious and that delaying immediate gratification will often bring greater rewards in the future. Thus, his interior vision of himself included a sense of personal efficacy (the ability to solve problems and overcome obstacles) and a belief that he has some control over what happens to him. Such experiences fundamentally affect behavior in school, making it easier to succeed subsequently as an adult.

In addition, the Jones child was "affluent" in a second way as well. Harriet and Edward were mature when Everett was born. Secure in their adulthood, they responded to him as consistently as possible and tried to create a family environment in which he could thrive. One result is a high level of verbal and interpersonal skill. Such characteristics produce more success in school and increase the level of achievement as an adult.

Finally, Harriet and Peter were able to provide Everett with many experiences—preschool, lessons, camps, computers at home, and the like—that increased his cognitive skills. So Everett entered school knowing his colors, able to count, and capable of using the computer to find sites his parents did not want him to see. Nonetheless, it became apparent in the first grade that Everett was a low achiever. Harriet and Peter attacked the situation directly: They consulted with the teacher and principal, volunteered to work in the classroom, had Everett tested, worked with him daily at home, had him tutored over the summer, and requested (and got) a more structured second grade teacher. Everett was working at grade level by the end of second grade. He is now in middle school, performing well, and is a good athlete. Last summer he attended a baseball camp, a basketball camp, a music camp, and computer camp. One suspects his eventual educational and occupational prospects are bright.

To use jargon again, Harriet and Peter Jones have financial, human, and social capital. Some of these advantages came from their parents. The house down payment is a tangible example; less tangible, but no less real, were the development of aspirations that led them to attend college and delay marriage. Other advantages reflect their own hard work. The long-term result is the probability of relatively high educational and occupational achievement for their child.

A caveat: As indicated earlier, I intend these examples to portray how the status attainment process occurs and the relative advantages middle-class people enjoy. You should understand, however, that some middle-class people have children but dodge parenting; they are unable to put their children's needs before their own. Some are absent due to their occupational ambitions. Some abuse their children. Some use their children as weapons during divorce. At the same time, many working-class and poor families are stable and nurturing. So you should take the Smith and Jones examples as illustrative of the impact of social class on status attainment, not definitive.

### Socialization and Status Attainment

*Socialization,* you should recall, is the lifelong process of learning norms and values, internalizing motivations and (unconscious) needs, developing intellectual and social skills, and enacting roles. Although this process continues throughout life, its importance is greatest when one is young. As summarized in Chapter 1, childhood interaction, primary group interaction, interaction with significant others, and long-term interaction are usually very influential on individuals. In the language of status attainment research, which is one way of restating socialization theory: Parent's occupation and income affect children's abilities, school performance, teachers' encouragement, aspirations, education, and occupation. Of course, children have increasing say in this process as they get older. The vignette comparing the Smith and Jones families is designed to suggest some aspects of this process, as revealed by research. A key finding is that *the higher the family income (especially in early childhood), the greater the achievement of children.*[47] The reason for this relationship is that family income affects the quality of the home environment: the nature of parent-child interaction, opportunities for learning, and the physical condition of the home, among other factors.

Think about the differences in parent-child interaction portrayed in the vignette. The Smiths are good people who struggled mightily, indeed heroically, to establish a stable family life—and they succeeded. Nonetheless, much of their interaction, between themselves and with their children, was harsher than what occurred within the Jones family. The finding is this: *The lower the family income, then the greater the economic pressures and the greater the stress between parents—which leads to harsher parent-child interaction.*[48] It follows that *the harsher the parent-child interaction, the lower children's self-confidence and the lower their achievement.* These findings are why I speculated that Mary Smith's future looks bleaker than that of Everett Jones. But such results are not inevitable. Recall that significant others besides parents affect status attainment. This is why I had a minister recognize Emma Smith's musical talent, altering the odds of her finishing high school and, perhaps, attending college. The future is not given; it is impossible to know what will happen to Mary, Emma, or Everett. There is no question, however, that the quality of the home environment—in this case parent-child interaction (along with that of others who are emotionally significant)—affects their future.

Opportunities for learning, defined broadly to include all aspects of one's life, not just schooling, also affect people's future. Consider, as just one example, the different way Mary and Emma Smith spend their summer compared to Everett Jones. Formal schooling is vital. The status attainment literature shows that *the higher the parents'*

---

[47]Mayer (1997), Duncan et al. (1998), Mayer and Peterson (1999), Lin (1999).
[48]Conger et al. (1997).

*social class, the higher the children's educational attainment.* And, of course, *the higher the educational attainment, the higher the occupational attainment.*

One reason for these findings is that middle-class people dominate the public schools. They are most capable of attending a school board meeting, a parents' night, a teacher conference, or a disciplinary meeting with the principal. People whose work makes them less physically tired at the end of the day, who possess private transportation, who have access to child care, and who enjoy paid leave time built into their jobs will attend such meetings at higher rates. As a result, their children's educational needs are better served: Teachers take a more personal interest, are more tolerant, and are quicker to spot (and resolve) potential problems. The different experiences of Mary Smith and Everett Jones were based on research that explores the way in which and the effectiveness with which middle- and working-class parents interact with teachers.[49] A hypothesis follows:

> *The less knowledge and self-confidence parents have, the less likely they are to see themselves as the status equal of teachers.*

If the hypothesis is correct, working-class parents who see themselves as unequal to teachers are likely to be less forceful and less effective than middle-class parents. This is why the vignette portrayed different outcomes for Mary and Everett, with long-term consequences. Social class of one's family of origin matters: The domination of the public schools by middle-class people means that their children have a better chance to succeed.

Another reason for these findings is that the educational resources available to children vary by class. For example, it has been estimated that youngsters whose parents are in the top fifth of the income distribution benefit from twice the educational resources, in simple dollar terms, as do children whose parents are in the bottom fifth.[50] Such variation means that poor and working-class children have fewer opportunities to learn than do middle- and upper-class children. For example, it is my impression that the availability of computers in the classroom is directly related to the socioeconomic status of the students served. In addition, exposure to computers outside the school—at computer camps, at private after-school workshops, or at home—is undoubtedly class related. As you will see in Chapters 9 and 10, the budgets of poor and working-class families make the purchase of home computers more difficult. Yet computer literacy will be an essential skill in the next few years. This example could be extended to class size, laboratory equipment, library materials, and the like. Again, these differences in educational resources mean that middle-class and rich children have a better chance to succeed.

A final reason for the findings cited above is that school success does not depend solely on ability; it also reflects preparation for school along with such personality traits as self-discipline, being able to take direction, intellectual (as opposed to emotional) behavior orientations, and hard work independent of intrinsic task orientation. Fewer poor and working-class children are likely to have these characteristics (especially when they are the children of young parents), and there is considerable evidence that the educational system does little to build such traits.[51] Rather, those students who lack self-discipline,

---

[49]Lareau (1989).
[50]Jencks et al. (1972).
[51]Bowles and Gintis (1976), National Center for Educational Statistics (2000).

who are less able to follow direction, who too often react emotionally, and who are unable to work without immediate rewards, are frequently stigmatized. Such students are often behind academically when they arrive in kindergarten or first grade, have negatively charged personality traits, and end up staying behind academically—regardless of their abilities. More generally, as noted earlier, students from all classes are usually placed in ability groups—tracked—with others like themselves.[52] Such tracks are correlated with social class. So children and their peers belonging to the same track function as role models for one another and reward each other's behavior, whether it is appropriate or not. This is fine for middle-class youngsters, less fine for people from other backgrounds, for it means there exist built-in differences in the chance to succeed. These experiences constitute an essential aspect of the socialization process.

As a final comment, many individual teachers try hard to help children who appear less able or less well adjusted. They usually fail over the long run. Yet the impact of the minister (it could have been a teacher) on Emma's life suggests that we ought to notice that some succeed. What these facts mean is that poor and working-class children more often enter school behind others and when this occurs they usually do not catch up. This failure means, in turn, that the educational system reproduces the stratification structure.

This description of the social psychological basis for status attainment provides a rather different view of the structure of stratification than that held by many researchers.[53] They emphasize, rightly, the high rate of mobility, and show how education and other achievement variables contribute to that process. I emphasize, rightly, the stability of the class structure, and show how family background and education facilitate that process. Both of us are correct. Can you and I become billionaires? We are more likely to win one of those state-run lotteries.

## *Summary*

The study of mobility focuses on changes in people's occupation, either intra- or intergenerationally. The study of status attainment focuses on how individuals enter specific occupations. Together, they indicate the relative emphasis on ascription and achievement in a society. The occupational structure has changed over time (Table 5.1) as people moved off the farm and into working- and middle-class jobs.

The major findings in the study of mobility are as follows (Table 5.2): (1) Inter- and intragenerational stability occurs most often, (2) mobility is widespread, and (3) most movement is short distance. The combination of stability and mobility has characterized the United States since the seventeenth century. Women and men show similar patterns of mobility. Historically, mobility for African Americans, Hispanic Americans, and other minority groups has differed significantly from that of Whites, with less occupational inheritance. Since the 1960s, however, racial and ethnic differences have been declining.

Although economic development produces higher rates of mobility, considerable variation exists across modern societies. Rates in the United States are not uniquely high or low compared to those in other nations.

[52]Oakes (1985), Lucas (2001).
[53]For example, Blau and Duncan (1967).

The class structure is stable across generations because people in each class pass their resources (wealth, education, interpersonal contacts) on to their children. When U.S. society is examined historically, the most important factors affecting mobility rates are structural: economic development, class differences in fertility rates, immigration, and affirmative action for white males. Thus, the rewards of hard work go mainly to those who start out with some advantages. The literature on mobility focuses on occupations and does not recognize the significance of a capital-owning class whose members' prestige and power in the society are not dependent on their jobs.

The status attainment process reflects an interrelated chain of ascribed and achieved variables, as shown in Figure 5.1: family background, ability, academic performance, encouragement, aspirations, and educational attainment lead to occupation. Subsequent work shows that the basic status attainment model also describes the experiences of African Americans and women, with the caveat that it does not take the impact of discrimination into account. The status attainment process in other Western industrial nations resembles that in the United States. Underlying the status attainment process is socialization, which varies by social class. Because children from different classes often (not always) have different experiences at home and at school, their status attainment varies accordingly.

# 6

# Political Participation and Power

In a democracy, citizens elect their representatives and thereby hold those who exercise power accountable for their decisions. Democratic societies have other attributes as well. For example, they are capitalist.[1] Democracy and capitalism fit together, in part, because in both goals are achieved via competition under the rule of law, which is another distinctive quality of democratic societies. The law not only regulates conflict, channeling it in nonviolent directions, but also reflects still another characteristic: a respect for individual dignity and ambition. In addition, democratic societies also emphasize the use of science to solve problems. Finally, democratic societies are buttressed by a set of unique cultural values, called the culture of capitalism. As described in Chapter 1, these structural at-

---

[1]Moore (1966), Berger (1986). Recall from Chapter 1 how all these factors are interconnected.

tributes have what Max Weber called an "elective affinity" for one another; in some form, they are typical of modern nations.

In this context, the democratic political process should display, at least ideally, two features.[2] First, competitors would act within the rules (the law) to influence public policy. When correct procedures are followed—as when citizens vote, representatives decide, and judges interpret—decisions about societal goals and priorities among them are accepted as legitimate by the people, even those whose interests are harmed because they lose money, privileges, or other resources—thus affecting their life chances. Second, access to the political arena would be open so that any person or group can compete for power. When everyone can vote, support candidates and causes, and lobby representatives, then decision makers are held accountable. Political scientists often use the term **pluralism** to describe this state of affairs.

The democratic political process, then, provides a nonviolent, competitive mechanism for dividing up shares in the available goods and services: jobs, income, wealth, and other resources that affect people's life chances. Of course, not every decision a modern society faces affects the stratification structure; some are moral or aesthetic. The three systems of ranking outlined in Chapter 1 constitute axes of conflict over the distribution of resources. Although race/ethnicity and gender remain salient (as shown in Chapters 2 and 3), the dimensions of inequality in modern societies are increasingly shaped by class conflict.[3] And make no mistake: There are always winners and losers. Even so, democracies are stable because the outcomes of political decisions are perceived by the people (especially the losers) as fair and just. The key to such stability, however, is widespread **political participation,** which refers to people's attempt at influencing who gets elected or the appointments, policies, and laws passed by government at all levels—federal, state, and local.

In fact, however, no democratic society displays the two characteristics described above in pure form, mainly because political participation is not equal in any society.[4] Nor is political power. Those classes with the most resources inevitably want to limit the ability of other classes to increase their share. Inequality results. As stated in the *Political Power Hypothesis* in Chapter 1:

> *The higher the social class, the greater the influence over the distribution of resources in the society.*

In this chapter, I suggest that decision makers in the United States are held accountable mainly by two constituencies: the middle class via votes and the rich via campaign contributions. It follows that the structure of stratification in the United States reflects their interests.

[2]Dahl (1967).

[3]Some would disagree with this assertion. See Kingston (2000), Grusky and Weeden (2001).

[4]This portrayal of a democratic society is an "ideal type," to use a phrase of Max Weber's (1920:6). The strategy consists of setting up an example that is logically perfect and then assessing empirically (by observation) how actual occurrences differ from the "pure" construct. See Turner, Beeghley, and Powers (2002).

# Types of Political Participation

## Voting

Democracy is usually taken to mean rule by the people, either directly or through their elected representatives, who compete with one another for the opportunity to make decisions. Elections function simultaneously as a method for citizens to express their desires and to hold decision makers accountable. If a democratic political system is to resemble the pluralist ideal, however, electoral procedures ought to maximize participation so that decision makers depend on voter constituents (defined as the voting-age population). One way to achieve this goal is to make voting as easy as possible. The United States, however, makes voting difficult because, unlike other nations, it requires individuals to register first. Once registered, people can vote on Election Day, but satisfying this two-step requirement is more difficult for poor and working-class people, who vote at a much lower rate.

Although elections provide an important mechanism for holding decision makers accountable, they do not end the political process; they begin it. After all, people pursue their interests (they exercise power) as public issues are defined, policies considered, and laws implemented. In a democratic society, will decision makers listen to their constituents who vote or to someone else?

## Partisanship

The "someone else" refers to **partisans,** people who identify with, work for, and try to influence a party, candidate, or issue. Average middle- and working-class citizens sometimes become partisans. During elections, they may wear a button, put a sign on their car, do volunteer work, or contribute small amounts of money. Between elections, the main form of partisanship consists of **lobbying,** the attempt at influencing legislators or other decision makers in favor of (or against) a specific decision. Again, average citizens sometimes lobby. They might, for example, telephone a member of the school board or write a note to their congressional representative. These contacts are taken very seriously by decision makers; they know that people who contact them in this way are especially likely to have voted and to vote again. Also, those who contact officeholders can then be solicited for campaign contributions at the next election.

The most influential partisans, however, are those constituents with large amounts of cash to spend. This is a key point: Contributions provide the lubricant for successful lobbying, which is mostly done by very wealthy people and hired professionals. They are effective precisely to the extent they can funnel cash to candidates, either directly to their campaign funds or indirectly via a political party. Candidates, both liberal and conservative, Republican and Democrat, rely on cash constituents to get elected. Thus, understanding the twin issues of accountability and power in a democracy requires recognizing the role of money in elections.

Both voting and partisanship involve "working within the system" or, perhaps, "working the system." No matter which interpretation you prefer, participation in these ways means that people follow the rules. They win and lose, and go on to fight other battles—without disruption, without violence. Yet a tension exists between these types of participation: voting versus money. Everyone can vote—if they are registered. Only a few can contribute money to campaigns. Once again, the question in a democracy is this: To what degree are decision makers accountable to voter constituents or cash constituents? Some people are left out.

### Unruliness

Without the ability to participate effectively (which is to say that participation makes a difference in people's lives), democracy is a sham. Those left out sometimes become unruly. This tactic, the only power the weak have, is not necessary for those who participate in the system. When participants become dissatisfied, they elect a new mayor, senator, or president to represent their interests, either by voting, campaign contributions, or both. Those who do not participate do neither. They often feel powerless—the jargon term is **alienated**—and this feeling is realistic. When those left out become angry, as periodically happens, they sometimes take to the streets, acting out in violent and destructive ways. During the 1960s, poor people and racial and ethnic minorities took to the streets repeatedly. Similar events have occurred in the last decade or so in Los Angeles, Miami, and other cities.[5] The obvious interpretation is to see such episodes as riots. From this point of view, the perpetrators are criminals, who should be prosecuted for vandalism, mugging, and even murder. Although this interpretation is correct, a nonobvious explanation also exists: One can see anger in the streets as rebellions on the part of oppressed and disenfranchised people. They are political acts by individuals for whom few options exist. From this rather different angle of vision, violence and other forms of unruliness are not merely protests; they constitute political claims to be considered.[6] But collective violence only occurs under conditions of extreme frustration; it is a form of political participation, a signal to those with power from those left out of the system. Unruliness, then, constitutes the political underbelly of a democratic system. It is ignored with peril.

## The Rate of Voting

Voting is the primal democratic act; it is the first and most important indicator of a democratic society. All other modes of participation are adjuncts to this act. After all, while cash constituents may contribute money to candidates, gain access to the winners, and lobby for the creation of laws beneficial to themselves (and against laws that would harm them), even if they are successful, elected representatives must ultimately appeal to ordinary citizens. Voters, then, can hold decision makers accountable—at least in principle—against the interests of those with money. Alas, many Americans do not vote.

---

[5]Gamson (1975), Piven and Cloward (1977), Special Advisor to the Board of Police Commissioners on the Civil Disorders in Los Angeles (1994).
[6]Coser (1967:84).

### *Voting in the United States*

Historically, the number and characteristics of citizens eligible to vote has steadily expanded in all democratic nations.[7] As explained in Chapters 2 and 3, voting in this country was restricted to white male property owners over age 21 when the *Constitution* was adopted. Over the years, however, all adults have gained the ability to participate, regardless of property ownership, immigrant status, race, or gender. In the United States, as in other nations, this process occurred mainly because those left out of the democratic process fought to be included.[8] There is a lesson here: The extension of the franchise resulted from unruly (and often illegal) activities—riots, demonstrations, and other forms of rebellion—by those excluded from a presumably democratic system. Such persons and groups had no other option. Historically, then, the U.S. political system has responded to the unruliness of those left out by including them. The outcome has been, at least in principle, a more democratic society.

That principle is not fully realized today. Although every person over age 18 is eligible to vote, relatively few do. This fact is revealed by Figure 6.1, which displays the rate of voting in presidential elections from 1876 to 2000. In the 2000 presidential election, only 51 percent of the adult population voted. The figure shows that electoral turnout has not always been this low. In fact, among those eligible, there was a time when most people voted; almost 80 percent of all eligible citizens took part in presidential elections during the last quarter of the nineteenth century. Moreover, in the non-Southern and most densely populated states, turnouts during the years 1876 to 1896 were much higher than the rates displayed in the figure. For example, average turnouts in presidential elections were 93 percent in Indiana, 92 percent in New Jersey and Ohio, 89 percent in New York, and 83 percent in Pennsylvania.[9] In nonpresidential election years during this period, these same states had average turnouts of 84 percent in Indiana, 77 percent in New Jersey and Ohio, 68 percent in New York, and 71 percent in Pennsylvania. It thus appears that nearly all eligible citizens—rich and poor alike—voted in those states where most of the population lived.

This, then, is the first important lesson: The current low rate of voting is not inevitable. Even so, you might remember that during the late nineteenth century, women and young adults could not vote by law. Moreover, although African Americans gained the franchise for a brief time after the Civil War, it was taken from them after 1876 by Whites' imposition of Jim Crow laws.[10] So the argument that low rates of voting can be avoided should be interpreted with caution for now.

In addition, some have argued that turnout data during this period may be artificially high because of vote fraud.[11] Most scholars conclude, however, that the data are reasonably accurate, at least with regard to the total rate of participation.[12] The problem of fraud

---

[7]Acemoglu and Robinson (2000).
[8]Gamson (1975), Williams (1977), Keyssar (2000), Acemoglu and Robinson (2000), Rusk (2001).
[9]Burnham (1980).
[10]Woodward (1966).
[11]Converse (1972).
[12]Burnham (1980).

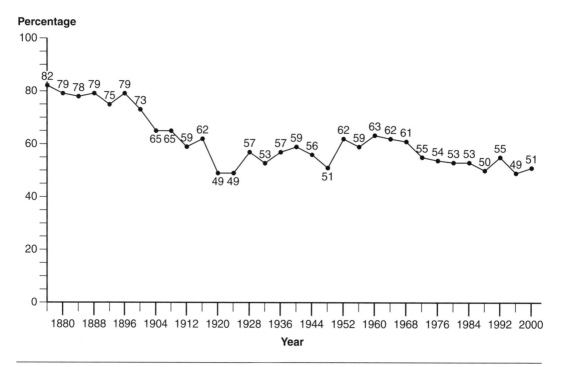

**Percentage**

**FIGURE 6.1** *Rate of Voting in U.S. Presidential Elections, 1876–2000*
*Source:* U.S. Bureau of the Census (1975:1071; 2001:252–53), Federal Election Commission (2001).

during elections of this period is separate from the issue of electoral turnout. All observers agree that most elections were controversial and competitive—usually decided by small margins. So high rates of participation make sense. Moreover, as will be shown in a few moments, the levels of voter turnout reported in Figure 6.1 for the late nineteenth century United States resemble the proportion of middle-class and rich people who vote today, the proportion of registered citizens who now vote, and European turnout rates. These similarities suggest that reported levels of participation in the last quarter of the nineteenth century are plausible.

Most fraud during this period involved vote buying, voter intimidation, miscounting of votes, and the manipulation of small numbers of ballots in highly competitive elections.[13] Thus, the nature of the ballot is extremely important. Before 1890, each party printed and distributed its own ballots, called "party strips" or "tickets," which listed all its candidates. These ballots were of varying size and color, which made it difficult to conceal one's preference as the ballot was dropped into the box. Voting during this period was raucous and public. Citizens selected one ticket, sometimes for a price, and turned it in—in full view of everyone gathered around the polling place. Adoption of the Australian ballot at the turn of the century changed this situation.[14] This type of ballot identifies

[13]Argersinger (1986), Allen and Allen (1981).
[14]Rusk (1970; 2001).

all the nominees for office on one piece of paper and asks voters to mark their choices. It not only reduces the possibility of fraud but also makes it easier for people to vote a "split ticket." That is, they can select candidates for various offices from either party.

Figure 6.1 shows that electoral turnout began dropping with the presidential election of 1900. As I will explain later, laws requiring registration were introduced in every state during this period. Participation rates fell steadily through the election of 1924. Part of this decline occurred because women obtained the franchise for the first time in 1920, which depressed rates for two elections. But as they developed a sense of political effectiveness and began voting in greater numbers, turnout rates rose somewhat, averaging about 56 percent during the elections from 1932 to 1948. With this exception, however, the decline in turnout was concentrated among the working class and poor.[15] Turnout rose again for the next five elections, averaging 61 percent from 1952 to 1968. But voter turnout has not been above 60 percent since that time, averaging about 52 percent in the presidential elections of 1972 to 2000. As shown below, those who do not vote are still mainly working class and poor.

Since just over half of all adults in the United States now vote, the necessary majority to choose the president and other public officials elected at the same time is about one-quarter of the voting age population (half of 50 percent). Electoral turnout during off-year congressional elections is even less; for example, only 39 percent of the population voted in House of Representative races in 2002.[16] Although part of the reason for low turnouts in off-years is the large number of relatively uncontested House seats, the more important reason (as I will show later) has to do with registration laws and other structural factors. These low voting rates in off-year elections mean that many decision makers—senators, representatives, governors, and state legislators—are selected by only 20 percent (or less) of all eligible citizens (half of 39 percent). Turnout in local elections that occur separately from off-year congressional elections is lower still. In my community, as in many others, voting rates of 25 percent are common in local elections, which mean that local officials (city and county commissioners, school board members) can be selected by only 13 percent of residents (half of 25 percent).[17] Low voting rates mean that a relatively small proportion of the population, mainly the middle class, chooses elected public officials. They, in turn, orient their decisions to the interests of those who voted. Such low turnouts, as I will suggest later (in Figure 6.2), have become self-perpetuating: Nonvoters are not contacted or mobilized and do not develop a sense of political effectiveness; so they do not vote. This pattern suggests that the United States has departed rather far from the democratic ideal.

Because this country makes voting contingent on registration, it is important to examine the relationship between them. Table 6.1 displays the proportion of all adults who reported they registered and voted by income, an important measure of inequality. Please look down columns (2) and (3). Note that as family income increases, the percent reporting that they registered and voted increases as well. Now look down column (4). While the percentage of those registered who reported voting rises with income, the rate of in-

---

[15]Arneson (1925), Gosnell (1927), as cited in Lijphart (1997).
[16]Lester (2002).
[17]Teixeira (1992:7), Ansolabehere and Iyengar (1995:145–46).

TABLE 6.1    *Self-Reported Participation in the 2000 U.S. Presidential Election by Family Income*

| (1)<br><br><br>*Family Income* | (2)<br><br>*Percent<br>Registered* | (3)<br><br>*Percent<br>Voted* | (4)<br>*Percent<br>Registered<br>Who Voted* |
|---|---|---|---|
| **All Incomes** | **70%** | **60%** | **86%** |
| < $9,999 | 56% | 38% | 68% |
| $10,000–14,999 | 59% | 44% | 75% |
| $15,000–24,999 | 65% | 51% | 79% |
| $25,000–34,999 | 69% | 58% | 84% |
| $35,000–49,999 | 72% | 62% | 86% |
| $50,000–74,999 | 78% | 69% | 88% |
| > $75,000 | 82% | 75% | 91% |
| **Percent Difference<br>Lowest to Highest** | **26%** | **37%** | **23%** |

*Source:* U.S. Bureau of the Census (2002b:7).

crease is not nearly so great as in the other columns. Finally, observe in column (4) that most of those who are registered actually vote, and this is so at all income levels. This fact has been true for many years: In the last nine presidential elections, the proportion of those registered who voted has ranged from 83 to 91 percent.[18]

These data lead to the second lesson you should remember: The turnout rate among those registered resembles that which existed in the nineteenth century. About 80 percent of the people vote once they are registered, and this is so among the poor and working class as well as the middle class. Thus, the low turnout among working-class and poor persons cannot be explained away as due to lack of motivation. Some observers try; they argue that those who do not vote must be satisfied with public policy.[19] This argument, a sort of "don't worry, be happy" orientation, implies that poor and working-class people must be the most satisfied of all citizens, since they vote at the lowest rates. This interpretation not only is absurd, but also masks a hidden reality: The middle class and rich dominate the political process in the United States and receive most of the benefits.[20]

## Voting in Cross-National Perspective

The pattern of electoral participation is greater in other Western nations, which come closer to the democratic ideal than does the United States. In Western Europe as a whole,

---

[18]U.S. Bureau of the Census (2002b:4).

[19]Conway reviews this argument (2000).

[20]The variation in turnout reported in Figure 6.1 and Table 6.1 occurs because self-reports of registration and voting tend to be higher than the actual numbers recorded. Although this difference may be important for some purposes (Bernstein et al., 2001), the logic of the analysis presented here remains accurate (Cassel, 2003).

turnout levels at 70 to 80 percent and above are common. This fact is illustrated by voting turnout in recent elections for the five nations shown below:[21]

| | |
|---|---|
| Sweden, 2002 | 80% |
| Germany, 2002 | 79% |
| Canada, 2000 | 61% |
| United Kingdom, 2001 | 59% |
| United States, 2000 | 51% |

Moreover, in most of these nations the lower classes have voting levels nearly as high as the middle class and rich. For example, the data below display turnout in the most recent Swedish parliamentary elections by family income in Swedish Crowns:[22]

| | |
|---|---|
| ≤ 49,000 | 73% |
| 50,000–109,999 | 78% |
| 110,000–165,999 | 77% |
| 160,000–219,999 | 85% |
| ≥ 220,000 | 89% |

Thus, nearly everyone votes and turnout hardly varies by class in Sweden, with only a 16 percent difference in turnout between the poor and rich. This variation is far less than occurs in the United States, which displays a 37 percent variation (see column (3) of Table 6.1). In fact, class differences in Swedish voting resemble those found in the United States among people who are registered, as shown in column (4) of Table 6.1.

The third lesson you should remember, then, is that cross-national data show turnouts resembling both the level of voting seen in this country in the late nineteenth century and the percent of registrants who vote. Neither low rates of participation nor vast differences by social class are inevitable.

But why do people vote? Well, partly as an act of patriotism. Voters are aware of the issues facing the society and develop a sense of political (and personal) effectiveness. More importantly, however, they support candidates and causes that will protect their interests.[23] In so doing, they want to hold decision makers accountable for the policies they enact. In other Western nations, where nearly everyone votes, decision makers must take everyone's interests into account in forming public policy. In the United States, by contrast, where only half the population votes in presidential election years and much less in off-years, middle-class people dominate voting. It should not be surprising that public policy often caters to the interests of this group. Yet, as indicated earlier, money talks. And it affects public policy as well.

---

[21]International Institute for Democracy and Electoral Assistance (2003).
[22]Statistics Sweden (2001).
[23]Thompson (1970), Conway (2000).

## *The Role of Money in Elections*

To the ordinary citizen, elections seem straightforward. Candidates present themselves in a campaign via television commercials, sound bites on the nightly news, public forums, and other venues. Based on this presentation, ordinary citizens select the winners on Election Day. Although this view is accurate, it is incomplete. Behind the veil, the real business of campaigns is conducted over the telephone, at cocktail parties, and at private meetings with wealthy contributors. The real business of any political campaign is money. Money is attracted to political campaigns like a moth to light. This is because money provides a source of power (the ability to achieve one's goals and a bigger share of the distribution of resources) not available to ordinary voters. This fact means that those with money (called "cash constituents") constitute another set of people to whom decision makers must be accountable. In order to see why money provides power, consider the cost of winning.

### *The Cost of Winning*

In the straightforward version, winning an election at any level requires a candidate with a timely and articulate message, appropriate experience, an effective campaign organization, and an attractive presentation of self and issues. In addition to these necessary attributes, however, a candidate requires money. In the 2000 presidential campaign, the two main national parties raised a total of $1.236 billion in "hard" and "soft" money (terms to be defined later), divided as follows:[24]

|  | *Democrats* | *Republicans* |
|---|---|---|
| "hard money" | $275,200,000 | $465,800,000 |
| "soft money" | 245,200,000 | 249,900,000 |
|  | $520,400,000 | $715,700,000 |

These enormous sums imply a fundamental truth: It costs so much money to be elected to public office that one must be wealthy or well-connected or both to conduct an effective campaign. In fact, millionaires and multimillionaires now comprise more than one-third of the United States Senate.[25] Listed below are the average amounts spent by the winner and loser, respectively, in congressional campaigns during the 2000 election:[26]

|  | *Winner* | *Loser* |
|---|---|---|
| Senate | $7,300,000 | $3,900,000 |
| House of Representatives | $ 840,000 | $ 307,000 |

[24]Center for Responsive Politics (2003).
[25]Lewis (2000:11).
[26]Center for Responsive Politics (2003).

These averages hide sharp variations in expenditures.[27] Representative James W. Humphreys of West Virginia, who spent $7,000,000 to retain his seat, ran the most expensive House campaign that year. Campaign expenses are usually much higher in Senate races because they are statewide. Senator Jon Corzine of New Jersey, who spent $63,200,000 (mostly his own money) to obtain his seat, ran the most expensive Senate campaign. The principle that running for office costs a lot of money applies to campaigns at all levels: governor, state legislator, or city commissioner. Money is necessary to pay for television and radio spots, staff salaries, transportation, and the myriad tasks that must be performed in a modern campaign.

## *Money, Winning, and Reelection*

Here is an empirical generalization:

*The more money spent on a political campaign, the greater the odds of winning.*

There are exceptions, candidates who lack a credible message or other necessary attributes (does anyone remember Steve Forbes or care about his message?). Even so, money is essential to winning. Look, for example, at the gap between the amount spent by winners and losers in House of Representative elections displayed in the informal table above. In 2000, winners outspent losers by an average $533,000, or 64 percent. Most House races, in fact, are financial mismatches: The winner vastly outspends the loser. This principle applies, of course, to elections at any level. And most winners are incumbents being reelected.[28] In 2000, 98 percent of members of the House of Representatives who ran for reelection won, which is about average since 1960. Similarly, 79 percent of senators running for reelection won, also about average since 1960. Again, this principle—that incumbents usually win reelection—is true at every level: city, county, and state. This result occurs partly because incumbents have many natural advantages. Their name recognition is high; they provide services to their district or state; they receive regular news coverage; and they enjoy the congressional franking privilege, which allows them to mail "newsletters" and other items to constituents without paying postage. The most important reason for their reelection, however, is that incumbents have an established network of contributors, both wealthy individuals and Political Action Committees (PACs).

Incumbent members of Congress get most of their campaign contributions from two sources: (1) individuals and industries in their district or state and (2) interest groups that are aligned with the member's committee assignment. In addition, many Democratic incumbents obtain contributions from labor unions. For example, members of the Financial Services Committee in the House will receive disproportionate contributions from people associated with credit companies and the securities industry, regardless of the location of their district. In fact, the financial sector (banks, accountants, real estate, etc.) is usually the single largest contributor of campaign funds in U.S. elections.[29] Members of Con-

---

[27]Center for Responsive Politics (2003).
[28]Center for Responsive Politics (2003). See also Gerber (1998).
[29]Center for Responsive Politics (2003).

gress, then, have loyalties to two groups: voter constituents and cash constituents. Both must be (and usually are) kept satisfied. Thus, except when challengers are already wealthy or have personal ties with people who can generate huge funds, they face a difficult race. Most lose.

### *Where Does the Money Come From?*

Challengers lose because interested individuals and PACs support incumbents with money—lots of it. For example, Table 6.2 depicts the sources of campaign contributions during the 2002 congressional elections. The business contributions of $707.9 million come from every industry imaginable: finance, agriculture, communications, utilities, defense, medical treatment, law, transportation, and many others. Labor contributions of $62.2 million come from some of the same industries, at least where unions exist. Ideological contributions come from special interest groups, both liberal and conservative, such as abortion groups (both sides), human rights groups, organizations interested in reducing or enhancing gun availability, and the like. The data reveal that business contributors overwhelm labor and ideology. The table shows that at least 75 percent of all contributions to congressional campaigns come from business interests ($707 out of $945 million).

I say "at least" because the data do not include other sources of money, most of which also come from business interests. Under the law, candidates for public office at all levels can spend as much as they can raise. The presidency is the only exception, and here is where the distinction between "hard" and "soft" money becomes important. "Hard money" is given directly to a presidential campaign. Under the Bipartisan Campaign Finance Reform Act passed in 2002, individuals can contribute $2,000 to a candidate per election (primary and general elections are separate), $25,000 to a national political party, and $10,000 to a Political Action Committee—up to a limit of $95,000 in any two-year election cycle. You might wonder what kinds of people have a spare $95,000 to give to a presidential candidate, an issue that will be discussed later. "Soft money" is given to the national Republican or Democratic Party for issue ads, get-out-the-vote drives, and anything else they wish to spend it on. Such "soft money" is now illegal under the law. The

**TABLE 6.2**   *Campaign Contributions, Congressional Elections, 2002*

| *Sector* | *Amount of Contribution* | *Percent to Democrats* | *Percent to Republicans* |
|---|---|---|---|
| Business | $707,900,000 | 42% | 57% |
| Labor | 62,200,000 | 92 | 8 |
| Ideological/Single Issue | 40,000,000 | 55 | 45 |
| Other | 68,000,000 | 43 | 57 |
| Unknown | 67,000,000 | 29 | 71 |
| Total | $945,100,000 | Average 45% | 55% |

*Source:* Center for Responsive Politics (2003).

impact seems potentially significant; recall from the data presented earlier that the national Democratic and Republican parties each raised about $250 million in "soft money" during the 2000 presidential campaign. The law prohibits the national parties from doing this.

"Soft money" will not, however, disappear.[30] Rather, it will reincarnate in a different location, as both national parties have set up state organizations that will now collect unregulated and unlimited contributions. In addition, both parties have established "Governors Associations" that will also raise unlimited amounts of money. Of course, "informal" coordination between presidential campaigns and the state organizations will occur, as it has in the past. As before, both parties will combine "soft" and "hard" money to fund their presidential campaigns. Remember the metaphor and pierce the veil behind elections: Money is attracted to power like a moth to light.

## An Example

One of the most powerful individuals in the United States is Dennis Hastert, a Republican from Illinois, who is Speaker of the House of Representatives. His 2002 campaign for reelection provides a convenient example of the role of money in elections.

Representative Hastert raised $3 million for his reelection campaign.[31] His Democratic opponent raised only $18,000. This vast difference meant that the election in this district was basically uncontested. Hastert won 74 percent of the vote. Nearly all the money Hastert raised, 91 percent, came from business interests. The top five sectors contributing to his campaign are shown below.

The data refer to both individual and PAC contributions.

| | |
|---|---|
| Finance/Insurance | $511,000 |
| Miscellaneous Business | 287,000 |
| Health | 256,000 |
| Communications | 180,000 |
| Lawyers/Lobbyists | 125,000 |

Although the amounts received and their sources will vary, every member of the House and Senate who gets elected and reelected—liberal and conservative, Democrat and Republican—must raise funds in this manner.

In addition, Representative Hastert formed his own political action committee, called "Keep Our Majority," during the 2002 election. This PAC raised an additional $1.8 million, again nearly all from business interests. Hastert distributed this money to the campaigns of 65 other members of the House of Representatives, many of whom were in contested elections in which a little more money helped a great deal. As noted, this tactic is not unique. Every House and Senate leader (along with other prominent members) has a personal political action committee designed to aid other members. Money thus distributed becomes a favor that can be called in when a vote is close. The point is clear: Elected

[30]Van Natta and Oppel (2002).
[31]All the data in this paragraph come from Center for Responsive Politics (2003).

officials at every level depend on large contributions from cash constituents to maintain themselves in office.

The aggregation of these contributions by category (finance and so forth) leads to an important insight: PACs and individuals run in packs, like wolves on the hunt. And such animals want to be fed. Less polemically, people do not spend such large sums of money on a whim. Campaign contributions are investments, and those making them expect results. They expect their interests to be protected. Where does that leave ordinary citizens? What about the public's interest?

## Social Structure and Political Participation

Ideally, people act within the rules to influence public policy, everyone has access to the political arena, and voters hold decision makers accountable for their decisions. Yet data show that people in different classes participate at different rates and in different ways. In effect, elected decision makers are held accountable by two constituencies: voters (who are mostly middle class) and contributors (who are mostly rich).

### Voting

In a society that comes closer to the democratic ideal, money would have less impact and cash constituents less influence on public policy because parties and candidates would have to appeal to the interests of and mobilize all citizens. This process occurs more in most Western European nations than in the United States. These differences reflect the impact of the social structure on voting, which restricts the poor and enables the middle class and rich. My hypothesis is as follows:

> *The rate of voting in the United States reflects the impact of (1) Election Day, (2) registration requirements, (3) voting procedures, and (4) the degree of inequality.*[32]

***Election Day.*** The day on which elections are held influences participation rates. In many Western European nations, as in Sweden and Germany, elections occur on Sunday or a national holiday, which means there is leisure time available to vote. This fact helps to explain why turnout rates are very high in these nations, often 70 to 80 percent or more, and class differences minimal. In contrast, Election Day is a working day in some nations, such as England, Canada, and the United States, and one result is that turnout rates are significantly lower and class differences greater. Voting on a working day is a structural

---

[32]Beeghley (1986; 1992). Omitted here (but included in my earlier analyses) is "the separation and frequency of elections." The argument is that Americans go to the polls so often in off-year and local elections that "voter fatigue" reduces turnout (Boyd, 1981; 1986; 1989). My guess, however, is that this factor is relatively unimportant compared to the other variables included in the hypothesis. Moreover, the usual solution proposed is to combine local and national elections (Lijphart, 1997), but this would involve an unfortunate trade-off because campaign costs at the local level would inevitably increase. Both the importance of this variable and the impact of the trade-off need to be debated.

barrier to participation. Those who overcome this obstacle in the greatest numbers have longer lunch hours, leave time built into their jobs, more physical energy at the end of the day, child care available, and a belief in their own political effectiveness. These traits, however, are class related, which is one reason why voting is also class related.

***Registration Requirements.***   In all Western European nations, the state automatically registers citizens to vote, another fact that partly accounts for their high voting rates. Only in the United States are citizens responsible for their own registration. Voting and registration differ in place, kind, and time, which make them fundamentally different tasks. Voting is a political decision in which voters decide whose positions best reflect and protect their own interests. Registration is an administrative act in which citizens must deal with regulators who assess their credentials and process forms, a situation that makes some people uncomfortable—especially those who are unfamiliar with professional settings.

In the past, registering to vote was rather difficult because citizens had to appear during working hours at a registration office (usually city hall or the county seat) well before Election Day. Moreover, in many states, registration deadlines were—and still are—60 to 90 days before the election. Passage of the National Voter Registration Act (NVRA, or "motor voter" law) in 1993 made registration easier by increasing the number of locations where it could take place.[33] Seven states are not subject to the act; they are North Dakota, which does not have registration, and Idaho, Maine, Minnesota, New Hampshire, Wisconsin, and Wyoming, which use Election Day Registration (more on this later). As of January, 1995, when the act went into effect, the other 43 states are supposed to offer citizens the opportunity to register when they appear at Department of Motor Vehicle offices, public assistance offices, and certain other state agencies. In addition, the NVRA also stipulates that citizens be allowed to register by mail. The act has been effective to some degree; registration levels nationwide increased by about 6 percent between the 1992 and 2000 presidential elections.[34]

The impact of the NVRA on turnout, however, has been minimal.[35] First, many states (about 18) refused to implement the law by mounting legal challenges or simply by ignoring it (or some of its provisions, such as not allowing registration at public assistance offices). Second, many states (about 17) implemented the law passively such that while citizens could register to vote at motor vehicle and other offices, they were not encouraged to do so. Third, in many states citizens who registered at motor vehicle or other offices found that their names had not been added to the voter lists given to poll workers or that their names had been illegally purged, even though registration had occurred well before the deadline. As a result, it is estimated that between 1.5 and 3 million registered citizens could not cast votes in the 2000 presidential election because of problems with the voter lists.[36] This issue was significant in Florida, where the election was decided.

[33]Tobias and Callahan (2002).
[34]Federal Election Commission (2001).
[35]See Martinez and Hill (1999) on one and two; see Tobias and Callahan (2002) on three. For a different view, see Wolfinger and Hoffman (2001); they blamed citizens' unwillingness to take advantage of a "costless" registration process.
[36]Caltech/MIT (2001:8).

In addition to these three problems, the NVRA does not and cannot solve the inherent difficulty presented by the registration requirement: The deadline for registration occurs before the election, often well before it. Nationwide, the average closing date for registration is three weeks before Election Day. A century and a half ago, the French observer Alexis de Tocqueville noted the significance of this time difference: "As the election draws near, intrigues grow more active and agitation is more lively and wider spread."[37] He thought a presidential election is like a national crisis, which motivates people to get involved—by voting—as it draws near. And he was right. As an election approaches, debates occur, candidates increase their advertising in order to get their messages across, and many races tighten, especially for the presidency. As a result, citizens become increasingly interested and develop a sense of political effectiveness; they think their vote matters. In the 2000 campaign, for example, 59 percent of the public reported they were giving "quite a lot" of thought to the campaign in September, nine weeks before the election. This figure rose steadily to 75 percent by the week before the election.[38] As another indicator of increasing interest, registration rates also increased during the run-up to the election—at least in those states where the deadline had not passed.

Table 6.3 illustrates how the registration deadline affects turnout by focusing on the six states that use Election Day Registration (EDR) along with North Dakota, which does not have a registration law. In the three states that instituted EDR in 1976, more than two-thirds of the voting age population turned out to vote in the 2000 presidential election. Even the three states that only recently instituted EDR, in 1996, had turnouts significantly higher than the nation as a whole. Taken together, average turnout in the seven states shown in the table was 65 percent, compared to only 50 percent for the remaining 43 states.

This, then, is the fourth lesson about electoral participation: If voting is made easier, turnout goes up. Indeed, this finding is consistent over several elections.[39]

The original rationale for imposing registration was to prevent electoral corruption. Yet fraud occurs rarely.[40] There has been no fraud in North Dakota, which does not require registration. Nor has it occurred in states using Election Day Registration. Nor does it happen in other Western nations. Finally, as noted earlier, it is likely that introducing the Australian ballot reduced fraud more than registration did. If registration is unnecessary to prevent corruption, then such requirements must have a less obvious purpose. One guess is that it helps to insure middle-class dominance of this aspect of the political process.

*Voting Technology.*    Assuming citizens are registered, nearly all of them vote—either at public polling places on Election Day or by absentee ballot obtained in advance (recall Table 6.1). In this country, five quite different technologies are used for voting. Each has strengths and weaknesses. Each affects the accuracy of the count and probably affects electoral turnout.[41]

---

[37]Tocqueville (1954:135).
[38]Gallup Poll (2001). See also Tobias and Callahan (2002).
[39]Highton (1997).
[40]Minnite and Callahan (2003).
[41]Caltech/MIT (2001:18–23).

**TABLE 6.3** *Turnout in States with Election Day Registration (EDR) or No Registration, 2000 U.S. Presidential Election*

| State | Year EDR Instituted* | Turnout |
|---|---|---|
| Minnesota | 1976 | 69% |
| Maine | 1976 | 67% |
| Wisconsin | 1976 | 66% |
| New Hampshire | 1996 | 63% |
| North Dakota* | — | 60% |
| Wyoming | 1996 | 60% |
| Idaho | 1996 | 55% |
| **Average in 2000 for the 7 states** | | **65%** |
| **U.S. turnout in 2000, excluding the 7 states** | **50%** | |

*North Dakota abolished registration in 1951.

*Source:* Federal Election Commission (2001).

First, hand-counted paper ballots are still used, mainly in rural areas. This is the simplest, least technologically sophisticated way of voting. Recall that in the nineteenth and early twentieth centuries, Americans simply dropped a preprinted ticket into the ballot box or marked their ballots with an "X." Even today's use of the Australian ballot makes voting easy, especially if there is only one choice to make. Paper ballots make auditing the election relatively straightforward: They are simply recounted. But there are drawbacks: Counting is slow, labor intensive, and can be error prone when more than one choice is marked on the same ballot. This is important because up to 20 offices and 20 initiatives may appear on each ballot in some elections and jurisdictions today. The advantage, then, of using more advanced technology is that it provides a speedier and, presumably, more reliable count. But does it? And do fewer people go to the polls because they are uncomfortable with the machines?

Second, mechanical lever machines require that citizens record their votes and then pull one or more handles. These machines eliminate paper but make auditing the election difficult because there is no separate record of each voter's intent, only the results captured by each machine. Also, this equipment can be intimidating and confusing to voters, making them less likely to turn out. Although many jurisdictions still use these machines, they are being phased out.

Third, electronic machines (sometimes touch screens) also require that citizens record their votes on an "interface," and then push one or more buttons. These machines have the same strengths and weaknesses as their mechanical cousins: They eliminate paper, which speeds counting, but make auditing each voter's intent impossible. Moreover, they can easily confuse and intimidate voters, especially those unused to computers. These machines are also very expensive to purchase and maintain.

Fourth, punch card ballots require citizens to depress a lever that creates a hole in a card, which is then counted by a sorting machine. This technology is not as daunting as electronic machines, nor is it difficult to use. Moreover, the count goes quickly and auditing voter intent during a recount is possible. But punch cards are, alas, the most error prone of all voting technologies. The experience in Florida in the 2000 presidential election, where the phrase "hanging chad" entered the national consciousness was not unique. Several other states had similar problems, which occur whenever an election is close and this technology is used.

Fifth, optically scanned paper ballots require citizens to mark their selections and then insert the ballot into a scanner, which reads and counts the votes. Like all paper ballots, they are less intimidating to voters, the count goes swiftly, and it can be audited relatively easily. Optically scanned paper ballots also display fewer errors than any other form of voting technology. Moreover, these machines are much less expensive to purchase than other equipment, such as touch screens.

Voting technology clearly affects the accuracy of the count and of a recount, if necessary.[42] In this regard, optically scanned paper ballots seem to provide the best choice. Citizens mark their ballots on paper. The count is quick. Each voter's intention can be accurately assessed. And these machines are cheaper to purchase.

Unfortunately, quantitative data on how voting technology affects turnout does not exist. It is plausible to speculate, however, that some citizens—especially those who are poor, uneducated, or simply unfamiliar with computers—are affected and turn out at lower rates when advanced technology is used. If so, I would guess that the impact is probably less than either day of the week or registration. In the trade-off between the possible effect on turnout and efficiency of recount, optically scanned paper ballots seem like the best choice.

***Degree of Inequality.***     Unequal possession of resources occurs in every society. Measuring the extent of this inequality can be done in a variety of ways. You have seen in previous chapters that occupational prestige scores are sometimes used. So are differences in educational attainment. Because income is fundamental to people's life chances, it provides a straightforward measure, as will be shown in subsequent chapters. But comparing income inequality across societies is tricky, so researchers often employ an index, called the **Gini Coefficient.** It translates the income distribution of each country into a standard score that varies (at least in principle) between zero and 100, with a higher number indicating greater inequality. Thus, a score of zero would mean that all incomes are completely equal, while 100 would mean that one person receives all the income. Of course, neither of these extreme results occurs in any nation.

Shown below are Gini Coefficients for the same five Western nations whose electoral turnout was compared earlier. All the data are for 1995 and are the most recent available.[43]

---

[42]Caltech/MIT (2001).
[43]Ritakallio (2001:15), U.S. Bureau of the Census (2002:19).

| Sweden | 21 |
| Germany | 27 |
| Canada | 28 |
| United Kingdom | 34 |
| United States | 45 |

As the data reveal, the United States displays much greater income inequality than do these other nations, and the gap has become greater over the past quarter-century. On this issue, the United States is consistently described as being in a world of its own. In fact, as will be discussed in subsequent chapters, the level of income inequality has increased in this country to a point not seen since the 1920s, just before the Depression.

Income inequality affects electoral turnout in all Western nations.[44] The finding is straightforward: The higher the degree of income inequality, the lower the turnout. In addition, the finding also occurs in subnational units within these societies. For example, in this country, states displaying higher levels of inequality also display lower turnout. This fact should not be surprising. At every level, people with power try to obtain a larger share of the pie, the implications of which are mentioned in a moment.

In sum, the impact of Election Day, registration, and degree of income inequality on voter turnout is displayed in Table 6.4. (The importance of voting technology is omitted here because it is more difficult to illustrate.) The table shows that nations with the highest rates of voting maximize the opportunity to vote by holding elections on a rest day and by not imposing registration requirements. Nations holding elections on working days have, in effect, imposed a barrier to voting that some people cannot cross and, hence, they display lower levels of participation. The United States—which places the most restrictions on the opportunity to vote by holding elections on a working day and requiring registration—reveals the lowest rate of electoral participation. Finally, it is not accidental that the United States also displays the highest level of income inequality. Recall the difference between this country and Sweden in electoral participation: The turnout gap between the rich and poor is 37 percent in this country but only 16 percent in Sweden. Most people vote in Sweden. Why not here? What are the implications?

***Implications.***    The short answer is that low electoral turnout is concentrated among the working class and poor (recall Table 6.1), and the result affects both who gets elected and the public policies they espouse. The great political scientist, V. O. Key, explained why, more than half a century ago: "The blunt truth is that politicians and officials are under no compulsion to pay heed to classes and groups of citizens who do not vote."[45] Regardless of the issue—job benefits (such as health insurance), housing policies, educational spending, or income protection—voters hold decision makers accountable. This is also true of issues unrelated (at least directly) to the distribution of resources, such as abortion policy, gun policy, or environmental policies. Thus, unless threatened with unruliness from be-

---

[44]Lijphart (1997), Mahler (2002).
[45]Key (1949:527). See also Verba, who commented that elected officials' "responsiveness depends on citizen participation" (1996:2).

**TABLE 6.4**    *Social Structure and Electoral Turnout in Five Countries*

| Country, Election | Electoral Turnout | Election on Work Day | Registration | Index of Income Inequality* |
|---|---|---|---|---|
| Sweden, 2002 | 80% | No | No | 21 |
| Germany, 2002 | 79% | No | No | 27 |
| Canada, 2000 | 61% | Yes | No | 28 |
| United Kingdom, 2001 | 59% | Yes | No | 34 |
| United States, 2000 | 51% | Yes | Yes | 45 |

*Measured by the Gini Coefficient.

*Sources:* International Institute for Democracy and Electoral Assistance (2003), Ritakallio (2001), U.S. Bureau of the Census (2002:19).

low or (more likely) co-opted by money from above, decision makers represent the interests of voter constituents.

There is, however, another interpretation of low electoral turnouts that ought to be mentioned. Some studies show that nonvoters do not differ much from voters and the authors conclude that the absence of nonvoters from the voting pool has little effect on government policy at any level and so low electoral turnouts do not matter.[46] The problem with this argument (a sophisticated version of "don't worry, be happy") is that nonvoters are typically citizens who have not given much thought to the way policy issues affect their lives or their life chances. They have not, in short, developed a sense of class consciousness and become politically mobilized. People come to believe in their own political effectiveness when opinion leaders, candidates, or parties contact them—face-to-face contact is especially important.[47] When this does not happen, nonvoters remain uninvolved and their interests go unrepresented. In fact, low turnouts do matter; they lead to public policies favoring the middle class and rich, and thereby affect the structure of stratification.[48] As a sidebar, while most observers assume that working-class and poor nonvoters would be "liberal" and more likely to vote for the Democratic Party, this is not necessarily correct; they may also be more conservative on some issues and display more racial prejudice.[49]

Regardless of the political attitudes of nonvoters, it should not be surprising that low turnouts have become part of a self-perpetuating electoral system. Figure 6.2 presents a model of the impact of structural inhibitions on the ability to vote that depicts this process.[50] As described in the model, structural inhibitions on voting lead to lower electoral

---

[46]Teixeira summarized the conclusions of several studies (1992:100). More recently, Highton and Wolfinger simulated the impact of nonvoters on the 1992 and 1996 presidential elections, and showed that their participation would have meant little (2001). Perhaps.

[47]Rosenstone and Hansen (1993), Gerber and Green (2000).

[48]See Hibbs (1977), Hicks and Swank (1992), Pacek and Radcliff (1995). Lijphart summarized this literature (1997).

[49]On the assumption, see Piven and Cloward (1988). Highton and Wolfinger offered the qualifying note (2001).

[50]The model is adapted loosely from some comments made by Piven and Cloward (1988:16–23).

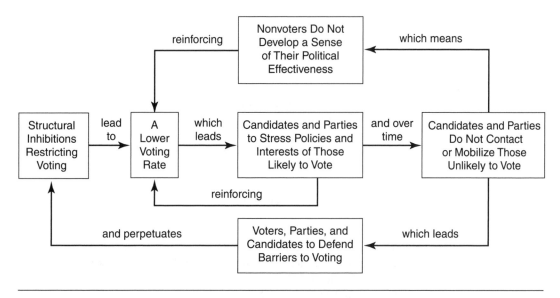

**FIGURE 6.2**   *The Impact of Structural Inhibitions on the Rate of Voting in the United States*

turnouts, which in turn lead candidates and parties to stress policies of interest to likely voters, who are mainly middle class. This emphasis, of course, reinforces the low voting rate. Over the years, the candidates and parties have stopped contacting nonvoters and trying to mobilize them. As a result, nonvoters do not develop a sense of their potential political effectiveness, which again reinforces low turnouts. In addition, since they do not contact (or care about) nonvoters, those who vote, candidates, parties, and some academic researchers find themselves defending barriers to voting, which perpetuates structural inhibitions (such as registration). Fear of fraud, worry about "uninformed" voters, and an amorphous—perhaps unarticulated—sense of self-interest buttress this position. And the cycle continues. But voting constitutes only one source of power. The rich have others.

## Partisanship

Although anyone can be a partisan, few citizens actually try to influence decision makers. They vote (or do not vote) and let it go at that. Ordinary people have jobs, spouses, and children, plus assorted other obligations—which keep them busy. In addition, most decisions made "inside the beltway" (the freeway that surrounds Washington, DC) or "downtown," seem remote to their daily lives, but the policies that result mean tens of millions of dollars to companies and large fortunes for individuals. It is a rarefied world, one where business and politics converge. The rich predominate in this world. In order to protect their interests, they are active partisans, trying to influence legislation at every stage. The structural basis for their effectiveness is wealth; but other factors also exist that are correlated with wealth. My hypothesis follows:

> *The sources of partisanship are (1) money, (2) class background, and (3) institutional location.*

***Money.***     The first and most important political resource in the United States is money. As an analysis of family budgets will show (to be described in Chapters 7–10), ordinary citizens have little money to contribute to political campaigns. This is why hardly anyone does—less than 5 percent of the population.[51] Those who do have the money to give are wealthy. For example, 81 percent of donors to congressional campaigns have incomes of more than $500,000 per year, which places them in about the top 3 percent of all earners. More than 90 percent of congressional donors are white, 80 percent are men, and most are in very high prestige occupations (such as business executives, lawyers, or doctors). About 49 percent are Republicans and 31 percent Democrats. And they are well connected: 61 percent personally know their congressional representative, 39 percent know one of their senators, and 32 percent know both. Not surprisingly, they want to preserve their income and wealth: More than half support tax cuts, even if government services must be reduced. Donors give in two ways, either directly to candidates themselves or to professional lobbyists employed by PACs who work for or against specific issues.

There are more than 14,000 registered lobbying firms and individual lobbyists in Washington, DC.[52] If the total of each firm's professional staff were included, the number of individual lobbyists would be much higher. A similar army of lobbyists exists, of course, in every state capital and large city. These are the professionals whose job it is to affect legislation and policy implementation. About 159 former members of Congress comprise a special category of lobbyists, since they retain access to the floor of the House and Senate chambers, members' dining rooms, the House gym, and parking. Like most lobbyists, former members of Congress have policy expertise, an understanding of the legislative process, and personal contacts with key representatives and senators. The most important task of the lobbyist and individual donors who contact decision makers is to explain their views about the nature and impact of pending legislation to members and staffers—with the goal of obtaining their support.

The mechanism for succeeding in this task is the campaign contribution and other gifts. Thus, because of the need for money, it has become common for members of Congress to solicit a campaign contribution soon (sometimes immediately) after concluding a meeting with a lobbyist.[53] One lobbyist described the procedure this way: After meeting with a member of Congress, a lobbyist will be invited to the member's next fundraiser. If the lobbyist gives, he or she will get another meeting. If the lobbyist does not give, then access dries up. Thus, the millions of dollars raised by candidates in order to get elected and reelected sets up a simple exchange relationship in which each side has something the other wants.

Campaign contributions are not necessarily bribes. Nor are the vacations, payments for "speeches," skybox tickets to the Super Bowl and Kentucky Derby, and other gifts that members of Congress casually accept.[54] One would have to be cynical to see them in this way. Rather, as noted, what contributors and gift givers say they are "purchasing" with their monetary support is access, the ability to make their case, to be heard in the policy-

[51]Green et al. (1998).
[52]Ota (2002).
[53]Public Campaign (2002).
[54]Barlett and Steele (1994:213).

making and rule development process. This is how power works. The empirical generalization follows:

> *The higher the social class and the greater the campaign contribution, then the greater access to public officials.*

Thus, since rich people contribute disproportionately, they have more access to decision makers, more ability to have their interests get a hearing.

A simple thought-experiment can illustrate why: Imagine yourself as a member of Congress considering legislation to "reform" the tax code. This issue is important because it affects how much money people get to keep for themselves rather than contributing to the common good. Now suppose your secretary tells you that two telephone calls have come in at once; one is from an ordinary voter constituent and the other from a wealthy contributor. Which call would you take? And whose position would be more persuasive to you? This logic is why public policy often favors the interests of those contributing to campaigns: cash constituents. It is why elections are like auctions, with the winner being the highest bidder.

It should be noted that campaign contributions constitute only one way lobbyists (whether wealthy individuals or professionals) influence legislators. Decision makers often rely on lobbyists for information, since in many cases they are experts in the field, capable of explaining complex and difficult subjects clearly. Moreover, on specific issues, lobbyists can often generate "grass roots" support for their positions by having ordinary citizens write, telephone, and visit legislators.[55] These contacts work because members of Congress (and decision makers at every level) want to please their constituents, especially those who are likely to vote. For these reasons, then, the rich often have access to policy makers.

***Class Background.***    Recall that many donors report they "personally know" their representatives and senators. They know one another because they often share a similar class background.[56] This similarity makes them intellectually and psychologically compatible with one another, easing talk. Thus, while dairy farmers and physicians form PACs and often influence legislation by means of campaign contributions and lobbying, their impact is rather specialized. In contrast, social ties stemming from class background give many wealthy people far-reaching political influence. These connections are reflected in the exclusive prep schools they attend, the exclusive fraternities and (to a lessor degree) sororities they belong to, and the private clubs they join.[57] These groups not only provide an informal context in which business deals are made, but they also serve as forums for political discussions with decision makers. The poor, along with the working class and middle class, are systematically excluded from such groups. In general, the rich often come from a class background similar to that of decision makers, and this fact, combined with their financial resources, allows them access.

---

[55]Mitchell (1998).
[56]Davidson (1995).
[57]Domhoff (1970; 1974), Ingham (1978).

***Institutional Location.***     In addition to money and class background, a third source of partisanship is institutional location. In this context, the term *institutional location,* refers to one's job, but not just any old job. Rich people have their interests represented simply because they occupy positions of power in the United States. For example, it has been argued that there are about 7,300 elite positions in the United States.[58] Approximately, 4,300 of this total are in the corporate sector, comprising the heads and boards of directors of large corporations; another 2,700 are in the "public interest" sector, comprising the owners and heads of mass media companies, philanthropic foundations, law firms, and civic organizations; and 300 are in the governmental sector, comprising the highest elected and appointed officials in the United States. Although these numbers are imprecise, the principle is correct: The people occupying these elite roles are atypical of the U.S. population; that is, they are predominantly rich, white, male, and have high prestige jobs—just like the donors described earlier. Ordinary people do not perform these roles. Those few who do enjoy access and influence.

In sum, money and status (in the form of class background and institutional location) count. Those who possess these traits have access to decision makers; and those with access can often make their case.

***Implications.***     Access means influence. Envision a common scenario on Capital Hill in Washington (or in your state capital or city hall). A serious problem is identified. Various ways of dealing with the issue are debated. Instead of adopting the best alternative, however, the "solution" passed actually protects the interests of those contributing to congressional campaigns—reflecting the outcome of the auction. Lawmakers, of course, describe the act as a reform and stress that it is in the public interest. This is a veil. Politics in a democratic society is never about finding the "best" solution to a problem. Politics is about finding the answer that can be passed by a legislative body. In figuring out what can pass the House and Senate (or your state legislature or city commission) one of the oldest sayings in politics should be kept in mind: "You gotta dance with them who brung ya." In most cases, "them who brung ya" are those who supplied the cash for political campaigns. Thus, you will not understand politics in America until you see it as a series of exchanges between candidates who need votes and those who have the money to pay for campaigns. Their "purchase" is effective. As one veteran observer commented, "There is no . . . investment with a greater return on capital than political contributions."[59] Figure 6.3 presents a model of the relationship among campaign contributions, access to members of Congress, and their votes.

So how is the distribution of resources affected by the relationships depicted in Figure 6.3? In part, it depends on the industry: Banking, insurance, resource extracting, telecommunications, agriculture, food processing, pharmaceuticals, accounting, and many more all reap benefits from their campaign contributions in the form of bills passed, bills passed in weakened form, bills defeated, or loopholes added to bills. As discussed in Chapter 7, the very rich own most of the stock in these industries.

The rich benefit personally and directly as well, affecting their life chances. Inequality has increased in recent years. For example, top tax brackets were reduced from

---

[58]Dye (2002).
[59]Quoted in Morgenson (2002).

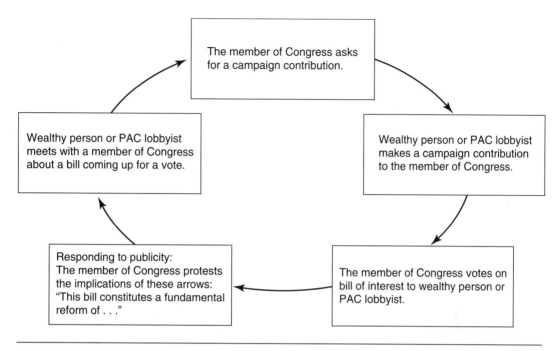

**FIGURE 6.3**　*Campaign Contributions, Access, and Congressional Voting*

70 percent to 50 percent in 1981, and then to 28 percent in 1986, before rising to 39 percent in 1993. As a result, the rich can now retain an enormous amount of income and become even wealthier than in the past. In addition, as will be shown in subsequent chapters, a "hollowing out" of the income and job structure occurred during these same years such that lower-middle class, working-class, and poor people are increasingly left behind; they get a smaller share of the available goods and services. More recently, high-income people contributed over $1.8 billion to political campaigns during the years 1999–2002.[60] It is probably not accidental that the most recent round of tax cuts amounts to $1.35 trillion over ten years, $769 billion of which will go to high-income Americans. Moreover, Internal Revenue Service audits of the wealthy, who have much greater ability to hide income, have declined. One result will be huge governmental deficits over the next few years, necessitating cuts in services. There will be less money for disaster relief, staffing the Internal Revenue Service offices and Head Start, research into the causes of disease at the Centers for Disease Control, and myriad other tasks. There will be less money for Medicare, Medicaid, and Social Security. It will be said that the nation cannot afford to protect the public. Actually, however, the Congress chose to enact these tax cuts.

Once again, this is how power works.[61] Whenever tax bills are passed, members of Congress develop sound bites for the nightly news, making statements like "this is a major effort to reform the tax law and make it more equitable."[62] Such sonorous platitudes have

[60]Public Campaign (2003).
[61]Scott (2001).
[62]Barlett and Steele (1994:252).

little relationship to reality. Rather, they are exercises in lowering the veil—in deceiving ordinary citizens.

## Conclusion

The veil hides the reality of class conflict over the possession of resources. Although this process occurs in every modern society, as suggested by the hypothesis presented earlier—*the higher the social class, the greater the influence over access to resources in the society*—it leads to greater inequality in the United States compared to other nations. In this country, the electoral structure inhibits voting, especially among the working class and poor, and those with the most money finance the campaigns of elected officials. As a result, candidates for office find themselves in a peculiar situation. To be successful, they must campaign as though they care about improving the lives of ordinary citizens. In governing, however, politicians as decision makers must satisfy the interests of those who voted and those who provided the money to be elected—usually in that order.

The game is rigged. Why is this so? In *The Culture of Contentment,* the economist and iconoclast, John Kenneth Galbraith offered an answer.[63] He speculated that those at the top of the class hierarchy develop a sense of entitlement, a feeling that their wealth and other benefits reflect merit: their virtue, intelligence, and hard work. This is a myth, of course, but a powerful one. Economic doctrine, Galbraith proposed, accommodates that view. In his pithy description, supply side economics argues that "if the horse is fed amply with oats, some will pass through to the road for the sparrows." Phrased this way, the crackpot nature of the argument becomes clear. Nonetheless, it provides an intellectual veil for what is really class conflict over possession of resources. Moreover, Galbraith suggested that middle-class people accept the enormous benefits going to the rich as "the price the contented electoral majority pays for being able to retain what is less but what is still very good."[64] In effect, it appears that the middle class allows the rich to be favored in return for some limited economic protection for itself. The result can be seen in the distribution of wealth and income, and the lifestyle of each class, as described in the following chapters.

## Summary

In a democratic society, people act within the rules to influence public policy and access to the political arena is open so that everyone can compete fairly. A dilemma results, however, because classes with resources want to limit the ability of other classes to increase their share. Three types of participation were reviewed: voting, partisanship, and unruliness.

Although the proportion of adults eligible to vote has expanded steadily over time, the actual rate of voting has declined, especially over the last 40 years (Figure 6.1). To-

[63]Galbraith (1992:27).
[64]Galbraith (1992:26).

day, only about half of those eligible participate in presidential elections, and the middle class dominates voting. But this fact is not inevitable: (1) About 70 to 80 percent of those eligible voted during the last quarter of the nineteenth century, (2) today, about 80 percent of those registered actually vote (Table 6.1), and (3) about 60 to 80 percent of adults vote in other Western industrial societies.

In order to understand elections, it is important to understand the role of money. The cost of winning has risen steadily over time. Most officeholders are reelected, mainly because they spend the most money. Incumbents raise money from large contributors, both individuals and political action committees, or PACs (Table 6.2). Contributions from people and organizations tied to business overwhelm those with labor and ideological affiliations. Decision makers are accountable, then, to those who supply the money necessary to win elections.

Voting rates are influenced mainly by the day on which elections are held, the registration requirement (Table 6.3), voting technology, and the level of inequality (Table 6.4). A model of the structure of elections shows the impact of a situation in which middle-class people dominate: Candidates lose interest in the working class and poor because they do not vote, the working class and poor fail to see their interests, and everyone defends barriers to participation (Figure 6.2).

Although anyone can be a partisan, the rich possess the resources to pursue their interests most effectively. Money, class background, and institutional location mean that the rich have more access to decision makers than members of other social classes. The rich take advantage of access in order to receive benefits (Figure 6.3).

# 7

## *The Rich*

They are the most talked about social class. Its members are both resented and envied, and for the same reason: They have so much. In the jargon, their life chances far surpass those of other social classes. Their notoriety is, perhaps, the reason why few people admit to being a member (recall the results of the class identification question in Chapter 4). They are the rich. Americans like to believe that ours is a society of opportunity and the existence of this class of people appears to epitomize the American dream: Anyone can become rich, or so it seems.

But, in fact, the rich—especially the very rich—are not like you and me. The poor are characterized by relatively low wages and periodic dependence on public aid as a source of income. Working and middle-class people rely on their occupations for income and prestige. Indeed, because these three classes comprise nearly the entire population, the usual tendency is to focus on people's occupations and the incomes they produce as the key to understanding their life chances and lifestyles. And this is a reasonable strategy. It is the logic, for example, underlying the literature on social mobility and status attainment reviewed in Chapter 5. But the rich are different. As you will come to see, they own capital—a great deal of capital.

# The Characteristics of the Rich

## Counting the Rich: Income and Wealth

Surprisingly, however, little agreement exists about the criteria for inclusion in this small class of people. One argument is that the rich are simply those with the highest incomes. And, in fact, most discussions of economic inequality begin with the distribution of **income,** which refers to the flow of dollars received during a period of time, usually a year—whether from one's job, the sale of goods, or profit from investments. This emphasis occurs because the vast majority of people derive nearly all their income from their jobs, but the distribution of income is rather limiting if the goal is either to count the rich, especially the super-rich, or to understand their true economic circumstances.

In order to see why, consider physicians and lawyers. It is common for people in these and other occupations to have incomes of $150,000 per year or more, which places them in the top 5 percent of the income distribution.[1] Although they live well, most people would see them and they would see themselves as middle class. They live in nice neighborhoods; in fact, most of their incomes go to purchasing their house; it is their biggest asset. They can pay for new cars, college for their children, country club memberships, and the like, but their income-producing assets are minimal. It is hard to call them rich, even though their incomes are so far above average.

Consider, however, people whose occupations lead to truly high incomes. Some football coaches make $1 to 2 million per year, placing them in the top 1 percent of the income distribution. They are clearly rich. So, too, are the small number of professional athletes and entertainers who make the big bucks, say $10 million per year or even more. They live in rarefied economic circumstances. But coaches get fired. Athletes get injured. Entertainers stop selling records. More important, people who earn a high income and spend it are living well and accumulating nothing. Income, even extraordinary income, is unstable—unless it is converted into wealth.

**Wealth** provides a much better measure for counting the rich. It refers to the value of everything a person or family owns minus its debts. The things owned can be consumer durables, like housing or automobiles, which satisfy people's needs. They can also be various forms of capital, such as stocks, bonds, commercial real estate, or other income-producing assets. Debt includes mortgage and auto loans, credit card balances, and the like. Although wealth can vary over time, it provides more stable long-term security for a family. Wealth is also more unequally distributed than income. For example, while the top 5 percent of all households obtain about 22 percent of all the income in this country each year, the top 1 percent of all households possesses 33 percent of all the wealth.[2]

If the rich are defined as those households possessing wealth of more than $1 million, then the size of this class has increased a great deal over the past few decades. For example, the percent of households possessing wealth of more than $1 million increased from about 3.3 percent in 1983 to about 7.0 percent in 2001. This figure translates into

---

[1]U.S. Bureau of the Census (2002:19).
[2]Income data are from U.S. Bureau of the Census (2002:19). Wealth data are from Kennickell (2003:9).

about 17.5 million persons, or roughly 5 percent of the population that can be considered rich. Although this estimate is a little high, it provides a rough guide.

The reason it is a little high can be seen when this small aggregate of people is divided into two types. First, most of those with wealth above $1 million (but sometimes much higher) are job-rich. They have acquired their wealth based on their jobs and frugality.[3] It is plausible, although rare, for example, for a professional couple (say, a college professor and a lawyer) to acquire over time, by means of the value of their pensions and small investments, wealth of greater than $1 million. Although they live well, often in large homes in exclusive neighborhoods, it remains true that their most valuable assets are their house and pensions. Again, many of these people, especially at the lower end of the wealth continuum, would define themselves as upper-middle class. So the dividing line between the middle class and rich is not precise. Second, the owner-rich comprise a much smaller group; they live off their ownership of capital: mainly stocks in large corporations, government and corporate bonds, business ventures, and commercial real estate. Only about 0.9 percent of households possess wealth greater than $5 million, which translates (roughly) into about 2.3 million people—less than 1 percent of the population. These wealthy people are super-rich. They comprise a tiny apex that owns most of the wealth in the United States.[4]

### The Basis of Great Wealth

The basis for great wealth is ownership of capital, especially corporate stocks and bonds, but other income-producing assets as well. Information from income tax returns not only provides an initial way of visualizing this fact but also shows once again that the truly rich comprise a very small aggregate of the population. Table 7.1 presents the distribution of tax returns and the percent of "adjusted gross income" from wages and salaries. Tax returns, of course, can be filed individually or jointly (by couples). I have placed "adjusted gross income" in quotes to remind you that it is income for tax purposes, not total income received during a year. It represents taxable income after a series of transfer payments and exclusions are subtracted from couples' and individuals' gross (or total) income. These deductions (called tax expenditures) occur for business expenses, depreciation of income-producing assets, individual retirement accounts, capital gains exclusions, and the like. They make it possible for people, mainly the upper-middle class and rich, to show an income for tax purposes that is lower (often much lower) than their total income. Observe again that, as shown in column (2), the rich constitute a very small segment of the population.

The importance of capital as the basis for wealth is shown in column (3) of Table 7.1. Those tax returns displaying "adjusted gross incomes" of less than $200,000 receive nearly all their income from wages and salaries. Thus, for the vast majority of the population—more than 97 percent—their jobs constitute the center of their lives, determining their life chances. Those returns showing "adjusted gross incomes" above $200,000 reveal a steadily decreasing proportion of income resulting from wages and salaries. At the

[3]Stanley and Danko (1996).
[4]Wolff (2002:15).

**TABLE 7.1**   *The Distribution of Tax Returns and Adjusted Gross Income from Wages and Salaries, 2000*

| *(1)*<br><br>*Adjusted Gross Income (AGI)* | *(2)*<br><br>*Percent of Tax Returns* | *(3)*<br>*Percent of AGI from Wages and Salaries* |
|---|---|---|
| $1 – < $15,000 | 29.4% | 76% |
| $15,000 – < $30,000 | 23.4 | 80 |
| $30,000 – < $50,000 | 18.7 | 81 |
| $50,000 – < $75,000 | 13.3 | 80 |
| $75,000 – < $100,000 | 6.7 | 79 |
| $100,000 – < $200,000 | 6.3 | 72 |
| $200,000 – < $500,000 | 1.7 | 61 |
| $500,000 – < $1,000,000 | 0.3 | 49 |
| $1,000,000 – < $2,000,000 | 0.11 | 41 |
| $2,000,000 – < $5,000,000 | 0.052 | 38 |
| $5,000,000 – < $10,000,000 | 0.010 | 34 |
| $10,000,000 and higher | 0.008 | 25 |
|  | 100% |  |

*Source:* Campbell and Parisi (2002:23).

top, among individuals and couples showing an "adjusted gross income" above $10 million, only about a quarter of their incomes are obtained from salaries; the remainder comes from capital. Finally, not shown in the table, data for the 400 wealthiest taxpayers in 2000, whose income averaged $174 million, show that their incomes accounted for less than 1 percent of the total.[5] These numbers reflect an empirical generalization:

> *The higher the income, then the greater the reliance on capital as the source of income.*

And, it should be added, the greater their share of the available goods and services in the society.

This fact has important implications, for those who obtain income based on capital have several advantages over those who live on wages and salaries. One advantage is economic security. People without capital who work for a living can be injured, laid off, or see their occupational skills erode if they pause to start a family. Their life chances are always precarious as a result. Another advantage is lifestyle. People who derive high income from assets can choose to be employed or not and, since nearly all do work, they can select an occupation that suits their interests and develops their human potential most fully. Persons without capital do not enjoy this luxury. A final advantage—one discussed in Chapter 6—is political influence. Although they constitute a very small segment of the

[5]Internal Revenue Service (2003).

population, those with great wealth also possess considerable political clout, which affects the structure of stratification in the United States.

## *The Concentration of Wealth*

At the extreme end of the stratification structure, wealth is very concentrated, as shown in Table 7.2. The top 1 percent of the population possesses a stunning 33 percent of all the wealth in the United States, $13.85 trillion. The top 10 percent holds 69 percent of all the wealth, which does not leave much for the remainder of the population. Thus, percentile 50 to 90 percent possesses 27 percent of the wealth while the bottom half of the population possesses a meager 3 percent. In considering the table, the most astonishing indicator of the degree of inequality is the fact that the top 1 percent of the population is wealthier than the bottom 90 percent. And this estimate of wealth concentration is probably low.[6]

Table 7.3 elaborates on this issue by displaying the assets owned by the rich and the rest of the population. The richest 1 percent own most of the capital that provides significant income. They own 64 percent of bonds, 58 percent of business assets, and 46 percent of trust funds. As financial advisors constantly remind investors, the single asset that goes up in value the most over time is stocks; the richest 1 percent of the population own 53 percent of all privately held stocks. Although many ordinary people invest in the stock market, the poorest 90 percent of the population own only 12 percent of all stocks. In fact, the table shows that the poorest half of the population owns almost no capital, nothing that produces an income. The ownership pattern is reversed for other kinds of assets. The poorest 90 percent of the population owns 63 percent of residential housing, most of which is mortgaged (often heavily). This debt means that an average family that purchases a home for, say, $100,000, will pay three or four times that amount in interest to a lending agency—owned by the rich. As will be shown in Chapter 8, this interest is deductible from income tax, which placates middle-class people. Similarly, 86 percent of all installment debt is owed by the poorest 90 percent of the population. Although this statement simplifies the situation, it can be said that a few people live rather well off the interest payments of middle-class families. The combination of assets and liabilities shows again that wealth is concentrated in this country.

The data in the table focus on individual wealth. Using individuals as the unit of analysis makes sense as long as they serve as a proxy for a nuclear family. Most people today think of the family as comprising adults living together, often with their immediate children. Family members typically have much less contact with relatives in their extended family, such as aunts, uncles, and cousins, but such ties are vitally important to the owner-rich. This is so for two reasons.[7] First, kinship indicates who can share in the family fortune. Thus, the founders pass on wealth to children; they, in turn, marry and bear children, passing on wealth again. This continuing process involves an ever-widening range of people and, it would seem, diminishes the fortune. Yet, great wealth usually remains intact. This fact leads to the second reason family ties are important to the rich: Family members combine their assets via trusts and holding companies so as to control

---

[6]Keister and Moller (2000), Internal Revenue Service (2003).
[7]Allen (1990).

**TABLE 7.2**  *The Concentration of Wealth, 2001*

| Population Percentile | Value of Wealth | Share of Wealth (Percent) | Cumulative Share of Wealth (Percent) |
|---|---|---|---|
| Top 1% | $13.85 trillion | 33% | 33% |
| Next 90–99% | 15.75 " | 37 | 70 |
| Next 50–90% | 11.60 " | 27 | 97 |
| Bottom 0–50% | 2.80 " | 3 | 100% |
| | 44.00 | 100% | |

*Source:*  Kennickell (2003:21).

**TABLE 7.3**  *Assets and Debts by Level of Wealth, 2001*

| | Share of Wealth | | | | |
|---|---|---|---|---|---|
| | Population Percentile | | | | |
| | Top 1% | 90–99% | 50–90% | 0–50% | Total |
| **Assets** | | | | | |
| *Owned Mainly by the Richest 10% of the Population* | | | | | |
| Bonds | 64% | 32% | 4% | 0%[*] | 100% |
| Business Assets | 58% | 32% | 10% | 0%[*] | 100% |
| Trust Funds | 46% | 40% | 13% | 0%[*] | 100% |
| Stocks | 53% | 35% | 11% | 1% | 100% |
| Other Assets[**] | 40% | 38% | 17% | 4% | 100% |
| *Owned Mainly by the Poorest 90% of the Population* | | | | | |
| Checking and Money Market Accts. | 26% | 35% | 33% | 6% | 100% |
| Pension Accounts | 14% | 47% | 36% | 3% | 100% |
| Life Insurance (cash value) | 13% | 34% | 47% | 7% | 101% |
| Home | 9% | 28% | 51% | 12% | 100% |
| Automobiles | 5% | 19% | 48% | 28% | 100% |
| **Debts** | | | | | |
| Installment and Credit Card | 4% | 11% | 38% | 48% | 101% |
| Home Mortgage and Home Equity | 5% | 20% | 52% | 24% | 100% |

[*]Less than 1/2 of 1%.

[**]Antiques, paintings, jewelry, oil leases, and all other economically valuable assets.

*Note:*  Some totals do not add to 100% because of rounding.

*Source:*  Kennickell (2003:21).

many large corporations. It turns out, then, that families, not individuals, own most fortunes.

Here is a simple example: In one tabulation, J. Paul Getty was included in a list of the 50 wealthiest people of the last 1,000 years.[8] Prior to his death in 1976, Getty controlled a majority of stock in Getty Oil, receiving dividend income of about $29 million per year (look back to Table 7.1 to see where this amount would place him). This stock was worth at least $1 billion at the time, but Getty was not really a billionaire. The reason is that while he controlled the stock, he did not own it. He served as the trustee of a trust established by his mother, voting the stock and receiving dividends from it. Both he and his sons were lifetime beneficiaries—entitled to the income but unable to touch the principal. The trust will not be dissolved until the death of the last surviving grandchild. At that time, a holding company will probably be formed in order to preserve the principal for subsequent generations. In effect, the assets of this fortune constituted the collective property of the entire family. According to Michael Patrick Allen in *The Founding Fortunes: A New Anatomy of the Super-Rich Families in America*, this pattern is typical among the rich and it carries important implications.[9] In the data displayed above, the many individual members of the Getty family are included in the top 1 percent even though in reality they function as a unit. Allen presented data and a host of interesting stories about 160 families, each of which was worth at least $200 million in 1986 and much more today. This is a rather small community of people who have tremendous economic and political resources.

## The Historical Trend in the Distribution of Wealth

The historical trend in the distribution of wealth, especially the share possessed by the very rich, is a matter of considerable controversy. Many people, even today, agree with the French observer, Alexis de Tocqueville, that the United States is and always has been a relatively egalitarian society.[10] In *Democracy in America,* originally published in 1835, Tocqueville argued that in the United States an equality of "condition gives some resources to all members of the community [and] prevents any of them from having resources to any great extent." Furthermore, Tocqueville asserted, "most rich men were formerly poor" and when wealth is amassed it is not passed on to relatives but circulates with "inconceivable rapidity." In contrast to this argument, other observers claim that wealth always has been highly concentrated in the United States. Gabriel Kolko, for example, argued that "a radically unequal distribution of income [and wealth] has been characteristic of the American social structure since at least 1910 and despite minor year-to-year fluctuations . . . no significant trend toward income equality has appeared."[11] The way to resolve this controversy, of course, is with data and a hypothesis that interprets them.

---

[8]Phillips (2002:206). The data on Getty come from Allen (1990).
[9]Allen (1990).
[10]Pessen (1971), Tocqueville (1954:250–58).
[11]Kolko (1962:13).

### The Kuznets Hypothesis

Like Gerhard Lenski, the economist Simon Kuznets hypothesized that when less economically developed societies, such as Brazil and Nigeria, are compared to more economically developed societies, such as the United States and Sweden, the relationship between economic growth and inequality is curvilinear in the form of a bowl turned upside down.[12] Phrased formally, the *Kuznets Hypothesis* goes like this:

> *Inequality of wealth and income increases during the early phases of economic development when the transition from pre-industrial to industrial society is most rapid, stabilizes for awhile, then decreases in the later phases of economic development.*

This pattern is not accidental, Kuznets said. Economic development, especially in the early stages, cannot occur without large-scale capital formation. Those who are not rich spend all or nearly all their income. Only rich persons can invest their incomes in sufficient quantity to transform a society from preindustrial to industrial. The result, however, is greater inequality, as wealthy people reap a considerable return on their investments. Kuznets argued that a variety of factors produce a stable and then a declining level of inequality as economic development continues. One of them is what Kuznets called "legislative interference" with the "free market," by means of inheritance taxes, government-induced inflation (which erodes the value of wealth), and other policies designed to redistribute wealth. Such "interventions," Kuznets suggested, "reflect the view of society on the long term utility of wide income inequalities."[13] As described in Chapter 6, voters hold decision makers in a democracy accountable—at least in principle—which can (at least in some societies) lead to more egalitarian public policies. Another factor reducing inequality over time is continued economic development combined with political freedom. The occupational structure changes, stimulating upward mobility as workers shift from agricultural and low-skill jobs to higher-paying blue- and white-collar occupations (recall Chapter 5). In addition, the more or less constant growth of new technology based on scientific advances (remember that capitalism, democracy, and science are all interrelated in modern societies) leads to the rise of new industries, which means old wealth declines in value and is superseded by new wealth. Thus, the Kuznets Hypothesis says that the impact of these changes first raises, then stabilizes, and, over time, reduces inequality as economic development continues.

This hypothesis implies that a historical process occurs. Yet the data used to test it are nearly always cross-sectional: comparisons of less- and more-developed societies existing today. One reason for this strategy is that such information is readily available. In any case, the hypothesis implies a historical pattern that needs to be traced empirically. In the following paragraphs, I sketch the trend of wealth inequality in the United States from colonial times to the present. The result will show that the Kuznets Hypothesis must be modified.

---

[12]Lenski (1984), Kuznets (1955).
[13]Kuznets (1955:9).

## *The Colonial Era*

The colonial era constituted a preindustrial period and the overall level of wealth inequality remained relatively low. It was greater, however, in colonial cities than in rural areas. For example, as early as 1693, the richest 10 percent of the population owned about 24 percent of the wealth in Chester County, Pennsylvania. This figure rose steadily. A century later, in 1793, the richest 10 percent owned approximately 38 percent of the wealth in Chester County.[14] Wealth appears to have been similarly concentrated in Salem, Boston, and New York.[15] But cities comprised a very small proportion of the total population, less than 10 percent. The vast majority of people lived in rural areas and on the frontier, where conditions were much more equal. Thus, the most reasonable estimate is by Williamson and Lindert in *American Inequality: A Macroeconomic History*.[16] They surmise that in 1774, on the eve of the Revolution, the richest 1 percent of free households owned about 13 percent of the wealth (see Figure 7.1).

## *The Nineteenth Century*

The first half of the nineteenth century is often called the "age of equality" in America. Yet this is the period in which industrialization began in the United States, and it is also a period of sharply increasing inequality. Millionaires appeared. The first was probably Elias Derby, of Salem, Massachusetts, whose wealth reportedly rose above $1 million in the 1790s. If so, the estimated ratio of his assets to the median income at the time is about 4000/1. In 1804, William Bingham of Philadelphia died, leaving an estate of $3 million.[17] Figures for various cities show increasing inequality.[18] In New York City, for example, the richest 4 percent of the city's population owned about 49 percent of the wealth in 1829, rising to 66 percent by 1845. In Brooklyn, a separate city then, the richest 1 percent owned 42 percent of the wealth in 1841; in Boston, the richest 1 percent owned 37 percent of the wealth in 1848. A similar trend occurred in the South, where the richest 10 percent of families held about 72 percent of the wealth in 1830 and 82 percent in 1860. By 1848, the richest man in America was John J. Astor, who was worth about $20,000,000. The estimated ratio of his wealth to the median income at the time is about 50,000/1.[19] Note how much greater this ratio is compared to Elias Derby's. Thus, the first really great fortunes were amassed in the early nineteenth century. This pattern contrasts with Tocqueville's assertion but fits the Kuznets Hypothesis.

Not only did wealth inequality increase during these years, but also most wealth was inherited and very stable over time. For example, on the one hand, economic development provided opportunity, just as Kuznets suggested. John J. Astor, for example, entered this country as a poor immigrant.[20] On the other hand, between 1828 and 1848, 92 to 95 per-

---

[14]Pessen (1971:1019).
[15]Williamson and Lindert (1980).
[16]Williamson and Lindert (1980:38).
[17]Phillips (2002:9, 19, 39).
[18]Pessen (1971:1022; 1973:36, 133).
[19]Phillips (2002:39).
[20]The data are from Pessen (1973:85). The quote is from Pessen (1971:1006). The point about Astor comes from Phillips (2002).

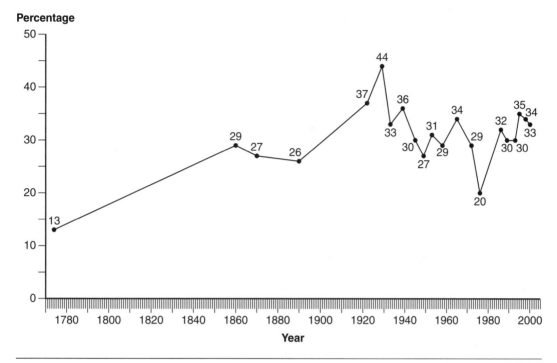

**FIGURE 7.1**   *Share of Personal Wealth Held by Richest 1% of Population, 1774–2001*
*Sources:* Williamson and Lindert (1980:38–39), Wolff (2002:81), Kennickell (2003).

cent of rich persons also had rich parents in the cities of New York, Philadelphia, and Boston. Only 2 percent had poor parents. Thus, even allowing for increased opportunity that accompanies economic development, the dominant pattern was for inherited wealth to be built up to higher levels with each generation. As one historian concluded, "the extent of an individual's early wealth was the major factor determining whether he would be rich later." This conclusion remains true today.[21]

During the second half of the nineteenth century, the economy continued its transformation and the distribution of wealth stabilized at very high levels of inequality. For example, in 1860 the richest 20 percent of the population probably owned more than 90 percent of the wealth in Baltimore, New Orleans, and St. Louis.[22] Data for ten other cities show a similar pattern. As today, the distribution of wealth was skewed. Consider now the richest 1 percent in those same three cities: This small aggregate owned 39 percent of the wealth in Baltimore, 43 percent in New Orleans, and 38 percent in St. Louis.[23] As was typical in the nineteenth century, however, urban areas displayed more inequality than rural or frontier regions. Thus, for the nation as a whole, Williamson and Lindert reported

[21]Allen (1990), Solon (1992).
[22]Gallman (1969). The other ten cities are in Soltow (1975).
[23]Pessen (1973:41).

that in 1870 the richest 1 percent probably owned 27 percent of the nation's wealth and the richest 10 percent owned 70 percent (see Figure 7.1).[24] They concluded that the best interpretation of the pattern to this point in time is that "wealth concentration rose over most of the period 1774–1860, with especially steep increases from the 1820s to the late 1840s. It should also be noted that these two or three decades coincide with early industrial acceleration." By 1890, the richest person in America was William H. Vanderbilt, with a fortune worth about $200,000,000. The estimated ratio of this wealth to the median income at the time is about 370,000/1.[25] Thus, the expansion of wealth inequality over the course of the nineteenth century roughly corresponds to that predicted by the Kuznets Hypothesis.

## *The Twentieth Century*

The extraordinary concentration of wealth reached in the nineteenth century continued to increase in the early years of the twentieth century. The richest 1 percent of all adults owned about 37 percent of the wealth in 1922 and 44 percent in 1929, an all-time high to that point in history. During these years, the richest person in America was John D. Rockefeller, whose wealth totaled more than $1,000,000,000. The estimated ratio to the median income at that time is 800,000/1.[26] Beginning with the Depression, however, wealth inequality declined. The extent of its decline is shown in Figure 7.1, which depicts estimates of the share of the wealth held by the richest 1 percent of the population for selected years over the past two centuries.

In addition to scattered data for the period 1774 through the 1920s, which have been mentioned previously, the figure shows that the years between about 1945 and 1980 displayed the lowest levels of wealth inequality during the twentieth century. Thus, the share of the wealth held by the richest 1 percent of all adults fell to about 27 percent in 1949, rose slightly during the 1950s, and dropped again in the 1960s and 1970s. By 1976, the richest 1 percent of American adults held approximately 20 percent of the total wealth, its lowest point in the century. One indicator of declining inequality during this period lies in the assets of the richest person during this period: In 1962, this distinction fell to J. Paul Getty, whose wealth totaled about $1,000,000,000, more or less the same as John D. Rockefeller's 33 years earlier. More telling, perhaps, the ratio of his wealth to the median income was "only" 138,000/1, a much lower ratio than Rockefeller's.[27] Thus, these years marked a relatively low degree of wealth inequality. Hold this thought, as I will return to it.

As Figure 7.1 reveals, the long-term historical pattern through the 1970s suggests—tentatively—that the Kuznets Hypothesis may be correct. Wealth inequality apparently increased with the onset of accelerated economic growth in the early part of the nineteenth century, remained very high between the Civil War and the Depression, then declined and stabilized at a relatively low level. On this basis, Williamson and Lindert, writing in the

---

[24]Williamson and Lindert (1980:46).
[25]Phillips (2002:39). The richest 1 percent is from Williamson and Lindert (1980:38–39).
[26]The richest 1 percent is from Williamson and Lindert (1980:38–39). Richest person is from Phillips (2002:39).
[27]Phillips (2002:39).

late 1970s, concluded that "the American record thus documents a 'Kuznets inverted U' for wealth inequality."[28] Alas, sometimes conclusions, even tentative ones, do not last long in the social sciences. Figure 7.1 shows that the story does not end in the 1970s.

## The Trend Since 1980

The figure presents data for the 1980s and 1990s revealing sharply increasing wealth inequality. The richest 1 percent now own about 35 percent of the wealth, an amount not seen since the 1920s. As one indicator of this huge increase, the richest person in the United States is now Bill Gates, whose wealth totals about $85,000,000,000. The ratio of his wealth to the median income today is far greater than ever before: 1,416,000/1.[29] Recall that in 1790, the ratio for the first millionaire, Elias Derby was 4,000/1 and that as recently as 1962 the ratio of J. Paul Getty's wealth to the median income was 138,000/1. And Bill Gates is not alone. As shown in Tables 7.1 and 7.3, a relatively small aggregate of about 229,000 households (comprising a few thousand families) now possesses 34 percent of the nation's wealth—approximately $10 trillion ($10,000,000,000,000).

These data show that Kuznets is wrong, or at least partially wrong: Inequality does not necessarily decline with advanced economic development.[30] Rather, modernity—based on industrialization, capitalism, science, democracy, the rule of law, and the culture of capitalism—leads to greater control over all aspects of the environment, physical and social. The level of inequality, whether by wealth, income, or any other measure, is now chosen. This new fact means that the Kuznets Hypothesis must be modified in the following way:

> *Inequality of wealth and income increases during the early phases of economic development, when the transition from preindustrial to industrial society is most rapid, stabilizes for awhile, and then becomes subject to political negotiation.*

It is known, of course, from Lenski's work, that power determines the distribution of surplus in most societies.[31] So the issue will be which classes can influence public policy so as to garner as much wealth and income as possible, ideally without prompting the losers to revolt. This is tricky business. I am arguing in this book that the rich and the middle class dominate the political process—the rich because they have the most money to spend and the middle class because they have the most votes. The data presented in Figure 7.1 suggest that the rich had enormous influence over public policy during the 1980s. They won the auction.

As noted in Chapter 6, during the 1980s so-called "supply side" economic theory was used to justify reducing taxes on the rich on the grounds that the benefits of their investments would "trickle down" to the rest of the population via increased jobs and increased tax revenue. The logic behind the assertion that reducing taxes would increase tax revenues was never clear, at least to me.[32] Even so, the crackpot nature of the argu-

---

[28]Williamson and Lindert (1980:63).
[29]Phillips (2002:39).
[30]Nielsen and Alderson (1997).
[31]Lenski (1984).
[32]Galbraith (1992).

ment was ignored, with the results shown in Figure 7.1. As the modified Kuznets Hypothesis suggests, the present level of wealth inequality in the United States is not inevitable; it reflects the outcome of class conflict.

## Cross-National Variations in Wealth Inequality

Other Western nations display far less wealth inequality than does this country. For example, the richest 1 percent in France possesses 26 percent of the wealth and in Canada 17 percent. The Gini Coefficients for wealth inequality in these nations are correspondingly lower as well.[33] Historical data are available for Sweden and the United Kingdom. In Sweden, the share of the wealth possessed by the top 1 percent steadily declined between 1920 and 1970, from about 40 percent to 17 percent. Since that time, it has risen to about 19 percent, still far lower than in the United States. A similar pattern has occurred in the United Kingdom: The richest 1 percent of the population held 61 percent of the wealth in 1923, far higher than that in the United States at that time—37 percent in 1922 (look back to Figure 7.1). Over the next half century, however, the proportion fell more or less continuously in the United Kingdom—to 23 percent. Table 7.4 takes up the story from that time, comparing the United Kingdom to the United States. As shown in the table, the two nations resembled each other during the 1970s, with the richest 1 percent possessing about one-fifth of the wealth. Since that time, however, the two nations have diverged. In the United States, as is now familiar, wealth inequality increased greatly. In the United Kingdom, by contrast, the richest 1 percent held only 18 percent of the wealth during the 1980s and early 1990s, and then increased it to 22 percent in 2000. In other Western nations, the rich are, indeed, very rich, but the distance between them and the rest of the population is not nearly so great as in the United States.

These differences between the United States and other Western nations have not developed accidentally. Public policies in Sweden, the United Kingdom, and other nations have lead to greater equality in wealth. Class conflict occurs in every nation. Its outcome varies.

## The Origin and Expansion of Wealth

In the United States, most people believe that hard work and ability will produce occupational and, by extrapolation, economic success. From this point of view, the way to wealth is through a process of long-term, self-limiting behavior in which savings and investments accumulate over time. This strategy works, especially for middle-class people who manage their pensions and other investments wisely. Truly great wealth, however, is another matter. There are at least five strategies for wealth creation and expansion, and probably others. I use those described below to illustrate the interplay between the great opportunity that exists in modern societies and the continuing role of inheritance.

---

[33]Wolff (2002:35). The Swedish historical data are from Wolff (2002:32–34).

**TABLE 7.4**  *Share of Wealth Possessed by Richest 1%, United Kingdom and United States*

| Year | United Kingdom | United States |
|------|----------------|---------------|
| 1974 | 23% | — |
| 1975 | — | 20% |
| 1986 | 18% | 32% |
| 1992 | 18% | 30% |
| 1998 | 23% | 34% |
| 2000 | 22% | — |
| 2001 | — | 33% |

*Sources:* Wolff (2002:33), Inland Revenue (2003), Kennickell (2003:21).

The first is windfall profit, which is to say that an asset generates a sudden, extraordinary return on an investment of time or money.[34] In the jargon economists use, the financial markets capitalize an asset at an extraordinary rate of return. In plainer language, a person possesses something the value of which increases exponentially, leading to what economists call capitalization: a high rate of investment. This development can lead to the creation of large fortunes in a very short time. Patient saving and investment have little to do with this process. The great fortunes mentioned earlier—of John J. Astor, John D. Rockefeller, and Bill Gates—all illustrate how, in a modern society, a few persons armed with insight, hard work, and luck can either generate or select an asset in which an extraordinary rate of return is about to be capitalized. The early years of the Apple Computer Company provide another good example. Steven Jobs and Stephen Wozniak produced the first microcomputer in a garage in 1976. A year later, they found a wealthy investor to underwrite their fledgling corporation. When Apple offered stock to the public in 1980, the value of the company suddenly ballooned. Their 37 percent share of Apple stock became worth $630 million, and much more today. Thus, once again, two middle-class men parlayed a certain genius, hard work, and a peculiar asset into great wealth in just a few years.

But windfall profit is a limiting case. The great fortunes of the owner-rich are rarely created in such a short time. Rather, they often take one or more generations to reach their zenith as the family builds its assets. This argument fits with the nineteenth century pattern described earlier: Most of the great fortunes today constitute inherited wealth that has expanded over time.[35]

A second strategy for wealth creation and expansion is to own a small company in a new field that becomes a growth industry and to pass it on to one's family heirs. The Motorola Corporation provides an example. The Galvin brothers founded the predecessor of Motorola in 1928 with an investment of about $1,300. The company became the sole supplier of radios to the fledgling automobile industry, which expanded steadily for over a

---

[34]Thurow (1975:149).
[35]All the examples that follow come from Allen (1990).

half-century. By 1952, the Galvin family (including children and grandchildren) owned only 31 percent of Motorola stock, but it was worth $21 million dollars. The company has continued to prosper, expanding into new areas of electronics, such as cellular phones, and the family's stake is now worth well over $550 million. The Johnson & Johnson Company provides another example. It sells medical equipment, supplies, and drugs to both hospitals and individuals. When Robert Johnson died in 1910, his estate, including shares in Johnson & Johnson was worth "only" about $3 million, still a lot of money in those days. By the time the company went public in 1944, however, that same stock was worth $30 million. By 1971, the 34 percent of Johnson & Johnson stock held by the descendants of Robert Johnson was worth $2.2 billion. It is worth considerably more today. Note that both companies started small but were part of growth industries. Note also that in both cases the family fortunes continued increasing long after the founding entrepreneurs left the scene. Like J. Paul Getty, family members receive incomes of millions of dollars each year based on their assets.

A third strategy for creating and expanding wealth is to own a corporation that radically increases its share of an important market, with the benefit going to family heirs. The Anheuser-Busch Company provides an example. Incorporated in 1875 by Adolphus Busch, it was for many years simply one of several hundred breweries supplying local markets around the country. As recently as 1952, Anheuser-Busch produced only 7 percent of the beer sold in the United States. At that time, the company had a market value of about $100 million, which meant the 50 percent share held by the children and grandchildren of Adolphus Busch was worth "only" about $50 million. Since that time, however, the company has become the dominant brewery in the nation, producing about 37 percent of all beer sold. The Busch family, which now owns only 20 percent of the stock, is worth at least $1.1 billion. Again, wealth expansion continued long after the founder left the scene and family members receive huge yearly incomes based on this asset.

A fourth strategy for wealth creation and expansion is for inventors of new products to establish their own companies, which then grow in value over time—to the benefit, again, of the family heirs. Thus, unlike the inventors of the personal computer (who found a wealthy investor to underwrite their company), Cyrus McCormick developed the mechanical reaper and, along with his brothers, founded McCormick Harvester Machine Company in order to sell it. The company eventually became International Harvester. Similarly, Charles Kettering invented a number of automotive devices, such as the self-starter, and founded Dayton Engineering Company to sell them to auto manufacturers. The company later merged with General Motors. A more recent example is Edwin Land. He founded the Polaroid Corporation in 1937 to sell polarizing filters he had invented. Other inventions followed, such as instant photography. By 1978, the 12 percent of Polaroid stock held by Land and his family was worth over $330 million. In all these cases, the inventors are also entrepreneurs, creating fortunes through their own efforts and passing them on to their descendants.

In most cases, as the examples suggest, the members of rich families watched their wealth grow over many years, benefiting from hard work by others. To use a baseball analogy, these are (mostly) people who are born at third base and think they hit a triple. In saying this, I do not mean to denigrate the importance of hard work and ability in producing success. I do mean, however, to suggest that these characteristics do not distinguish those who become very rich from those who do not. What separates most of those who are extremely wealthy from people in other social classes is, quite simply, luck. Many rich persons work hard, but then so do most people in all social classes. For the rich, however, the result is the possession of political resources (money) that can be used to protect their interests even though their numbers are relatively small.

## Power and Wealth Inequality

Power is difficult to observe, especially with the methods normally used in the social sciences. Its effect can be seen indirectly in terms of who decides what issues are important and the outcome of key decisions. Many issues that roil the public are of little interest to the rich, who are mainly concerned with the preservation of wealth. As a general principle, those classes possessing the most resources want to preserve them and limit the ability of other classes to increase their share. Recall that this argument can be stated formally as the *Political Power Hypothesis:*

> *The higher the social class, the greater the influence over the distribution of resources in the society.*

Tax law provides an important indicator of the ability of the rich to preserve their wealth. Taxes have two purposes. One is to finance government activities that provide for the common good. These tasks include national defense, highway construction, immunization programs, public aid for the poor, disaster relief, harbor dredging, medical insurance, old age support (Social Security), regulation of industries to protect the public (food, water, air), and much more. The other purpose of taxes is to redistribute income. Many people believe that taxes are too high; in fact, the very rich always believe this, no matter at what level they are set. In any case, the real problem is not the size of the tax burden but its distribution.[36] Consider: Taxes can be set so that the rich have enough money left to buy several houses and everyone in the middle and working classes can buy one house. Or taxes can be set so that the rich are left with enough money to buy many houses and large estates while middle- and working-class people cannot buy even one. This relative ability to buy one or many houses is, of course, a metaphorical way of describing people's life chances, their ability to share in the available goods and services. The house metaphor suggests that taxes affect this ability by channeling income up or down the class structure.

This fact results in two dilemmas. First, the political dilemma is who benefits; that is, which class can keep most of its income and wealth. Do not be naïve; fairness is never a choice. For example, cutting back in the Medicare program hurts elderly people; similarly, a tax increase for the top 1 percent makes the rich worse off. The issue is always whose ox will be gored. Even though politicians often use the phrase "tax reform" when describing changes in tax law, this is really a euphemism for making someone else pay. Second, the value dilemma is the common good; that is, should taxes be set so that everyone has plenty or that some have plenty and others not enough? Over the past 30 years or

[36]Barlett and Steele (1994:26).

so, these dilemmas have been resolved to the advantage of the rich, as federal income tax rates declined, especially at the top, and this decline is one (but not the only) reason inequality increased.[37]

Figure 7.2 suggests this result by displaying the top bracket for each year since the income tax was imposed in 1913. Observe that the two periods with low top tax brackets were the 1920s and since about 1980. By contrast, between the years 1945 and 1980 the top bracket was set very high, 70 percent and above. Now look back to Figure 7.1 and recall my suggestion that you "hold this thought." The two periods when wealth inequality has been greatest were during the 1920s and since 1980 or so, and the period with the lowest degree of wealth inequality was between 1945 and 1980. Moreover, recall as well, the cross-national data on wealth mentioned earlier: The United States displays much more wealth inequality than do other Western nations, and these other nations also have significantly higher top brackets than does the United States.[38] These correlations are not accidental.

They are achieved, in part, by establishing only a few brackets and setting the highest at a relatively low income. For example, from 1945 to 1964, there were 24 brackets.[39] The impact of having so many brackets is that people at similar income levels were treated similarly. In contrast, as of 2002, there were only six brackets, as listed below:[40]

| *Income Bracket Tax* | *Rate* |
| --- | --- |
| $0–12,000 | 10% |
| $12,000–46,700 | 15% |
| $46,700–112,850 | 27% |
| $112,850–171,950 | 30% |
| $171,950–307,050 | 35% |
| Over $307,050 | 38.6% |

The impact of having only a few brackets is that people with different economic problems and possibilities are treated as if they are the same.[41] Families with incomes of $46,000 and $112,000 face different economic obstacles. Families with incomes of $171,000 and $307,000 have different abilities to purchase a home and send their children to college. And families with incomes of $307,050, $1 million, $5 million, or $10 million have vastly different lifestyles—and ability to acquire wealth. By the way, the top bracket is scheduled to fall to 35 percent in 2005. The existence of so few tax brackets allows better off individuals and families (the rich) to retain more of their income. The few tax brackets channel income upward, improving the life chances of the rich and creating more inequality.

You should remember, however, that this analysis deals with the top tax brackets rather than effective tax rates—which are lower because of expenditures for deductions

[37]Feenberg and Poterba (1993), Auten and Carroll (1999). For a review of the issues surrounding the relationship between tax structure and inequality, see Slemrod (2000). For a historical overview of tax policy toward the rich, see Brownlee (2000).
[38]Century Foundation (1999:20).
[39]Barlett and Steele (1994).
[40]Tax Policy Center (2003a).
[41]Barlett and Steele (1994).

**Top Tax Bracket (percentage)**

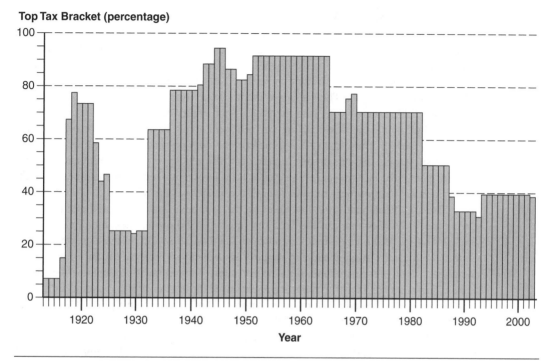

FIGURE 7.2   *Federal Income Tax: Top Bracket Rates, 1913–2002*

*Sources:* U.S. Bureau of the Census (1975:1095), Tax Policy Center (2003).

and exemptions. Even so, the point remains. Although most people benefit from deductions and exclusions that reduce their tax obligations (explained in Chapter 8), the rich benefit the most.

One indicator of how the rich benefit is the number of persons with "adjusted gross incomes" greater than $200,000 who paid no taxes whatsoever in various years:[42]

| Year | Number |
|------|--------|
| 1966 | 155 |
| 1974 | 244 |
| 1980 | 198 |
| 1990 | 1,183 |
| 1999 | 2,525 |

Although this threshold seems low ($200,000 is what the Internal Revenue Service uses to define high-income taxpayers), only the very rich have sufficient deductions to allow them to avoid paying taxes altogether and retain their income. During the 33 years between 1966 and 1999, Congress amended the tax code 30 times.[43] Many of these "re-

[42]Barlett and Steele (1994:40), Balkovic (2002:11).
[43]Century Foundation (1999:4)

forms" reflect the success of various groups that lobby members of the tax-writing committees of Congress to obtain special treatment—against the interests of the majority of the population. The overall effect, once again, has been to increase the ability of the rich to retain their income, which is one factor leading to an increase in wealth inequality.

Another indicator of how the rich benefit from changes in tax law is revealed by the 400 wealthiest taxpayers. Their average income rose from $47 million in 1992 to $174 million in 2000, a nearly four-fold increase in just eight years. The main reason for this huge windfall is that their average tax rate fell from about 29 percent to about 22 percent during this period. These data do not include tax cuts passed since that time.[44] As one observer suggested, tax cuts targeted to the very affluent "give people with plenty of cash to spare even more cash to spare." Yet, as will be shown in a few moments, these tax cuts do not increase employment rates or overall prosperity very much.[45]

The arguments justifying low taxes on the rich have a time-honored quality. Thus, during the 1920s, Secretary of the Treasury (and one of the wealthiest men in the United States) Andrew Mellon asserted that low taxes on the rich would produce greater tax revenue and reduce tax evasion and avoidance.[46] He added that high rates reduce investment, retard economic prosperity, and, besides, constitute a communist plot against the United States. These are precisely the same arguments used during the 1980s, recycled as "supply side" economics. The only difference is that instead of a "communist plot," it was argued that high rates constitute a form of "class warfare" that is somehow unfair. As a United States senator argued a few years ago, there is something "very dangerous taking place in this nation. . . . It is class warfare under the theory of 'let's get the rich guy, the richest 1 percent.' So we set them up, target them; those are the people we are going to get."[47] Of course, members of every class want a bigger piece of the economic pie and describe dieting as unfair; that is the essence of class conflict in a modern society.

The federal income tax only constitutes part of the story about taxes. In general, as the federal income tax has been reduced over the years, especially to benefit the rich, other taxes have been increased to make up at least part of the revenue shortfall. In addition to income taxes, the federal tax system also comprises payroll taxes (for Social Security and Medicare), excise taxes (on gasoline, alcohol, tobacco, and more), the estate tax (on very high-income estates), and corporate income taxes. Under current law, taxes on estates will be eliminated and taxes on corporations are very low. I focus here on the payroll tax, which is higher than the income tax for most households. But the payroll tax is regressive, meaning that lower-income people pay at a much higher rate than do those with higher incomes. Thus, the maximum payroll tax rate for each individual taxpayer who is employed amounts to 7.65 percent on the first $84,900 of income (employers pay a matching amount).[48] So the payroll tax for a middle-class person who earns precisely that amount will be $6,495. In comparison, the person with an income of $1 million will also pay $6,495, a rate of only 0.65 percent. And the few individuals with incomes of $10 million will also pay $6,495, a rate of 0.065 percent. In addition, taxes levied by states, counties,

[44]Internal Revenue Service (2003).
[45]Krugman (2003).
[46]Mellon (1924).
[47]Quoted in Barlett and Steele (1994:93).
[48]Social Security Administration (2003).

and cities are also very regressive and have been raised over the last few years. This fact is illustrated in Table 7.5, which shows the percentage of state and local taxes paid by the poorest 20 percent of the population, the middle 20 percent, and the richest 1 percent. As revealed by the table, state and local taxes take a greater share of income from middle- and low-income families—which lowers the tax burden on the rich. The disparity is even greater in the nine states without an income tax and those states whose income tax is either nominal or regressive.

Taken together, the overall tax structure now bears far more heavily on working- and middle-class people than it did only 30 years ago. Remember, this change reflects deliberate decisions. As the modified Kuznets Hypothesis states, the level of inequality is now subject to political negotiation. The nature of this negotiation was described in Chapter 6: Those who donate money to political campaigns have access to decision-makers, and access means influence. Moreover, donors and legislators come from similar class backgrounds; many personally know their senators and representatives. Finally, decision makers themselves are often wealthy. This is how the rich, as a social class, affect the distribution of resources in the United States.

For many years, people like Andrew Mellon and "supply side" economists have argued that reducing taxes on the rich and shifting more of the burden to the middle and working classes would lead to greater economic prosperity for all, such as higher employment rates and an overall increase in prosperity. Alas, it probably does not, as suggested by Table 7.6, which juxtaposes the average top bracket over three periods during the last half century and average annual productivity growth. In economics, one measure of prosperity is change in the level of **productivity.** The term refers to the percent of the total output of goods and services in private business. The table shows that when tax brackets (and by extrapolation, effective tax rates) are higher, productivity is higher; when brackets are lower, productivity is lower. In considering this relationship, however, you should understand that the table hides a lot of "statistical noise." Prosperity reflects the impact of a great number of factors and varies significantly from year to year, even when taxes remain the same.[49] Even so, the data suggest that the "supply siders" have it exactly backwards; there is an association between high taxes on the rich and the level of economic prosperity—which benefits the entire population.

Instead, we have chosen to allow the rich to retain their income, to have plenty of cash to spare. Their lifestyle is more opulent as a result. It is worth thinking about whether this fact adds to the common good.

## Social Class, Life Chances, and Lifestyle

In 1899, Thorstein Veblen published *The Theory of the Leisure Class,* a satirical look at the attempts by wealthy people in the late nineteenth century to appear sophisticated.[50] They did this by purchasing items that were both expensive and superfluous. In effect, the rich at this time were trying to express (and gain) social status by displaying the extent of

[49]Slemrod and Bakija (2000:96–99).
[50]Veblen (1979).

**TABLE 7.5**    *The Distribution of State and Local Taxes, Two Quintiles and*
*Richest 1%, 2002 (Non-elderly Taxpayers)*

|  | Poorest 20% | Middle 20% | Richest 1% |
|---|---|---|---|
| Average Income in Group | $9,300 | $31,900 | $1,081,000 |
| Sales and Excise Taxes | 7.8% | 5.1% | 1.1% |
| Property Taxes | 3.1 | 2.5 | 1.4 |
| Income Taxes | .6 | 2.3 | 4.8 |
| Deduction from Federal Income Taxes | –0.0 | –0.3 | –2.0 |
| Total | 11.4% | 9.6% | 5.2% |

*Source:* Institute on Taxation and Economic Policy (2003:118).

their wealth. Veblen, a mordant critic, had a gift for descriptive phrases. Thus he portrayed a wealthy class engaged in "conspicuous consumption," "vicarious consumption," "conspicuous leisure," and "conspicuous waste." One of his many examples was the walking stick, a popular affectation in those days. Excluding the infirm, this item is entirely without purpose—for walking. Its function was to demonstrate idleness based on wealth. Hence, walking sticks (as opposed to ordinary canes) were often very ornate. Such forlorn efforts still occur today, especially among the job-rich and people who are new to wealth. They seek out publicity so that the public (middle- and working-class people) will know about their glitzy lifestyle: the collection of expensive automobiles, the $10,000 watches, the appearance at swank clubs—all designed to draw attention to themselves.

In contrast, most of the rich, especially those with truly great wealth, lead "intensely private lives" organized so as to make themselves as invisible as possible.[51] This orientation reflects a desire to elude those searching for money, to enhance their personal security, and to avoid becoming a focus of political attention. The emphasis on privacy means that consumption tends to be inconspicuous.

Privacy combined with wealth brings much more personal autonomy than the rest of the population has. Although they are concerned with many political issues, especially those (such as tax law) that are related to the preservation of their wealth, many of the disputes that vex the public appear less important to the rich. Thus, they tend to be uninvolved in issues like the abortion controversy. A wealthy woman wishing to terminate her pregnancy has always been able to do so, precisely because she possessed economic resources. Since Medicaid money cannot be used to pay for abortions, many poor women do not have a choice: They must bear children. Without medical insurance, many working-class women lack a choice as well (see Chapter 8). More generally, it seems to me, the fight over cultural values (for example, sex, abortion, and drugs) in the United States over the last several decades provided useful political cover for the rich, who were able to increase their wealth without much reaction from ordinary people.

In addition, the combination of privacy and wealth brings luxury that adds to the quality of life, such as larger homes, longer vacations, and amenities that are more pleas-

[51]Allen (1990:2), Stanley and Danko (1996).

**TABLE 7.6**  *Top Tax Brackets and Economic Productivity, 1950–2002*

| Years | Average Top Tax Bracket | Average Annual Productivity Growth |
|---|---|---|
| 1950–1964 | 91% | 3.6% |
| 1965–1981 | 71% | 2.1% |
| 1987–2002 | 37% | 1.9% |

*Note:* Productivity refers to percent of gross domestic product (the total output of goods and services) produced in private business sector.

*Sources:* Tax Policy Center (2003), Bureau of Labor Statistics (2003),

ant. These purchases tend to be designed to ensure their status within the upper class itself rather than to demonstrate it to ordinary (nonrich) people.[52] Hence, rather than purchasing useless items, "the ideal expenditure [today] is one that represents a sound financial investment and that simultaneously enhances the social status and political influence of the family."[53]

Here are several examples. First, a ranch in Montana not only provides a second home for vacations in a pristine location, but also serves as an income-producing asset. Second, an art collection not only demonstrates taste and brings pleasure, it constitutes an investment. This is because the prices paid for original works can multiply in a very short period.[54] Thus, paintings by Chagall increased in value by about 50 times between 1951 and 1969, while those by Picasso increased about 37 times during this same period. This process of price appreciation has continued to the present. The impact can be seen with a hypothetical but plausible example. Suppose you buy a painting for, say, $50,000 and enjoy it for 20 years. Assuming its value increases by 30 times, you then donate it to a museum at its new market price of $1,500,000 (30 × $50,000) and take a tax deduction in that amount. Third, owning racehorses provides a certain cachet while also producing a profit or a tax deductible loss. In all these cases, the search for status combines with a financial investment. According to the tax code, breeding racehorses constitutes a farming business. So, owners can deduct from their taxes the cost of food, housing, employees, insurance, transportation, state and local taxes, interest charges, depreciation (as horses age), stud fees, attending horse shows, and visiting (friends at other) horse farms.[55] Thus, racehorses provide the perfect expenditure in that a rich person's lifestyle is underwritten by the majority of taxpayers.

A similar process occurs with elite education, a topic on which I wish to elaborate because it affects life chances—the share of goods and services people possess. In order to place this issue in perspective, it is useful to recall the literature on mobility and status attainment reviewed in Chapter 5. This research shows that occupational status attainment

[52]Higley (1995).
[53]Allen (1990:248).
[54]Keen (1971).
[55]Barlett & Steele (1994:217).

reflects the impact of ascription and achievement, with the latter having greater impact over time. The dominant image in this literature is of an increasingly meritocratic society in which ability provides the key to occupational success.

This image is consonant with the ideology of middle- and upper-middle-class parents, who see education as an investment in their children's occupational future and, hence, white-collar status. So it appears that much anguish occurs over getting their children into "gifted" programs, into select public high schools, and into good universities. For some, the latter translates into the state-supported Flagship University; for others, the goal is one of the elite private schools, especially in the Ivy League. Because the vehicles for admission are typically test scores and grades, middle-class parents see this process as based on merit. In comparing themselves to the poor and working class, they do not wish to recognize the impact of family background, with its advantages and disadvantages.

The rich are not so myopic. They know the meritocratic image is misleading, that family background is fundamental. In Chapter 5, I used a fictional vignette about the game of Monopoly to illustrate both the reproduction of the class structure as a whole and the existence of the rich, a group whose position in society does not depend on occupation but source of income. Since their children's economic future is assured, education is designed to facilitate their children's entrance into the exclusive social circles of the upper class.[56] This process begins with attendance at one of the elite private prep schools.

The prep school has always served as the means for inculcating upper-class values, preparing students for socially desirable universities (the Ivy League plus a few others), and building networks of friends and acquaintances who will become important in the future for both business and marriage.[57] About 16 of these schools form the elite core; among them are Phillips Exeter Academy, Groton School, Kent School, Deerfield Academy, and Woodberry Forest School. All are located in the northeast. Most are unknown to middle-class people, which constitutes another example of the ability of the rich to keep their lifestyles relatively private.

It should not surprise you that those attending such schools enjoy a decisive advantage over public school applicants in gaining admission to Ivy League universities.[58] This is, of course, a form of affirmative action for the rich, most of whom are white (recall Chapter 3). Unlike public school advisors, college advisors at these prep schools typically have long-standing personal relationships with college admissions officers. During the spring, when decisions are made, prep school college advisors often sit-in on admissions committee meetings. In addition, universities apparently make an effort to recognize applicants from elite prep schools; for example, by color-coding their files. This process means that the public high school student from the Midwest with outstanding credentials who applies to Harvard is sometimes denied admission in favor of an undistinguished prep school applicant. When merit and pedigree clash, the latter often wins.

The result is the reproduction of the class structure over time. For example, graduates of elite prep schools are much more likely than nongraduates to rise in the hierarchy

---

[56]Allen (1990:249).
[57]Baltzell (1958; 1964).
[58]Persell and Cookson (1985).

of Fortune 500 corporations.[59] Of course, as seen earlier, such graduates are also more likely to own or control stock in these corporations. Over the long-run, then, the rich comprise a relatively well-integrated network of people who know one another, marry one another, share similar experiences and values, and—most importantly—have access to resources that allow them to exercise political power.

## *Summary*

Wealth refers to the value of everything a person or family owns, minus its debts. The source of great wealth in the United States is ownership of capital, income-producing assets. This chapter explored some of the implications of this fact. The rich comprise a relatively small proportion of the population, about 7 percent of households—roughly 17.5 million persons. This is a liberal estimate. The reliance of the wealthy on assets is shown by the fact that only 41 percent of the income from tax returns with an adjusted gross income above $1 million comes from wages and salaries; the remainder comes from capital (Table 7.1). The higher the income, the greater the reliance on capital as the source of income.

The concentration of wealth is shown by the fact that the richest 1 percent of families own 34 percent of the nation's wealth. In fact, the richest 1 percent of families in the United States is worth more than the poorest 90 percent (Table 7.2). The rich own most of the bonds, business assets, trust funds, and stock (Table 7.3). The table understates the concentration of wealth because it focuses on individuals rather than families.

The historical trend in the distribution of wealth in the United States shows that the Kuznets Hypothesis of an upside down U must be modified to take into account the huge increase in inequality since 1980 (Figure 7.1). Thus, it appears that wealth and income inequality increase with economic growth, stabilize, and then become subject to political negotiation. Cross-national data show that other Western nations display far less wealth inequality than does the United States (Table 7.4).

Although wealth can result from hard work and thrift, this characteristic does not distinguish the truly rich from those not so fortunate. Rather, most rich people inherited their wealth. It is created or expanded by means of windfall profit, owning a small company in a growing industry, owning a company that increases its market share, or developing a new product and founding a company to market it. Other strategies probably exist.

Increasing inequality reflects the power of the rich, especially their ability to obtain reduced taxes while shifting the burden to middle- and working-class people (Figure 7.2). This change was justified by asserting that low taxes on the rich would produce greater tax revenue, encourage economic prosperity, and prevent a form of "class warfare" against the rich. Over the last few decades, the tax burden has been shifted from the rich to the remainder of the population (Table 7.5). Whether the common good is served by low taxes on the rich can be questioned, especially since economic prosperity seems to be related to high taxes on the rich (Table 7.6).

[59]Persell and Cookson (1985).

Finally, with some exceptions, the lifestyle of the rich reflects an attempt at preserving privacy. In this context, wealth allows for personal autonomy and considerable luxury. In expressing their lifestyle, most people with a lot of money try to combine social status with sound financial investments. These can range from second homes that are working ranches to art that appreciates in value. Education in elite prep schools provides a vehicle for both preserving the lifestyle of the rich and access to power.

# 8

# *The Middle Class*

The middle class has not always existed. The essence of middle-class life is to do nonmanual labor. Persons in white-collar jobs usually sit at desks, nearly always stay physically clean while they work, often supervise others, sometimes engage in entrepreneurial activity, and frequently have high incomes. More polemically, they do not "bend, lift, scrub, shovel, haul, or engage in other potentially damaging exertions for a living."[1] They join fitness clubs instead. But the rise of a class of people who need physical activity as a respite from work is new in history.

In colonial times, the structure of stratification did not include a large segment of the population who could survive and prosper doing nonmanual labor. Nearly everyone worked with their hands; most plowed the land using their own muscles as the energy source. A few people, however, were anomalies—pointing to the future. For example, in *Paul Revere's Ride,* the historian David Hackett Fischer observed that Revere saw himself as both an artisan (a silversmith) and a gentleman—without any sense of contradiction.[2] As a gentleman, he was part of the political elite of Massachusetts. He was not the

---

[1]Ehrenreich (1990:233).
[2]Fischer (1994).

loner described in the myth of "Paul Revere's Ride." Rather, he organized and directed resistance to the British in the Boston area during the 1770s. The ability of such a man to rise to the top suggests that the stratification structure was simple. Indeed, all societies before industrialization can be divided into two main classes: a small ruling class and the great mass of people.[3] Colonial America was no different; the vast majority of people farmed small plots of land while an elite group of large landowners and entrepreneurs dominated the new society. The colonial stratification structure was unique in history, however, because it was relatively open, which meant that exceptional individuals like Revere could rise to the top and plausibly claim to be "gentlemen." But he worked with his hands. Indeed, Fischer shows that Revere was one of the finest silversmiths in the colonies. He was an artist. Today, the combination of artisanship and elite membership is unlikely; few silversmiths get elected to Congress or belong to the clubs of the rich. Revere's position was significant historically and sociologically because he was part of a very small group of "middling sorts," people who were highly skilled, relatively autonomous, earned a cash income, and on that basis had sufficient leisure time to be able to participate in the political life of the community.

Over the years, as Max Weber recognized, the stratification structure became more complex and these "middling sorts" eventually turned into what we now call the middle class. What happened, of course (as you should recall from Chapter 5), is that economic development during the nineteenth century led to the creation of more and more white-collar jobs, which resulted in a great deal of upward mobility. People in these new occupations began being paid by salaries instead of hourly wages, and the spatial separation of blue- and white-collar jobs occurred because the latter worked at desks in offices.[4] In this context, a unique **lifestyle** gradually developed that set the nascent middle class off from the working class. You should recall that the term refers to people's way of living as indicated by their consumption habits, use of leisure time, and fundamental choices and values. Thus, the greater income of the middle class allowed for larger homes equipped with amenities and filled with more elaborate furnishings. Patterns of housing segregation by class developed and those doing white-collar work tended to live in one place for many years, indicating that their jobs were stable. For example, in Boston during 1840 to 1850, only 36 percent of unskilled manual workers remained residentially stable for the entire decade, compared to 69 percent of white-collar workers.[5] Although the emerging middle class was very small, its stability meant that people with similar characteristics began associating with one another—in neighborhoods, churches, clubs, and the like. They began keeping their children in school and even sending them to college. Young people with similar backgrounds and experiences began marrying one another. This pattern continued with economic expansion over the decades and the middle class developed a historically unique lifestyle, one that still exists today. As these similarities became clear, the middle class crystallized as a more-or-less self-aware aggregate around the turn of the twentieth century.

Yet, surprisingly, intellectuals often disparage middle-class people because they are presumably unaware of their true political interests. C. Wright Mills, for example, pro-

---

[3]Marx and Engels (1848), Lenski (1984).
[4]Blumin (1989).
[5]Archer and Blau (1993).

vided one of the most provocative accounts in *White Collar*.[6] Mills contrasted the "old middle class" of the nineteenth century, which he characterized (inaccurately) as independent, self-employed, and self-sufficient, with the "new middle class" of the present, which he depicted (also inaccurately) as mere employees who are politically impotent and alienated. In sociology, remember, the term **alienation** refers to people who feel powerless, so much so that dominant norms and values seem remote. While any book by Mills contains more interesting ideas than most sociological treatises, this one is fundamentally flawed by the fact that he has an intellectual's dislike for the "little people" who constitute his subject. They do not share his interest in ideas, his definition of freedom, or his fantasies about nineteenth-century life. It is true that most middle-class people today are employees; for Mills, this fact indicates that they are essentially proletarians, such as those Marx described, and Mills condemned them as a result. Erik Olin Wright continued this tradition in *Classes*.[7] He argued that middle-class people occupy a "contradictory class location," meaning that they do not own capital yet have authority over working-class people—at least on the job. The implication is, once again, that middle-class people are really proletarians, like the working class, who do (or should, if they were more self-aware) feel alienated.

Most middle-class people do not share either Mills's or Wright's vision of what they ought to be like. Middle-class people define themselves as representing what is best about the United States: hard work, frugality, economic and occupational success, and individual autonomy. These attitudes seem—to them—to be characteristic of this country, to be uniquely middle class. Thus, as shown in Chapter 2, the class identification question reveals that most people with white-collar jobs say they are middle class, and, along with the rich, they dominate the political process in the United States. In the case of the middle class, they do so as voters. And they are perfectly aware of their interests. They want "perks" to go along with their jobs—medical insurance, pensions, and the like—and they want a decent income to follow from their labor. As a result, their life chances, while not as great as those of the rich, are nonetheless very good.

## Social Class and Job Perquisites

**Job perquisites** (the jargon term for the more common "perks") consist of any protections, privileges, or benefits tied to one's employment status. They have a long history. For example, a 1913 Bureau of Labor Statistics study described 50 companies that provided employees with such perquisites as on-site eating facilities, pension plans, paid vacations, and the like.[8] Although such benefits were the exception then, they are common now. Today, the list of potential perquisites includes such benefits as holidays, disability insurance, on-site child care, parental leave, free parking (very important in large cities), college tuition for children, and much more. In addition to these sorts of "perks," many companies provide upper echelon employees with rather special benefits, such as expense

[6]Mills (1951).
[7]Wright (1997).
[8]Mitchell (1992).

accounts, use of company-owned cars, membership in private clubs, entertainment, and stock options. Often called "fringe benefits," job perquisites are not fringe at all; rather, they are fundamental aspects of remuneration and constitute an important element in the structure of stratification in the United States, significantly affecting people's life chances. Indeed, they are so central to middle-class people that they cannot envision being without these benefits and privileges; they act politically to protect them and ignore the fact that members of other classes often go without them.

Despite Mills's and Wright's arguments, the pervasiveness of job perquisites reflects the power of middle-class people, who obtain a greater share of the distribution of resources than do the working class and the poor. Yet the importance of perquisites is not salient to many observers, partly because they are difficult to measure and partly because they are so taken for granted. My argument is that people with higher-prestige jobs and higher incomes generally have the best protections, privileges, and benefits, as expressed by the *Job Perquisite Hypothesis:*

> *The higher the social class, the greater the job perquisites.*

Although the hypothesis is probably accurate, I do not describe the relationship as an empirical generalization because measurement problems exist and the research literature omits certain topics. For example, while considerable work has been done on the job perquisites available to ordinary workers, there is very little social scientific research on the additional perquisites enjoyed by top-level executives. Hence, the most conservative strategy is to pose a hypothesis and present what data do exist. The job perquisites reviewed in the following paragraphs are typical of those available in private industry.

### Paid Time-Off Benefits

Many employees—but not all—are paid for certain amounts of time even though they are not required to be at work, such as holidays and vacations. **Holidays,** for example, are days of special significance—for religious, patriotic, or cultural reasons—for which many employees receive time-off with pay. Typical paid holidays are New Year's Day, Memorial Day, Independence Day, Thanksgiving Day, Christmas Day, and some others. Moreover, when a holiday falls on the weekend, a compensatory day off is sometimes scheduled on Friday or Monday. Table 8.1 shows that a higher proportion of professional and technical workers (higher-prestige white-collar jobs) have more paid holidays than any other aggregate. A lower proportion of clerical and sales workers enjoy holidays off, as do a still lower proportion of blue-collar workers. In addition, not shown in the table, white-collar workers usually have more paid holidays than do blue-collar workers. Also not shown in the table, the people at the bottom, low-paid hourly workers, often do not get paid holidays. When the business shuts down for Christmas or New Year's Day, they are out of luck.

Similarly, nearly all professional and technical workers in private industry receive paid vacation time, while significantly fewer blue-collar workers enjoy this benefit. For those eligible, this perquisite usually begins after a certain length of service. For example, among large- and medium-size firms, professionals and technical workers obtain about 16

**TABLE 8.1**   *Percent of Workers with Access to Employee Benefits, by Occupational Category, Private Industry, 2000*

| | Paid Time-Off | | Employee Benefit Medical | | | | Cash & Family | | Pension | |
| --- | --- | --- | --- | --- | --- | --- | --- | --- | --- | --- |
| *Occupational Category* | *Holidays* | *Vacation* | *Medical Insurance* | *Short-Term Disability* | *Long-Term Disability* | *Long-Term Care Insurance* | *Severance Pay* | *Child Care* | *Defined Benefit* | *Defined Contribution* |
| Professional and Technical | 84 | 87 | 63 | 49 | 50 | 14 | 35 | 11 | 26 | 52 |
| Clerical and Sales | 80 | 80 | 50 | 32 | 27 | 7 | 24 | 5 | 18 | 40 |
| All Blue Collar | 72 | 77 | 47 | 27 | 14 | 4 | 12 | 2 | 17 | 26 |

*Source:* U.S. Department of Labor (2003:4–5).

days vacation after 5 years of service while blue-collar employees get 12 days or less.[9] The pattern for smaller companies is similar. Moreover, as above, white-collar workers tend to receive longer vacations compared to blue-collar workers.

It should be emphasized that the data on paid time-off understates class differences because very few white-collar workers punch time clocks, which means their working hours are less regulated. Even among the lowest-prestige white-collar workers, informal norms often develop that allow for daily and situation-specific variations in established schedules. White-collar workers, in short, are much more capable of coming and going— as long as their work gets done. In any case, the benefit of more paid time-off goes disproportionately to middle-class people, who see it as an occupational right.

The data in the first section of Table 8.1 conform to the Job Perquisite Hypothesis. You should note that this pattern is invariant across the rows of the table: Those at the top of the prestige hierarchy receive more "fringe benefits" and their life chances improve as a result.

## Medical Benefits

**Medical insurance** pays for treatment when people become sick or injured. The earliest known coverage for medical treatment in this country occurred in 1798, with the establishment of the U.S. Marine Hospital Services.[10] Under this plan, seamen had deductions taken from their salaries in order to pay for hospital services. Several mining, lumber, and railroad companies in the Far West developed insurance plans in the 1870s and 1880s. They set up clinics and prepaid doctors to provide their employees with medical services. But, overall, very few people had medical insurance coverage in this country at the turn of the twentieth century. A movement advocating some form of nationwide medical insurance developed during those years, partly because most European nations had already enacted such plans. It was opposed in this country, however, by unions (which thought they would be weakened), physicians (who assumed their salaries would be lower), and private insurance companies (which wanted to retain a lucrative business for themselves).[11] This movement failed. Legislation mandating nationwide health insurance also failed in 1994.

This failure means that for most people today, about 71 percent of the population, medical insurance is tied to employment. Another 14 percent of the population obtains insurance via a government program unconnected to employment, most often Medicaid (which serves the poor). By arithmetic, then, about 15 percent of all Americans, 41 million people, have no insurance coverage.[12] This means they cannot get medical treatment when the need arises. By contrast, in other Western nations, everyone is covered by medical insurance; it is viewed as a right of citizenship. As a result, everyone has better life chances in these nations.

Among those with medical insurance, their plans typically cover hospitalization, surgery, and treatment in a physician's office—although the way this process occurs var-

---

[9]U.S. Department of Labor (1998:7).
[10]Scofea (1994).
[11]Scofea (1994).
[12]U.S. Bureau of the Census (2002c:3).

ies considerably. Some plans, especially those held by middle-class persons, provide more complete coverage than others. People become eligible to participate in these plans when they are hired and for as long as they continue employment with the sponsoring company. Companies frequently pay half or sometimes more of the cost of medical insurance for employees, thereby helping them to pay lower income taxes. The remainder—paid by employees—will often come out of pretax income, which means they do not pay taxes on that portion of their wages or salaries. (These savings are called tax expenditures, explained later on.) People who are laid off, fired, or quit for any reason lose insurance benefits—just when they are most needed.

Medical insurance coverage varies by social class. For example, as shown in Table 8.1, 63 percent of professional and technical employees in private industry have coverage, compared to 50 percent of clerical and sales, and 47 percent of all blue-collar employees. The problem is especially serious among low-income earners: Almost a quarter of those earning less than $25,000, 23 percent, have no coverage.[13]

These data illustrate that individuals not participating in employer-based group medical insurance plans are disproportionately working class and poor, and nearly all of them do not participate because they cannot. Their employers do not give them a choice. Although Medicaid presumably aids poor persons without other means of obtaining medical treatment, Chapter 10 will show that coverage is inconsistent and a significant proportion of the poor are not eligible. Middle class people, however, do not suffer from these problems and, hence, are relatively unconcerned.

**Short-term disability** (often called "sick leave") refers to protection against income loss for short periods of physical incapacity, usually providing full pay for several weeks. As shown in Table 8.1, the percentage of employees with this employer-paid benefit varies by social class. About half of professional and technical workers, 49 percent, can stay at home and still get paid if they get the flu. Or, let's say, they have to undergo minor surgery; they can stay home and recuperate—and still get paid. In contrast, 73 percent of blue-collar workers (100 – 27 percent in the table) have a stark choice: work and get paid, or stay home and do not get paid. Moreover, among those with short-term disability, the number of days people can receive their wages varies by occupation. In general, higher-prestige employees can stay home sick for more days than lower-prestige employees.[14] Put differently, middle class people, who are least likely to become sick or hurt, are most likely to have sick leave benefits and, when this perquisite is available, have more days in which to recuperate.

**Long-term disability insurance** constitutes protection against income loss from long periods of physical incapacity. Thus, given coverage, long-term disability payments can be combined with Social Security disability, workman's compensation, and other government benefits such that total compensation provides a relatively high proportion of full pay for an extended period of time.

The first long-term disability insurance policy was probably written in Massachusetts in 1850. For a premium of fifteen cents, a policy holder would be paid $200 in case of injury due to a railway or steamboat accident—a lot of money in those days.[15] The

[13]U.S. Bureau of the Census (2002c:3).
[14]U.S. Department of Labor (1997; 1998).
[15]Scofea (1994).

nation's first group health policy was long-term disability insurance purchased by Montgomery Ward and Co. for its employees in 1910. It provided benefits up to half of an employee's weekly salary. Benefits today are somewhat greater but participation in employer paid long-term disability plans varies by occupation, as revealed in Table 8.1. About half of professional and technical workers in private industry have employer-paid long-term disability plans, compared to 27 percent of clerical and sales staff and only 14 percent of blue-collar workers. Those working for companies not offering disability insurance must pay for it themselves, something middle-class people find easier to do, since they earn more than their working-class counterparts to begin with. Many of the latter simply go without, even though their jobs are more dangerous and more likely to lead to serious injury (and even death, see Chapter 9).

**Long-term care insurance** covers some or all of the cost associated with nursing home care, home care, or adult day care for aged persons.[16] These benefits are usually initiated when an insured person or an insured spouse can no longer perform several activities of daily living, such as dressing, eating, bathing, going to the toilet, or taking medicines. The cost of living in a nursing home or some other facility can range from $36,000 to well over $100,000 per year, not amounts most families can finance by themselves. Neither Medicare nor its supplemental insurance covers long-term custodial care. The odds of needing such care rise with age. For example, only about 1 percent of those aged 65 reside in nursing homes, a figure that increases to 18 percent by age 85.[17] The necessity for other forms of care rises in a similar way. The implications can be bleak: In the Star Trek movies, Mr. Spock often closed conversations by saying "live long and prosper." In today's world, in which many people live into advanced old age, a more accurate comment might be "live too long and face financial ruin."

In order to avoid this fate, people increasingly purchase long-term care insurance, at rates ranging from $500 to $2,000 per year or (much) more, depending on the age of the insured, whether a spouse is covered, and the extent of coverage desired. Given their income (described later in this chapter), white-collar people are better able to afford these rates. A lucky few, however, obtain long-term care insurance for themselves and sometimes their spouses as a perquisite of their employment. As shown in Table 8.1, about 14 percent of professional and technical employees in private industry enjoy this benefit, compared to only 7 percent of clerical and sales, and 4 percent of blue-collar workers. People's life chances in old age are decisively affected by their possession of long-term care insurance.

### Cash and Family Benefits

Some perquisites come in the form of cash payments. **Severance pay** is a lump sum or installment payment to employees who have been fired, laid off, or for some other reason separated from the company. Among top-level people at major corporations, these sums can be very high—millions of dollars. For most employees, however, this payment is equivalent to several months' salary or wages. As shown in Table 8.1, about 35 percent of

---

[16]Katt (1997).
[17]U.S. Bureau of the Census (2001d:7).

professional and technical employees are entitled to severance pay, compared to 24 percent of clerical and sales and only 12 percent of blue-collar workers.

Other perquisites are designed to help employees and their families by paying for various obligations. In addition to saving employees money, these perquisites reduce their tax bill as well. One example is **child care,** which fully or partially subsidizes the cost of caring for employees' children in a nursery or day care center, or by a sitter. Such care is important not only for preschool children, but for after school care as well. As shown in Table 8.1, about 11 percent of professional and technical workers in private industry receive this benefit, compared to 5 percent of clerical and sales workers, and only 2 percent of blue-collar workers. Those who do not receive this benefit must either pay for child care out of pocket (in after tax dollars), leave their children at home alone after school, or one parent must remain at home. Any of these choices affects the life chances of employees and their families.

### Pension Benefits

**Pensions** constitute earnings deferred until retirement. Pensions were unnecessary until recently because so few people lived into old age. In 1890, for example, only 4 percent of the population was over age 65. But that figure was an all-time high and apparently triggered the discovery of "old age" as a social problem and the need for pensions.[18] Thus, in 1903 Edward Everett Hale (himself more than 80 years old at the time) published an article titled "Old Age Pensions" in *Cosmopolitan* magazine. He proposed that workers contribute $2.00 per year to a pension fund until they were 69, after which they would receive an annuity of $100 for the remainder of their lives.[19] This principle—contributions during people's working years (either by the employer, employee, or both) and yearly payments after retirement—remains the basis of all pension plans.

Although the principle remains the same, pension plans today can be divided into two types: defined benefit and defined contribution. Defined benefit plans provide participants with annuities equal to a percentage of employees' preretirement earnings, usually calculated based on years of service to a company. An annuity is a monthly income. Under defined contribution plans, usually both the employer and employees contribute a percentage of employees' wages to a pension fund each month, with the eventual benefits after retirement dependent on the employees' ability to manage their money. Participation in such plans is important, as people live longer now and the proportion of the population over age 65 has increased to 13 percent today. This figure will rise to 20 percent or (probably) more during the next century.[20] Today, about 44 percent of all workers participate in employer or union-sponsored retirement plans in addition to Social Security.[21] This relatively low level of participation means that only about a third of all persons over age 65 actually receives a pension (from any source—private or public) in addition to Social Security.[22] Aged persons living only on Social Security benefits endure a very restricted lifestyle.

[18]U.S. Bureau of the Census (1975:15), Fischer (1978).
[19]Hale (1903).
[20]U.S. Bureau of the Census (2002c:15).
[21]U.S. Bureau of the Census (2002c:350).
[22]U.S. Bureau of the Census (2002c:342).

Participation in an employer-funded private pension plan varies by occupation, as shown in Table 8.1. About 26 percent of professional and technical employees in private industry participate in defined benefit plans, compared to 18 percent of clerical and sales, and only 17 percent of blue-collar employees. About 52 percent of professional and technical employees participate in defined contribution plans, compared to 40 percent of clerical and sales, and only 26 percent of blue-collar employees. Thus, regardless of the size or type of plan, blue-collar workers are least likely to participate in pension plans. This is so even though the law requires that if a pension plan is offered to some employees it must be offered to all. Companies find all sorts of ways around this requirement. These data are important because they mean that pension benefits and, hence, lifestyle after retirement reflect the preretirement class structure.

In sum, it appears that the Job Perquisite Hypothesis accurately summarizes the relationship between social class and employee fringe benefits. And these benefits not only make life easier and more pleasant, but also improve people's life chances. Paid time-off in the form of holidays and vacations allow those who have them to maintain their lifestyle while they refresh themselves through leisure. Medical insurance means that sickness or injury does not represent a financial catastrophe. Short- and long-term disability insurance allows people the time they need to recover from ill-health without loss of income. Long-term care insurance means that aged people do not have to spend down their assets in order to qualify for nursing home care paid for by Medicaid. Severance pay tides people over between jobs. Child care benefits reduce the daily expenses that families face. And pensions mean that people who have worked for many years can have a pleasant retirement. All these benefits accrue mainly to the middle class, and especially for those in higher-prestige and higher-income white-collar jobs. They are not "fringe benefits"; those who have them possess a greater share of the resources available in the United States. This fact suggests that middle-class people have a greater ability to protect their economic situation and lifestyle than do working-class or poor people. They possess a greater share of the resources in U.S. society.

The advantages enjoyed by middle-class people and the way job perquisites increase inequality can be illustrated by the experience of Mary Mendez, a 40-year-old single mother.[23] She sorts apples in a packinghouse in Wenatchee, Washington, for $8.00 per hour. After a minor injury at work forced her to stay home for a few days to recover, her employer simply did not pay her for the time off. It is hard to imagine such harshness toward white-collar employees. Moreover, although the firm she works for offers medical insurance to employees, it does not cover other family members. Ms. Mendez, therefore, must spend $21 per month out of pocket to cover her child. She does this on a budget that is only slightly above the poverty line. By cross-national contrast, the state takes care of all pension, medical, and disability needs in most Western European nations, which means that class differences are minimal. Hence, the millions of European citizens in jobs like that held by Mary Mendez have much more economic security than she does. As a result, these nations display less inequality. But this fact is irrelevant to most middle-class people in the United States because they have all the job perquisites they need. So they do not demand the development of government programs that might provide such benefits

---

[23]Passell (1998).

for everyone. Hence, those working-class and poor people who remain without adequate income protection are politically isolated and ineffective. Compared to the middle class, they lack power, especially (as shown in Chapter 6) voting power.

C. Wright Mills argued that white-collar people are politically impotent and alienated. Yet those who are powerless should not be able to garner for themselves more paid time off, better medical insurance, more cash and family benefits, and better pensions. Moreover, these differences in perquisites indicate that middle-class employees have greater control over their lives, both on and off the job, than do working-class employees. So perhaps white-collar people are not as alienated as Mills and others suggested.

## *Top-Level Perquisites*

The job perquisites available to middle-class people, however, are far less than those enjoyed by those at the top of the class structure. Although top-level people in private industry are paid a great deal of money, sometimes millions of dollars, companies believe that high salaries alone are not enough to recruit and retain them. "Perks" are the thing. After all, many of them are tax free to the recipients.

People in upper management receive essentially the same holidays and vacations as others, although the length of the latter may be longer. They also get additional leisure time amenities.[24] Examples of a few of them are country club memberships (such as at Augusta National Golf Club, for example, site of the Master's Tournament), memberships in private clubs (such as the Union League in Philadelphia and similar organizations in other cities), and access to sky boxes and season tickets to sporting events. As an example of the latter, someone gets to sit at courtside at National Basketball Association games, such as those played by the Los Angeles Lakers or the New York Knicks. Ordinary people, in contrast, watch the games on television, the leisure time amenity of the middle and working classes.

The medical benefits available to top-level executives are juiced-up versions of those offered to ordinary employees.[25] Their medical insurance, for example, may have no deductibles, no co-payments, no yearly dollar limits. Their yearly physicals may be paid for by the company. Even when they are insured, middle- and working-class people pay for these things out of pocket. The disability insurance offered to top-level executives may contain higher benefit levels and be written more restrictively so that policy holders would not have to take a lower-paying job, even if qualified. Their long-term care insurance premiums may be paid for life, with more expensive benefits guaranteed.

Cash and family benefits, however, are what really distinguish top-level people from the middle class.[26] To begin with, many companies provide amenities that save top executives significant amounts of money, regardless of how well the company performs. Housing subsidies, expense accounts, and personal use of company cars and airplanes are some common examples. Private dining rooms, and laundry and dry cleaning facilities, and financial planning services are some others. These "perks" go tax free to top-level people; everyone else pays for them out of pocket.

[24]Yaqub (1999).
[25]Yaqub (1999).
[26]Yaqub (1999), Useem (2003).

Companies also protect top executives' jobs and salaries. Recall from Table 8.1 that about 35 percent of professional and technical employees receive severance pay, typically equal to a few months' salary. The severance package for top-level people is often called the "golden parachute" (in the jargon, a "change of control agreement"). If the company changes hands and an executive is forced out, she or he may receive a package worth millions of dollars, along with what is called "gross-ups," which is additional money to cover the cost of excess taxes stemming from such large lump-sum payments.

Finally, companies add to top executives' compensation with stock options, guaranteed bonuses, and no-interest loans (often forgiven). Stock options can bring a huge financial windfall.[27] Although many white-collar employees also receive stock options, most companies reserve nearly all of them for top executives. A stock option gives the holder the right, but not the obligation, to purchase a certain number of shares of a company at a fixed price (called the "exercise price") over a specified time. The exercise price usually equals the stock price at the time the option is granted. The profit can run to millions of dollars, as illustrated with the following example. Let us say the Widget Corporation grants its CEO 50,000 stock options, which can be exercised any time after one year but before ten years from the date of granting. Let us also say the stock price on the day of granting is $50, so the cost of 50,000 shares would be $2.5 million at that time. Finally, assume that the stock goes up in value by exactly 10 percent a year (this keeps the arithmetic simple). In the tenth year, the stock price will be $100 and the cost of 50,000 shares would be $5 million. The executive then takes (or borrows) $2.5 million and exercises his options and buys 50,000 shares of the Widget Corporation at the exercise price of $50. This is so even though it is currently selling at $100. The result is a windfall of $2.5 million. Although simple, the amounts in this example are not extreme. In order to offer these options, many firms simply issue new shares of stock—thereby diluting the value of all the other outstanding shares, such as the 200 owned by a middle-class person in a retirement account. But stocks do not always go up in value or do not go up very much. In such cases, companies have been known to lower the exercise price retroactively. Ordinary middle-class people do not get many stock options and, when they do, the exercise price remains unchanged regardless of the direction of the stock price.

In addition to ordinary pensions, companies offer top-level executives Supplemental Executive Retirement Plans (SERPS) designed to insure that their huge incomes continue after they withdraw from the workforce.[28] In fact, use of SERPS is increasing, even though an estimated 40 percent of large companies either have or are considering reducing pension benefits for rank-and-file employees. The advantage of SERPS is that, unlike the pension plans available to middle- and working-class people, there are no upper limits on contributions. Moreover, executives are eligible for these pension plans, often amounting to millions of dollars per year, immediately on employment. Companies simply credit a newly hired Chief Executive Officer with 20 or 25 years service. They then place the money in trust funds so that top executives get them even if the company goes bankrupt in the meantime. Such protection is not available to ordinary workers.

As mentioned in Chapter 6, the political game is rigged in the United States, and the structure of stratification reflects this fact. The structure of elections means that the

---

[27]Financial Markets Center (2000).

[28]Yaqub (1999), Fryer (1999), Revell (2003).

middle class dominates the electoral process. They appear to accept the huge share of the distribution of resources (life chances) going to the rich as the price of their own contentment: The middle class obtains a lesser share, but what they do obtain remains very good—much more than that which goes to the working class.[29]

# Social Class, Income Inequality, and Income Transfers

The job "perks" discussed above, while very important, are not the same as a pay check. Income makes a lifestyle possible and it is lifestyle (as will become clear) that separates the middle class from the working class.

## Social Class and Income

The top row of Table 8.2 reveals that the median income for people working full-time all year long was $38,300 for males and $29,200 for females in 2001. As it turns out, the median highlights class differences, since most white-collar workers earn more than the median while most blue-collar workers earn less. Thus, the average male white-collar worker, an administrator of some sort or a professional worker, earns well over the median (for men), about $57,000 or so per year. Similarly, the average female professional also earns well over the median (for women), about $40,000. Among men, the only white-collar job category in which people do not earn more than the median is administrative support. Among women, those in technical, sales, and administrative support usually do not earn above average wages. Even so, most people in white-collar jobs find that their work pays off, not only in pleasure and prestige, but monetarily as well. In contrast, individuals in blue-collar jobs nearly always earn less than the median. The typical male machine operator earns about $29,700 each year, not much to live on, even with a spouse who is, say, a secretary. The only exception to this pattern is male precision production workers (such as skilled electricians, probably union members) who earn about $35,200 on average. More generally, however, as one looks down the table, each occupational category includes a higher proportion of jobs with lower prestige and income. So work pays off for these people, but barely.

The income distribution shown in Table 8.2 reveals the importance of both spouses in maintaining family lifestyle—even though the table reveals that women earn less than men in every occupational category (recall Chapter 3). It is an empirical generalization that husbands and wives tend to be from the same social class; that is, white-collar men usually marry white-collar women, and blue-collar men marry blue-collar women.[30] The most prevalent cross-class marriage pattern is for blue collar men to marry women in administrative support jobs.

This finding of class homogeneity can be used to suggest the implications family income has for class differences in lifestyle. For example, assume that a male physician is married to a female lawyer. Although not shown in the table, their incomes would usually

[29]Galbraith (1992).
[30]Eshleman (1994).

TABLE 8.2   *Median Income by Occupation and Gender, 2001*

| Occupation | Male | Female |
|---|---|---|
| **All Workers** | **$38,300** | **$29,200** |
| **White Collar** | | |
| Executives and Managers | 57,300 | 40,300 |
| Professional Specialty | 57,600 | 40,900 |
| Technicians | 40,500 | 26,600 |
| Sales | 41,900 | 25,700 |
| Administrative Support | 33,000 | 26,400 |
| **Blue Collar** | | |
| Precision Production | 35,200 | 26,000 |
| Machine Operators | 29,700 | 20,800 |
| Transportation | 32,000 | 23,400 |
| Handlers and Laborers | 30,200 | 27,300 |
| Service | 25,000 | 17,700 |
| Farming, Forestry, and Fishing | 21,000 | 13,600 |

*Note:* Data are for year-round, full-time workers.

*Source:* U.S. Bureau of the Census (2002a).

be above the average for professional workers. Let us assume for a moment that the physician earns $200,000 and the lawyer $150,000. These plausible figures mean that their total income of $350,000 makes them rich—statistically, at least. In identification, however, they would undoubtedly see themselves as upper-middle class. A few years ago they were called "Yuppies," young urban professionals, with unflattering connotations. In comparison, assume that a female nurse marries a male high school teacher. Again, both are professional workers. She earns, let us say, $50,000 per year, and he $45,000. Their combined income of $95,000 makes them solidly middle class and they would undoubtedly identify as such. But their lifestyle is much restricted compared to the physician-lawyer couple. Finally, consider a male police officer married to a female secretary. Police officers are service workers, and they usually earn above the average for that category. Let's assume he earns $35,000 per year, and she earns $30,000. Their combined income of $65,000 requires a more restricted lifestyle. That is to say: These three couples live in different neighborhoods, shop in different stores, take different vacations, and usually send their children to different colleges (although working-class youth are less likely to attend college). Such variations suggest what it means to be upper-middle, middle, and working class in the United States. All these people have been buffeted, although in different ways, by changes in the distribution of income over the past half-century.

## Trends in Income Inequality

Whether the United States has become more unequal over time is a controversial topic, and not just among academics. During the quarter century after World War II, real incomes (adjusted for inflation) rose among all social classes.[31] Hence, most people were better off and could afford an improved lifestyle. For example, rates of home ownership among Whites expanded significantly during this period. But the degree of income inequality remained more or less unchanged during these years. Since about 1970, however, income inequality (like wealth inequality) has increased significantly.

***Income Inequality, 1950–1970.***     Two alternative hypotheses describe income inequality during the years after World War II until about 1970: the Inequality Reduction Hypothesis and the Inequality Stability Hypothesis. The *Inequality Reduction Hypothesis* states that

> *The lower the social class, the greater the benefit from income transfers and the lower the level of inequality from 1950–1970.*

The term **income transfers** in the hypothesis refers to government spending that provides money or benefits to individuals without obtaining goods or services in exchange, which means there is no increase in the gross domestic product (GDP). Thus, an income transfer occurs whenever money or an in-kind benefit, such as medical treatment, is simply given to recipients by the government with no expectation of receiving goods or services in return. Beginning in the mid-1930s, the federal government developed a variety of programs providing economic benefits to various segments of the population. Some of the most well-known assist the poor and the aged. Welfare programs are especially salient to the public and appear (the word is important) to reduce income inequality. After all, cash programs like Temporary Assistance to Needy Families (or its precursor, Aid for Families with Dependent Children) provide income, while noncash programs like Medicaid and Food Stamps provide economically valuable resources.[32] Other programs, such as Social Security and Medicare, target the aged. Social Security does reduce income inequality among the aged. So the Inequality Reduction Hypothesis sounds like common sense.

It turns out, however, that the hypothesis suffers from three problems. First, the literature supporting it fails to include all cash income transfers to various population groups.[33] One example would be the omission of the impact of farm price supports, which go mainly to the largest and richest farmers.[34] Farm price supports are income transfers from the government to farmers that make up the differences between the selling price of a crop and an arbitrary target price. Second, this argument assumes that public assistance reduces poverty, ignoring the fact that recipients must remain poor in order to continue receiving benefits and that the cash they spend ends up going into the pockets of middle-class people (see Figure 10.3). The different impact of such programs as Temporary Assistance to Needy Families and Social Security reflects the means test that characterizes the former but not the latter. Thus, precisely because it has no means test (that is, it does not require that recipients remain poor), the Social Security program reduces inequality

---

[31]Levy and Murnane (1992), Ryscavage (1999).
[32]Danziger et al. (1981).
[33]Danziger et al. (1981), Danziger and Plotnick (1977).
[34]United States Department of Agriculture (1998:40).

among the aged. Third, the Inequality Reduction Hypothesis flies in the face of theoretical understanding. Gerhard Lenski, remember, found that power has determined the distribution of resources over most of human history.[35] Now theory can be refuted by evidence, of course, but those proposing the Inequality Reduction Hypothesis fail to address the issue. In sum, despite the redistributive effect of Social Security, the Inequality Reduction Hypothesis does not explain the facts.

Rather, the best explanation of the pattern of income inequality between World War II and about 1970 is the *Inequality Stability Hypothesis:*

> *The higher the social class, then the greater the benefit from income transfers such that the overall distribution of income remained unchanged from 1950–1970.*

Table 8.3 illustrates the Inequality Stability Hypothesis in two ways. Please look first at Panel A for the years 1950–1970. These data show that the income distribution among households was relatively stable during this period. The poorest 20 percent of households received about 5 percent of the total income, the second 20 percent about 12 percent, the third about 18 percent, the fourth about 24 percent, and the richest fifth about 41 percent. The top 5 percent of households (included in the "richest fifth") received about 15 percent of the total income. Now look at the Gini Coefficients displayed in Panel B for the years 1950–1970. You should recall that the Gini Coefficient is an index that measures the degree of income inequality. It varies between zero and 100, with a score of zero meaning that all incomes are equal and a score of 100 meaning that one household receives all the income in a society. Again, the data show that income inequality was rather stable (it actually declined in 1960) during this period.

The reason for this stability lies in the impact of income transfers. The pattern shown in the left portion of Panels A and B is plausible because "income" includes cash received from virtually any source: not just earnings, but also unemployment and workers' compensation, Social Security and veterans' benefits, public aid, survivor and disability benefits, educational assistance, alimony and child support payments, and all other periodic cash income. Thus the impact of income transfers is included in the data. Moreover, the Inequality Stability Hypothesis makes sense theoretically, of course, because in most societies the more powerful classes make sure they obtain their "fair" share of the benefits from such programs. "Fair," of course, is defined as "more." Recall here the pie metaphor used earlier: Classes always want a bigger piece of the pie; some are more successful than others.

Several studies have shown that the pattern displayed in Table 8.3 for the years 1950–1970 is accurate. One investigation looked at the impact of governmental tax and spending policies in 1950, 1961, and 1970 and included a wide array of income transfers plus some that clearly go to middle-class persons, such as "farm income" (apparently price supports) and "housing expenditures" (apparently housing subsidies). In addition, the authors also took into account governmental outlays for such public goods as "auto expenditures" (apparently roads), "estimated expenditure on higher education," and "children under age 18" (apparently public school outlays). The term **public goods** refers to government expenditures for goods and services that, presumably, anyone can take ad-

---

[35]Lenski (1984).

**TABLE 8.3**  *Income Inequality among Households, 1950–2001*

|  | *1950* | *1960* | *1970* | *1980* | *1990* | *2000* | *2001* |
|---|---|---|---|---|---|---|---|
| **Panel A: Percentage of Income Received by Each Quintile and Top 5%** | | | | | | | |
| Poorest Fifth | 5% | 5% | 5% | 5% | 4% | 4% | 4 |
| Second Fifth | 12 | 12 | 12 | 12 | 10 | 9 | 9 |
| Third Fifth | 17 | 18 | 18 | 18 | 16 | 15 | 15 |
| Fourth Fifth | 23 | 24 | 24 | 24 | 24 | 23 | 23 |
| Richest Fifth | 43 | 41 | 41 | 42 | 47 | 50 | 50 |
|  | 100% | 100% | 100% | 101% | 101% | 101% | 101% |
| Richest 5% | 16% | 16% | 16% | 15% | 18% | 22% | 22% |
| **Panel B: Gini Coefficient of Income Inequality** | | | | | | | |
|  | 38 | 36 | 39 | 40 | 43 | 46 | 46 |

*Note:* Totals of 101% represent rounding error.

*Source:* U.S. Bureau of the Census (2002:19).

vantage of or use, such as lighthouses or airports. The finding of these authors is that the distribution of income after governmental taxing and spending decisions was unchanged between 1950 and 1970.[36]

Another analyst came to a similar conclusion after looking at the impact of government spending on a wide range of public goods, such as expenditures for national defense, science and technology, the administration of justice, government operations, energy, the environment, community and regional development, revenue sharing, and interest on the national debt. "Over time, greatly increased government activity has not led to more income equality. There is little indication that the United States government has done much net redistributing of income."[37]

Finally, in *American Inequality: A Macroeconomic History,* Williamson and Lindert examined income inequality in the decades after World War II and came to an unequivocal conclusion.[38]

> By almost any yardstick inequality has changed little since the 1940s. . . . The data that yield this conclusion differ greatly from one another. Several series are available: the Statistics of Income reported by the Internal Revenue Service, the Survey of Consumer Finances, the Census Bureau's Current Population Survey, the income distributions of the Social Security Administration, and the benchmark consumer surveys of the Bureau of Labor Statistics. . . . One would expect such diversity to produce a variety in the estimates, but in fact none of the inequality measures exhibits any dramatic trend.

[36]Reynolds and Smolensky (1977).
[37]Page (1983:144).
[38]Williamson and Lindert (1980:92).

So for the period between World War II and 1970, income inequality remained rather stable. Although income transfers to impoverished people became politically salient during these years as more programs benefiting the poor came into existence, the overall impact of transfers was to preserve the status quo. Two final points: First, I have made this discussion somewhat longer than it had to be in order to emphasize, once again, the importance of hypothesis testing in the social sciences. We proceed, very imperfectly, by conjecture and refutation, to get at truth. Second, I would like to remind you of Max Weber's aphorism cited in Chapter 1: The social sciences are granted eternal youth. The reason is that findings vary over time (and across societies). Thus, beginning around 1970 the pattern of income inequality changed.

***Income Inequality Since 1970.***    This change was not fate. It did not "just happen." It reflects, rather, the impact of human decisions on the structure of stratification. Please look at Panel A of Table 8.3 for the years 1980–2001. Data for this more recent period show that the income distribution became more unequal as the bottom quintiles began receiving less income and the richest fifth (and top 5 percent) began receiving more. Although the differences in percentage may not seem like much, the samples are so large that even small changes are significant. Just how significant can be seen by looking at the Gini Coefficients in Panel B. Note that the Gini rose steadily from 1970 to 2000, which means the United States became steadily more unequal. Moreover, these data provide a practical measure of how much better the lifestyle at the top is today compared to a few years ago: The increase in household income inequality between 1960 and 2000, as measured by the Gini, was 28 percent.

The reasons for this change are complex and illusive. Among the explanations are the following:[39] First, the Baby Boomer generation graduated from college in precisely these years and, hence, the supply of people looking for white-collar jobs increased. Salaries fell as a result, especially for the middle class. Second, the demand for people in blue-collar jobs fell with the decline of high-paying jobs in manufacturing industries and the rise of low-paying jobs in service industries. Third, the impact of so-called supply-side economic policies adopted during this period redistributed income to the rich. With regard to this last item, I want to suggest how certain elements of income tax policy contribute to income inequality.

### Tax Expenditures and Income Inequality

Taxes are the source of income for government—but all governments use tax policy to influence behavior; that is, they enact spending programs via tax policies that stimulate some activities rather than others and profit some citizens rather than others. So it follows that individuals and groups compete to see who can benefit from such programs. The result affects the level of income inequality.

The name for such programs is **tax expenditures.** They constitute the least well known type of income transfer. The term refers to provisions of the tax code that provide special or selective reductions in taxes for certain groups of citizens and corporations,

[39]Levy and Murnane (1992), Ryscavage (1999:109–30).

thus increasing their income. Tax expenditures are "analogous to direct outlay programs." As such, the two are "considered as alternative means of accomplishing similar budget policy objectives."[40] For example, if the goal is to insure that the population has adequate housing, one way to do this is to provide cash assistance or vouchers to people, as is done for some poor persons. Another, more or less equivalent, way is to allow middle-class people to deduct or exclude from their taxes certain aspects of the cost of obtaining housing. In addition, of course, such housing programs also stimulate the economy and thereby provide people with jobs. Thus, both direct budget outlays and tax expenditures cost money and often serve similar goals. For such reasons, the cost of tax expenditures is routinely included in calculations of the federal budget.

On a more cynical level, members of Congress who belong to the Joint Committee on Taxation (a plum assignment) see tax expenditures as a vehicle for enhancing their influence. They can enact spending programs by creating pockets of privilege within the tax code.[41] The advantage of such programs is that they receive far less scrutiny during enactment than do direct budget outlays. Perhaps this is why a corporation that pays for season tickets to professional baseball games for its top-level employees can deduct their cost as a business expense, while parents who take their children to the same games cannot. One wonders if this type of program would be passed if it had to be justified to voters.

Table 8.4 displays the most significant tax expenditures by budget category. Individuals received about $748 billion in benefits during fiscal year 2003, many of which went to middle-class and rich people. The table has a (rough) orderliness to it. The items at the top (#1-8) refer to the value of some of the job perquisites discussed earlier, such as pensions ($108 billion), medical insurance ($75 billion), life and disability insurance ($2 billion), transportation ($4 billion), and child care ($1 billion). Of course, most of the remaining tax expenditures also benefit the middle class and rich. The exceptions are items #29–30 at the bottom of the table, which go mainly to the poor. I have selected two examples from the table to illustrate how these programs work. In considering them, remember that the issue is not whether these and other governmental spending programs are good or bad, wise or unwise; the issue is how such programs benefit the middle class compared to the working class and poor.

**1.** The deductibility of mortgage interest on owner-occupied homes (item #13) provided individuals with $70 billion in fiscal year 2003, more than twice the $32 billion spent on Housing Assistance for the poor.[42] What these benefits mean on an individual level is that a middle-class family in the 27 percent tax bracket which paid $20,000 in mortgage interest in that year received a $5,400 income transfer from the government. This amount is more than a poor family receiving cash via the Temporary Assistance to Needy Families program (see Chapter 10). Moreover, the mortgage interest deduction is supplemented by other benefits to homeowners. For example, items #14–17 in the table provide an additional $87 billion to individuals. Again, most of them increase the incomes of middle-class people. These programs are not means tested. Individuals qualify for them

---

[40]Joint Committee on Taxation (2002:2). See also Beeghley and Dwyer (1989).
[41]Brownlee (2000).
[42]U.S. Bureau of the Census (2002c:307).

**TABLE 8.4**    *Tax Expenditures by Budget Category, Fiscal Year 2003*

| Individuals | Program Cost (in billions) |
|---|---|
| **Selected Employment Fringe Benefit Programs** | |
| 1.  Exclusion of employer provided pension contributions | $107.6 |
| 2.  Exclusion of employer contributions for medical insurance | 75.1 |
| 3.  Exclusion of employer provided life & disability insurance | 2.4 |
| 4.  Exclusion of employer provided transportation (cars, limousines) | 3.7 |
| 5.  Exclusion of employer provided group term life insurance | 2.4 |
| 6.  Exclusion of employer provided child care | 0.8 |
| 7.  Exclusion of various other employer provided fringe benefits | 22.6 |
| 8.  Exclusion of investment income on employer provided life insurance & annuities | 24.2 |
| **Selected Investment Programs** | |
| 9.  Reduced rates on long-term capital gains | 57.4 |
| 10.  Exclusion of capital gains at death | 40.1 |
| 11.  Exclusion of interest on state & local bonds | 3.5 |
| 12.  Exclusion of interest on state & local debt | 15.8 |
| **Other Programs** | |
| 13.  Deductibility of mortgage interest on home | 69.8 |
| 14.  Deductibility of state & local property tax on home | 22.1 |
| 15.  Exclusion of capital gains on home sales | 13.8 |
| 16.  Deductibility of state & local income & property taxes | 46.3 |
| 17.  Other housing programs | 4.9 |
| 18.  Deductibility of charitable contributions | 32.9 |
| 19.  Credit for child care expenses | 3.1 |
| 20.  Tax credit for children less than age 17 | 26.9 |
| 21.  Deductibility of medical expenses | 6.0 |
| 22.  Deductibility of long-term care expenses | 6.0 |
| 23.  Exclusion of untaxed Medicare benefits | 29.1 |
| 24.  Other medical exclusions & deductions | 12.8 |
| 25.  Exclusion of worker compensation benefits | 5.6 |
| 26.  Exclusion of Social Security benefits | 23.5 |
| 27.  Exclusion of veterans benefits | 2.6 |
| 28.  Credit for Elderly, Disabled, & Blind | 2.3 |
| 29.  Exclusion of Public Assistance Benefits | 0.7 |
| 30.  Earned Income Tax Credit | 35.0 |
| 31.  All Other | 49.2 |
| **Total Individual Programs** | **$747.8** |
| **Total Corporate Programs** | **94.6** |
| **Grand Total** | **$842.4** |

*Note:* Some program categories have been combined for ease of presentation. Fiscal year 2003 begins on July 1, 2002.

*Source:* Joint Committee on Taxation (2002:20–28).

merely by having sufficient income to purchase a house and make their mortgage payments—but these programs provide people with real cash to spend on whatever they want.

**2.** The exclusion of employer contributions for medical insurance premiums (item #2) provided individuals with $75 billion in fiscal year 2003, not counting the benefits of various other medical exclusions shown in the table. What this program means for middle-class people can be illustrated with a simple example from my own medical insurance plan (many of your parents have similar plans). My yearly premium for family coverage is $7,918, of which the University of Florida pays $6,106 (77 percent) and I pay $1,812. Thus, because of the exclusion of employer contributions, I receive an income transfer of $1,649, assuming a 27 percent tax bracket (27 percent of $6,106). In addition, because my share of the payment is taken out of pre-tax income I also receive an additional $489 income transfer (27 percent of $1,812). The reason for this result is that if an employer pays the total premium directly to its employees (in my case $7,918), who then use it to purchase medical insurance, they will have to pay taxes on the income. While the amounts will vary, those who have medical insurance as a job perquisite have a great deal more money to spend each year as a result. Again, this is real cash that can be used to take a vacation cruise or for anything else they desire. Medicaid benefits to the poor constitute an analogous program. As will be pointed out in Chapter 10, however, since the poor do not have extra money to begin with, those who do not receive Medicaid benefits simply go without medical treatment. As before, the exclusion of employer contributions for medical insurance is not means tested; one member of a family must merely have a job with a group insurance plan.

Table 8.5 illustrates the way tax expenditures distribute benefits across social class by examining six programs. The data are arrayed according to adjusted gross income. The table shows that most of the benefits of the earned income tax credit go to those with low incomes. Although Social Security benefits are spread throughout the class structure, most go to people in the middle income brackets. Finally, the ability to deduct mortgage interest payments, state and local property taxes, and charitable contributions mainly provides benefits to relatively high-income people. You should remember that "adjusted gross income" as used in the table is not people's total income; rather it is income for tax purposes, after various deductions. The pattern in the table is meant to be instructive: As one looks from left to right, from column (2) to (7), the benefit of tax expenditure programs go increasingly to middle-class and rich people. I mentioned earlier that job perquisites exaggerate income inequality. Tax expenditures constitute one way this process occurs. Middle-class and rich people have more money to spend on the good things in life.

A final note: Tables 8.4 and 8.5 do not take into account the benefits individuals receive from public goods purchased by the federal government. While public goods are presumably for everyone, they actually provide benefits for specific groups. For example, everyone can take advantage of harbor dredging, drawbridge erection, lighthouse construction, and buoy maintenance financed by the federal government so long as they own a sailboat. This amenity, of course, is mainly reserved for upper-middle class and rich people. People with lower incomes are much less likely to take advantage of it. Similarly, everyone can use the government-financed commercial and general aviation facilities at airports so long as they are rich enough to fly commercially, own a private plane, or use corporate aircraft. Again, these amenities are primarily reserved for middle-class and rich

TABLE 8.5 *Distribution of Selected Tax Expenditures by Adjusted Gross Income, Fiscal Year, 2003*

| (1) Adjusted Gross Income | (2) Exclusion of Earned Income Tax Credit | (3) Deductibility of Medical Payments | (4) Exclusion of Social Security | (5) Deductibility of Mortgage Interest | (6) Deductibility of State and Local Property Taxes | (7) Deductibility of Charitable Contributions |
|---|---|---|---|---|---|---|
| < $10,000 | 19% | 0% | 0% | 0% | 0% | 0% |
| $10,000–20,000 | 46 | 4 | 4 | 0 | 0 | 0 |
| $20,000–30,000 | 27 | 6 | 14 | 1 | 0 | 1 |
| $30,000–40,000 | 6 | 8 | 20 | 2 | 1 | 2 |
| $40,000–50,000 | 1 | 12 | 20 | 3 | 1 | 3 |
| $50,000–75,000 | 0 | 24 | 33 | 12 | 6 | 10 |
| $75,000–100,000 | 0 | 18 | 5 | 19 | 11 | 12 |
| $100,000–200,000 | 0 | 17 | 3 | 37 | 26 | 22 |
| > $200,000 | 0 | 11 | 1 | 26 | 55 | 50 |
| | 99% | 100% | 100% | 100% | 100% | 100% |

*Note:* Some totals do not add to 100% because of rounding. Fiscal year 2003 begins on July 1, 2002.

*Source:* Joint Committee on Taxation (2002:30–34).

people. About half of the federal budget goes for such public goods—for example, internal affairs, science and technology, natural resources, commerce, community development, education, the administration of justice, general government, fiscal assistance, and interest on the national debt. These general categories include hundreds of programs. Although one could question whether such public goods are income transfers, many economists treat them as such.[43] Thus, the impact of spending on public goods amplifies that of tax expenditures specifically and income transfers generally.

## Income Inequality and Economic Prosperity

I mentioned earlier that in the years after World War II most people's real incomes rose, especially among Whites, even after taking inflation into account. So economic prosperity meant that they became better off, even though the level of inequality remained unchanged during that period. In the years between 1970 and the present, however, the level of inequality increased, with most of the benefit going to the rich and middle class—in that order. As mentioned earlier, part of this increase reflected the entry of the well-educated Baby Boomer generation onto the job market at a time when the economy was being transformed such that demand for blue-collar skills declined and demand for white-collar skills increased. But, in addition, part of this increase reflected political decisions about the nature and extent of income transfer programs—as illustrated by tax expenditures.

An important question is whether the two processes, income inequality and economic prosperity, are related to one another and, if so, how. Considered metaphorically, think of economic prosperity as a pie and the degree of income inequality as the proportion of the pie going to each social class. If the pie gets bigger and each class is getting the same size slice, then everyone is better off. If the pie stays the same size, but one social class gets a larger slice, then a few people are better off and most others worse off. If the pie gets bigger and one class also gets a bigger slice, it gets most of the benefit of the increase in size while the share of everyone else remains the same. The empirical issue is whether and to what degree income inequality leads to greater economic prosperity, as indicated by investment and worker productivity.

The usual hypothesis is *the greater the income inequality, the greater the economic prosperity in economically developed societies*. In the customary interpretation, "any insistence on carving the pie into equal slices would shrink the size of the pie. That fact poses the trade-off between economic inequality and efficiency," another word for greater investment and worker productivity.[44] The logic underlying this interpretation is that greater inequality increases investment and work incentives, thus leading to an expanding gross domestic product—the size of the pie increases—and everyone prospers at their own level. This argument is, of course, a variation on supply side economics. It also allows those who benefit the most to claim that their riches are good for the society as a whole, an argument that should remind you of the Davis-Moore thesis described in Chapter 1. There is a self-serving quality to this analysis that ought to arouse suspicions.

[43]Page (1983), Reynolds and Smolensky (1977).
[44]Okun (1975:48).

The hypothesis can be tested, and the empirical answer is mixed. For example, one study suggests, indeed, that nations in which the level of inequality increased during the 1990s (such as the United States, United Kingdom, and Japan) also experienced a greater increase in the gross domestic product. During this same period, however, nations in which the level of inequality did not increase so much or actually decreased (such as Germany, France, Canada, and Italy), experienced a slightly less increase in the GDP but—and this is important—most of the benefit went to working- and middle-class people.[45] In another study, covering the years 1974–1990, the results refuted the hypothesis: (1) Greater income inequality corresponded to lower levels of investment. (2) Variations in income inequality were not related to differences in worker effort and productivity. The author concluded that the hypothesized trade-off between income inequality and economic performance has little credence in advanced industrialized nations.[46] Interpreting these results requires some care. My guess is that a very high level of equality would, in fact, lower investment and worker productivity. But no Western nation displays this profile. At the opposite end, it can be argued that a very high level of inequality can be detrimental to economic performance over the long term by reducing consumer demand and reducing motivation on the part of those left behind. In any case, in modern societies, decision makers have a lot of room to maneuver such that inequality can be reasonably low and economic prosperity can be reasonably robust. And the distribution of benefits from the latter reflects the distribution of power in a society.

## Power and Income Inequality

The benefits of income transfers, whether as budget outlays or tax expenditures, are legislatively enacted. Politics, the process of producing legislation in a democracy, is a competitive process in which the most powerful usually receive the most benefits. This is why laws rarely constitute the "best" solution to problems; rather, they reflect compromises among competing groups. So despite the public salience of transfers to the poor, the overall impact of transfers was to maintain income inequality for many years (1950–1970) and increase it since then.

This increase constitutes one of the great social experiments of our time. It was justified by "supply side" economic theory, which argued that placing more money in the hands of the rich through reduced taxes would ultimately benefit everyone. This is because the rich invest (or supply) money, creating jobs and (presumably) increased tax revenues. Hence, the result of making the rich richer would "trickle down" to the rest of the population. Note what went on here: The majority of the population gave money to the upper-middle class and rich on the grounds that everyone would benefit. Regardless of your opinion about this experiment (mine is that we got snookered), these data imply a simple fact described in Chapter 1: Modern societies determine how much inequality exists, how much poverty exists, and the forms they take. Other Western societies, such as Sweden and England, display a more equal distribution of income than does the United States. In addition, poverty in these other nations is significantly less. The social structure in each case reflects these choices.

[45]Burtless (2001).
[46]Kenworthy (1995).

Once again: Although C. Wright Mills and others claimed that middle-class people are politically impotent and alienated, the evidence suggests otherwise. Rather, as theory predicts, middle-class people appear to have sufficient political power to insure that they obtain the highest proportion of income transfers. Moreover, earlier sections of this chapter showed that middle-class people possess higher incomes and more job perquisites than do working-class people. The enjoyment of these benefits implies, therefore, that middle-class people are very much in control of their lives; they are not alienated. Their lifestyles are better as a result.

## Social Class, Life Chances, and Lifestyle

The majority of the American population today is middle class. Its members not only survive, but also prosper doing nonmanual labor. Their **life chances** are pretty good. The term, you should recall, refers to people's share in the distribution of the resources available in the society, their share of the pie. Although the middle class possesses considerably less than the rich, what they do have is very good; it is considerably greater than that of the working class or poor. And the lifestyle that follows is, if not unique, also much better than that of the working class and the poor. **Lifestyle** is often taken to refer to the stuff people surround themselves with, such as houses, cars, and other amenities that one can purchase, and to the way in which people amuse themselves, such as their modes of entertainment or avocation. These issues do indeed provide important indicators of social class, but lifestyle also refers to how people organize their lives at home. For example, prior to World War II, it was common for middle-class families to employ working-class women as servants, mainly nannies, cooks, and maids.[47] Over time, however, they have been, as the new saying goes, outsourced. The nanny now works for the day care center, often without job perquisites. The cook now works at McDonalds or one of the food delivery outfits—again, without benefits. And the maid now works for a janitorial or cleaning service—without perks. When middle-class families do employ a housekeeper, the impression one gets is that many (most?) cheat her out of Social Security benefits. Think of it as a small way of keeping a bigger piece of the economic pie. Lifestyle and stratification are inherently connected.

This connection is also revealed in terms of people's moral choices, another aspect of lifestyle. Put bluntly: Middle-class families cannot maintain their lifestyle if they cannot control their fertility.

Some background is necessary. As it developed during the nineteenth century, the middle class acquired some peculiar values regarding family life and gender roles that distinguished it from the working class. As the economy was being transformed, working-class families continued to need the income generated by children and wives. In an urban environment, children in the working class often brought in 30 to 40 percent of the total family income.[48] Hence, even though both parents may have been employed, many families' survival depended on their children's earnings. It is important to understand that I am referring to the wages of young people, aged six to fourteen years. Historically, such indi-

---

[47]Palmer (1989).
[48]Zelizer (1994:58).

viduals had always labored on the farm. (They continued doing so in the late nineteenth century.) Urban living did not change this condition for working-class women and children. Thus, families in this situation continued the age-old practice of having many children.

The nascent middle class, however, found itself in a different situation and, hence, developed different interests. Upwardly mobile, often working in occupations that had not existed previously, by the second half of the nineteenth century, husbands were earning a "family wage"; that is, they could support their wives and children without them having to work for pay. As always, most housework remained labor intensive and it was asserted that women, often with the help of servants from the working class, ought to take primary responsibility for it. In this context, middle-class people began wanting smaller families and the birth rate declined as a result. Thus, for every 1,000 white women of childbearing age, the birth rate fell from 275 in 1800 to 131 in 1900, with much of this reduction occurring among the middle class.[49] In this context, child rearing became central to the middle-class lifestyle, and norms about appropriate levels of care and attention became stricter. Childhood became a distinct stage of life, and women, it was said, ought to be the primary caretakers of children because men had to earn a living and lacked nurturing instincts. (This was, of course, an ideological stance.) Men's and women's roles, at least in the middle class at this time, became rather narrowly defined. It was during this period that what we now call **traditional gender norms** emerged. As described in Chapter 3, these rules specified that women and men ought to have separate spheres: Women should bear and raise children and take care of their husbands while men should provide for the family economically and dominate public life. Such norms grew widespread in the middle class during the latter part of the nineteenth century. They extended to the working class later.

But these norms became unstable over time. The reduction in the birth rate referred to above was achieved by use of birth control (condoms, douches) and abortion.[50] The rising incidence of abortion among middle-class women ignited the first abortion controversy during the latter years of the nineteenth century.[51] As a result, restrictions on access to abortion were enacted in every state around the turn of the century. They served as a legal buttress to traditional gender norms, since the inability to regulate fertility kept women, especially middle-class women, from pursuing occupations requiring long training or cumulative expertise. This is because pregnancy could occur at any time, changing the direction of a woman's life. The situation remained this way for many years. Eventually, however, gender norms began changing—albeit mainly in the middle class. One (not the only) expression of these changing norms was the desire to regulate fertility. That goal meant, in turn, access to birth control and, if necessary, to an abortion. Thus, the second abortion controversy developed in the 1960s and continues today. Although the ability to control fertility is an issue affecting all women (and all couples) regardless of social class, middle-class people—especially women—have always been predominant among activists favoring abortion rights. They have interests to protect.

[49]U.S. Bureau of the Census (1975:49).
[50]Sanderson (1979).
[51]Luker (1984), Reagan (1997).

But abortion is a moral issue. All discussions of this topic revolve around the question of whether the developing embryo is a person or a potential person. If it is assumed to be a person, a baby, it follows that abortion can never be morally right because it is murder. In contrast, if the developing embryo is assumed to be a potential person, a fetus, then abortion can be morally justified and the issue becomes women's right to control their fertility. You should observe that each moral stance reflects an unverifiable assumption about the nature of developing life. This suggests that an underlying social division exists.

Some perspective on this division can be obtained by looking at data. Here are cross-national rates of abortion per 1,000 women aged 15 to 44 during the mid-1990s:[52]

| United States | 23 |
| Sweden | 19 |
| United Kingdom | 12 |
| France | 12 |
| Germany | 8 |
| Netherlands | 7 |

Abortion is legal in each of these nations. In each, it is relatively unregulated early in the pregnancy with increasing restrictions over time. These data suggest that a solution exists to the "abortion problem," that we do not have to live with such a high rate. That solution is contraception. The low rate of abortion in other nations reflects an emphasis on preventing pregnancy. It is probable that encouraging contraceptive use in the United States would reduce the level of abortions by half or more, a result that would make our rate similar to that in Western European nations.[53]

In general, whenever relatively obvious solutions are rejected, you can be sure that hidden social divisions exist. In this case, the debate about abortion is not only about moral values, but also—and perhaps more importantly—about the nature of the family and the centrality of motherhood in women's lives. It is, in short, about lifestyle. Those on each side of the abortion debate in the United States want to live in different worlds.

In a sense, they do live in different worlds, framed by their social class. Abortion is often seen as a cornerstone of the feminist movement, a movement dominated by middle-class white women acting in their interests. There is some truth to this assertion. Phrased simply, restrictions on the possibility of abortion are taken by many (not all) middle-class people as a threat to their economic interests and lifestyles. At the same time, as mentioned earlier, abortion is a moral dilemma. Most people try (albeit imperfectly) to live by their values. In this regard, most people find themselves in the middle—supporting women's right to an abortion with some ambivalence.[54] Yet, as it turns out, people's moral positions often fit with their economic interests. So it is with abortion. This is because the conflict over abortion is one aspect of the larger conflict over fertility control and the nature of the family. These are, to some degree, class struggles. Needless ones?

---

[52]Henshaw et al. (1999).
[53]Westoff (1988), Marston and Cleland (2003).
[54]Beeghley (1996).

## *Summary*

The middle class originated in the nineteenth century as the number of white-collar jobs increased, people in these jobs began being paid by salaries, and blue- and white-collar jobs became spatially separated. As a result, middle-class people developed a unique lifestyle: They became residentially stable, lived near one another, and interacted with one another. By the end of the nineteenth century, the middle class had coalesced into a more-or-less self-aware aggregate. Following from theory, the Political Power Hypothesis asserts that that the middle class and the rich have greater influence over the distribution of resources than the other social classes.

The Job Perquisite Hypothesis specifies that middle-class people receive much more from such job perquisites as paid time-off benefits, medical benefits, cash and family benefits, and pension benefits (Table 8.1). Perquisites to top-level people are even greater, especially severance packages and stock options. Job perquisites add to the level of inequality in the United States, making middle-class and rich persons unwilling to demand government programs to provide such benefits to everyone. They illustrate the ability of middle-class people to influence the distribution of resources.

People in white-collar jobs nearly always earn more than those in blue-collar jobs (Table 8.2). Although the Inequality Reduction Hypothesis states that income transfers reduced income inequality between 1950 and 1970, this argument appears to be wrong. Rather, the Inequality Stability Hypothesis better explains the facts. That is, income transfers served to maintain the level of inequality for many years (Table 8.3). Since 1970, however, income inequality has risen, primarily because of (1) the increased supply of white-collar workers as the Baby Boom generation matured and (2) the reduced demand as a result of so-called "supply side" economics. Tax expenditures are provisions of the tax code that allow reductions in taxes for selective groups of citizens and corporations. They constitute an important, if relatively unknown, form of income transfers. Tax expenditure programs are analogous to direct outlay programs, often attempting to achieve similar goals, such as providing housing or medical insurance for the population. Examining the array of tax expenditures by budget category suggests that some programs exist to benefit people at every class level (Tables 8.4). Nonetheless, the benefits of tax expenditures appear to go primarily to middle-class and rich people (Table 8.5).

The last section of the chapter looked at how lifestyle reflects people's values by examining the abortion issue. People's moral stance often corresponds to their economic interests.

# 9

# *The Working Class*

Does the working class differ from the middle class? The Embourgeoisement Hypothesis suggests that it does not.[1] Although the word *embourgeoisement* is unwieldy, it stems from Karl Marx's work and attempts to account for the lack of working-class radicalism in the United States. To use his terminology for a moment, it asserts that the bourgeoisie have allowed proletarians to become sufficiently affluent that they are not very interested in political activity aiming at income redistribution, greater economic equality, or other forms of radical change. In plainer language, the hypothesis proposes that there has been long-term improvement in the occupational characteristics, income, and lifestyle of working-class people such that they now resemble middle-class persons, with the result that the members of the working class do not display distinctive political attributes.

    If this argument is correct, then it should be observable. For example, researchers should find that the occupational settings of blue- and white-collar people are similar, that they have similar life chances (as indicated by, say their incomes), and as a result that they have similar lifestyles. Such findings would mean that a separate analysis of the working class, like that undertaken here, is unnecessary because most people in the United States, excluding the very rich and the poor, are reasonably affluent and middle class. I intend to

[1]DeFronzo (1973).

**211**

show that this hypothesis is incorrect, that the working class differs from the middle class in fundamental ways.

This is an easy argument to make. Few social scientists think the Embourgeoisement Hypothesis accurately portrays the working-class situation because the evidence does not support it.[2] But the argument is useful for my pedagogical purposes as a way of showing how an interesting idea can be put forth and refuted empirically. Phrased formally, the *Embourgeoisement Hypothesis* is:

> *The greater the similarity in the occupational characteristics, income, and lifestyle between the working class and the middle class, then the less emphasis on radical political change by the working class.*

As stated, the hypothesis presupposes that middle- and working-class people are similar and uses this "fact" to explain why working-class people are not politically radical. As it turns out, however, the presupposition is not correct, which means the hypothesis is false.

Previous chapters have shown that working-class and middle-class people differ in ways that are relevant to the hypothesis. For example, as revealed in Chapter 4, people who have blue-collar jobs usually display lower occupational prestige than do their white-collar counterparts and their class identification is with the working class rather than the middle class. Moreover, as described in Chapter 3, the division between blue- and white-collar work serves as a semipermeable barrier to mobility such that children of working-class parents usually end up in working-class jobs themselves. Finally, Chapter 8 revealed that working-class people enjoy fewer job perquisites (such as paid time-off, various medical benefits, severance pay, and pensions) and lower incomes than do middle-class people. Thus, the information already available casts doubt on the hypothesis: If working- and middle-class people differ so much, then the Embourgeoisement Hypothesis obviously cannot be correct.

In spite of these differences, however, other similarities are possible that have relevance for the Embourgeoisement Hypothesis. For example, perhaps the work settings of blue- and white-collar people do not differ so much as is thought. If so, that would be evidence for the argument. Or perhaps their level of job security is about the same. Although income is obviously vital, a secure income—even a low one—determines lifestyle. Or, finally, perhaps there are similarities in consumption habits, tastes, use of leisure time, or other elements of lifestyle. If it can be shown that middle-class and working-class people resemble each other along these dimensions, then the plausibility of the Embourgeoisement Hypothesis would be greater.

## Social Class and Occupation

Like the middle class, the working class has not always existed. In preindustrial societies, work was "a game against nature" as people used human and animal muscle power to obtain necessities for living.[3] Reliance on an inefficient source of energy meant that productivity was low. As a result, most people lived a rural life for nearly all of human his-

---

[2]van den Berg (1993).
[3]Bell (1976).

tory, struggling with the soil for subsistence.[4] In such contexts, a working class did not exist. In comparison, beginning in the nineteenth century, work increasingly became "a game against things" as people linked new, more efficient forms of energy (mainly steam and fossil fuel) with machines, and productivity rose greatly. As a result of industrialization, the class structure changed dramatically. Increasing numbers of people became urban and labored at new kinds of jobs in which the tasks were routinized, systematic, and mechanical—not to mention dangerous to health and safety. These are the people Marx called proletarians in the 1840s. They coalesced as a recognizable working class over the remainder of that century.

## *Working-Class and Middle-Class Occupations*

Today, as you may recall from Chapter 2, about 45 percent of the population answers the class identification question by saying they are working class. This answer correlates with the occupational distribution, as shown in Table 9.1. Column (2) reveals that about 40 percent of the population does blue-collar work. Taken together, these figures provide a reasonable estimate of the size of the working-class population in the United States.[5] But significant racial and ethnic differences exist, as also shown in Table 9.1. About 61 percent of Hispanic Americans, 48 percent of African Americans, and 33 percent of Asian Americans do blue-collar work. Nearly all of them identify with the working class as well. These different occupational distributions by race and ethnicity suggest that while most working-class people are white (since they are the largest group by far), a higher proportion of minority group people are working class—a fact that has important implications for differences in life chances and lifestyles.

The millions of people referred to in the lower portion of Table 9.1 wear some form of work clothes on the job. This is so they can do manual labor, the essence of working-class life. These are the people who fix, haul, lift, scrub, shovel, help, and otherwise engage in potentially damaging exertions for a living. Hence, one gets the impression that working-class people are less likely to join fitness clubs. Their jobs are exhaustive enough. And often dirty.

In *Families on the Fault Line,* one of Lillian Rubin's respondents talks about the implications of getting dirty on the job: "I used to work in an upholstery factory. . . . The only thing I wanted to do when I got home was take a bath."[6] The clean-dirty divide serves as a metaphor for the division between the middle class and working class. This same respondent now works as a word processor, making slightly less money but glad for the difference in job characteristics:

> You're a real person. . . . If you want to stop a minute and go talk to the other girls, nobody says anything. Or you can go to the bathroom and grab a smoke, and it's no big deal. I mean, they expect you to work, but they know you can't do it every minute. If it got slow in the factory, you got laid off. But in this job, they don't just dump you if there's a couple of slow days.

[4]Lenski (1984).
[5]Zweig argues that the working class is the majority of the population (2000).
[6]Rubin (1994:41).

**TABLE 9.1** *Occupational Distribution by Race and Ethnicity*

| *(1)* <br><br> *Occupation* | *(2)* <br><br> *All* <br> *2001* | *(3)* <br> *White* <br> *American* <br> *2001* | *(4)* <br> *African* <br> *American* <br> *2001* | *(5)* <br> *Hispanic* <br> *American* <br> *2000* | *(6)* <br> *Asian* <br> *American* <br> *2000* |
|---|---|---|---|---|---|
| **White Collar** | | | | | |
| Executives and Managers | 15% | 16% | 11% | [ 14% | [ 39% |
| Professional Specialty | 16 | 16 | 12 | [ | [ |
| Technicians | 3 | 3 | 3 | | |
| Sales | 12 | 12 | 10 | }25 | }28 |
| Administrative Support | 14 | 13 | 17 | | |
| Total White Collar | 60% | 60% | 53% | 39% | 67% |
| **Blue Collar** | | | | | |
| Precision Production | 11 | 12 | 8 | 14 | 6 |
| Machine Operators | 5 | 5 | 7 | | |
| Transportation | 4 | 4 | 6 | }22 | }11 |
| Handlers and Laborers | 4 | 4 | 5 | | |
| Service | 14 | 12 | 21 | 19 | 15 |
| Farming, Forestry, Fishing | 2 | 3 | 1 | 6 | 1 |
| Total Blue Collar | 40% | 40% | 48% | 61% | 33% |

*Note:* Data for All, White Americans, African Americans, and Hispanic Americans are for persons aged 16 and older; data for Asian Americans are for persons 25 years and older. Some totals do not add to 100% because of rounding.

*Sources:* U.S. Department of Labor (2002:175), U.S. Bureau of the Census (2001e; 2002d).

Being laid off is always a threat if you are working class. Nonetheless, as Rubin commented, working-class people provide the wheels and services that make the nation turn.[7] She meant this not as a metaphor but literally. Someone—almost half the population—has to build, fix, haul, cut, and scrub. And they often do so in rather difficult contexts.

## *Social Class and Job Setting*

Recall that the embourgeoisement hypothesis presupposes that middle-class and working-class people are fundamentally alike. But, as the quotation above suggests, the environment within which middle-class and working-class people must labor differs in fundamental ways that are logically incompatible with the hypothesis. Working-class job

[7]Rubin (1994:26).

settings are frequently unpleasant and dangerous, characterized by intense production pressures, and feature close supervision and petty work rules.

***Unpleasant and Dangerous Working Conditions.***    Average middle-class Americans use electricity generated by coal that others have to mine, consume meat that others have to grind, work in buildings that others have to build, and use paper made from trees that others have to log. Those "others" are working-class people. Indoors or out, even if the tasks inherent to blue-collar work involve some degree of autonomy and satisfaction, which is sometimes the case, the tasks are often unpleasant and difficult. One result is a high level of job-related deaths and injuries, which occur at all skill levels.

Those who work inside frequently operate machines that are very hazardous if unreliable or handled incorrectly, such as a meat grinder or hand-held power tools.[8] In addition, they must often face high noise levels as machines clatter and grind, a great deal of noxious dust, dirt and other airborne particulates, toxic odors that are poorly ventilated, inadequate lighting, and extreme temperature variations because work stations have too little heat, air conditioning, or simply air movement. All of these factors can lead to long-term health problems and physical deterioration. For example, miners and textile workers must inhale toxic fumes and dust while doing their jobs.[9] Similarly, forge and hammer operators must endure the tremendous heat and cacophony of sound created by their own and others' machines.

Those who work outside must face the weather, the seasons of the year. Garbage collectors, mail carriers, soft-drink drivers, and land-fill workers must toil in the rain and the snow and the heat and the cold.[10] Electricians and telephone line repairers must work in the middle of storms, in the middle of the night, no matter what the temperature, with equipment that is often dangerous; electrocutions are a constant threat.[11] Bricklayers, carpenters, and others who construct homes and office buildings, usually cannot wear gloves and still do their jobs. So if it is cold they just suffer; if it is hot they just suffer. If they fall, they simply go to the hospital and sometimes die; if they have a heart attack, they sometimes die.[12] Probably the most dangerous form of work, however, is logging; the odds of loggers dieing on the job are 27 times greater than the average for all occupations. Yet their work is vital. In one year, the "average American uses wood and paper products equivalent to what can be produced from one 100-foot, 18-inch tree."[13] Someone has to build, fix, haul, cut, and scrub, and these tasks are often dangerous.

Every day, about 16 people die in work-related accidents, roughly 6,000 each year. Most of them are working class, as a look at the distribution of fatalities at work by occupation in 2001 shows. These data exclude the 2,900 work-related deaths that resulted from the attack on September 11 of that year.[14]

---

[8]Orr (2000), Brown (2003), Armstrong et al. (1999).
[9]Reardon (1993), Hertzberg et al. (2002).
[10]Personick and Harthun (1992), Kitsantas et al. (2000).
[11]Taylor et al. (2002).
[12]Johansen et al. (2002).
[13]Sygnatur (1998).
[14]Bureau of Labor Statistics (2002:1, 11).

| | |
|---|---|
| Executives and Administrators | 6% |
| Professionals | 4 |
| Technicians | 3 |
| Sales | 7 |
| Administrative Support | 2 |
| Precision Production | 19 |
| Operators and Laborers | 35 |
| Service | 9 |
| Farmers, Foresters, and Fishers | 14 |
| Military | 1 |

Most fatal work-related injuries, about 78 percent, occur to people in working-class jobs, mostly those who operate or come into contact with heavy equipment. Another way of seeing this fact is to look at the manner in which workplace fatalities occurred (again excluding September 11).[15]

| | |
|---|---|
| Transportation Accidents | 43% |
| Assaults and Violent Acts | 15 |
| Contact with Objects and Equipment | 16 |
| Falls | 14 |
| Exposure to Harmful Substances | 9 |
| Fires and Explosions | 3 |

The most common source of injury leading to death is connected to operating a vehicle. Some white-collar workers, such as those in sales, use cars regularly. But even more blue-collar workers must do so as they go from work site to work site, or operate moving equipment—such as forklifts. Ignoring homicides, a high proportion of deaths on the job reflects its inherent dangerousness: operating machinery or tools, the impact of structures on which people work, environmental conditions, toxic liquids, and the like.

Behind the statistics are people whose lives have ended.[16] Rolan Hoskin, 48 years old, lived in Tyler, Texas. He was married with one daughter. He worked at a pipe foundry that produces cast iron sewer and water pipes, the kind found under neighborhood streets in most U.S. cities. One day he was trying to adjust a conveyor belt and got caught in the machinery, which crushed his head. Rick Slusack, 29 years old, lived in Steven's Point, Wisconsin, near a branch of the University of Wisconsin. He was married with one child. Each working day, he was supposed to load large plastic bags filled with bark chips and wood shavings into tractor trailer trucks. These bags end up at suburban shopping malls and garden stores, where they are sold as mulch to middle-class people. One morning the forklift he was operating skidded on gravel, overturned, and pinned him underneath. He was dead within the hour. Dereck Hubbard, 42 years old, lived in Muscle Shoals, Alabama, where he was an iron worker. One afternoon, he was locking roof panels into place on an office building when he fell to his death. A wife and two children survive him. Danny Newman, 46, married with three children, was an oil rigger in south-

---

[15]Bureau of Labor Statistics (2002:9).
[16]Barstow and Bergman (2003; 2003a; 2003b), Nordheimer (1996).

eastern New Mexico who died when a mechanical failure caused a piece of equipment to crush him. Finally, an electrician named Lynda Gertner, a 31-year-old married woman with one child, died when a chemical explosion ripped through the plant where she was working and spread poisonous fumes throughout.

I have focused on fatalities on the job because they are the ultimate price some people pay to keep the nation running—literally. Sewer pipes are manufactured and laid in the ground to carry our water; mulch is ground and transported to stores so we can decorate our yards; the iron framework for the office buildings we work in is hoisted and fastened; meat for our tables is cut, sliced, and ground at huge processing plants. Working-class people must perform these and myriad other tasks.

Behind the work-related deaths, however, are many more injuries. About 1.5 million people are injured on the job every year.[17] Nearly all of them occur in the working class. The people most likely to become injured work as truck drivers, laborers, nursing aides and orderlies, janitors, machine assemblers, construction workers, carpenters, electricians, stock handlers, cashiers, and cooks. About 40 percent of all injuries are sprains and strains, most often involving the back from all the lifting involved, but many are disfiguring. Bobby Lee Cantley was only 15; he was not supposed to be there. But there he was anyway, working in a beef processing plant in Ohio in order to help support his family. He slipped and fell into a meat grinder and lost his entire arm. About 11,000 nonfatal workplace amputations of arms, hands, legs, and feet occur every year.[18] Less than 1 percent of all job injuries, they can serve as a symbol of all the burns, lacerations, cuts, respiratory problems, blurred vision, and headaches to which people in working-class jobs become accustomed.

Journals like *Monthly Labor Review, Compensation and Working Conditions,* and several others carry articles with titles such as "Work-Related Injuries, Illnesses, and Fatalities in Manufacturing and Construction," "Exposure to Different Forms of Nickel and Risk of Lung Cancer," "Blurred Vision and Occupational Toluene Exposure," and (my favorite title) "Logging Is Perilous Work."[19] There are no titles like "Workplace Injuries in the Office Suite." Apart from injuries due to repetitive motions at the keyboard (that is, carpel tunnel syndrome), I cannot think of any way in which white-collar work compares to the dangerousness of blue-collar work. And no one dies from carpel tunnel. This difference in degree of dangerousness is why working-class people lose an estimated 32 percent more days from work each year than do middle-class people.[20] Of course, when they become injured, working-class people are less likely to have health insurance, sick leave, or other job perquisites that protect their income (recall Chapter 8).

Middle-class jobs are different. Even in menial white-collar occupations, work stations are relatively quiet, reasonably clean, without offensive odors, and maintained at a constant temperature. In addition, it is common for office workers, even the lowest paid, to have windows and to surround themselves with flowers and pictures on the walls. Those who think, administer, sell, and push pencils or type keys for a living are, quite

[17]Bureau of Labor Statistics (2003a:1).

[18]Orr (2000), Brown (2003).

[19]Webster (1999), Grimsrud et al. (2002), Campagna et al. (2001), Sygnatur (1998).

[20]Hamermesh (1998), Bureau of Labor Statistics (2003a).

simply, subjected to fewer health hazards and, hence, injuries. Thus, even if the tasks that white-collar workers must do are routinized, the environment within which they are accomplished is, most of the time, reasonably pleasant and safe. Working-class jobs are much more dangerous than middle-class jobs.

***Production Pressures.***     By the phrase "production pressures," I mean the attempt at regulating the rate and rhythm of work. This characteristic is especially true of assembly line occupations. In a pipe foundry, a certain number of sewer pipes must be produced each hour because, as it was put, "time equals pipe, and pipe equals money."[21] What happens is that employers measure the amount of time it takes a competent person to perform a task and then set the pace of the line accordingly. It does not matter if a person has a sprained hand or was up last night with a sick child. Production pressures occur in most manufacturing and some service tasks, whether an assembly line exists or not. The installation of new sky boxes and renovation of a college football stadium must be completed on time, or the contractor faces significant financial penalties. So does the road builder if the repaving of an interstate highway is not finished on time.

Their inherent dangerousness constitutes part of the reason for so many deaths and injuries in blue-collar jobs. But production pressures and the company's orientation to those pressures constitute another. Companies in the same industry often take rather different approaches. In the pipe foundry industry, for example, some companies emphasize keeping the line running regardless of safety or environmental hazards. If 80 pipes are supposed to be produced each hour, then management expects 80 pipes—not 79. These companies have high rates of work-related deaths and injuries, constant accusations of polluting the environment, and high employee turnover. But the dilemma may be false. Other companies in that same industry are very profitable while emphasizing job safety and environmental responsibility; they also have high employee morale and low turnover.[22] This emphasis reduces (although it does not eliminate) the level of danger inherent to many jobs.

***Close Supervision and Petty Work Rules.***     Close supervision and petty work rules distinguish many working-class job settings. The pervasive time clock, at which people punch in when they arrive to work and punch out when they leave, suggests immediately how closely supervised blue-collar workers are. Along with supervision, of course, come rules to enforce. Working-class jobs are often characterized by work rules that resemble those in elementary school or, perhaps, boot camp. There are rules against talking, against going to the bathroom without authorization, against pausing for a moment to stretch tired muscles, against everything that would make a job more pleasant or enjoyable.[23] The enforcers of these rules are the foreperson and line-level white-collar managers. Although the power of these supervisors is somewhat circumscribed in union plants, the millions of nonunion workers face a simple choice: do what they are told, toe the line, or be fired. Workers report that this kind of supervision makes them feel as though they are being

---

[21]Barstow and Bergman (2003a).
[22]Barstow and Bergman (2003a).
[23]Barstow and Bergman (2003; 2003a; 2003b).

treated like machines instead of human beings. This is a metaphorical way of describing what it means to feel powerless or, in the jargon, alienated.

Most middle-class jobs are rather different. For one thing, time clocks rarely exist; most people are paid annual salaries rather than hourly wages, which means punching in and out is viewed as less necessary. In addition, while nearly everyone has a supervisor or boss, the nature and quality of the supervision is often quite different. For example, it is hard to imagine college professors, engineers, computer programmers, salespersons, or even clerical workers having to justify going to the bathroom or a few moments on the telephone talking to their spouse. (Recall the quotation from the word processor a few pages ago.) To propose such rules is to propose an absurdity. Yet many blue-collar workers live by them everyday. In most middle-class jobs, getting the task done is the important issue, and this is accomplished with far less direct supervision and far fewer work rules.

This emphasis on production pressure and close supervision reflects a specific managerial approach that is peculiarly American. In *Fat and Mean: The Corporate Squeeze of Working Americans and the Myth of Managerial "Downsizing,"* David Gordon argued that American companies rarely emphasize raises, bonuses, and other "carrots" as mechanisms to motivate workers.[24] Rather, compared to other nations, U.S. companies typically develop rather large bureaucracies that emphasize a "stick strategy": arbitrary commands and threats of loss of job for failure to obey. This "fat" bureaucracy and "mean" management style is supposed to lead to greater productivity. It probably lowers productivity, however, as most people respond better to positive reinforcers ("carrots") than negative ("sticks"). Gordon argued that one—not the only—reason for rising inequality in this country (recall Table 8.6) is the existence of bloated bureaucracies in U.S. corporations whose personnel require income that might otherwise go to blue-collar workers. So working-class people toil harder, with less job security, just to stay in place. From this angle, the presupposition underlying the Embourgeoisement Hypothesis is incorrect.

## Social Class and Job Security

I mentioned earlier that working-class men and women provide the wheels and services that make this nation turn by fixing, hauling, lifting, shoveling, and helping. Although one might think that people employed in these sorts of jobs would be paid rather well for the extra danger and other difficulties, the income and job security of working-class people are less today than in the past. This fact was illustrated in the last chapter in Table 8.2, which shows median income by occupation for men and women. Please pause and look back at the table now. These data reveal that, despite the Embourgeoisement Hypothesis, reality for most working-class individuals and families is that they are not affluent; they are, rather, economically insecure. Nonetheless, popular stereotypes abound of the plumber, the teamster, and even the garbage collector as members of a new well-to-do working class. This perception reflects considerable misunderstanding because most

[24]Gordon (1996).

people do not realize who gets the money when they employ skilled people, such as precision production workers. For example, when customers take their automobiles to be fixed, they are often charged $35 to $50 per hour for the job. While such figures seem like a high rate of pay for a "simple car repair" most of the money does not go to the mechanic; it goes, rather, to the owner of the dealership or repair shop to cover overhead and profit. Owners are classified as businesspersons, not blue-collar workers. The latter make $10 to $15 per hour ($21,000 to $31,000, if they work full-time all year long—many do not). This same point applies when people employ plumbers, electricians, and other skilled blue-collar people. Those who actually do the job often earn far less than the price paid by the customer and, as a result, are much less affluent and more economically insecure than white-collar employees.

Although income is fundamental to families' economic circumstances, those who are assured a regular income, even if it is relatively low, can organize their lives to a greater degree than those for whom a steady income is more doubtful. Thus, if working-class people have job security similar to that of middle-class people, then this fact could be taken as evidence of embourgeoisement.

Unfortunately, job security, as indicated by the unemployment rate, is far less for those engaged in working-class occupations. This fact is illustrated in Table 9.2, which shows that unemployment rates are much higher in all working-class occupations. For example, the unemployment rate among professional specialty workers was only 2 percent in 2001, compared to figures between 5 percent and 8 percent in most working-class occupations, up to 10 percent for those in handling and laboring occupations (a category I will return to in a few moments). These differences in likelihood of unemployment mean that of all those out of work at any time, most were previously in working-class jobs.

Moreover, most people who are unemployed do not leave their jobs voluntarily. Table 9.2 shows that the overall rate of unemployment was about 5 percent in 2001. This figure can be broken down in the following way.[25]

| | |
|---|---|
| 51% | Lost job |
| 12 | Left job |
| 30 | Reentering the job market |
| 7 | Entering job market for the first time |

Thus, very few of the unemployed find themselves in that situation because they left their jobs by choice. Nearly all those without work, 81 percent (51 percent + 30 percent), either lost their jobs or, overcoming their discouragement, reentered the job market. Discouragement, by the way, is a major issue in discussing the unemployment rate. This is because people are only classified as unemployed if they are looking for work. If they have become so demoralized that they have stopped looking, then they are no longer unemployed—at least officially. This paradoxical phenomenon is why you occasionally see newspaper articles describing hundreds or even thousands of applicants appearing when a new plant opens up. When jobs, real jobs, become available then people reenter the labor market—another way of saying they become hopeful of actually finding work. I placed

---

[25]Bureau of Labor Statistics (2003b).

**TABLE 9.2**  *Number Unemployed and Unemployment Rate by Occupation, 2001*

| Occupation | Number Unemployed | Unemployment Rate |
|---|---|---|
| **White Collar** | | |
| Executives and Managers | 491,000 | 2% |
| Professional Specialty | 482,000 | 2% |
| Technicians | 133,000 | 3% |
| Sales | 794,000 | 5% |
| Administrative Support | 772,000 | 4% |
| **Blue Collar** | | |
| Precision Production | 711,000 | 5% |
| Machine Operators | 573,000 | 8% |
| Transportation | 298,000 | 5% |
| Handlers and Laborers | 610,000 | 10% |
| Service | 1,150,000 | 6% |
| Farming, Forestry, Fishing | 259,000 | 7% |
| Overall | 6,742,000 | 5% |

*Note:* Data refer to persons 16 years of age and older.

*Source:* Bureau of Labor Statistics (2003b).

the number of unemployed people in Table 9.2 in order to emphasize that millions of people are reflected in the percentages. You should remember, however, that the figures understate the number of unemployed and discouraged people. There are 15 million poor persons in this country (to be discussed in Chapter 10).

One last point: Although it is not shown in the table, the mean duration of unemployment across all social classes was about 13 weeks in 1998.[26] This time has been fairly typical over the years, and it implies that a far higher proportion of the total workforce, three to four times the overall rate, experience some unemployment in any specific year. The vast majority of these persons are working class, which is a typical situation, and many are poor for at least part of the time. Thus, the people who have the least job security, who have the most to fear from unemployment, are in working-class families. This finding is not consonant with the Embourgeoisement Hypothesis, since those who are economically insecure cannot be considered like the middle class.

The experience of unionized asbestos workers in New York City provides a good illustration of the economic problems and dangers many working-class people face.[27] Recall from looking back at Table 8.5 that the median income of male handlers and laborers working full-time, all year round, was $30,200 in 2001. In addition, Table 9.2 reveals that

[26]Bureau of Labor Statistics (2003b).
[27]Passell (1998).

handlers and laborers display the highest rate of unemployment of any occupational category. Asbestos is widely used in the mining and construction industries. Further, anyone involved in the manufacture of insulation, fireproofing materials, cement products, and automobile brakes must work with asbestos. In many cases, they are classified as handlers and laborers. Members of unions, however, make considerably more than average, partly because they are organized and (in this case) partly because the substance they are handling is incredibly dangerous. Inhaling the dust leads to asbestosis—a progressive lung disease that kills the victim in a painful way. Respirators (which often function very imperfectly) are essential to prevent this result. The death toll among people doing this sort of work has always been high. During the early 1980s, unionized asbestos workers in New York City were earning about $31 per hour. Over the next few years, however, an influx of immigrants willing enough and desperate enough to do this work (often without the protection of either a union or a respirator) meant that wages fell to about $13.50 per hour during the early part of the 1990s. More recently, they have rebounded to about $19, as the union recruited many of these new workers. Although this wage is still not very high given the degree of danger involved, it is worth calculating what it means in practice. A person making $19 per hour who works 40 hours per week all year long will make $41,392 (before taxes). But if he (nearly all asbestos workers are men) is unemployed for part of the year—a likely possibility—income drops. Let us assume an average duration of unemployment, 13 weeks. This person's actual income (before taxes) becomes $30,248. Not many people can take a one-quarter drop in income without significant economic and familial consequences.

These consequences are more serious for racial and ethnic minorities. Their incomes are usually lower than Whites at every occupational level (see Chapter 2). So they have fewer resources to begin with, on average, which means they are worse off when the axe falls. Table 9.3 compares the experiences of African Americans and Whites with unemployment. It reveals that African American men and women are about twice as likely to lose their jobs as Whites and to be out of work for significantly longer when they do. Most of these job losses afflict working-class people.

As an editorial aside, economists often describe unemployment as "unpaid vacation," presuming, I guess, that people benefit from being thrown out of work because they have leisure time in which to enjoy themselves. I wish to comment on this image and those who use it.

Economists are usually employed in colleges and universities or come from an academic background, experiences that fundamentally influence their vision of reality. For example, college professors are generally employed on nine-month contracts and paid sufficiently well that they frequently view the summer as free time, as unpaid vacation. Those who publish often use the summer to do research, which means that (no matter how much they enjoy their jobs) they see themselves as giving up leisure time in order to work. Moreover, college professors have unpaid leave built into the academic year at Thanksgiving, Christmas, and Spring Break. Once again, this time is often used for research, which involves giving up leisure. Thus, from economists' points of view, those who (like themselves) are sometimes unemployed have "unpaid vacation" and those who (like themselves) work anyway are particularly virtuous. It seems to me, in other words, that economists' rather privileged position in the society leads them to make inappropriate generalizations about those in other situations, such as working-class people.

**TABLE 9.3**   *Unemployment Rate by Gender and Race, 2001*

| Race | Percentage Unemployed | | Average Duration in Weeks | |
|---|---|---|---|---|
| | *Men* | *Women* | *Men* | *Women* |
| Whites | 4% | 4% | 12 | 11 |
| African Americans | 9% | 8% | 17 | 17 |

*Note:* Data refer to persons 16 years of age and older.

*Source:* Bureau of Labor Statistics (2003b).

This mistake illustrates a fundamental difficulty that is peculiar to social science research: How are observers to be objective about society even as they participate in it? This is the problem Max Weber alerted us to a long time ago. Alas, there remains no easy answer to the question, and those of us in sociology and economics rely on the disciplined skepticism of our colleagues to point out implicit bias in our work.

Reality, in fact, is far different from the image conveyed by the phrase "unpaid vacation." Any period without a job, especially long-term unemployment, is devastating to working-class families, often destroying their lifestyle completely and sometimes creating poverty where none had existed before. This threat is a fundamental and pervasive source of stress among working-class people. It means they are not affluent, that the embourgeoisement thesis is incorrect. In the next section, I examine the human consequences of unemployment in more detail.

## The Human Consequences of Unemployment

As will be explained in more detail in Chapter 10, a trade-off usually occurs between inflation and unemployment, and U.S. policy makers typically choose to allow unemployment to be higher than inflation. While this choice can be defended as one that benefits the nation as a whole (the argument is that "everyone is hurt by inflation"), poor and working-class people are hurt more by unemployment than inflation. There is, however, surprisingly little research on the human consequences of unemployment. I am using the phrase "human consequences" to distinguish the suffering of individuals from the macroeconomic effects of unemployment: loss of productivity. Economists emphasize, correctly, that billions of dollars worth of goods and services are not produced when people, factories, and other resources stand idle.

The lack of research on the impact of losing one's job is important because unemployment has far-reaching economic and noneconomic consequences for those who go through it, sometimes lasting long after the experience is over. Furthermore, it is possible that these results, nearly all of which are negative, redound (or spill over) into other arenas of society. This situation means that macroeconomic policies are made in relative ignorance, buttressed by stereotypes of unemployed people enjoying unpaid vacations, rather than social scientific evidence.

### A Note on the Meaning of Work

Max Weber emphasized that in modern societies people's jobs have both economic and noneconomic implications.[28] Jobs not only provide a way to earn a living, they also affect people's identity. When unemployment occurs, this identity is threatened.

One indicator of this fact is that the vast majority of people would, if given a choice, continue working even if they had enough money to live comfortably.[29] This is because many individuals view their jobs as relatively interesting and enjoyable, as a way of staying physically and mentally healthy, and as a means for justifying their existence and seeing themselves positively. Others, mainly those in less engaging and more physically arduous occupations, say they would keep working (although not always at the same job) because they do not want to be idle or bored, because their self-respect is tied to earning a living and providing for their families, and because they would "go crazy" if their work did not keep them occupied.

But work appears to have different meaning for middle-class and working-class people. Those in middle-class occupations tend to emphasize that their jobs are interesting and carry a sense of accomplishment as well as a concern with self-respect and a desire not to be idle. It should be recognized that people in white-collar jobs are often in competitive environments where individual initiative can pay off—a fact that carries intrinsic interest. (Administrative support workers constitute an obvious exception to this generalization.) In contrast, working-class people tend to say that their jobs occupy their time, provide them with companionship, and give them a sense of earning an "honest living," which they define as working with their hands. This orientation leads to some harsh judgments. It appears that many working-class people see white-collar jobs as scams for avoiding "real work."[30] Moreover, from this angle, the work middle-class professionals do often takes the form of harassing those below them—working-class people. Hence, they believe that working with your hands is more honorable than "shuffling paper" or "working with your mouth." Whatever one thinks of these judgments, they indicate how central employment is to the lives of working-class people. Observers consistently find that "one of the best indicators of the importance of the job to these men is their discomfort when they cannot work."[31]

I mention men here because it appears that the possibility of unemployment raises different issues for women and men, at least in the working-class couples Lillian Rubin talked to.[32]

> Ask a [working class] man for a statement of his identity, and he'll almost always respond by telling you first what he does for a living. The same question asked of a woman brings forth a less predictable, more varied response, one that's embedded in the web of relationships that are central to her life.

[28]Weber (1920).
[29]General Social Survey (1998).
[30]Ehrenreich (1990:137–38).
[31]LeMasters (1976:26.
[32]Rubin (1994:104).

Among these couples, women tended to have multifaceted self-identities that include their roles as mother, wife, friend, daughter, and sister. So even for those women who were divorced and single mothers, their job only represented part of their sense of self. Hence, while losing a job (or the potential for doing so) might be painful and anxiety producing, it did not call their identity into question. For men, however, even though they also assume many roles (as husband, father, friend, son, and so forth), going to work is what they are. Their job is what they are, the core of their being. As will become clear, these differences in orientation affect the impact of unemployment on families.

## Economic Deprivation

For young couples of any race or ethnic group, usually saddled with high debts and little savings, unemployment of either spouse is an immediate catastrophe. For families in the prime earning years, however, getting laid off usually does not result in poverty—at least immediately. But it is a constant specter. In order to see why, I have sketched plausible income and expenses for a working-class Hispanic couple, whom I will name Margarita and Alberto Martinez. They have two teenage children and are active in their church. They are a more or less typical family. They are now doing pretty well economically because, after many years of struggle, Alberto, age 42, recently became a member of Local 78 of the Asbestos, Lead, and Hazardous Waste Laborers in New York City. Following from the discussion earlier, I am going to assume that he works full-time all year long and earns $41,000. Margarita, 38, is a bank teller. She also works full-time all year long and earns the average for clerical workers, $26,000 (see Table 8.2). Although their total gross income is well above average for blue-collar workers, I use it to illustrate the precariousness of lifestyle in the working class.

This uncertainty can be seen by looking at the breakdown of their gross income in Table 9.4. Although the figures in the table are tailored to fit this hypothetical example, they are comparable to amounts shown by consumer expenditure surveys for families at this income level.[33]

Although the Martinezes' gross income is $67,000, this amount is reduced in a variety of ways. Following from the discussion of job perquisites in Chapter 8, I assumed that they obtain medical insurance through her employer, which pays most of the cost of medical insurance. In addition, each of their employers matches their retirement contribution. Their share of the cost of these two benefits is $1,600 and $5,000, respectively, which is paid before taxes (another small perquisite). So their total taxable income is reduced to $60,400.

Their income is reduced further by taxes. After normal deductions, the Martinezes' federal income tax rate is 8 percent, about the same as their payroll tax rate (for Social Security/Medicare) of 7.65 percent. It is common for millions of ordinary citizens to pay a higher payroll tax than federal income tax. Finally, their income is reduced by state and local taxes on property, income, and sales that combine to total 11.1 percent. This figure is somewhat higher for the Martinezes and others who live in New York City than they

---

[33]Bureau of Labor Statistics (2003c).

**TABLE 9.4**   *Income and Expenses for a Hypothetical Working-Class Family (Two Adults, Two Children)*

| Income | |
|---|---:|
| Gross Income from Husband's Job | $41,000 |
| Gross Income from Wife's Job | 26,000 |
| Total Gross Income | 67,000 |
| Minus Expenses Taken before Taxes | |
| Employee share of cost of Medical Insurance | – 1,600 |
| Employee share of Retirement Contribution[a] | – 5,000 |
| Total Taxable Income | $60,400 |
| Minus Taxes on $60,400 | |
| Income tax at 8%[b] | – 4,800 |
| Social Security/Medicare tax at 7.65% | – 4,600 |
| State & Local Taxes at 11.1%[c] | – 6,700 |
| All Taxes = 27%, Yielding Net Yearly Income | $44,300 |
| Net Monthly Income (44,300 ÷ 12) | $3,700 |
| **Monthly Living Expenses[d]** | |
| Total Food (home and away, plus personal supplies) | $900 |
| Mortgage Payment | $600 |
| Utilities (including telephone) | 250 |
| Transportation (car payment, insurance, public trans.) | 450 |
| Life Insurance | 50 |
| Health Care (deductibles, non-insured expenses) | 100 |
| Church Contribution | 100 |
| Education (for children) | 50 |
| Entertainment | 200 |
| Tobacco and Alcohol | 100 |
| Saving for children's education | 300 |
| Non-allocated | 600 |
| Total Nonfood | $2,800 |
| Total Monthly Living Expenses (total food + total non-food) | $3,700 |

[a]$3,000 for him, $2,000 for her, see Bureau of Labor Statistics (2003c).

[b]Assumes normal deductions for a family of 4. All income is from wages.

[c]Assumes couple lives in New York. Includes sales, property, and state/local income taxes. The nationwide average for a couple like this would be 8.8%. See Institute on Taxation and Economic Policy (2003).

[d]These figures are a loose extrapolation from Bureau of Labor Statistics (2003c).

would be for people in the rest of the nation, where the average is 8.8 percent.[34] This family pays about 27 percent of its taxable income in taxes, a rate higher than that of many rich persons and families, but typical at this income level. On that basis, the Martinezes have a net monthly income of about $3,700, from which they must pay their living expenses.

In order to ease comparison with a similar table to be presented in Chapter 10, the monthly living expenses depicted in Table 9.4 are divided between those for food and nonfood. Note, however, that I have lumped in with food (purchased both home and away) the cost of personal supplies people normally buy in a grocery store, such as toothbrushes, vitamins, and the like. As sketched in the table, Margarita and Alberto Martinez have relatively fixed expenses totaling almost two-thirds of their take-home income: mortgage, utilities, transportation, life insurance, and health care not covered by insurance. This leaves about one-third for expenses and purchases of the sort that every family makes. Even so, note that this budget contains no provision for credit card debt, a new transmission for the car, dental work, or shoes for their children (endorsed by a popular athlete, of course), to name some obvious unallocated but plausible expenses. Nor does it take into account expenses for holidays, birthdays, or vacations. All in all, then, a family like this gets by. Although it is not poor, the fear of poverty is always there: What happens if (or when) Alberto gets laid off? Because he has only recently joined the union, Alberto has little seniority. Like many other minority persons, he will get the axe before others do and remain unemployed for a longer time.

When he loses his job, the family's income is cut by 60 percent. Although Alberto is eligible for unemployment benefits (not everyone is), this supplement is time limited and only covers a portion of his lost pay. Hence, the Martinezes' first task is to cut back on expenses. The family will retain medical insurance because they get it through Margarita's employer, but she will stop contributing to her retirement fund (as will Alberto, of course, since he is not working). Church contributions, holidays, entertainment, and optional purchases (dentist?) are also eliminated. Selling the car is a possibility, especially in New York City, but it limits Alberto's work options because jobs are increasingly located in suburban areas that are difficult to commute to via mass transit. This would be much more of a problem, of course, for a family living in a city without good public transportation. If Alberto's unemployment persists, the basic elements of the family's lifestyle will be affected: the car is sold, heat is set lower, and the like.

The second task is to generate new resources. Like many working-class men, Alberto has a variety of skills and is resourceful; he works off-the-books whenever possible to generate income. But the pay at these kinds of jobs is nearly always at or near the minimum wage. In addition, the modest funds in Alberto's and Margarita's retirement funds can be tapped, albeit with a tax penalty. Of course, that strategy means for a leaner old age. Finally, when they become truly desperate, they can obtain a small amount of financial help from kin or have one of the children leave high school and enter the labor force. Although none of these strategies will be effective for very long, they do tide families like the Martinezes over (remember, the sketch here is hypothetical). The single most important priority in cutting expenses and generating resources is to continue paying the

---

[34]Institute on Taxation and Economic Policy (2003).

mortgage. "We could be on the street." This is the primordial fear that rises in working-class families when unemployment occurs.[35]

If the period without work is short-term—a few weeks or months (at most)—families like the Martinezes can often recover their lifestyle. If, however, it persists for very long, the consequences are catastrophic. Here is an empirical generalization that expresses the relationship between unemployment and economic deprivation: *The longer the duration of unemployment, the greater the economic deprivation and the more likely impoverishment.* And homelessness.

Furthermore, remember that unemployment does not happen gradually. Rather, a person is suddenly laid off or fired, just before the mortgage payment is due, just before a holiday, just before something—there is no convenient time. Most unemployment, it will be recalled, occurs among working-class people, precisely those who have the least amount of money in savings and the least economic flexibility. The suffering that results can permanently erode people's sense of self-worth and confidence in the world, and often causes familial disruption.

### *Psychological Stress*

Although research on the human consequences of unemployment is rather sparse, some work has been done. For example, studies undertaken during and after the depression of the 1930s showed consistently that men who are thrown out of work—who are forced to be idle because no jobs are available—interpret this experience as a threat to their self-worth.[36] More recent literature indicates that this remains the case.[37] It shows that the economic deprivation, loss of social support, abrupt changes in daily routine, and the disruption of long-term financial plans that accompany unemployment lead individuals to suffer depression, anxiety, and physical ailments. Ethnographic studies of working-class families portray these results vividly.[38]

In effect, people without jobs feel small. They speak of their insignificance, their impotence, their boredom, of their inability to control their own lives.[39]

> I've been lost in the general scheme of things. . . . I don't even know what I'm doing, you know? I'm just what they call "free falling." There's not plans or anything. I used to try to make plans; there's no concentration. I feel like I'm in a fog. I have been called a vegetable. I don't read the newspaper. I try. It's just that I can't really concentrate. I used to.

"I can't really concentrate. . . ." This statement is a sign of depression, something that often accompanies unemployment.[40] What happens is that most people in the United States are socialized (or taught) by parents, teachers, and clergy that the work ethic is a fundamental value. (You should recall here the four principles of socialization presented

---

[35]Rubin (1994:114).
[36]Bakke (1940), Komarovsky (1940).
[37]Glyptis (1989), Feather (1990; 1992), Breslin and Mustard (2001).
[38]LeMasters (1976), Rubin (1994).
[39]Cottle (1994:78), Murphy and Athanasou (1999).
[40]Rubin (1994), Khan et al. (2002).

in Chapter 1.) This value becomes part of people's sense of self, of who and what they are. When people who have internalized the work ethic as part of their sense of self and who have been steadily employed all their lives suddenly find that they can no longer be active, productive members of the society, they lose confidence in themselves and display other indications of stress. This argument can be summarized as a simple empirical generalization: *Individuals who are or have been unemployed display more psychological stress than those who have not.* One manifestation is depression. Another is excessive drug use, especially alcohol. These results can be long-lasting.

### *Familial Disruption*

Although the available evidence is scant, it appears that individuals who experience unemployment also endure family disruption. By the phrase "family disruption," I refer not only to unhappiness and divorce but also to spouse abuse and child abuse.

In a context where families are dealing with economic deprivation and the unemployed person is trying to cope with his or her own stress, disruption becomes likely. Ethnographic studies, for example, report that working-class men not only had financial problems when they were unemployed, but also drank excessively and displayed more tense marital relationships.[41] What happens, apparently, is that unemployed people—especially men—experience economic deprivation and stress, which leads them to become more irritable, tense, and hostile. Such feelings are acted out on those immediately around them: children and spouses. So the discipline of children becomes more arbitrary, punitive, and violent.[42] Marital relations also suffer, with spouse abuse and divorce more likely.[43] This argument can be expressed as a simple, albeit hard to demonstrate, hypothesis:

> *Families in which one of the spouses is or has been unemployed have a higher probability of familial disruption than those who have not.*

This hypothesis is hard to demonstrate because the relationship between unemployment and familial disruption is probably not a simple causal connection.[44] Thus, the overall strength of the marriage, the personality characteristics of the spouses and previous experience with unemployment and income loss are all probably related to the degree of and form of familial disruption. For example, a couple in which the spouses are nurturing and supportive of one another and emotionally stable is probably going to have less familial disruption as it adjusts to economic deprivation and job loss than one in which the spouses are consistently critical of one another and display emotional instability. It is likely that these characteristics are class related.

In sum, one premise underlying the Embourgeoisement Hypothesis is that the working class has become as affluent as the middle class. Unfortunately, those doing blue-collar work not only earn less money, but also have less job security than those doing white-collar work. Their lifestyles are not secure.

[41]LeMasters (1976), Rubin (1994), Dooley and Prause (1998), Gallo et al. (2001).
[42]Lenton (1990), Elder et al. (1992), Catalano et al. (2002).
[43]Gelles (1990), Sander (1992), Rubin (1994).
[44]Liker and Elder (1983), Rubin (1994).

## *Social Class, Life Chances, and Lifestyle*

The Embourgeoisement Hypothesis also presumes that working- and middle-class people have essentially similar lifestyles. **Lifestyle,** you might recall, refers to people's way of living, as indicated by their consumption habits, use of leisure, and fundamental choices and values. One easy indicator of how consumption differs by class is the kind of clothes people wear, both on the job (work clothes versus suits, for example) and at play. Other examples are the type of car or truck owned, leisure time activities, furniture purchased, magazines subscribed to, mail order catalogues bought from, even the sweetness of drinks. All give fairly obvious clues about people's social class and way of living.[45] Moreover, there is an enormous amount of pretension inherent in lifestyle—at all class levels. One result of such hubris (or undue pride) is that people act to protect their way of life by discriminating against others whom they consider inferior or, at least, different (recall Chapter 5).

Housing provides an important way of illustrating the differences in lifestyle displayed by the working and middle classes. Some of these differences are subtle, but easily noticed. For example, house color, lawn decorations, number of pets running loose, and many other external features. Moreover, the interior of people's houses provides countless clues to their occupants' class identity and, hence, their lifestyle. For example, it appears that the television often occupies the central place in working-class living rooms.[46] Patterns of interaction vary as well. For example, my impression is that working-class persons often evaluate middle-class neighborhoods as too impersonal, since people nearby do not interact much and may not even know one another. Conversely, middle-class people are often suspicious of working-class neighborhoods precisely because there is so much street life. People become familiar with and develop an emotional affinity for a particular kind of neighborhood, and they make negative judgments of other areas in terms such as these. These alternative value judgments reflect the lifestyle of each class.

These differences in lifestyle, of course, reflect taste and skill combined with economic necessity—another way of talking about life chances. As described in Chapter 2, most U.S. cities are divided into neighborhoods by class, race, and ethnicity, and residents accurately perceive these differences. When they are asked by researchers to identify how neighborhoods differ, most persons refer to the relative income characteristics of people living in different sections of town or, in suburban areas, entire communities. Thus, particular areas will be seen as poor, working class, middle class, or rich by observing their housing characteristics and imputing income.

My suspicion, however, is that when respondents mention income to interviewers asking about housing location and neighborhood, it serves as a convenient proxy for invidious judgments they make but are reluctant to talk about openly and, sometimes, are only partly aware of. For example, my guess is that working-class neighborhoods are characterized by higher housing density, more garages converted into extra rooms, and more cars being repaired in driveways or on the street. While people recognize these

---

[45]Fussell (1983).
[46]Rubin (1994).

differences, they are not the first thoughts that come to mind when asked to compare neighborhoods.

People's housing, whether a home or an apartment, is usually their biggest single expenditure, and it symbolizes their share of the distribution of resources in the society. As such, it has positive consequences for individuals and families.[47] For example, it leads to preferential tax treatment (recall the discussion of tax expenditures in Chapter 8) and wealth accumulation. Homeowners have greater ties to the community, and their children often do better in school. But differences exist among homeowners, differences that call the Embourgeoisement Hypothesis into question.

As most observers know intuitively, the quality of housing differs by social class. In order to illustrate some of these differences, I have selected a few easily quantifiable measures. Table 9.5 compares the housing of families at three income levels. That between $40,000 and $59,000 is typical of a working-class household (note that it is just below that of the hypothetical Martinez family), while the other two are typical middle-class income levels (see Table 8.2).

Table 9.5 displays data for households that own their homes. It shows that working-class families usually live in older houses, which means that repair costs are higher. At some point, the roof begins leaking or the water heater stops functioning. Yet, the budget for working-class families is usually stretched pretty thin; Table 9.4 does not include the cost of replacing a leaky water heater. Where is the money going to come from? Newer homes are less likely to have these kinds of problems, which means that middle-class people do not have to use resources for them. Given different income levels, it follows that working-class people own homes that are less expensive than those of middle-class people. But in order to obtain housing, working-class people must pay a higher proportion of their income. Thus, families with incomes around $50,000 who own their homes spend about 18 percent of their incomes for housing, compared to 15 percent and 11 percent for families with higher incomes. Although data for renters is not shown, the pattern displayed in Table 9.5 is the same. Hence, these differences can be expressed as an empirical generalization that applies to both:

> *The lower the social class, then the older the housing, the lower the value of housing, and the higher the proportion of income spent on housing.*

This empirical generalization has important implications for life chances. The relatively high proportion of income spent on housing means there is less money available to working-class families for other things that bring pleasure and express lifestyle: going bowling or to the opera, buying a pickup truck or a car, contributing to a church or a political campaign, and saving for children's college education. It also means that since the value of their house is often less, when working-class people sell late in life, as at retirement, they have less money (and, hence, fewer choices) to take them through old age. Finally, the houses themselves have fewer amenities and, perhaps, depending on one's point of view, do not look as nice.

The bottom portion of Table 9.5 displays selected differences in housing amenities, another way of assessing the quality of housing. As mentioned, some things people do to

---

[47]Green and White (1997), DiPasquale and Glaeser (1999), Aaronson (2000).

**TABLE 9.5** *Social Class and Housing: Owner-Occupied Units*

| Housing Characteristics | Household Income | | |
|---|---|---|---|
| | *$40,000–59,000* | *$80,000–99,000* | *120,000+* |
| **Housing Age** | | | |
| Median Year Built | 1970 | 1975 | 1977 |
| **Housing Cost** | | | |
| Median Value of Home | $112,000 | $160,000 | $256,000 |
| Monthly Costs as % of Income | 18% | 15% | 11% |
| **Housing Amenities** | | | |
| Median Square Footage | 1,700 | 2,000 | 2,500 |
| Percent with 2+ Baths | 54% | 68% | 80% |

*Source:* U.S. Bureau of the Census (2002e:158–65).

their homes indicate their taste: color of paint, kind of yard decorations, and the like. Class differences in things like this reflect varying values as well as relative economic situation. In the table, however, I am using some expensive amenities—fundamental choices people make in purchasing and renting their homes—and in each case, working-class families are significantly less well off. Thus, on the average, families with lower incomes have significantly less square footage available to them: an average of 1,700 square feet in the working class, compared to 2,000 and 2,500 in the middle class. Each 300 to 400 increase in square footage means the house is about one room larger. Similarly, only 54 percent of owners in the $50,000 range have homes with two or more baths, compared to 68 percent and 80 percent at higher-income levels. Again, the pattern is the same for renters, although the square footage and percentages are lower in each case. Such variations are expressed in the following empirical generalization:

*The lower the social class, then the fewer amenities built into housing.*

Items like those used in the table are significant because they indicate families' levels of physical comfort and convenience. Not shown in the table are differences in the availability of air conditioning, quality of insulation, and other factors that decisively influence comfort and convenience. The square footage and bathrooms are important in another way as well, however, for they indicate the degree of crowding that occurs. Part of this is "just" daily hassle: Getting into and out of the bathroom each morning as family members prepare for work and school is much easier if more bathrooms are available. In addition, however, crowding has more serious implications. Smaller houses (or apartments) make daily life more difficult because people have less privacy. A couple's sex life is more restricted, there is less space for children to do homework, and there is less ability to get away from each other when someone is angry, among many other problems. Recall that unemployment leads to stress and family disruption; crowded living conditions exacerbate these problems. Ultimately, it does not matter whether these variations in amenities reflect comparative cost—which means in every case that the working class is less well off—or simply taste. As Max Weber emphasized, people make subjective invidious judgments of others based on their sense of sharing a common way of life. The working class is different from the middle class.

## On the Working Class

The Embourgeoisement Hypothesis does not accurately describe the condition of the working class in the United States. As you may recall, I have used this argument as a pedagogical device, an example of hypothesis testing in the social sciences. Thus, the available evidence shows that working-class people labor at inferior occupational settings that carry with them lower incomes and less job security. Furthermore, the life chances and lifestyles of the working and middle classes differ. Thus, based on the empirical data, the Embourgeoisement Hypothesis should be rejected because its premise is incorrect.

For contemporary Marxists, however, the Embourgeoisement Hypothesis implies a rather different kind of analysis. Karl Marx saw capitalist society as divided into two great classes: the bourgeoisie, consisting of a small group of capitalists who own the means of production, and the proletariat, consisting of the vast majority of people who own nothing and must sell their labor power to survive. The relationship between the two was inherently exploitive, Marx believed, and he predicted that over the long run an impoverished proletariat would rebel and usher in a new society. The problem for contemporary Marxists is to explain why this scenario has not occurred.

For this reason, the size, composition, and political orientation of the working class is a matter of some controversy.[48] Although the circumlocutions (or excessive words) become very complex in Marxist writings, a typical strategy is to downplay the differences between the working and middle class and argue, in some form or another, that the vast majority of people are still essentially proletarians who have been temporarily bought off by the bourgeoisie. Thus, it is asserted, engineers, real estate sellers, electricians, and police officers are "really" proletarians because they possess few assets and have nothing to sell but their labor power.[49] Ultimately, contemporary Marxists are still presuming that all those who do not own capital will eventually disregard their middle- or working-class location, recognize their true interests, unite, and overthrow a repressive regime.[50] The Embourgeoisement Hypothesis implies this type of analysis. Thus, contemporary Marxists remain committed to an evolutionary interpretation of history: A communist revolution and the destruction of capitalism are historically inevitable. This position is as much a leap of faith today as it was in 1848, when the *Communist Manifesto* was published.

Yet, even if a Marxist explanation is rejected, the question remains: Why are working-class people in the United States not politically radical? In Western Europe, working-class persons have organized socialist and labor political parties, some of which are quite radical, to represent their interests. This has not happened in the United States. Part of the reason, as shown in Chapter 6, is that working-class persons in the United States do not have the political resources comparable to their counterparts in Western

[48]van den Berg (1993).
[49]Wright (1997).
[50]Gagliani (1981).

Europe and participate in politics at a much lower rate than do middle-class and rich persons. Furthermore, Americans consistently say they do not want economic equality.[51]

While the reasons for these attitudes are unclear, a few suggestions can be made.[52] The transformative impact of the Protestant Reformation (especially Puritanism) was much greater in the United States than in other nations, mainly because of the absence of a feudal tradition in the New World. Moreover, the existence of the Frontier probably served as a sort of safety valve, diluting class conflict and allowing opportunity.[53] Further, as seen in Chapter 3, the very real possibility of upward mobility over the past century has buttressed the dream of success through hard work. The result is a unique emphasis on individual rather than collective action. Finally, the half-century conflict between the former Soviet Union and the United States made the "American dream" with its emphasis on individual responsibility into an ideology, relatively impervious to contradictory facts. While the impact of these phenomena cannot be demonstrated empirically, they constitute plausible reasons for the lack of working-class radicalism in the United States.

## Summary

This chapter used the Embourgeoisement Hypothesis as a pedagogical vehicle for sketching some of the characteristics of the working class in the United States. About 40 percent of the population does blue-collar work, with somewhat higher percentages among minorities (Table 9.1). Coupled with the class identification question in Chapter 2, this figure provides an approximate estimate of the size of the working class in the United States.

The occupational setting in which working-class people labor is often unpleasant due to heat and cold, noise, noxious and toxic fumes, dangerous machines, and other factors. It is also dangerous, as data on work-related fatalities reveal. Working-class people typically endure very close supervision, petty work rules, and intense production pressures as employers attempt to regulate the rate and rhythm of work.

As shown in Chapter 8, working-class people have lower incomes, on the average, than do middle-class people and less job security (Table 9.2). Minority people (both men and women) have higher unemployment rates than do Whites, as illustrated by the experiences of African Americans (Table 9.3). Most people without jobs do not leave them voluntarily. The human consequences of unemployment include economic deprivation (Table 9.4), lowered self-concept, and increased familial disruption.

The lifestyles of working- and middle-class people are quite different. I argued that this is true for a wide range of indicators and used housing as an example (Table 9.5). Working-class persons own houses at lower rates, own less expensive houses, and spend a higher proportion of their incomes paying for housing than do middle-class people. Furthermore, the houses working people live in have fewer amenities, such as extra bedrooms and bathrooms. The chapter concluded by describing some possible reasons why the working class in the United States is not radical.

[51]Hochschild (1981), General Social Survey (1998).
[52]Lipset (1977).
[53]F. J. Turner (1920).

# 10

# *The Poor*

We are two nations. One of them is familiar. It comprises the vast majority of the population—working-class and middle-class people who earn a decent living and enjoy the fruits of their labor. Although their level of affluence varies considerably, previous chapters have shown that they usually possess the resources necessary to deal with personal crises. Thus, when faced with a failed marriage, a pregnant daughter, an auto repair, a cavity, or any of the other tribulations and difficulties of modern life, they have a range of effective choices. The other nation is unfamiliar. Yet hand-lettered signs, "Will work for food," announce it. So does being accosted by a panhandler: "Can you spare some change?" So do those who walk the street: the drunk, the mentally ill, possessed by their peculiar demons. Such behavior suggests they have become so poor and so desperate that they are willing to debase themselves in public. This response is inexplicable to most people, but not every member of this unfamiliar nation displays extreme behavior. Many work, often full-time. Many are aged. Many are children. All live poorly in the United States. Recall the Class Structure Hypothesis from Chapter 1: The poor have fewer choices and find it harder to solve their personal dilemmas compared to members of other social classes. Coping is often the best they can do.

Sometimes the result of trying to cope with adversity is heartbreaking.[1] Maria Sanchez telephoned the emergency room at Boston's City Hospital. Her nine-month-old baby had diarrhea. A doctor told her to go to the pharmacy and buy Pedialyte (water with electrolytes added). She went to the pharmacy but did not have enough money, since the medicine costs about $6.00 per bottle. Medicaid will pay for it in her state (most would not), but only with a written prescription. Instead of going to the hospital immediately, Ms. Sanchez took the child home. The little boy became worse. She brought him to the emergency room 36 hours later, moribund. He eventually died.

This example, although extreme, illustrates the dilemmas the poor face and how difficult it is for those with few resources to solve the problems they face. Ms. Sanchez had a medical emergency and no money. (I know it is hard to imagine not having $6.00. But, as you will see, that is reality for millions of people.) More affluent persons faced with the same problem would simply pay for the medicine, however overpriced. If short of cash, they would use credit cards. This was not a choice for Ms. Sanchez. Rebuffed at the pharmacy, she had no car and no money to pay for transportation. Also, she spoke little English. Hospital bureaucracies are hard to deal with, even for well-educated, reasonably affluent, English-speaking persons with insurance. For the poor, such organizations are even more intimidating. So, given these limitations, Maria Sanchez tried to care for the baby herself.

It is easy to view this decision harshly, and the harshness with which the nonpoor judge the poor ought to alert you to the fact that the poor inhabit an unfamiliar nation. In fact, Ms. Sanchez's decision does not appear irrational—given her options. While the result was tragic, such events are rather common among the poor, who frequently find themselves in extreme situations. For them, coping with problems requires a degree of wisdom and heroism that few possess, and even these traits often do not help.

The example also illustrates the dilemma faced by those who would assist the poor. When physicians diagnose an illness, they confront not only a medical problem but also poverty. When teachers send work home or want a conference with parents, they confront not only education but also poverty. When counselors deal with a drug abuser, they confront not only self-destructive behavior but also poverty. Poverty affects every dimension of life. If the physician who talked to Ms. Sanchez on the telephone had told her to come for a prescription prior to going to the pharmacy, the baby's death might have been avoided. The physician, although well-meaning, did not appreciate the difficulties Ms. Sanchez faced. When would-be helpers are unfamiliar with the reality of poverty, they often fail to recognize its connection to the problem at hand.

In order to consider such connections, a definition is necessary. Definitions of poverty are of two types: absolute and relative. **Absolute definitions** refer to a standard below which basic needs cannot be met. **Relative definitions** compare a person or family's eco-

---

[1]Klass (1992).

nomic position to that of the rest of the population, often using the distribution of income as the metric. In the United States, an absolute definition is employed. Thus, **poverty** refers to a minimum income level below which individuals or families find it difficult to subsist. The word *subsist* should be taken literally. As you will see in a few moments, it is hard for poor people to obtain food, shelter, and medical treatment. Maria Sanchez provides an example of the last dilemma. Other Western nations employ relative definitions. In the European Union, for example, the official line equals 60 percent of the mean (or average) income.[2] Because the mean is influenced by the outliers—in this case, the income of the very rich—individual nations and most scholars doing cross-national research use some proportion of the median income (the midpoint of the distribution).

## Dimensions of Poverty

An initial step toward making the poor seem more familiar is to count them. How many people live in poverty? And how poor are they? It turns out, however, that counting the poor requires a series of subjective decisions in order to produce a realistic figure.

### Poverty in the United States

Standards of living change over time, which makes assessing the long-term trend in the poverty rate tricky.[3] In 1900, only 1 percent of all families owned an automobile, which meant it had no impact on people's economic circumstances because social life was organized without requiring ownership of high speed transportation.[4] Today, those without a car find it difficult (sometimes impossible) to get to and from work. Similarly, only 12 percent of the population had running water in their homes in 1900, which meant that most people used outhouses to relieve themselves. Although this practice exposed people to disease and, hence, had negative health consequences, it was free. Today, it is impossible to use an outhouse in any city, where most people now live. The poor must pay—with cash—for water, heat, electricity, and all other items necessary for living.

One way to resolve the problem of changes in the standard of living is to ask a simple question that stems from the definition offered earlier: What proportion of the population has difficulty subsisting? The answer provides an estimate that takes into account the changes mentioned above. These data are presented in Figure 10.1.

The figure shows that about 45 percent of the population was poor during the latter part of the nineteenth century. This percentage, however, is squishy. A review of estimates for this period shows that they range between 40 percent and 60 percent.[5] Hence, by selecting a relatively low estimate in this range, I have chosen to avoid overstating the

---

[2]Eurostat (2000).

[3]Fisher (1997).

[4]U.S. Bureau of the Census (1975:717).

[5]Patterson (2000). Plotnick et al. estimated poverty rates back to 1914 (1998). They show a pattern similar to that in Figure 10.1, but the percentages are higher: 70 percent prior to World War I, more than 30 percent after World War II. As they suggest, the former seems unreasonably high. What you should learn is that such estimates are tricky and involve a large amount of guessing and a large error term.

level of impoverishment during the late 1800s. The poverty rate apparently dropped around the turn of the century, primarily because of industrialization. In assessing the long-term trend, ignore the spikes caused by World Wars I and II, and the Depression. Immediately after World War II, the poverty rate probably stood around 30 percent, with a much narrower range of error. By 1960, it had declined to about 22 percent, then to 11 to 12 percent during the 1970s. This is the lowest level ever attained, at least in the United States. The poverty rate rose during the 1980s to about 14 to 15 percent and remained at that level until recently. During the last few years, the poverty rate has declined to about 12 percent. It is too soon to know if this change represents a trend (I doubt it). Note that the data for the last 30 years reflect the official poverty line adopted by the government. They comprise the most accurate information available—assuming you agree that the poverty line provides a realistic measure. As will become clear, the key word is "realistic," not "valid" or "objective," or "correct."

The historical data presented in Figure 10.1 reveal that a long-term decline in poverty occurred in the United States. These data, however, need to be supplemented with information from other nations in order to place the U.S. poverty problem in perspective.

### Poverty in Cross-National Perspective

As described earlier, most other nations employ relative definitions of poverty, usually some proportion of the median: 40 percent, 50 percent, or 60 percent of the income distribution. The most frequent one defines as poor all those earning less than 50 percent of the median. The results are shown below.[6]

| | |
|---|---|
| United States | 17% |
| United Kingdom | 13 |
| Canada | 12 |
| Netherlands | 8 |
| France | 8 |
| Germany | 8 |
| Sweden | 7 |

No matter how it is measured, poverty has declined in all Western nations over the last century and a half. Yet these cross-national data show that the U.S. rate remains much higher compared to other nations. Moreover, because these nations provide more in-kind (noncash) benefits for all citizens, regardless of ability to pay, being poor is not nearly as onerous as it is in the United States. For example, access to medical treatment is regarded as a right of citizenship in all these nations, which means that women like Maria Sanchez can obtain treatment for their infants at no cost. These differences suggest that, unlike the United States, most Western nations apply notions of fairness to society's victims, to those least able to cope with life's crises. These differences also suggest that public policies that place fewer people in situations like Maria Sanchez can be devised. Modern societies are not helpless in the face of problems. The United States, however, chooses to maintain a rather large impoverished population and to live with the consequences—in

---

[6]Jesuit and Smeeding (2002).

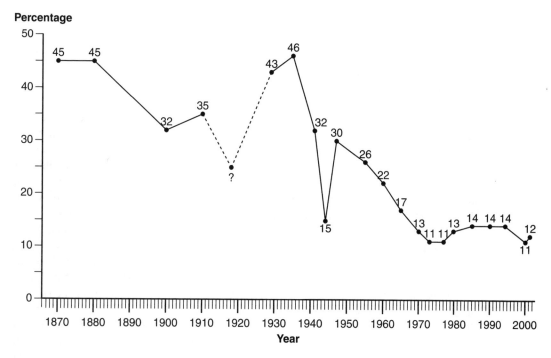

**FIGURE 10.1**   *Poverty Estimates in the United States, Selected Years, 1870–2001*

*Note:* There are no data for World War I (but see Plotnick et al., 1998). I have used a dashed line to suggest that the poverty rate probably fell around 1918.

*Sources:* 1870–1910 (Hartley, 1969:19), for 1929–44 (Ornati, 1966:158), for 1947–55 (Council of Economic Advisors, 1969:154), for 1960–2001 (United States Bureau of the Census, 2002f:21).

this case, a higher infant mortality rate and the human tragedy that follows, but also (as will be described later) hunger, homelessness, and other problems.

But is the U.S. poverty line realistic? The official rate is 12 percent, which is about 40 percent of the median income in this country. Does 12 percent of the U.S. population find it hard to subsist? The answer to a question like this inevitably involves issues of measurement and the limits of the social sciences.

## The Measurement of Poverty

The official poverty line for a family of four in 2001 was $18,022.[7] Because most people still think in terms of the stereotypical family of four, this figure is the most commonly recognized poverty threshold. The cut-off varies, however, by family size, being lower for a two-person family and higher for a six- or seven-person family. The line also varies depending on the age of the head of the household, being slightly lower if the head is over

[7]U.S. Bureau of the Census (2002f:5).

65 and higher if less than 65. The poverty threshold does not vary by region or rural-urban residence, mainly because the methodological problems are great. Taking all these permutations into account, about 12 percent of the U.S. population lived in poverty in 2001: 33 million people. Of this total, approximately 12 million were children. Thus, about one in six young persons in the United States lives in poverty. It would be wise to consider the long-term consequences, both for them and for society.

Right now, however, my interest is with the logic underlying the poverty line. Developed in the 1960s, the poverty line embodies a series of arbitrary decisions.[8] First, it is based on the cost of a standard market basket of goods, using the U.S. Department of Agriculture's Thrifty Food Plan. Second, it assumes that poor persons spend one-third of their income on food and two-thirds on everything else (rent, utilities, medical treatment, and so forth). Third, the threshold is adjusted each year in light of changing prices, using the Consumer Price Index. Finally, the poverty line refers to cash income before taxes from any source, such as a job, alimony, Social Security, or public aid. Again, all of these decisions are arbitrary and subjective, and this was true at the time the line was adopted.[9]

The most common criticisms of the poverty line are that the food plan does not provide a nutritionally adequate diet over the long run, the ratio between food and non-food expenses is wrong, the focus on before-tax income fails to account for the (lesser) amount of money really available to families (after sales and other regressive taxes), and it does not include the value of in-kind benefits, such as Medicaid or food stamps, which improve the lives of recipients. By dealing with these criticisms, policy makers could define a smaller or larger population as poor.

And there lies the rub. If, for example, the ratio between food and nonfood costs was changed to reflect the actual percentage of income spent on food, then more people would be labeled poor. Alternatively, if in-kind income (such as the value of food stamps) was counted as income, then fewer people would be labeled poor because they had higher "incomes." The Census Bureau has experimented with alternative poverty lines, most of which would increase the number of people defined as poor.[10] The point to remember is that either result—raising or lowering the number of impoverished persons—carries political implications.

Because any decision about the poverty line would be a political one, the search for a "more accurate," more "valid," or "more scientific" threshold is fruitless.[11] It is, nonetheless, a perennial siren song for social scientists, often involving logic traps.[12] For example, it is argued that the benefits of various public assistance programs lift people out of poverty. Thus, food stamps allow (some) poor people to purchase more food than they could otherwise. Medicaid allows (some) of the poor to obtain medical treatment. Housing subsidies allow (some) of the poor to rent apartments. And cash programs, such as Temporary Assistance for Needy Families (TANF) and the Earned Income Tax Credit provide extra cash for (some) poor families. Impoverished people who receive such ben-

[8]Orshansky (1965), Citro and Michael (1995), Fisher (1998), Garner et al. (1998), Bernstein (2001), Jesuit and Smeeding (2002).
[9]Orshansky (1965).
[10]U.S. Bureau of the Census (2002f:13-19). See also Citro and Michael (1995).
[11]Beeghley (1984).
[12]Citro and Michael (1995), Bernstein (2001), Jesuit and Smeeding (2002).

efits are indeed better off as a result, but they remain poor. This assertion is correct substantively, as an analysis of their budgets will show. It is also correct logically. Because these programs are means tested, people must become poor in order to be eligible for benefits and stay poor in order to keep receiving them. It is an illusion to think that a family so destitute that it receives TANF or food stamps or a housing subsidy or Medicaid is not poor.[13] A scientifically accurate poverty line is a contradiction in terms. Recall for a moment the limits of the social sciences discussed in Chapter 1 (in the section on Max Weber's work). These disciplines can discover the facts, explain them, and describe the implications that follow. The most important question about the poverty line is not whether it is accurate, but whether it is realistic.

## *Are the Poor Really Poor?*

In order to illustrate the difficulties impoverished people face, I have constructed a budget for a hypothetical family of four living at the poverty line.[14] Before proceeding, however, you should understand that any family (or household) used as a point of reference is inevitably arbitrary. For example, the needs of a family composed of two parents and two small children will differ from the needs of a family composed of one parent and two teenagers. Also, families will have different needs depending on where they live. For example, the cost of living in Alaska and Hawaii is significantly higher than in the 48 contiguous states. Similarly, costs vary in rural Florida compared to New York City. So in considering the vignette that follows, make mental adjustments for families with different characteristics and situations. I would like to suggest, however, that no matter what variations are considered, any analysis of family budgets at or near the poverty line will show they have limited lifestyles and life chances compared to other citizens. They are poor.

Please recall the Smith family. I used the vignette about them in Chapter 5 to illustrate how people in their situation cope, thus affecting the status attainment process. Since we last saw them, however, Edward Smith lost his job because the food-processing plant in which he worked closed. He now stays home to care for the two children and maintain the household. Jane Smith continues working 40 hours a week, 52 weeks per year in the textile mill. Contrary to commonsense assumptions, there are no two-week paid vacations, paid time-off, or holidays at this economic level. Those who do not show up for work do not get paid. If, for example, they must go to the welfare office to get certified for food stamps, or take a child to the doctor, or go to the dentist, they lose time at work—and income. As shown in Table 10.1, Ms. Smith has worked at the mill for many years and earns $8.75 per hour or $18,200 annually, before taxes. This places the family barely above the poverty threshold of $18,022. While her income is high for the kind of work she does, setting it at the minimum wage would leave the family far below the poverty line.

The income and expenses shown in the table involve several assumptions. It is assumed, for the moment, that Edward Smith earns no money informally and that Jane Smith is employed on the books and must have Social Security taken from her pay check. But she is smart and has no income tax withheld. Although the Smiths are eligible for the

---

[13]Beeghley (1984).

[14]Ehrenreich makes this same point, more evocatively (2001).

**TABLE 10.1   *Income and Expenses for a Hypothetical Poor Family (Two Adults, Two Children)***

| Income | |
|---|---|
| Gross Income from Husband's Job[a] | $      0 |
| Gross Income from Wife's Job | 18,200 |
| Total Gross Income[b] | 18,200 |
| Minus Expenses Taken before Taxes | |
| Employee share of cost of Medical Insurance | – 0 |
| Employee share of Retirement Contribution | – 0 |
| Total Taxable Income | $18,200 |
| Minus Taxes on $18,200 | |
| Income tax | – 0 |
| Social Security/Medicare tax at 7.65% | – 1,392 |
| State and Local Taxes at 14.4%[c] | – 2,621 |
| All Taxes = 22.5%, Yielding Net Yearly Income | $14,187 |
| Net Monthly Income (14,187 ÷ 12) | $  1,182 |

| Monthly Living Expenses[d] | |
|---|---|
| Total Food (home and away, plus personal supplies) | $    323 |
| Housing Payment (usually rent) | $    318 |
| Utilities (including telephone) | 228 |
| Transportation (car payment, insurance, public trans.) | 264 |
| Life Insurance | 0 |
| Health Care | 119 |
| Church Contribution | 38 |
| Education (for children) | 41 |
| Entertainment | 63 |
| Tobacco and Alcohol | 40 |
| Saving for children's education | 0 |
| Nonallocated | 0 |
| Total Nonfood | $  1,111 |
| Total Monthly Living Expenses (food + total nonfood) | $  1,434 |
| Monthly Balance (income – living expenses) | $  – 252 |

[a]Assumes the husband receives no off-the-books income.

[b]Assumes the family receives no public assistance income.

[c]Assumes couple lives in Florida. Includes sales, property, but no income taxes. If they lived in New York (as in Table 9.4), the tax rate would be 12.7%. The nationwide average for a couple like this would be 12.7%. See Institute on Taxation and Economic Policy (2003).

[d]These figures are typical of a family at this income level, see Bureau of Labor Statistics (2003c).

Earned Income Tax Credit, I will introduce this fact later; for now, the table assumes they do not receive that or any other form of public aid. It is assumed that the Smiths live in Florida (this was established in the vignette in Chapter 5), which relies on regressive taxes. Thus, the family must not only pay Social Security tax but also a variety of sales and other taxes; these total 14.4 percent—higher than a similar family living in New York would pay. Finally, the table outlines typical monthly expenses for a family living at this income level.

For comparison purposes, the format of Table 10.1 makes it easy to contrast the Smiths' budget with that of the Martinez family described in Chapter 9 (Table 9.4). Such a comparison will suggest how constricted the lifestyle of a poor family is compared to that of a working-class family. In their new circumstances, the issue for the Smiths is no longer whether they can purchase a computer for the children or send them to camp; the issue is survival. Can they subsist on $18,200?

The food budget of $323 translates into $2.69 per person per day, assuming a 30-day month. It will be slightly more in February (because it has only 28 days) and the Smiths will fast one day in each month that has 31 days. This last is sarcasm, of course, but with a serious message: The Smiths cannot obtain a nutritionally adequate diet on $2.69 per day. (Actually, you cannot even go to Burger King and get a Whopper meal on that amount.) Moreover, poor persons nearly always pay more for food because nearby markets are either mom-and-pop operations or franchised small stores. (Large supermarkets rarely serve impoverished areas.) This amount is not enough to cover their food costs, so the Smiths cannot remain within their food budget. They are, however, eligible for food stamps. The formulas for determining how much they receive are very complex, depending not only on their income but also on their assets and other factors. I am assuming they would receive $300 per month in coupons, $2.50 per person each day. Assuming they actually obtain the coupons, they now have the equivalent of $5.19 per person per day for food. (They can afford a Whopper Meal, except that the coupons cannot be used in restaurants. The coupons are like money, but not the same as money.) But even with this supplement, the Smiths find it hard to eat nutritionally. The benefit of food stamps does not change their basic situation: The Smiths cannot remain within their food budget, they must use part of their nonfood budget in order to eat.

A sidebar: Assuming the Smiths receive food stamps (many poor families do not), their total value would be the equivalent of $3,600 per year. If the coupons are seen as like money, their "income" is now above the poverty line. Does it make sense to argue, either substantively or logically, that this family is no longer poor? Since the program is means tested (requiring low income and few resources as a condition for receiving benefits), is it not more accurate to say that their poverty makes them eligible for aid?

The Smiths' nonfood budget is not adequate to cover their living expenses either, even if none of it is used for food. Table 10.1 shows a very modest nonfood budget of $1,111 per month to cover the cost of rent, utilities, automobile use and maintenance, medical and dental bills, clothing, educational expenses for children, and everything else necessary for living in the United States. Although the table presents living expenses that are more or less typical of low-income families, it is hard for many people to secure housing for the amount shown: $318 per month. The specter of homelessness arises constantly. Utility expenses refer to the price of gas, electricity, and a telephone, which costs many poor families a lot because their homes are so badly insulated. Finally, transportation costs are about $264. This figure can be less in large cities, assuming a person's house and job are both near public transportation stops. The vast majority must rely on their cars. What happens when the brakes go out? The Smiths' budget now has $301 left each month to pay for medical and dental bills, clothing, purchases necessary for a school-age child, entertainment, and everything else. Even purchasing birth control pills is difficult. And if Jane becomes pregnant, the family's finances fall apart completely. Although none of these amounts is very high and much variation occurs from one location and family to another, no matter how these numbers are manipulated, it is clear that the Smiths probably cannot stay within the nonfood budget for very long. New and unexpected expenses always occur. Yet, as noted, this family cannot stay within its food budget either. In fact, as shown at the bottom of Table 10.1, the typically modest living expenses incurred by a poor family put it in the hole by $252 each month.

The income and expenses shown in Table 10.1 reveal that families like the Smiths face a conundrum: They must often choose between paying for utilities and food, or housing and food, or medical treatment and food. It should not be surprising, then, that hunger and homelessness occur among the poor. Remember, the example used here has been for a family living just above the poverty line. About 12 percent of the population lived below it in 2001. The average poor family had a cash income $7,200 below the cutoff.[15] Put differently, imagine the problems a household of four would have with an income of $11,000. Yet millions of people did just that. Thus, it seems reasonable to assert that the 33 million persons living below the poverty line, of which 12 million are children, were really poor and that the official threshold provides a realistic indicator of the extent of poverty in the United States today.

Another sidebar: A partial solution to the Smiths' conundrum exists. They filed federal income tax forms and received Earned Income Tax and Child Credits of $3,960. These are tax expenditures, as described in Chapter 8 (see Tables 8.4 and 8.5). Let us say that they used the money to pay two months' back rent of $650 and old medical bills of $800. They also spent $300 on new clothes and shoes for the children and themselves, and $180 on tires for the car. The remaining $2,750 they set aside for emergencies. As the analysis of the income and expenses shown in Table 10.1 reveals, these are perfectly plausible uses of this money. And as that analysis also reveals, the set aside will not last very long because the Smiths' monthly expenses exceed their income. This family simply does not have enough money to meet its expenses.

Now let us add the value of food stamps (treating them as equivalent to cash) and the two tax credits to the Smiths' earned income:

| | |
|---|---|
| Net income | $18,200 |
| Food Stamps | 3,600 |
| EIT/child credits | 3,960 |
| | $25,700 |

Based on this amount, it can be argued that the Smith's are no longer poor. After all, their "income" is above the poverty line. But once again: Does this argument make sense, ei-

---

[15]U.S. Bureau of the Census (2002f:13).

ther substantively or logically? Since both public assistance programs are means tested, is it not more accurate to say that their poverty makes them eligible for aid?

As the situation in which the Smiths find themselves illustrates, the millions of families living at the poverty line are not simply short of cash—a problem everyone has sometimes. Such families are desperate. They do not, on their own, have enough money to meet the basic expenses necessary for living in a modern economy. This fact can be summarized by the Class Structure Hypothesis presented in Chapter 1: *The lower the social class, the fewer choices people have and the less effective they are in solving personal problems.* People who have few options often must turn to public assistance in order to survive.

# Public Assistance and Poverty

Because people are poor, public assistance alleviates some of the problems inherent to living poorly but does not change people's station in life. In fact, it can be argued that public assistance programs provide as many (if not more) benefits to those who are not poor as to those who are poor. In order to see why this paradox is possible, it is necessary to understand how the programs are organized and what actually happens to the money.

## The Characteristics of Public Assistance Programs

There are two types of public assistance programs: those providing cash to recipients, such as Temporary Assistance to Needy Families (TANF) and Supplementary Security Income (SSI), and those providing noncash benefits, such as food stamps and Medicaid. These are the four programs reviewed here.

***Temporary Assistance to Needy Families.*** This program originated with passage of the Personal Responsibility and Work Opportunity Reconciliation Act of 1996. All states were required to replace Aid to Families with Dependent Children (AFDC) with TANF by July 1, 1997. TANF is financed by block grants from the federal government to the states and by state-appropriated funds. States have a great deal of discretion in how they use federal money to implement the goals of the program.

Although the details of the new program are devilishly complex, among its most important elements are the following: All "needy" families with children are eligible to receive aid, but each state determines the definition of "needy." A parent (typically a woman) must assist in identifying the other parent (typically a man) and sign over child and spousal support to the state. There is a five-year lifetime limit on eligibility, regardless of work effort or earned income. Parents must work after two years of receiving aid, but states can choose to require work prior to that time (even immediately). "Work" is defined as having a job, obtaining on-the-job-training, actively looking for a job, being in a vocational training program, attending school, or engaged in community service. Under complicated criteria, states can exempt certain parents from the work requirement. Nonetheless, states must encourage employment by disregarding some earnings in calculating benefits. How this goal is accomplished, however, is left to each state's discretion. At state option, limits can be set on receipt of Medicaid during the "transition" from public assistance to work. States must subsidize childcare, but have discretion as to the amount and duration. States may allow recipients to establish "individual development accounts" in order to save money. Finally, states must set a minimum level of resources a family may possess (mainly checking and savings account balances, but also other economically valuable assets) and benefit levels. This resource limit combined with income constitutes the means test.

As implied by these requirements and its name, the primary goal of Temporary Assistance to Needy Families is to reduce the number of people receiving assistance by encouraging them to work. Indeed, the Department of Health and Human Services claims that the nation has "made dramatic progress [over the past few years] on the critical goal of moving families from welfare to work."[16] Nationwide, those receiving TANF declined by 57 percent between 1996 and 2001, to about 2.1 million families or 5.4 million persons.[17] But considerable variation occurred by state. For example, the number of recipients plunged 70 percent in Wisconsin, 77 percent in Florida, 78 percent in Illinois, and 89 percent in Idaho. Such declines suggest that many people are not being encouraged, but pushed off the rolls. Leaving public assistance, however, is not the same as getting out of poverty. It is possible, of course, that some unknown number of these people obtained jobs and are no longer poor. Thus, it can be argued that the strength of the economy (as indicated by the relatively low level of unemployment in recent years) has led to the slight decline in the poverty rate shown in Figure 10.1. But many, if not most, of those who have left (or been pushed off) the rolls do not do very well.[18] In Wisconsin, for example, about two-thirds of former recipients had lower incomes after losing public assistance. In Milwaukee (Wisconsin's largest city), 86 percent of those who lost public assistance had incomes below the poverty line. The major barriers to work are the availability of jobs, the lack of child care, and transportation. As will be shown, the structure of the economy means that there are not enough jobs for public aid recipients.

While receiving TANF benefits, the program regulates people's lives (and lifestyles) in rather detailed ways. As mentioned, each state has a great deal of latitude in setting requirements. Table 10.2 illustrates how the program might operate for a family of three.

Panel A of Table 10.2 displays some program provisions that recipients must satisfy. Recall that these will vary considerably by state. I have selected some common requirements for the table. Thus, in this illustration the family can have assets worth no more than $2,000. This amount refers mainly to bank accounts and other financial resources. In reality, few recipients have any money at all. The applicant must begin working immediately—in the sense noted above (be employed, in school, looking for a job, and so forth). The only exemption would be if the applicant has an infant less than one year old. Although states can exempt some recipients from work, there are funding penalties if they do so too often. In this example, the reward for employment is that the state will allow a family to retain 50 percent of the TANF grant for every dollar earned. In a fit

[16]U.S. Department of Health & Human Services (1998:1).
[17]U.S. Department of Health & Human Services (2003).
[18]Children's Defense Fund (1998; 1998a).

**TABLE 10.2**   *Temporary Assistance to Needy Families (TANF): Illustrative Program Provisions and Public Aid Benefits at Three Earnings Levels for a Family of Three*

**Panel A: Illustrative TANF Program Provisions**

| | |
|---|---|
| Assets Allowed: | $2,000 (excluding a car) |
| Must begin Working: | Immediately on receiving TANF |
| Work Exemption: | If child is less than 12 months old |
| Earnings Disregard: | 50% |
| Medicaid: | Yes, for 12 months |
| Child Care Subsidy: | Yes, 20% of earnings for 12 months |
| Individual Development Account: | Yes, for education only; no dollar limit |
| Five-Year Lifetime Limit: | Yes, no benefits to children after limit reached |

**Panel B: Illustrative Public Aid Benefits at Three Earnings Levels, Family of Three**

| Earnings (+ Benefits, – Taxes) | Example (1) | Example (2) | Example (3) |
|---|---|---|---|
| Earnings | $ 0 | $ 7,000 | $11,000 |
| + Earned Income Tax (EIT) | 0 | 2,800 | 3,600 |
| + TANF | 4,800 | 2,700 | 1,500 |
| + Food Stamps | 4,400 | 2,700 | 2,500 |
| – Social Security Taxes | 0 | 500 | 800 |
| | $9,200 | $14,700 | $17,800 |

*Notes:* Program provisions in Panel A are common among states. Receipt of EIT (shown in Panel B) is not automatic. I calculated the EIT in (2) and (3) and found that it was not easy to do. In (1) I used TANF benefits from the state of Pennsylvania and calculated food stamp benefits based on reasonable assumptions. Sales and other regressive taxes are significant but excluded. The TANF benefit in (2) was obtained as shown below. The amount in (3) was obtained in a similar manner.

| | | | | |
|---|---|---|---|---|
| $7,000 | (earnings) | | $4,800 | (maximum TANF) |
| –3,500 | (50% earnings disregard) | | –2,100 | (net earnings) |
| –1,400 | (20% child care subsidy) | | $2,700 | (TANF benefit) |
| $2,100 | (net earnings) | | | |

*Source:* U.S. Department of Health and Human Services (2003).

of fantasy, the state in this example will allow recipients to save some money—in this case for educational purposes. It is a fantasy because, given their probable expenses, it is unclear how such a family will find any money to save. During the first year of employment, the state will provide both Medicaid coverage and a child care subsidy. After that time, however, the family is on its own. This fact is important because in the example, the family is at the end of its first year on the program.

Panel B of Table 10.2 illustrates the benefits from TANF and other programs that a family of three might receive at various income levels. As indicated in the notes to the table, I am using TANF benefits from the state of Pennsylvania in this example. As a point of comparison, the poverty line for a three-person family was $14,269 in 2001. In Example (1), the family resources of $9,200 are only 64 percent of the poverty line. It is hard to survive on this amount of money. Example (2) shows how employment is encouraged, since the family gets to keep half of its TANF grant as well as the Earned Income Tax credit. Hence, the available benefits (assuming food stamps are counted as equivalent to cash) push the family above the poverty line, but barely. Note, however, that Medicaid benefits and the child care subsidy are expiring. It is not clear how the mother will be able to continue working under these conditions. If a three-person family budget were calculated similar to that in Table 10.1, it would be clear that this family faces precisely the same difficult choices as shown there. In this regard, example (3) is most interesting. It posits that a recipient worked for nearly a year at the minimum wage and still retains some TANF benefits plus those from other programs. Observers arguing that public aid programs get people out of poverty, point to people in categories like this one. In this case, the family's income and benefits place them about $3,500 above the poverty line. Substantively, of course, the family remains poor, as a budget calculation will show. Logically, since the programs require that the family continues to have almost no assets, it must stay poor to remain eligible. Finally, the unstable job market for those earning the minimum wage combined with their limited resources mean that the odds are low of a family staying above the poverty line as Medicaid and child care subsidies are withdrawn. What will happen to this family if it hits the lifetime limit?

In thinking about the implications of this example, note that the TANF benefits it posits are about average for the nation as a whole. Nationwide, the average for a family of three is $4,716, just below that used in the example. Moreover, there is great variability by state, as shown in Table 10.3. At the lowest are the southern twins, Alabama and Mississippi, with maximum TANF benefits of $1,998 and $2,040 yearly. At the other end, Wisconsin and Massachusetts seem positively generous, with maximum benefits of $8,076 and $7,596 yearly. This "generosity" vanishes, of course, when families must meet their living expenses. These data suggest that the lifestyle (and life chances) of an impoverished family receiving assistance varies a great deal depending on where they live. Whether such variations should be allowed is, of course, a political question. Some might argue that the cost of living is less in Alabama than in Massachusetts. Perhaps. But is there an Alabama brand of shoes or pampers or cereal? Do manufacturers give TANF recipients in Alabama a 10 percent discount?

***Supplementary Security Income.***    Unlike TANF, which is administered by the states and displays considerable variability in benefit levels as a result, Supplementary Security Income (SSI) provides a minimum monthly income for poor aged, blind, and disabled persons that is relatively uniform throughout the nation. There were about 6.7 million recipients in 2001. They received a maximum benefit of $6,540 yearly if they were single, living independently, and had no other income, and $9,804 yearly if they were a couple and living independently.[19] Both individuals and couples who qualify for SSI are automatically eligible for food stamps in small amounts that vary by state. As the title of the program suggests, recipients can have a low income from other sources, such as Social Security or wages, and use SSI benefits to supplement it. In addition, 44 states provide

---

[19]Social Security Administration (2003).

**TABLE 10.3**   *Maximum Yearly TANF Benefit Levels in Least Generous and Most Generous States*

| Least Generous | | Most Generous | |
|---|---|---|---|
| *State* | *Yearly Maximum* | *State* | *Yearly Maximum* |
| Alabama | $1,968 | Wisconsin | $8,076 |
| Mississippi | 2,040 | Massachusetts | 7,596 |
| Tennessee | 2,220 | Vermont | 7,548 |
| Texas | 2,412 | California | 7,368 |
| South Carolina | 2,346 | New Hampshire | 7,200 |
| Arkansas | 2,248 | New York | 6,924 |
| Nationwide Average: | $4,716 | | |

*Note:* "Most generous" refers only to the continental United States. Both Alaska and Hawaii have significantly higher benefit levels because of the very high cost of living.

*Source:* U.S. Department of Health and Human Services (2003:Table 12:2).

small additional stipends to the basic SSI grant. The result, however, still leaves most recipients below the poverty line. Apart from being aged, blind, or disabled, eligibility requirements for SSI dictate that beneficiaries must satisfy a means test; they must become destitute and stay that way. Thus, their assets (again, everything they own) must be less than $2,000 for single persons and $3,000 for couples, excluding a car.[20] Like TANF, then, recipients must become poor and stay that way to remain eligible for SSI.

*Medicaid.*   Although the Medicaid program is the nation's primary mechanism for insuring that the poor obtain medical treatment, many go without. The Medicaid program only pays for treatment for about 40 percent of the poor. Among the poor, those covered vary by age, as shown by the following table:[21]

| Age with Medicaid | % of Poor |
|---|---|
| 0–5 | 61% |
| 6–10 | 58 |
| 11–18 | 48 |
| 19–44 | 30 |
| 45–64 | 30 |
| 65 + | 30 |

Those not covered are left to fend for themselves, which usually means not obtaining treatment or begging for it at an emergency room. Among those covered, states are

[20]Committee on Ways and Means (2000).
[21]Committee on Ways and Means (2000:902).

required to offer the following services: hospital (inpatient and outpatient), laboratory and x-ray, family planning (including supplies), physician and nursing treatment, and what is called "early and periodic screening, diagnosis, and treatment" for children.[22] This last is the only form of preventive treatment paid for by Medicaid. Beyond this minimum, the scope of health problems covered varies sharply from state to state.[23] For example, 11 states pay for optometrist's services and 12 pay for eyeglasses. Prescribed drugs are paid for in 14 states and psychologists' services in 6. Although TANF recipients are not automatically eligible for Medicaid coverage, most states provide it, usually for one year. Although impoverished persons who do not receive TANF qualify for Medicaid, many do not receive benefits. For example, in most states, poor children who cannot see clearly may or may not be examined by a doctor and get glasses. Similarly, in most states, poor children who need antibiotics may or may not get them. In most states, poor children who need psychological services because they have been abused or for some other reason, probably will not get them. Whether these limits are wise is a political question.

*Food Stamps.*     Poor persons may not get enough to eat either. The U.S. Department of Agriculture states that the food stamp program is "America's first line of defense against hunger" because "it enables low income families to buy nutritious food."[24] As with all other public assistance programs, eligibility for food stamps requires that recipients satisfy a means test; that is, they must use up all their assets and earn little or no income. Thus, while TANF and SSI recipients are automatically eligible for food stamps, all other persons receiving them can retain resources worth less than $2,000, not counting a car.[25] All adults without dependent children must work (defined, more or less, the same way as in the TANF program). But whether employed or not, benefit levels are very low. For example, as shown in Table 10.2, an average family of three with no income receives only $2,400 in coupons per year, about $4.07 per person per day. If they are treated as a form of cash and combined with TANF benefits, the total of $9,200 is only about 64 percent of the poverty line. Nationwide, food stamps provide an average benefit of $71.00 per person per month, about $2.37 per day.[26] But a significant proportion of those who are eligible for food stamps do not receive them. Although about 17.3 million people received coupons in 2001 (a sharp decline since 1996), about 33 million people were officially impoverished in that year and, presumably, eligible.[27] As will be discussed, this fact implies that many people go hungry—at least sometimes—with malnourishment following.

They do so because significant barriers exist to obtaining food stamps in many states.[28] (1) The application forms are often very long. Nationwide, the average length is 12 pages. In two states (Minnesota and West Virginia), they are more than 30 pages long. By comparison, when middle-class people apply for federally guaranteed home mortgages of several hundred thousand dollars, the average length is four pages. When people

---

[22]Committee on Ways and Means (2000:904).

[23]Committee on Ways and Means (2000:927).

[24]U.S. Department of Agriculture (2003).

[25]U.S. Department of Agriculture (2003a:3–7).

[26]U.S. Department of Agriculture (2003a:39).

[27]U.S. Department of Agriculture (2003a:13).

[28]America's Second Harvest (2003).

apply to carry a firearm, the average application is one page long. (2) The applications in many states are complex and employ bureaucratic terminology that is difficult for many people to understand, especially those with low levels of formal education. (3) The applications ask nonessential and threatening questions. (4) The process of obtaining the necessary interviews is complex and filled with pitfalls designed to prevent applicants from obtaining benefits.

In one study, researchers simply wrote to request a food stamp application in California.[29] It is 13 pages long and asks questions like the following: "If you are a non-citizen applying for Medi-Cal and you are not (a) LPR (an alien who is a lawful permanent resident of the U.S.), (b) an amnesty alien with a valid and current I-688, or (c) PRUCOL (an alien permanently residing in the U.S. under color of law), please do not fill in the shaded box for 'Birthplace.'" Near the end of the application, just above the required signature, is the following statement: I understand that "if I do not follow food stamp rules . . . I may be fined up to $250,000 and/or sent to jail/prison for 20 years." This can hardly be comforting thought for anyone nervous about the process. Once the application is completed, people are scheduled for interviews. In many states, the appointment date and time is mailed to applicants without regard to work or family considerations. In California, a sheet accompanying the application describes "What to Expect When You Come In For Your Intake Interview." It includes the following instructions: "At 7:25 AM report to window 8 to check in." "At 7:30 AM an orientation will begin that reviews your rights and responsibilities." "At 7:31 AM you are late for this appointment and you will be rescheduled for another day." "Please be prepared to spend **several hours (noon or longer)** completing the intake process" (emphasis in original).

Imagine a single parent, working at the minimum wage trying to support and feed two children. This is what she must go through to obtain food stamps. Similar bureaucratic processes exist for those applying for Temporary Assistance for Needy Families, Medicaid, and other programs. The problem of obtaining food stamps provides an example of what the Class Structure Hypothesis means: No matter what the task, the lower the social class, the fewer the choices people have and the less effective they are in solving problems.

## *The Paradox of Public Assistance*

Recognizing that public aid programs provide help while requiring that the poor remain poor reveals their paradoxical impact. On the one hand, they help the poor with income support and in-kind benefits. The result alleviates some of the problems they face. The word *alleviate* is important; it means to relieve pain, to make suffering more bearable. This is what public assistance programs do by reducing the level of deprivation. It is all they do. As a result they function to maintain the economic status quo because people must remain poor in order to stay eligible for benefits. The mechanism for achieving this result is the means test, which stipulates that if recipients obtain additional income or assets above specified levels they become ineligible for public assistance. What happens is that recipients receive aid, which is immediately returned to the taxpayers, either by the

---

[29]America's Second Harvest (2003:2–3).

beneficiaries themselves when they use TANF and SSI to pay bills or purchase necessities, or by the government when it reimburses providers of noncash benefits.

As an aside, I do not wish to imply that there is anything wrong with using a means test or asking people to remain poor in order to continue receiving benefits. I do wish to suggest, however, that grandiose notions about America's generosity toward the poor are misbegotten. Despite much rhetoric, the programs described in the previous section are not "antipoverty programs." The cycle of poverty and public assistance programs shown in Figure 10.2 suggests this fact.

Box (1) of the figure anticipates the discussion in the next section by showing that the main causes of a family's entry on to the public assistance rolls are lack of a job, low wages, or marital dissolution. As the Smith and Martinez vignettes illustrate, job loss is always a potential problem for working-class people, whose employment responds to economic fluctuations (recall Chapter 9). Thus, when a factory closes down or reduces its workforce, the persons laid off first and for the longest time are those in blue-collar occupations. Further, for many intact families, their receipt of public aid—especially food stamps and Medicaid—reflects low wages rather than lack of work. As indicated previously, a family in which the head earns the minimum wage, $5.25 per hour (nationally, it varies somewhat by state), lives well below the poverty line. Millions of jobs pay at or near this level. Finally, for many women with children, marital dissolution because of divorce or separation forces them to turn to public assistance.

Boxes (2) to (4) depict the obvious functions of public assistance. They describe what happens to recipients each month they receive aid: For reasons noted above, they become (2) poor enough to satisfy the means test, which leads to (3) the use of public assistance, so that (4) they obtain needed benefits. As indicated by the feedback loop, this sequence repeats itself each month while they remain in poverty. In this way, then, public assistance helps the poor to survive by alleviating some of their problems. The sequence does not stop until, as indicated in Box (5), recipients obtain an adequately paying job, remarry (in the case of women), or exceed the five-year lifetime limit and are kicked off the rolls.

Box (4a) depicts the nonobvious functions of public assistance. It describes what happens to the money recipients receive each month: They return it to the nonpoor and the economic status quo is maintained as a result. Middle-class people, of course, use this money to support themselves or to invest and better their lifestyles. In my *Living Poorly in America,* I described this process as the "trickle-up effect" in order to denote its artificial character.[30] In the physical world, water trickles down as a natural result of the force of gravity. In the social world, the trickle-down effect rarely occurs, despite claims by some economists (recall Chapters 6 and 7). Thus, simply because money is appropriated to help the poor, does not mean they get to keep it or that income has been redistributed by the nonpoor to the poor. Just as governments can construct elaborate pumping stations and aqueducts in order to make water flow upward, so they can (far more easily) insure that money appropriated to help the poor is not permanently redistributed to them. The means test is the key to understanding this paradox. It insures that public assistance programs do not reduce the rate of poverty while, at the same time, guaranteeing that those who are

[30]Beeghley (1983).

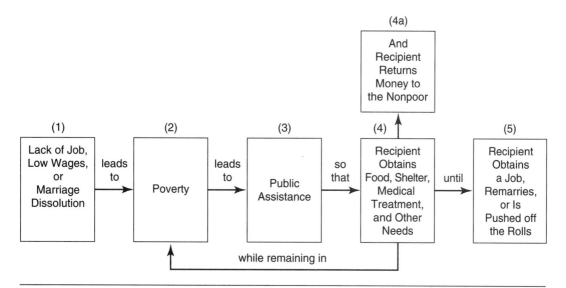

**FIGURE 10.2**  *A Model of the Cycle of Poverty and Public Assistance*

impoverished obtain help to alleviate some of their problems. Thus, while the poor endure less deprivation, they remain impoverished.

Before leaving this topic, it is important to resolve the paradox. It seems to me that neither conspiracies nor accidents happen very often in social life. Most of the time, there are relatively straightforward explanations for social arrangements, if observers care to look. Put simply, the paradox of public assistance results from who has power in this country. As the *Political Power Hypothesis* suggests:

> *The higher the social class, the greater the influence over the distribution of resources in the society.*

The nonpoor, especially the rich and middle class, who dominate the political process in the United States, control poverty policy; through their representatives, they enact public assistance programs. This fact means that the organization of these programs reflects the economic interests of the nonpoor. It is why the means test insures that only the very poor receive assistance and that the money is returned immediately to the nonpoor. The significance of the means test can be seen in its selective use. The many income transfer programs going to the middle class and rich are never called public assistance (or welfare), and none include a means test as a condition for aid (recall Chapter 7). Another problem remains. If public assistance requires people to remain poor and a large class of impoverished people persists, who benefits? And what implications follow?

## *The Benefits of Poverty*

I would like to suggest that the nonpoor, including readers of this book, benefit from the misery and deprivation of others. Moreover, I would also like to suggest that whenever harmful conditions persist over time, it usually means that some segment of the population is benefiting.[31]

First, poverty benefits the nonpoor by making a class of low-skill workers available who can and will perform vital tasks that others do not wish to do. Such jobs come easily to mind: making cloth and clothes, picking crops, cooking and serving food, cleaning buildings and streets, and all the other dirty, menial, dangerous, low-paying, and short-term occupations that must be performed in an industrial society.[32] Thus, the persistence of a high rate of poverty ensures that many people in the United States have so few options that they must fill positions no one else wants. This situation benefits the nonpoor.

An unexpected implication of this point of view is a recognition of the dual impact of the public schools mentioned in Chapter 5. On the one hand, schools facilitate achievement. On the other hand, they also weed out a sufficient number of individuals who become available for dead-end jobs. Thus, even though education can be a vehicle for upward mobility on the part of some individuals, by systematically failing to educate a certain proportion of students, the schools help to create and perpetuate a class of poor people who make up the cadre of low-skill workers our society needs. The irony here is that this process really is at least partly unintended, for it occurs despite the efforts of dedicated teachers.

Second, poverty benefits the nonpoor by keeping prices down. Because its members have no alternative to working for low wages, the existence of an indigent class subsidizes the consumption activities of the more affluent. Thus, clothes are cheaper, food is less expensive, mortgages are reduced, and taxes are kept low. What this interpretation means is that the lifestyle of the middle class and rich in U.S. society depends on the existence of a low-paid workforce.

The unexpected implication of this point of view is that nonpoor people have an economic stake in preventing the majority of hardworking poor persons—whose jobs include picking produce in the hot sun, making clothes in sweat shops, and picking up garbage in the streets—from obtaining education or job skills and thereby earning higher wages. It is easy to dismiss such people as low-skill workers and, hence, deserving of low wages. But they perform vital tasks, and if they were paid decent wages, the lifestyle of nonpoor people would suffer.

Third, poverty benefits the nonpoor by creating jobs and income for persons who would regulate, serve, or exploit those who are less fortunate. For example, people who cannot obtain work sometimes resort to illegal drugs and street crime to sustain themselves, thereby guaranteeing jobs for police officers, lawyers, judges, probation officers, and everyone else connected with the criminal justice system. By the way, this fact is not an apologia, merely a recognition that such illegal activities benefit the nonpoor population (which is least victimized). In addition, dependence on public aid guarantees jobs for social workers, clerks, and administrators employed in social service departments of government at all levels. This is because people who publicly declare their inability to provide for themselves and thereby receive aid from the state must be regulated by the nonpoor.[33]

[31]The source of my remarks in the following paragraphs is Gans (1972). See also Galbraith (1992).
[32]Ehrenreich (2001).
[33]Piven and Cloward (1971).

Less obvious, but just as important, the existence of a class of poor persons provides work for grocers, clerks, liquor store dealers, pawn shop owners, doctors, nurses, pharmacists, and many other individuals. Finally, there exist academicians who get huge grants to study the poor, write books about them, obtain tenure, and make money thanks to mass poverty. Thus, the jobs of millions of affluent people are dependent directly or indirectly, on the existence of a high rate of poverty.

An unexpected implication of the fact that poverty creates jobs and income for the nonpoor is the existence of the trickle-up effect associated with public assistance. As indicated earlier, this process occurs in two ways. On the one hand, public assistance programs require hordes of bureaucrats to administer them, social workers to regulate the recipients, physicians to provide medical treatment, pharmacists to supply medicine, computer programmers to keep track of the funds, and so forth. In this way, the government gives public assistance money directly to middle-class people. On the other hand, the trickle-up effect occurs as poor persons spend their "welfare" checks and stamp allotments. This money also ends up in the hands of the nonpoor: grocers, gasoline station operators, utility companies, landlords, and so forth.

Fourth, poverty benefits the nonpoor because destitute persons purchase goods and services more affluent people do not want. Indigents have so few alternatives that they must buy deteriorating or ill-constructed merchandise, patronize secondhand stores and thereby give new life to old products, and provide a market for stolen goods of all sorts (if they wish any amenities of modern life). In addition, poverty forces people to obtain services from badly trained or malevolent professionals who cannot make a living from middle-class customers. It should be emphasized that this argument is not just a repetition of the assertion above that poverty creates jobs and income; rather, the point here is that the poor are exploited more and have less legal protection than any other segment of the population.

The unexpected implication of a recognition that poor people purchase goods and services others do not want is that perverse consequences result when they try to plan ahead. Thus, by purchasing discount (often shoddy) or aging merchandise, indigent people are trying to save money, be frugal, and plan ahead for other expenses; they are, in short, trying to live by dominant values characteristic of the United States. And what they often learn from this attempt is that such efforts do not pay off, since what they buy is so frequently either useless or does not last. While it is easy to indict impoverished people for not being willing to plan ahead, to delay gratification, the experience of many low-income persons is that such strategies are fruitless. As a caveat, it should be recognized that some highly qualified persons do choose to serve or work for the poor, our most vulnerable citizens. Thus, the irony is that while impoverished people can be readily exploited, and this benefits the nonpoor, they also constitute an outlet for those with a more altruistic orientation, and this also benefits the nonpoor.

Although there are other ways in which the nonpoor benefit from poverty, the last one I want to mention here is that the poor are made to absorb the costs of economic policies. For example, whenever inflation has been high over the past 35 years, the federal government pursued fiscal and monetary policies that produced increasing unemployment. Such policies did reduce inflation, but at terrible cost to those who, through no fault of their own, were thrown out of work. Similarly, when reducing the federal budget deficit became an issue during the 1980s, 1990s, and today, the programs suffering the greatest cuts were those designed to aid the poor. Put bluntly, this interpretation means that the existence of mass poverty provides a class of people who can be exploited by the rest of the population—at least so long as they do not protest in some way or become unruly.

The unexpected implication of this point of view is the possibility that the political system in the United States is not really open to everyone, especially the poor. As consistent victims, perhaps they are kept from participating, except by disruptive or unruly behavior (recall Chapter 6). For now, however, I want to discuss the causes of poverty from two different angles, each of which provides a different kind of information. Thus, one way to understand the causes of poverty is to ask why individuals (like the Smiths) become poor. This line of analysis applies a basic sociological orientation to understanding impoverishment: Individuals act on and react to the situations in which they find themselves. In addition, another way to understand the causes of poverty is to ask how the social structure produces such a large class of impoverished persons. This question applies the notion that the social structure decisively influences rates of events to the study of poverty. Taken together, these angles of vision lower the possibility for self-deception and provide a clear, if cynical, view of U.S. society. They make the unfamiliar familiar.

## The Individual and Poverty

Poor persons in the United States are unfamiliar because they live on the margin in a land of plenty. They do not share in its material abundance. Given the exposition here and in previous chapters, the characteristics of those who are poor are just those you might expect.

*Age.*   *Children are more likely to be poor than people at any other stage of the life cycle.* Thus, about 16 percent of U.S. children are poor, compared to 10 percent of those between the ages of 18 and 64 and 10 percent of those over age 65.[34] One reason so many children are poor is that they are born of children and young adults, persons who have not acquired education or job skills, as illustrated by the vignette about the Smith family and their children in Chapter 5. It is a stereotype but nonetheless true that as people mature into adulthood and obtain job skills, the probability of poverty declines. Thus, even though it is usually unwise for young persons to marry or establish households independently of their parents, they sometimes try to do so—a fact that suggests how restricted their choices are. For example, one factor leading to this decision is pregnancy. Yet the United States makes it relatively difficult for young persons to obtain contraception and, thereby, prevent pregnancy.[35] This difficulty affects the poor most of all. In addition, sometimes girls become sexually active and pregnant as a reaction to an abusive home life or other deprivations.[36] In effect, they respond by confusing sexual intercourse with love, and by conceiving a child as evidence of their humanity, their adulthood. Boys from impover-

---

[34]U.S. Bureau of the Census (2002f:3).
[35]Luker (1996).
[36]Dash (1989).

ished backgrounds often react in similar ways. They make someone pregnant under the delusion that this result indicates their manhood.[37] Still another factor leading young persons to establish their own household is the desire to escape an impoverished home life.[38] Hence, young persons make unwise decisions in specific contexts in which their choices are limited and their experiences teach them (often falsely) that they will be better off forming their own families.

***Race and Ethnicity.*** *Whites are less likely to be poor than any other racial or ethnic group*, as indicated by the following data.[39]

| | |
|---|---|
| African Americans | 22% |
| Hispanic Americans | 21% |
| Asian Americans | 10% |
| White Americans | 8% |

You should note, however, that the pattern differs when absolute numbers are shown. Thus, the percentages refer to about 15 million white Americans, eight million African Americans, eight million Hispanic Americans, and one million Asian Americans. Hence, more Whites are poor than any other group. The reason a higher proportion of minorities endure poverty is discrimination (recall Chapter 2).

***Family Characteristics.*** Divorce, separation, or abandonment often lead to poverty for mothers and children: *Single-parent families are more likely to be poor than two-parent families.* Thus, 26 percent of female-headed and 13 percent of male-headed single-parent families are poor, compared to only 5 percent of two-parent families.[40] In considering the importance of a two-parent (hence, two-earner) family, I would like to return again to the Smiths. Recall from Chapter 5 that before Edward Smith lost his job, the family had a low but steady income, around $43,000 per year. They managed the stresses inherent to their economic situation. Since losing his job, however, Edward has battled feelings of meaninglessness and a sense of helplessness because he cannot provide for his family. Fights between Jane and Edward have increased. This is partly because Edward feels so badly and partly because money has become so tight. It will take courage for this family to remain together. Millions of couples find themselves in situations like this. Some break apart. And when this happens women usually get custody of the children.[41] As a result, more than half of all poor families are headed by women.[42]

***Low-Wage Job Skills.*** *The fewer the job skills people possess, the greater the likelihood of poverty.* Thus, people with higher education—such as those who write well, speak a foreign language, learn the law, and fill prescriptions—have job skills. They rarely be-

---

[37]Marsiglio (1993).
[38]Rubin (1994).
[39]U.S. Bureau of the Census (2002f:3).
[40]U.S. Bureau of the Census (2002f:3).
[41]Beeghley (1996).
[42]U.S. Bureau of the Census (2002f:3).

come impoverished. People without higher education—such as those who type, serve food, operate cash registers, and repair cars—also have job skills. But they are more prone to poverty. In modern societies, skills are traded for wages. One of the most important indicators of skill is education. Listed below are poverty rates among individuals aged 25 years and older by educational attainment.[43]

| | |
|---|---|
| Less Than High School Diploma | 22% |
| High School Diploma | 10% |
| College Diploma | 3% |

***Work Experience.*** *People who work less are more likely to be poor.* Thus, among the poor population aged 25 to 54 (the prime earning years), 49 percent were not employed during the previous year. Some observers take this fact as indicating laziness. My own observation, however, is that some people get beaten down by poverty. I will elaborate on this idea later. For now, I want to consider this finding in the context of the one above. Work experience often leaves people impoverished because their wages are so low. Put simply: A lot of employed people are poor. Jane Smith, for example, earns $8.75 per hour, an income that places her family at the poverty line even though she works full-time all year long. Of course, the Smiths constitute a hypothetical example, but they represent millions of people. Among the poor population aged 25 to 54 years, 33 percent work part of the year and 18 percent work full-time all year long.[44]

Poverty is thus a transformative event. In Chapter 1, I defined **socialization** as the lifelong process by which individuals learn norms and values, internalize motivations and needs, develop intellectual and social skills, and enact roles as they participate in society. Children whose parents go through the experiences described here learn quickly that life is neither predictable nor controllable. Such events can be defining episodes in people's lives. Not all of them suffer hunger and malnutrition, but many do. Not all of them endure homelessness, but some do. Not all of them withdraw into drug abuse or join gangs and express their rage, but a few do. All of them, however, even those whose families remain stable, go through hardship and deprivation.

Now the usual, commonsense approach to understanding poverty is to blame individual deficiencies: If only they would work harder, it is said, they could escape impoverishment. And there is truth to this adage, albeit partial truth. Some economists adopt the commonsense approach by seeing poverty as resulting from lack of **human capital.** As described in Chapter 3, the term refers to job skills or education, which can be converted into skills, that produce income. From this angle, people who are poor because they do not earn enough should simply augment their human capital so as to make their services more valuable and increase their income. At the very least, they should look for a job. And it is true, as common sense would have it, that individuals without a high school degree can often find a job if they look hard enough. A few vacancies exist even in central cities, despite declining employment opportunities in these areas. Yet, if successful, this strategy will only solve an individual's problem. It will not reduce the high rate of poverty. The reason is simple: There are not enough jobs. Thus, if a large proportion of those out of work sought all the jobs available, they would overwhelm the vacancies at the lower skill

---

[43]U.S. Bureau of the Census (2002a:Table 7).
[44]U.S. Bureau of the Census (2002a:Table 10).

levels.[45] This fact means that advocating self-help strategies to eliminate poverty—whether as common sense or dressed up in academic jargon—is not very practical. Such proposals affirm dominant values without increasing understanding. The latter occurs when structural questions are asked.

## Social Structure and Poverty

Throughout most of history, human beings lived at the mercy of nature. Productivity was low, based on muscle power. Nearly everyone scratched a living from the soil. The few amenities (goods that make life pleasant) were monopolized by an elite group. Life was short. Nearly everyone was poor. During the past century or two, however, this situation changed radically. Productivity is now high, based on nonliving sources of energy. Few people work the land. Amenities are spread throughout the population. Life is long. Relatively few people are poor. Today, nature lies at the mercy of human beings. Figure 10.1 revealed this transformation clearly. Poverty declined steadily over time, not only in the United States but in every Western society. This fact suggests that common structural changes occurred in all of them. At the same time data also reveal that the U.S. poverty rate is higher than that of comparable nations. This fact suggests that our country chooses to maintain a larger population of impoverished persons. In this section, therefore, I deal with two issues. First, why did a long-term fall in the rate of poverty occur? Second, why is the U.S. level so much higher than that of other societies?

### The Long-Term Fall in the Poverty Rate

Common sense, as mentioned earlier, suggests that people avoid poverty by working hard. Hard work, people are taught, produces success. Failure consists in giving up. From this point of view, it is easy for those who achieve some success to attribute it to their work ethic. After all, they sacrificed while training, found a job and labored for years to advance. Their lives confirm the idea that hard work pays off. By extrapolation, then, the conventional explanation assumes that in "a social context where plenty of opportunity existed," those who worked hard have been successful and those who are poor must not have worked very hard.

Students, of course, employ a similar orientation. They have learned that a correlation exists between hard work and success, in the form of grades and college matriculation. Thus, those whose good grades (and family background) enable them to attend Outstanding Private University assume that anyone can get in if they work hard. Similarly, those whose good grades enable them to attend the state-supported Flagship University assume that anyone can get in if they work hard. Finally, those attending Community College assume that anyone can go if they work hard. Thus, in both everyday life and higher education, people assume that hard work explains their success.

But this explanation is too facile. I mentioned above that the conventional account assumes "a social context where plenty of opportunity existed." The phrase was placed in

[45]Kasarda (1995).

quotes to alert you to the structural question: What factors produced a context in which hard work could pay off? My answer, in the form of a hypothesis, is as follows:

*The long-term fall in the poverty rate reflects (1) industrialization, (2) class differences in fertility rates, and (3) declining discrimination.*

*Industrialization.*    As you may recall, **industrialization** refers to the transformation of the economy as new forms of energy were substituted for muscle power, leading to advances in productivity. Now this definition, while accurate, is also rather narrow. Industrialization occurred in the context of other basic structural transformations: First, it is linked to the rise of **capitalism,** an economic system based on private ownership of the means of production—the machines and techniques used to produce goods and services.[46] Ownership produces a concern with profit, one motivation for increasing productivity. Second, industrialization is also linked to the rise of **work-centered values.** By the term, I mean ideals dictating that people should work hard, organize their lives methodically, delay immediate gratification, and earn money. Such sentiments do not develop in individuals by accident. People are taught them at home and at school. They emerged as unintended consequences of the Protestant Reformation.[47] Third, industrialization is linked to the value placed on personal freedom that arose in the West in the eighteenth century.[48] Free people choose for themselves what to produce and buy. Finally, industrialization is based on advances in scientific knowledge that occurred over the past 400 to 500 years. The terms *industrialization* and *industrial society,* then, are often used as shorthand ways of describing a historical watershed: the rise of new kinds of societies in the West over the last few centuries. So you should remember that the term *industrialization* implies more than merely a change in economic organization.

But precisely this change is of primary interest here. With industrialization, the proportion of white-collar jobs rose while farming jobs fell. Thus, as shown in Table 5.1 (in Chapter 5), the white-collar workforce rose from 18 percent to 60 percent between 1900 and 2001. In contrast, the farm workforce fell from 38 percent to 2 percent. The new job slots at the top of the class structure were, in effect, a vacuum that had to be filled. They "pulled" people upward, out of poverty. This is because an industrial society requires people in management positions. In addition, a host of new, highly skilled, white-collar occupations emerged in industrial societies. So people left farming and blue-collar jobs for better paying, higher prestige, ones. Poverty fell as a result.

*Class Differences in Fertility Rates.*    The **fertility rate** refers to the average number of children born to each woman. Although a two-century decline in fertility has occurred, the "baby boom" generation being the only exception, lower-class people have always displayed higher birth rates. This difference, greater in the past than today, meant that families in farming and blue-collar occupations had more children, on the average, than those in white-collar occupations. In the context of industrialization, in which the number of farming and blue-collar jobs was declining, these "excess" young persons were "pushed"

[46]Berger (1986).
[47]Weber (1905).
[48]Lenski (1984).

upward in the occupational hierarchy by population pressure. The result was upward mobility and, hence, a decline in the rate of poverty.

*Declining Discrimination.* **Discrimination,** you should recall, refers to the unequal treatment of individuals and groups due to their personal characteristics, such as their race or gender. In the past, the unequal treatment of racial and ethnic minorities was deliberate and overt, often legal. For example, the denial of civil rights kept racial and ethnic minorities from full citizenship. Other problems followed: unequal medical treatment, housing segregation, school segregation, and occupational discrimination, to name some obvious examples. Hence, Whites enjoyed tremendous advantages in the context of industrialization and class differences in fertility rates. Yet, while discrimination continues in all these areas, Chapter 5 showed that significant improvement has occurred in each of them as well. African Americans, Hispanic Americans, Asian Americans, and Native Americans suffer less discrimination than in the past. The result has been greater upward mobility and a lower rate of poverty.

The unequal treatment of women was similarly deliberate and overt, and also legal. For example, access to higher education and professional schools was restricted for women. Their ability to obtain credit in their own name was limited. **Traditional gender norms** dictated that women should remain home, bearing and raising children, and taking care of their husbands. Hence, males enjoyed tremendous advantages in seeking occupational and economic success over most of this century. Yet, while unequal treatment remains widespread, Chapter 2 showed that women suffer less discrimination today than in the past.

Now it remains true that, regardless of industrialization and class differences in fertility, people (usually white males until recently) only succeeded by hard work. These structural variables are important, however, because they provided a historical context in which hard work could pay off. A little counterfactual thought experiment suggests their impact. A century ago, the vast majority of people worked either on the farm or in blue-collar jobs, using muscle power to produce goods. Most were poor. If the job structure had not changed, then these people and their descendants (most of you) would have remained hard-working farmers. In the real world, however, people's options changed. Although no one was forced to be upwardly mobile, both the jobs and the people to fill them existed. These facts had nothing to do with each individual's motives or abilities. In Emile Durkheim's phrase, they reflected a change "in the nature of society itself."[49] The result has been a decline in the proportion of poor people in all industrial nations, more so in Western Europe than the United States.

### The American Poverty Rate Today

Despite the progress against poverty that has occurred throughout this century, the United States maintains a higher rate of poverty than other Western industrial societies. This difference can be accounted for in structural terms.[50]

---

[49]Durkheim (1895:128).
[50]Beeghley (1983; 1989).

*The rate of poverty in the United States reflects (1) the reproduction of the class structure, (2) the vicious circle of poverty, (3) macroeconomic policy, (4) the structure of elections, (5) the structure of the economy, and (6) institutionalized discrimination.*

***The Reproduction of the Class Structure.***     In the United States, as in all societies, the class structure is stable over time. The main evidence for this stability comes from analyses of mobility reviewed in Chapter 5, which document that most people end up in the same class as their parents. Although authors of these studies usually emphasize (correctly) how much movement occurs, the fact that most people remain in the same occupational category as their parents and go very short distances when mobility occurs means that the class structure is continually reproduced.

This stability exists because, as Max Weber emphasized a long time ago, people at each level use their resources to protect their advantages and pass them on to their children.[51] Thus, those who are most vulnerable to poverty—working-class families—tend to remain that way over time and across generations. Working-class individuals cannot alter the class structure into which they are born. It exists as a reality independently of them, limiting their choices. Thus, while a few near the top of the blue-collar hierarchy who work hard and have ability will move into white-collar jobs, most (including many who work just as hard and have just as much ability) will remain about where they began. Some of them will become impoverished during their lives. And, in turn, a small proportion of the poor become trapped.

***The Vicious Circle of Poverty.***     Sometimes impoverishment that would ordinarily be temporary combines with other difficulties, like a vicious circle, to snare people into long-term poverty. One way people become trapped is that their efforts at escaping poverty are thwarted and they become so discouraged they give up. Consider the Smiths, and remember they represent lots of families. As you may recall from Chapter 5, they live in Cedar Key, Florida, which has been a rural backwater for many years. It has always been a pleasant place to live. Although there is little crime (okay, a few locals run drugs up and down the coast), there are also very few (legal) jobs. In the last few years it has become something of a tourist haven and a few artists have moved there. Hence, Edward decided to set up a kiosk next to the town dock and sell locally made "art" (junk, but the tourists don't know that). The result was transformative. He became clean shaven and stopped drinking. He was bringing in an income. Alas, after protests to the police by the Chamber of Commerce, Edward was forced to stop because the law limits the number of street vendors. So Edward cleaned up his car and started using it as a jitney van, taking people staying in condominiums to the dock area at $1.00 per person. After protests by the local cab company, he was again forced to stop. Edward knows the "American Rule:" One is supposed to keep trying, to find work, and succeed over time. But this effort becomes hard after being repeatedly thwarted.

These imaginative illustrations are not exaggerated. Although some poor persons have so few job skills that years of training would be necessary for employment, many

---

[51]Weber (1920).

can operate small businesses. Lots of opportunities exist—cab drivers, jitney van operators, cosmetologists, and street vendors, to name a few—that do not require much capital or education. They require, instead, entrepreneurship. But such initiative is often restricted by local laws, in four ways.[52] First, limits are placed on the number of jobs in any one area. In New York City, for example, exactly 12,187 taxis, 4,000 food vendors, and 1,700, merchandise peddlers may operate—legally. Second, extensive training is required that has little relevance to public safety. In New York, one needs 900 hours of training to become a licensed cosmetologist, compared to 116 hours to become an emergency medical technician and 47 hours to become a security guard (with a gun). Third, outlawing certain jobs protects interest groups. Although jitney vans are in high demand in New York, the Transit Workers Union successfully lobbied the state assembly and city council to make such services illegal. Finally, bureaucratic sophistication is required, along with endless paperwork. In New York, the city's official directory contains 73 pages of directions about places to go and forms to fill out in order to get a license to repair videocassette recorders or open a parking lot. Thus, in New York as in other cities, thousands of bootstrap entrepreneurs operate illegally, on the economic margin, unable to expand their businesses. The long-term impact is to dull ambition, and people become trapped.

These limits on ambition mean that some illegal capitalists also rely on public aid. They are, of course, guilty of welfare fraud if caught. Moreover, the penalties for obtaining legal jobs can be severe. Let us suppose that one of Edward's friends works at a company where a janitorial position opens up and he gets the job (most jobs are obtained by word of mouth). He now earns $5.50 per hour, or $11,440 per year. (This assumes he works 40 hours per week for 52 weeks per year, including Christmas, and is never sick.) Alas, a major problem follows: The children have become ineligible for Medicaid because Edward and Mary's combined income of $29,640 is so high(!). The Smiths must choose between work and health insurance for their children. This is a *Catch-22* phenomenon.[53] In the novel of that title by Joseph Heller, if Captain Youssarian was crazy, he could get out of the war. But since he saw that the war itself was crazy, he was clearly sane. Hence, he could not get discharged. In the real world, people like Edward Smith sometimes choose not to accept employment. Is he lazy?

Assume for a moment that Edward turns down the job in order to maintain Medicaid coverage for the children. Their problems are not over. Young Samuel develops an earache. The nearest Medicaid provider is 90 miles away in Gainesville. Out-of-pocket expenses for gas and lunch while at the emergency room of the teaching hospital there will be at least $20. So the Smiths decide to wait and see if their son recovers. And he seems to. Although this is a reasonable strategy, since some medical problems improve over time without treatment, it has unfortunate results. Sam had otitis media, a common childhood ailment, easily diagnosed and treated. Left untreated, however, it results in hearing loss, even deafness. Thus, this little child has a long-term disability, one that increases the odds of him doing poorly in school and ending up trapped in poverty himself as an adult. This is the social context in which the Smiths and millions of real people must act.

[52]Mellor (1996)
[53]Heller (1961).

The Smith vignettes suggest how factors associated with poverty can sometimes form a vicious circle trapping people. Remember: Laws regulating small businesses and determining eligibility for welfare reflect policy choices made by middle-class and rich people. So do macroeconomic decisions.

***Macroeconomic Policy.***     **Macroeconomic policy** refers to the way government regulates the economy, especially inflation and unemployment. Ideally, there would be minimal amounts of both. In practice, however, a trade-off usually occurs such that one is higher than the other.[54] Although the government can regulate the economy in many ways, the most well known mechanism is interest rates as set by the Federal Reserve Board. In principle, when the Fed (as it is known) increases interest rates, it raises the cost of borrowing money for both businesses and consumers. This leads to deferred spending, slower economic growth, and lower inflation; it also leads to greater unemployment and poverty. In contrast, again in principle, when the Fed decreases interest rates, the reverse effects occur: greater spending, economic growth, and higher inflation, which in turn lower unemployment and poverty. The qualifier "in principle" should alert you to the fact that applying macroeconomic tenets to real-world problems remains a very imprecise process.

Even so, every few months the Federal Reserve Board meets and tries to do just that. In considering the impact of changing interest rates, you should understand that all economic problems are political problems. There is no politically painless way to decide whether to emphasize low inflation or unemployment. No matter what choice is made, someone's interests must be harmed while others benefit. In general, unemployment hurts the poor more than inflation. For example, a 1 percent increase in the unemployment rate increases the poverty rate by an almost identical .97 percent (note the decimal point). In comparison, a 1 percent increase in inflation increases the poverty rate by only .12 percent.[55] Thus, unless the situation is atypical, when macroeconomic policy decisions are made, the poor benefit by keeping unemployment low.

Since World War II, however, American policy has focused primarily on keeping inflation in check.[56] It has sought (not always successfully) lower levels of inflation, 2 to 3 percent, in exchange for higher levels of unemployment, 5 to 6 percent. In contrast, most Western European governments have sought (again, not always successfully) to have higher levels of inflation, 5 to 6 percent, in exchange for lower levels of unemployment, 2 to 3 percent. These different emphases have practical consequences: They influence the level of poverty. Put crudely, when macroeconomic policy is effective (which is not always the case), the United States seeks a higher rate and Western European nations a lower rate of unemployment.

The U.S. emphasis on keeping inflation down reflects the political priorities of middle-class and rich persons. They generally do not worry about unemployment and do not suffer its consequences. Rather, they see the value of their salaries and return on investments fall due to inflation, even if it is only moderate. Therefore, their representatives act to prevent it.

---

[54]Heilbroner and Thurow (1982).
[55]Blank and Blinder (1986:187).
[56]Hibbs (1977).

***The Structure of Elections.***   The phrase "their representatives" is deliberately provocative. I mean to suggest that public officials usually make choices reflecting the interests of the most powerful segments of a society. The fact that public policy in the United States creates more poverty than in other nations indicates the political dominance of middle-class and rich people. Quite simply, they participate in the political process (either by voting or contributing money) at a much higher rate than the working class and poor.

This fact means, as shown in Chapter 6, that the latter are relatively incapable of protecting their interests. Recall, for example, that holding elections on working days (rather than weekends or holidays) limits the ability of working-class and poor persons to vote. Those who overcome this handicap most easily have jobs that are less physically tiring, enjoy personal leave time as a job perquisite, have child care available, own a car, and live in safe neighborhoods. In addition, registration requirements limit the ability of the poor to vote. Those who overcome this handicap most easily are the middle class and rich, who are more aware of and able to deal with election laws. Finally, of course, people also participate by contributing money to campaigns. Rich persons always have an advantage here, and they gain access to decision makers as a result. It is not accidental that laws often favor their interests. As one example, macroeconomic and public aid policies reflect the interests of the nonpoor. In this context, the structure of the economy must also be recognized.

***The Structure of the Economy.***   Hard work often does not prevent poverty, mainly because of the structure of the economy. The pay attached to many jobs is low, as indicated earlier by the fact that 18 percent of the poor population aged 25 to 54 work full-time all year long. Such persons, like Jane Smith, are motivated, responsible, and have jobs. What they do not have is an income high enough to live on.

But those with employment are lucky. They earn something. Recall that the nation's main public assistance program, Temporary Aid to Needy Families, posits that families will move from welfare to work. But where are the jobs? Whenever this crucial question is asked, it is like the sound system goes out. Projections of the availability of low-skill jobs indicate that former public aid recipients alone (that is, not counting impoverished persons who are not on the rolls) will outnumber the net new jobs by about two to one.[57] And the problem is worst in those states with the highest public aid caseloads. This phenomenon is not new. The number of job seekers (especially at the low-skill level) has always exceeded the number of jobs.[58] Disregarding this fact, the TANF program is organized (by the nonpoor) on the assumption that public aid is temporary, that the poor will find work on their own.

The phrase "low-skill jobs" in the above paragraph refers to occupations in such industries as cleaning and building service, food preparation, and textiles and apparel—jobs that require little formal education and limited on-the-job training. These jobs are not likely to carry high wages. It has been estimated that the odds of one of these low-skill jobs paying a poverty level wage for a family of three are about 22 to one.[59] The odds of such a job paying a wage at 150 percent of the poverty line are about 64 to one. And the

[57]Weisbrot (1998).
[58]Abraham (1983).
[59]Weisbrot (1998).

odds of such a job paying a "livable wage" (arbitrarily set at about $25,000 for a family of four) are about 97 to one. "These numbers probably represent the most realistic estimate of the odds that a typical target of welfare reform will escape poverty through employment," and these results are consistent with other studies.[60]

The structural problem, however, is not only the availability of any jobs at all, but also the location of those jobs that do exist. A mismatch exists between the location of jobs and people.[61] In the past, cities were centers for the manufacture and distribution of goods, which meant that people (immigrants, for example) without much formal education could find work. Since about 1970, however, cities have lost hundreds of thousands of manufacturing jobs. Many of these jobs are now located in suburban areas.[62] Getting to them requires a long and expensive commute, usually by car. This job mismatch has especially affected minority groups, who are less able to live in suburban areas because of housing discrimination. Observers can only speculate about why these jobs have moved. One reason is probably cheaper land and easier access to transportation (interstate highways and airports). Another possibility is corporate aversion to African American workers.[63] Regardless of the reason, the result is massive unemployment in central cities, concentrated among minority people.

Thus, the structure of the economy insures that millions of people will be poor no matter how hard they work, no matter what their skills, no matter how much they try. This fact exists independently of their individual efforts. Institutionalized discrimination exacerbates this problem.

***Institutionalized Discrimination.***     I mentioned earlier that members of minority groups suffered from overt and legal forms of institutionalized discrimination in the past. As a result, they were unfairly confined to low-wage blue-collar jobs. Thus, one cause of a high rate of poverty among minorities today is their historical class of origin, not current discrimination.

Yet, as discussed in Chapter 2, discrimination still exists, only now it is covert and illegal. In its institutionalized form, discrimination is sometimes not intended. For example, African Americans, Hispanics, Asians, Native Americans, and Whites usually participate in different social networks. Thus, Whites work at different jobs, their children go to different schools, they live in different neighborhoods, and they attend different churches. In effect, these forms of segregation identify the boundaries of the social networks in which members of each group participate. Such boundaries indicate how the class structure affects interaction patterns, housing choice, educational attainment, occupational attainment, and virtually every other aspect of life. The fact of segregation, of participating in different social networks, often produces discrimination, even when no individual intends to do so. One result is a higher rate of poverty among minority groups.

I also noted earlier that traditional gender norms meant, until recently, that women were systematically denied the opportunity to work outside the home, prevented from competing with men when they did, and kept economically, politically, and psychologi-

---

[60]Weisbrot (1998:8). See also Danziger and Lehman (1997), Meyer and Cancian (1996), Burtless (1998).
[61]Kasarda (1990; 1995).
[62]Kasarda (1990; 1995).
[63]Williams (1987).

cally dependent on men. Although this situation has improved considerably in recent years, Chapter 3 shows that many people still govern their lives by such rules. Moreover, they teach their children, male and female, that such norms still provide guides for living. One result is that women are less successful occupationally, economically, and politically.

We are two nations: one poor, one not poor. In my experience, when presented with ethnographic accounts of poverty or the details of poor people's lives in some other way, nonpoor persons react with sympathy and understanding. When discussing "the poor," however, without specifics, these same persons revert to stereotypes about "deservedness." The structural analysis presented here should alert you to the fact that poor individuals acting in their own self-interest cannot reduce the level of poverty. No amount of moralizing about the importance of self-reliance and individual initiative will change that blunt fact.

## Concluding Comments

Some individuals believe that suffering brings purification, that through suffering one achieves nobility. I have never observed this phenomenon. Rather, suffering often mutilates people. It twists the spirit, sometimes breaking it. As stress piles on stress, some people lose hope. In sociological jargon, they become **alienated.** That is, they believe they have little control over their lives. For people living in poverty, this perception is often very realistic. It is easy to convince ourselves that we would behave differently, heroically, if placed in the situations in which the poor find themselves. Reality is usually far different. The poor have fewer and less effective choices than do members of other social classes. In order to illustrate this fact, I want to describe the effect of poverty by focusing on hunger and homelessness.

Although the United States does not display starvation like that occurring in some third world nations, many Americans go hungry for significant periods of time and suffer malnutrition as a result. By the term **hunger,** I mean the chronic underconsumption of nutrients. The most reasonable estimate is that 25 million people endure hunger in this country.[64] This figure makes sense in light of the family budget described earlier. For some, hunger occurs at the end of the month when food stamps run out and the cupboards are empty. For others, unable to obtain coupons, it is a pervasive, everyday affair. The presence of food distribution centers in every city suggests that the nutritional needs of many people go unmet. According to one study, such centers feed about 23 million people each year.[65] Of those fed, about one-third are employed adults, about 40 percent are children. These data suggest that hunger is widespread among the poor, that the food stamp program does not solve the problem.

The long-term consequences of hunger are catastrophic, especially for children. They display slow growth and mental deficiencies as a result of malnutrition. A six-year-old can look (and act) three years old. Many children, hence, become stupid because they have not had enough food to eat during the first years of life. They do not recover. Ever. Lack of nourishment makes people more susceptible to disease and less capable of recov-

[64]U.S. Department of Agriculture (2002:5).
[65]America's Second Harvest (2001), U.S. Conference of Mayors (2002).

ering. This is important because many common illnesses have a long-term impact. For example, if strep throat, a typical childhood disease, is not treated with antibiotics it can lead to heart and kidney damage. The result is a sickly adult who cannot be a productive person. A nutritious diet can help prevent strep.

Yet obtaining a nutritious diet requires difficult choices.[66] About 45 percent of clients at food distribution centers report they must choose between paying for food and paying for utilities. About 36 percent must choose between food and rent. And about 30 percent must choose between food and medicine or medical treatment. Forcing people to make these sorts of choices does not bring nobility. It does, however, provide a practical example of alienation. Moreover, the long-term impact redounds (overflows) to affect the entire society.

So does **homelessness.** By the term, I mean lack of access to a conventional dwelling: a house, apartment, mobile home, or rented room. Those without housing sleep in places not intended for these activities: cars, scrap-metal shacks, and public areas (such as bus stations or heat grates outside buildings). Some also sleep in shelters. The current estimate is that about 3.5 million people, of whom 1.4 million are children, experience homelessness each year.[67] This number is probably low, however, as precise counts are hard to obtain.

In surveys, it appears that most of those who are homeless are men, with many (about 40 percent) reporting they are veterans. A significant minority report problems with drug addiction, mental illness, or both. The fastest growing segment of the homeless population, however, comprises families with children.[68] One night in January, a reporter went looking for homeless people near the White House. Within a few minutes he found "an African American woman, eight months pregnant, sleeping on the lawn of the Justice Department" and "five veterans, sleeping on a heat grate for warmth." If he had gone to a nearby shelter, he would have found people like twenty-six-year-old Martha Harris and her two children.[69] After an abusive childhood, she fled a husband who beat her regularly. Her five-month-old daughter, Sara, is listless and underweight. She cannot hold down food or grasp a rattle. Her fifteen-month-old son, Mathew, does not speak, has trouble sleeping, and often refuses to eat. I mention them because you should always remember that real people underlie quantitative data, people whose range of choices is so restricted that they cannot even obtain a place to live.

The impact of homelessness is most obvious in children. One study reported that 40 percent of homeless pregnant women received no prenatal care, another example of the limited choices available to some.[70] So the odds of bearing low birth weight babies, with all the human tragedy and costs they entail, become much higher. Children in shelters or on the streets are more likely to be abused or neglected. They display chronic medical and psychological problems. They do not attend school or do so irregularly. The McKinney Act, by the way, requires school districts to provide extra educational help for homeless

[66]America's Second Harvest (2001).
[67]National Coalition for the Homeless (2002).
[68]National Coalition for the Homeless (2002a).
[69]DeParle (1993), Bassuk (1991).
[70]Bassuk (1991).

children. The logic, of course, is that such assistance can avoid long-term problems, misery, and societal costs. It is my impression, however, that most districts really wish homeless children would just go away.[71] And they do.

They live in grief and on grates. Such experiences do not produce nobility of soul. Without a home, they lack stability and nurturance. They lack friends, family, faith group, schools, and regular medical treatment. The consequences are catastrophic and, like hunger, redound to affect the entire society.

The high rate of poverty in the United States means that central cities, especially the largest ones, have the aesthetic flavor of some third world nations: Teems of homeless people wander around. Large areas are disorganized and dangerous. Drug abusers appear everywhere. People live amidst the rubble of empty buildings. An air of hopelessness pervades the streets. And this situation affects not only the unfortunate souls inhabiting these areas but everyone who is not poor as well. Yet it is not inevitable. As the cross-national data show clearly, the level of poverty in this country could be far lower. If so, its negative consequences would be less severe. One has to wonder why it is allowed to continue.

If we wish to reduce the rate of poverty and endure fewer of its results, the direction public policy should take is clear: The United States needs to redistribute money, benefits, training, and—above all—jobs. By benefits, here, I refer to programs that prevent poverty over the long term. Access to birth control, for example, could allow poor women to regulate their fertility. Access to medical treatment could prevent illness from becoming chronic, especially if the emphasis is on prevention. Access to housing could help prevent trauma to children and family break-up. Other types of programs should be considered, but these suggest the direction this country should take if it wishes to cut the poverty rate. But such programs imply an expansion of what is sometimes called the "welfare state."

When confronted with this possibility, however, we tend to throw up our hands in despair. There exists a pervasive fear that government creates problems, not solve them, but this is self-deceptive. Middle-class and rich people do not hesitate to use government. They seek tax breaks, contracts, and services. They protest mightily, and often effectively, when these benefits are taken away. Only when the issue is sharing benefits with the poor do questions about the deservedness of the recipients arise. Only when the issue is protecting all our children does the public resist.

Americans persist in believing that we can take income support from the poor and they will be able to get jobs and support themselves; that we can take training programs from the poor and they will somehow train themselves; that we can take child care from the poor and they will be able to go to work; that we can prevent the poor from access to medical treatment and they will be healthy; that we can prevent the poor from access to drug treatment programs and they will get off drugs; that we can limit access to birth control and abortion, and they will have fewer children; that we can reduce the amount of affordable rental housing and they will still find places to live; and that schools can be underfunded yet kids will learn. Is this wise? Should we divide ourselves into two nations?

---

[71]National Coalition for the Homeless (1999).

## *Summary*

The poor remain unfamiliar to nonpoor persons. Poverty refers to a minimum income level below which individuals or families find it difficult to subsist.

Although living standards have changed considerably over time, it appears that at least 45 percent of the population was poor during the last part of the nineteenth century. Ignoring declines during World Wars I and II, and a huge increase during the Depression, a long-term fall in the poverty rate occurred (Figure 10.1). It dropped to a low of about 11 percent in the 1970s, jumped to 14 to 15 percent during the 1980s and 1990s, and has declined slightly since then. The level of poverty in the United States is significantly higher than in other Western societies. The measurement of poverty is an arbitrary process. The question is not whether a "scientifically accurate" measure exists, but whether the line is realistic or not. Preparing a budget for a family near the cut-off shows that those living below it are desperate (Table 10.1). They have difficulty obtaining food, shelter, medical treatment, and other necessities.

Public assistance programs alleviate some of the problems poor people face, but do not eliminate poverty. This is because the means test requires that people become poor and remain poor in order to stay eligible (Figure 10.2). TANF provides very low cash benefits (Table 10.2) that vary greatly by state (Table 10.3) to people who must not have any assets. SSI provides low cash benefits to poor aged, blind, and disabled people, who must also be devoid of all assets. The food stamps program provides coupons for small amounts of food purchases, coupled with a means test. And Medicaid provides medical treatment for the poor, also coupled with a means test. Public assistance programs reflect the political priorities of the nonpoor population. It can be shown that the nonpoor benefit from a high rate of poverty: An impoverished population constitutes a class of low-skill workers who perform jobs others avoid. They subsidize consumption by the more affluent. They create jobs for nonpoor persons who regulate, serve, and exploit the less fortunate. They are exploited and have less legal protection than other segments of society. They absorb the costs of change. These are practical examples of alienation, an inability to control one's own life.

Young persons display a greater likelihood of poverty. Whites are less likely to be poor than members of other racial and ethnic groups. Female-headed families are especially likely to be poor. Individuals with low-wage job skills are more likely to be poor, even if they are employed.

The long-term fall in the poverty rate reflects the impact of industrialization, class differences in fertility rates, and the decline of discrimination. Industrialization created job openings at the top of the class structure while higher birth rates among the lower classes provided the people to fill those empty slots. Although discrimination continues, it has declined in every area.

The poverty rate today reflects the impact of the reproduction of the class structure, the vicious circle of poverty, macroeconomic policy, the structure of elections, the structure of the economy, and institutionalized discrimination. The reproduction of the class structure occurs because of the tendency for occupational inheritance. Poverty can be seen as a vicious circle that traps people, as indicated by the problems of obtaining work while on public aid and seeking medical treatment. Macroeconomic policy in the United States generally trades higher unemployment (hence, poverty) for lower inflation. The poor participate less in elections because they are held on working days and require advanced registration. The economy does not provide enough high-wage jobs, located in areas the poor live. Finally, institutionalized discrimination continues to prevent women and minorities from achieving.

A major implication of poverty is that it twists the spirit; people become alienated. This response reflects people's experience with hunger, homelessness, and violence. Yet modern societies like the United States determine how much poverty exists.

# *The United States in Global Context*

All societies display stratification, but the arrangement of classes and the level of inequality within and between them can vary a great deal. Consider the following societies:

In the first, everyone makes a living by fishing. People's incomes in this society will not be equal, of course, since some individuals are willing to work harder than others and some have more ability than others. Hence, over time a set of classes will develop and valued resources will be distributed unequally. In the process, however, the main criterion by which people are evaluated is achievement: how much fish they catch. Although people's life chances will vary by social class, it is likely that the level of inequality between the rich and poor will be low. In this context, most people will see the structure of stratification as fair. A nation like this one is likely to be democratic (in some form) and stable. There will probably be little need for the use of force (especially military force) to control the population.

In the second, everyone makes a living by gold prospecting. As above, people's incomes will not be equal, since a few will have discovered (or seized) mother lodes and become wealthy. Some may have found small deposits of ore and do reasonably well. Most, however, will not locate much and will end up with little to show for their efforts even though they work hard. As above, a set of classes will develop over time. In this case, however, distribution of valued resources will be very unequal and so will people's life chances. Of course, some of this inequality will reflect ability (since some individuals may have greater skill at spotting signs of gold) and some will be willing to spend more hours prospecting than others. For the most part, however, the stratification structure will reflect luck combined with rapaciousness. Over time, this result means that the main criterion by which people are evaluated will be ascription, non-performance-related characteristics. This is because no matter how much ability they have or how hard they work, most prospectors will end up poor. In this context, many people will see the structure of stratification as unfair. A nation like this one is likely to be undemocratic and, hence, it will sometimes be necessary to rely on force to control the population.[1]

These are, of course, hypothetical societies. They can be seen as ideal types, to use a phrase of Max Weber's, benchmarks against which our own and other real nations can be compared. Previous chapters have shown that inequality in the United States has increased over the past few years. The distribution of valued resources and the life chances that follow are more unequal than ever before. Thus, one can argue that the United States now resembles the gold-prospecting society more than the fishing society. And to the extent true, this result is cause for concern because, as mentioned in Chapter 6, people's dissatisfaction may erupt in violence or some other form of unruliness. But just how unequal is the United States compared to other nations? Does the United States really resemble the gold-prospecting society? As it turns out, the answer to this question depends on the angle of vision from which it is asked.

In this chapter, I deal with this question by looking at the structure of stratification in a global context. The focus will be on income inequality (although other points of comparison will be made as well), mainly because worldwide observations are available. It turns out that such observations are difficult, however, for the following reasons: (1) Although the data are the most recent available, they were gathered in different years. This fact means they reflect different economic and social conditions—both within each nation and between them. (2) The definition of income varies. For example, it may be before or after taxes. The latter is a measure of disposable income (and, hence, probably better). In addition, "income" may include transfer payments. As should be clear from Chapters 8 (the middle class) and 10 (the poor), transfers can significantly alter people's lifestyles. (3) The reporting unit varies. It can refer to individuals, families, or households. If households constitute the unit of analysis, which is most common, then it is usually assumed that income sharing occurs. But this is not always so. (4) The purchasing power of money varies. And (5), translating local currencies into dollar values is a very imperfect business. These difficulties mean that complete comparability is not possible, even with countries like Canada and the United States or the United Kingdom and the United States. Nonetheless, comparability is a matter of degree and it is possible to reach an acceptable and meaningful level. Scholars do what they can, knowing the pitfalls.

## Poverty and Inequality in the United States and Developing Nations

I have selected five developing nations from around the world to compare with the United States: China, Brazil, India, Mozambique, and Honduras.[2] They are chosen arbitrarily, but

---

[1]Krugman (1995).

[2]I am using nations as the unit of analysis throughout this chapter. For a different and very useful approach to understanding world income inequality, see Firebaugh (1999; 2000).

not accidentally. China, Brazil, and India represent what are called "semi-peripheral societies." That is, they display relatively diversified economies that may (or may not) become industrialized. See them as more or less in a middle stage of economic development. Honduras and Mozambique represent what are called "peripheral societies." That is, they display a much lower level of economic development. See them as on the edge. The reason for these labels will become clear in a few moments.

As has been true throughout history, most of the world's population is poor—often desperately poor. Although data on global poverty are tricky to obtain and interpret, partly because the ability to consume nonmarket goods (especially food) varies and partly because of the difficulties noted above, some cross-national observations about poverty are available. One standard measure is the percentage of a nation's population living on less than $2.00 per day ($730 per year). Such data are presented next for the five nations being used as a continuing example in this section:[3]

| | *% Living on < $2.00 per day* |
|---|---|
| Brazil (1997) | 47% |
| China (1996) | 54 |
| Honduras (1996) | 69 |
| Mozambique (1996) | 78 |
| India (1997) | 86 |

Two nations tie for the dubious honor of having the highest percentage of its population living on less than $2.00 per day: Nigeria and Mali at 97 percent. Although these nations are being used as examples here and much variability exists, a very high proportion of people living in developing nations are poor. And they are poorer than the poor in the United States. In comparison, the percentage of the population living on less than $2.00 per day in the United States and, indeed, in every Western nation, is zero. The World Bank does not even include this item for these countries in its analysis of "world development indicators." Another indicator of how poor these nations are is the Gross National Product (GNP) per capita.[4] This measure describes the value of all the goods produced in a society, as divided by the total population. It is $6,300 in Brazil, $3,300 in China, $2,300 in Honduras, $2,100 in India, and $800 in Mozambique. The nation with the lowest GNP per capita in the world is Sierra Leone: $400. By comparison, the rate in the United States is $30,600. All of these nations are extremely poor compared to the United States.

This high rate of poverty in developing nations translates into restricted life chances for their citizens. The infant mortality rate provides one indicator of just how restricted people's lives are because it reflects their overall living standards. You should recall that the infant mortality rate is defined as the number of live babies who die in the first year of life. The rate is 28 per 1,000 in China, 36 in Honduras, 37 in Brazil, 63 in India, and 139 in Mozambique.[5] The nation with the highest number of children dying during infancy is

[3]World Bank (2003).
[4]World Bank (2003:274–75).
[5]U.S. Bureau of the Census (2002c:829).

Angola: 193 per 1,000. These rates are similar to those seen in the United States during the nineteenth century. The current American rate is 7, and this is high by Western standards.

Their high level of poverty and restricted life chances imply that many developing nations exhibit a very unequal income distribution. And this is generally true, although some exceptions exist.

I shall begin with the "semi-peripheral" nations: China, Brazil, and India. One overall way of assessing income inequality is to look at the Gini Coefficient. As you may recall from Chapter 8, the Gini Coefficient is a standard index in which zero would mean complete equality (every household has the same income) and 100 would mean complete inequality (one household has all the income). In the United States, for example, the distribution of household income produces a Gini Coefficient of 46, which (as shown in Chapter 8) is substantially higher than in the past. In comparison, the Gini for Brazil is 60, indicating greater inequality in the distribution of income, while it is 38 in India and 40 in China, indicating less inequality. The main reason for these differences occurs at the extremes of the income distribution. Displayed in the following table are the shares of income going to the poorest and richest 20 percent of the population in these three nations and the United States:[6]

|  | Income Share to the | |
| --- | :---: | :---: |
|  | *Poorest 20%* | *Richest 20%* |
| Brazil (1996) | 3% | 64% |
| United States (1997) | 5 | 46 |
| China (1998) | 6 | 47 |
| India (1997) | 8 | 46 |

Thus, Brazil has a more unequal income distribution than the United States, mainly because the richest fifth of the population takes 64 percent of all the income. In comparison, India is less unequal than the United States, at least in terms of income distribution. The poorest fifth of Indian households receives about 8 percent of the nation's income, compared to 5 percent in the United States. A similar difference exists at the other end of the distribution: The richest fifth of all households receives 46 percent of the income in India, identical to that in the United States. But this relatively equal income distribution in India does not obviate the fact that it is a very poor nation: As pointed out earlier, nearly all its population subsists on less than $2.00 per day, and 63 of every 1,000 of its children die at a young age.

The "peripheral" nations also vary a great deal in terms of income distribution. Honduras, for example, displays a Gini Coefficient of 54, while Mozambique's is 60. The most unequal nation in the world, by the way, is Sierra Leone. In that sad nation, the Gini Coefficient is 63, and the poorest 20 percent of the population receives only 1 percent of the income.[7]

---

[6]U.S. Bureau of the Census (2002:19), World Bank (2003:282–83).
[7]World Bank (2003:283).

Although these data may understate the degree of income inequality in some nations, such as India and Brazil, some conclusions are nonetheless possible. First, most people in most developing nations are poorer than in the United States. Second, many developing nations display both more poverty and more income inequality than the United States. Third, some developing nations display more poverty but similar or even less income inequality. This last point is revealing: It suggests the extent to which recent increases in inequality in the United States reflect political choice. In general, however, these comparisons imply that the United States resembles the fishing society more than the gold-prospecting society.

This conclusion, however, depends on the question asked. I would like to pause here for an excursus (digression) and ask a different question, one that goes beyond simply comparing poverty and inequality in developing nations and the United States: Why is there so much poverty and inequality around the world?

One way of answering this question requires a change in the unit of analysis such that the focus becomes the worldwide circumstances in which poverty and inequality occur. In sociological terms, the unit of analysis must change from the nation-state to a world system. This orientation is useful because developing nations today must confront the already developed nations, like the United States—which have interests to protect. Thus, it can be argued that economic and distributive processes that appear to be internal to them—to Brazil or Mozambique, let us say—are actually affected by their location in the world system. When this change in the unit of analysis takes place, then the United States and other Western nations are viewed in a different way.

In the world system, nations can be seen as like classes.[8] Envision, if you will, a three-tiered global stratification structure.

The "core societies" are analogous to the rich: comprising the industrialized countries such as the United States, Sweden, Germany, France, and most of the other Western European nations. They control most of the world's wealth, military force, technology, and financial services. Their economies are diversified, with a focus on manufacturing and—increasingly—service industries. They do not export unfinished raw materials. These nations tend to be democratic, stable, and powerful.

The "semi-peripheral" societies are analogous to the middle class. Such nations are industrializing, or trying to. Achieving this goal is difficult because they are so dependent on the core societies. For example, developing nations often provide skilled labor to companies based in core nations, as when computer programmers and engineers from India work for American-based corporations. Or, to take another example, developing nations are exploited due to their low labor costs: companies based in the United States manufacture products or parts of products outside the United States that are destined to be exported back to the United States and to other nations (such as when an automobile plant is located in Brazil). Although some of these societies are democratic, like Brazil and India, they remain unstable. They have little military power compared to the United States and other Western nations.

The "peripheral" societies are analogous to the poor. Like the poor, these nations are relatively "unskilled" in the sense that their economies are simple (and sometimes so

[8]Wallerstein (1974), Chirot (1986).

disorganized that they are unable to take advantage of their resources). Hence, they depend on the "core" nations for financial aid, technology, and markets for their raw materials (for example, coffee from Honduras). Economic development is difficult in this context because decisions are made in terms of the interests of corporations based in core nations and their governments. Moreover, elites in such societies (called "compradors") are dependent for their wealth on these same foreign corporations and, hence, function as their agents against the nation's interests. Such nations are usually not democratic; they rely on military force (whose soldiers are often trained by core nations) to control their populations.

According to Immanuel Wallerstein in *The Modern World System,* the reason there is so much poverty and inequality in developing nations is because Western industrial nations like the United States exploit them.[9] The "semi-peripheral" and "peripheral" societies provide the cheap labor and raw materials that enrich the rich nations. From this point of view, the Western industrial nations (the "core societies") have an interest in keeping developing nations undeveloped; they have an interest in keeping them poor. In short, from this point of view, poverty and inequality around the world reflects the impact of Western imperialism.

This chapter opened with a comparison between a hypothetical fishing society and a gold-prospecting society. When nations of the world are compared in terms of this ideal type, then the United States appears to resemble the former more than the latter. But when the world system becomes the unit of analysis, the global stratification structure seems to resemble a single giant gold-prospecting society. From this point of view, the United States and other Western nations are the successful (and rapacious) prospectors.

Although Western exploitation provides one answer to the question of poverty and inequality around the world—and it is useful—it is not the only answer. Another answer involves looking at the developing nations themselves. This angle of vision requires shifting the unit of analysis from the world system back to nation-states.

I mentioned earlier that most people in most developing societies are poor. This is not always so. Some nations, such as Japan and South Korea, have successfully pursued economic development over the past half-century even though they were clearly economically and politically dependent on the United States. This fact has important implications, not only for understanding how development occurs but also for their levels of poverty and inequality.

Unlike Brazil and the other nations described earlier, there is very little poverty in either Japan or South Korea. As used before, one indicator of living standards is the infant mortality rate.[10] It is 8 per 1,000 live births in South Korea and 4 in Japan—the lowest in the world. Japan, in fact, has become the healthiest nation in the world. The U.S. rate, you should recall, is 7. (Remember that the infant mortality rate is 37 per 1,000 in Brazil, 63 in India.) Another indicator of economic development and its impact on poverty and inequality is the Gross National Product per capita.[11] In Japan, it is $24,000, while in South Korea it is $14,600. Although both figures are less than in the United States, $30,600, they

[9]Wallerstein (1974), see also Chirot (1986).
[10]U.S. Bureau of the Census (2002:829).
[11]World Bank (2003:282).

resemble the GNP in other Western nations: Sweden's is $20,800. And both are much higher than in China, Brazil, India, Honduras, and Mozambique.

The overall level of inequality in Japan and Korea also resembles that displayed in Western nations, and is lower than in the United States. The Gini Coefficient summarizing the income distribution among households is 25 in Japan and 32 in South Korea, both of which are lower than in the United States.[12] The income distribution in these nations reflects this development, as shown below by the proportion going to the bottom and top 20 percent, respectively:[13]

|  | *Income Share to the* | |
| --- | --- | --- |
|  | *Poorest 20%* | *Richest 20%* |
| Japan (1993) | 11% | 36% |
| South Korea (1993) | 8% | 39% |

Yet both Japan and South Korea were devastated in the aftermath of war, World War II and the Korean War, respectively. It is hard to imagine two nations more dependent on the United States. Both pursued aggressive policies designed to produce economic development, with considerable success.[14] The revised *Kuznets Hypothesis* describes what happened. As you may recall from Chapter 7, the argument is as follows:

*Inequality of wealth and income increases during the early phases of economic growth when the transition from preindustrial to industrial society is most rapid, stabilizes for awhile, and then becomes subject to negotiation.*

What apparently occurs is that the early stages of economic development require large-scale capital formation. Since only the relatively few who are rich have sufficient wealth to invest, they reap greater rewards initially and the level of inequality increases. Over time, however, as the economy is transformed, the combination of demographic factors (the rich do not reproduce themselves) and government regulation of the market results in a reduced level of inequality, or at least the issue becomes open to political intervention. There is logic to this explanation. This is why I used the Kuznets Hypothesis in Chapter 7 to explain the historical pattern of inequality in the United States. The experience of both Japan and South Korea appears to conform to that predicted by the hypothesis. Today, neither would be called a developing nation.

According to Peter Berger in *The Capitalist Revolution,* there are lessons to be learned from the experiences of Japan and South Korea.[15] As I understand it, what these nations did—in rather different ways—was to pursue an aggressive form of capitalism (what Berger described as "a growth-oriented private enterprise" strategy) with some attention to land ownership among the poor, attracting investment in labor-intensive projects that increased the wages of ordinary people and fostered industrialization, and

[12]World Bank (2003:282).
[13]World Bank (2003:282).
[14]Berger (1986).
[15]Berger (1986:138).

removing legal and social barriers to opportunity. Obviously the specific form of this strategy would vary from one society to another. But over time, Berger hypothesized, *the more a developing nation is included in the world capitalist system* (by these and other strategies), *the greater its economic development.* The impact of economic development will be, over the long run, to reduce poverty and inequality—as has happened in the West and in Japan and South Korea.

But nothing resembling this process has occurred in most countries around the world. To varying degrees, many developing nations can be described as "a Sweden superimposed on an India." That is, they display a relatively modern, technologically based, and (small) affluent sector of the population coexisting with masses who live in extreme poverty.[16] Those who have traveled to, say, Brazil, know that deviating only a little way from a rather narrow range of airports, modern hotels, and tourist venues will lead a person into areas of abject poverty. Such experiences are even more common in other nations. From this angle of vision, then, perhaps wealthy elites and the governments they control are the problem in developing nations. They are like the lucky and rapacious gold prospectors in the hypothetical society described at the beginning of this chapter.

Apart from the metaphor, my guess is that any explanation of poverty and inequality in developing nations will have to take into account both a world system and a nation-state explanation. In other words, it is probably true that Western industrial nations have exploited developing nations and it is also probably true that many of these nations have adopted policies that mainly benefit their own elites (keeping the masses impoverished). But my overall interest in this book is somewhat different than that developed in the above excursus: an understanding of the structure of stratification in the United States. Even though the distribution of valued resources in the United States has become more unequal in recent years, it seems less harsh when compared to that in developing nations. The level of poverty in this country, bad as it is, is far less than in many nations in the world. And the consequences of poverty, in the form of infant mortality (other indicators could have been used), are less widespread. But whether such comparisons are meaningful is unclear. The economic, political, and cultural differences are so great that it is hard to know whether the contrasts are useful for understanding. People who are poor or working class in the United States do not compare their situations to people in Brazil or India. Hence, another perhaps more useful way to look at the structure of stratification in this country is to compare it to that among Western European nations. These nations are similar to the United States economically, politically, and culturally.

## Inequality in the United States and Western Nations

The United States and other Western nations also display similar structures of stratification. In Chapter 4, for example, it was shown that an empirical generalization exists: *Hierarchies of occupational prestige are similar across all Western industrial nations.* This stable finding means that the social standing of the jobs people have is nearly the same in, say, the United Kingdom, France, and the United States. A physician and a lawyer, an

---

[16]Berger (1986:132).

automobile mechanic and a sales clerk, will all be similarly ranked. In Chapter 5, it was shown that, while some variability exists, all Western nations display high rates of occupational mobility. The U.S. levels of mobility are neither the highest nor the lowest. Finally, it was also shown in Chapter 5 that the variables affecting status attainment are similar in all these nations, a combination of ascribed factors (family background) and achieved factors (education), with increasing emphasis on the latter. These similarities suggest the degree to which all Western industrial societies resemble the fishing village described at the beginning of the chapter.

But there are differences as well, and they are significant. Chapter 6 showed that voting rates are much lower in this country. And these differences are class based: Those who participate at lower levels are primarily working class and poor. In the United States, the middle class dominates voting. The rich dominate by contributing money to political campaigns, which allows them access to decision makers. Ultimately, it can be argued that these differences result in greater income inequality in the United States. One aspect of the overall income distribution is the greater number of poor persons in this country. Chapter 10 showed that the poverty rate in the United States is more than twice that in Sweden, Germany, the Netherlands, and France, and significantly greater than that in the United Kingdom and Canada.

It follows that the United States displays much more inequality in the income distribution than does any other Western industrial nation. Gini Coefficients for the nations that have been compared to the United States in previous chapters follow:[17]

| | |
|---|---|
| Sweden (1995) | 21 |
| Germany (1995) | 27 |
| Canada (1995) | 28 |
| France (1995) | 31 |
| Netherlands (1994) | 33 |
| United Kingdom (1995) | 34 |
| United States (2001) | 46 |

Nearly all the difference in the income distribution occurs at the bottom and top. For example, as mentioned previously, the bottom 20 percent of the U.S. population receives about 5 percent of the total income while the top 20 percent takes 46 percent. In comparison, in Sweden, the most egalitarian of these nations, the bottom 20 percent gets 10 percent and the top gets 35 percent. The other nations shown above are in between. By the way, there tends to be a division among Western European nations such that those in southern Europe exhibit somewhat greater income inequality.[18] Even so, none of these nations approach the level of inequality found in the United States.

The result is that people have more restricted life chances in this country, as indicated by the infant mortality rates (per 1,000 live births) shown below for 1997:[19]

[17]Ritakallio (2001), World Bank (2003), U.S. Bureau of the Census (2002:19).
[18]Atkinson (1996).
[19]U.S. Bureau of the Census (2002:829).

| Japan | 3.9 |
| Sweden | 4.0 |
| Netherlands | 4.4 |
| France | 4.5 |
| Germany | 4.7 |
| Canada | 5.0 |
| United Kingdom | 5.5 |
| United States | 6.6 |

Taken together, these data suggest that when the angle of vision refers to other Western industrial societies then the United States is very unequal. It resembles the gold-prospecting society, in which a small elite has—by a combination of luck and rapaciousness—increased inequality for its own benefit. How can this situation be changed?

## Some Practical Strategies for Reducing Inequality

Although some practical strategies exist, they will not be easily implemented. Partly because of the difficulties described at the end of Chapter 10 (our federalist system, racial and ethnic divisions, the legacy of slavery, the ideology of individualism, and the existence of private benefit providers), reducing inequality in the United States will not be easy. For those who worry about how unequally the spoils are divided in this country, here are some suggestions.

First, eliminate federal and state income taxes on the poorest one-third of the population. Increasing the number of tax brackets and enacting modest increases in taxes on the top third could make up the lost revenue. As described in Chapter 7, nearly all the changes in tax law over the last two decades have allowed the rich to keep more of their income.

Second, perhaps an alternative to the (very difficult) first, expand the earned income tax credit. This is a cumbersome way of redistributing income, but it would work, and it has the advantage of being tied to employment.

Third, increase expenditures for communal services: day care (this would help poor and working-class people work), early childhood education, mass transit, even recreation opportunities. Policies like these would be one way of reducing the impact of income inequality and increasing people's opportunities for success.

Fourth, expand sex education and make birth control services free to young persons. Such policies would reduce the birth of unwanted children. They would also enable young adults to learn job skills and develop the ability to support themselves prior to making decisions about parenthood.

Fifth, develop some form of nationwide health insurance so that everyone can at least obtain medical treatment. Better yet, such an insurance program ought to emphasize preventive care. It is nearly always cheaper to prevent disease rather than treat it.

Sixth, build lots of low-cost housing, preferably near jobs. Access to housing and jobs would do much to reduce the level of inequality in this country.

These changes are, however, unlikely. Even when the greater poverty and inequality in developing nations is taken into account, the United States appears to resemble the gold-prospecting society. Is this the direction we should be heading?

## *Summary*

When the United States is compared to developing nations, such as Brazil, India, Mozambique, and Honduras, it becomes clear that they are much poorer. Many developing nations, but not all, also display greater income inequality.

Two explanations for these differences were discussed. In the first, the world system becomes the unit of analysis, with various nations being seen as analogous to classes. The "core nations" are like the rich. The "semi-peripheral nations" are like the middle class. The "peripheral nations" are like the poor. The argument is that both "semi-peripheral" and "peripheral" nations are exploited and kept dependent by the "core" nations. The second explanation shifts the unit of analysis back to nation-states and focuses on the elites and governments in developing nations. Japan and South Korea constitute examples of how economic development can occur, thereby reducing poverty and inequality.

When the United States is compared to other Western nations, it becomes clear that all have similar structures of stratification. It also becomes clear that the United States exhibits much more inequality than any other economically developed country. There are, however, a number of practical strategies that can be used to reduce the level of inequality in this country—if we have the will.

# 12

## Reflections on the Study of Social Stratification

*Objectivity in the Study of Stratification*
*Research Methods in the Study of Stratification*

*Paradox in the Study of Stratification*

**Sociology** systematically attempts to see social life as clearly as possible, to understand its various dimensions and their interrelationships, and to do so without being swayed by personal hopes and fears.[1] This book has attempted to illustrate the possibilities inherent to sociology by focusing on a specific aspect of social life—the structure of stratification—explaining it on different levels (individual and structural), and summarizing the relevant research results. In this last chapter, I would like to reflect on some implications that follow from this orientation. Although my comments will emphasize the study of social stratification, the topics are of general significance to all areas of sociological inquiry. The first issue is the problem of objectivity, because it is required if sociologists are to see the world clearly. The second is the problem of research methods, because they provide the key to understanding the dimensions of social life. The final issue is the paradoxical nature of sociological analyses, because this characteristic highlights people's hopes and fears about the future.

### Objectivity in the Study of Stratification

In order to see any aspect of social life clearly, such as stratification, a specific orientation is necessary—one not required of ordinary persons: Bias must be eliminated as much as

---

[1]Berger (1977).

possible. This goal is far more difficult to achieve in the social sciences than in other disciplines because observers are embedded in their subject. Thus those interested in the study of stratification also occupy a specific location in the class structure; they earn an income, they have a job with its level of occupational prestige, they own property, they are married and have children, and the like. These facts mean that a researcher's personal experiences, values, and economic interests can easily influence the researcher's analysis.

The reduction of bias requires that sociologists adhere to the norms of science, regardless of their personal experiences, values, or economic interests. These rules direct researchers to try to report findings without regard to their motives for undertaking the study. They require researchers to use the most systematic evidence available and to make logical deductions. And they adjure researchers to make their own values explicit so that others may assess whether bias enters their analysis. Such rules provide those studying stratification with a way of looking at the world that is decisively different from daily life. Moreover, two additional norms exist that influence the community of scholars who examine social scientific findings. Thus researchers are directed to critically evaluate others' work. This injunction also applies to students. It means, for example, that readers should ask themselves whether my personal values might have distorted the presentation in earlier chapters. Finally, researchers are taught to try to refute previous work. When these efforts fail and findings are replicated, especially if different types of data or methods produce similar results, then the probability of their being accurate reflections of reality goes up. Over the long run, these norms insure that objective, scientific findings about the structure of stratification will be produced. They help us to see social life as clearly as possible.

This orientation is why I emphasized the importance of hypothesis testing throughout the book. Thus some intuitively plausible ideas, such as the Job Perquisite Hypothesis (Chapter 8) or the Kuznets Hypothesis (Chapters 7 and 11), must remain tentative statements because either adequate data do not exist or testing has not yet occurred. Such hesitance is useful because some very good ideas, like the Embourgeoisement Hypothesis (Chapter 9), turn out to be false when systematically examined. Moreover, even empirical generalizations must be continually evaluated and sometimes modified, as with the finding that the prestige hierarchy is similar across Western industrial societies (Chapter 2). But over the long run, empirical generalizations emerge. These stable research findings constitute statements of fact. Although they are not immutable, since times change, they do indicate how the benefits of a stress on objectivity and the elimination of bias lead to knowledge.

## *Research Methods in the Study of Stratification*

Research methods, C. Wright Mills asserted in *The Sociological Imagination,* comprise the procedures sociologists use to apprehend social life in all its aspects.[2] No matter how objective research is, no matter how free of bias, if the procedures sociologists use do not take into account the various dimensions of stratification, then a full and accurate depic-

---

[2]Mills (1959).

tion of this topic becomes impossible. As it turns out, an understanding of each level of social life requires rather different procedures.

One dimension of social life involves the study of individuals and the way in which they act on and react to the situations in which they find themselves. As indicated in Chapter 1, most researchers, at least in the United States, are prone to focus on individuals when studying stratification. Thus a great deal of work exists that identifies the reasons why people move upward or downward occupationally, become poor, vote or participate in politics in other ways, and endure gender or racial inequality. The empirical generalizations summarizing these relationships are among the most significant results in sociology. Such studies typically involve survey data, statistical analyses, and quantitatively precise findings. An exclusive focus on individuals, however, is limiting because it omits the existence of other aspects of social life which, although less often studied, provide additional insight into stratification.

Yet sociologists in the United States tend to avoid asking any questions that cannot be answered in quantitative terms. In practice, this orientation means that "research" is usually defined as the analysis of survey data. Underlying this choice of methodology is a dominant value orientation shared by all U.S. citizens, regardless of class: a preference for seeing individuals as both cause and solution to social problems. Sociologists are no different from other people. They believe in and benefit from individual initiative, competition, and the rewards that ensue. This background leads many of them to adopt a nominalist methodological stance, which means that society is considered to be nothing more than the sum of its parts—individuals.[3] If this were true, then quantitative analyses of survey data ought to identify the true causes of the high mobility rate, the poverty rate, the rate of political participation, and the level of gender and racial and ethnic inequality. In fact, however, they do not, primarily because such an orientation excludes the structural dimension of social life from consideration.

In public policy terms, this preference for focusing on individuals, is why the United States lost the war on poverty in the 1960s. Virtually all the antipoverty programs developed at that time emphasized job training and education so that poor individuals could better themselves. While there is nothing particularly wrong with such programs, they did not and could not reduce the poverty rate in this country because individual characteristics are not responsible for the large number of impoverished people. Rather, as shown in Chapter 10, the high rate of poverty in the United States results from the reproduction of the class system, macroeconomic policy, and other structural factors. What is needed is a way of seeing the structural aspect of social life as clearly as possible. This alternative approach does not substitute for the study of individuals; rather, it complements such analyses and leads to greater insight into social stratification.

It was argued in Chapter 1 that the social structure determines rates of events and that this orientation can be seen in the work of sociologists as different as Marx, Durkheim, and Merton. The hypothesis offered there was that lower-class people have fewer and less effective choices in comparison to upper-class persons, with the result that rates of behavior are decisively effected. In subsequent chapters, this idea was applied to the analysis of mobility rates, poverty rates, political participation rates, levels of gender

---

[3]Bryant (1985).

inequality, and levels of racial and ethnic inequality. In each chapter, the account followed a similar pattern and none of the proposed explanatory factors dealt with individuals.

As shown in Chapter 5, for example, in order to explain the rate of mobility, variables such as industrialization, class differences in fertility rates, immigration, institutionalized gender discrimination, and institutionalized racial and ethnic discrimination are necessary. Note that the rate of mobility is accounted for in terms of other rates, not individual characteristics. Thanks to the explosion of research on status attainment over the past 25 years, it is clear in this case more than in any of the others that the factors affecting individual mobility (the status attainment process) are different from those influencing the rate of mobility.

An important but little recognized implication follows from the fact that rates of events must be explained by rates of other events. To use Durkheim's language, social facts (rates) are things and they must be explained by other social facts.[4] Methodologically, this injunction usually means that survey research or other analogous modes of data analysis often cannot be used. Although the topics dealt with in this book are amenable to quantitative methods in principle, the aggregate survey data needed for their analysis do not exist. Instead, it was necessary in each case to perform a mental experiment similar to Max Weber's in *The Protestant Ethic and the Spirit of Capitalism*.[5] Weber's research strategy involved the construction of a set of logically interrelated variables, which he called "ideal types," and the empirical assessment of how actual cases deviated from a purely logical formulation.[6] The analyses in this book proceeded in a similar way, that is, by identifying a set of structural factors, such as the rate of mobility, poverty, and so forth, and hypothesizing the manner in which they are affected by other structural variables. In each case, an implicit counterfactual hypothesis posited that if the proposed explanatory variables had different configurations, then the rate of mobility and the like would be far different. My argument is that this methodological procedure provides observers with a way to confront many significant issues for which survey data cannot be used.

In practice, this research strategy reflects a process Willer and Webster called abduction; that is, it attempts to identify, based on theory and empirical observation, those variables affecting the phenomenon of interest.[7] This procedure invites creativity, which is useful in any analysis. In this book, the process involved looking at how the major institutions—economy, family, education, and government—interact with the stratification structure. The resulting explanation did not identify new variables; it was, rather, synthetic: showing how well-known forces (many of which appear unrelated to one another) produce a high rate of some phenomenon, placing these factors into a coherent theoretical context, and systematically following through the implications of the analysis. In so doing, the way explanations focusing on individuals and structures complement one another became clear. For example, when the process of status attainment and the causes

[4]Durkheim (1895).
[5]Weber (1905).
[6]See Turner, Beeghley, and Powers (2002).
[7]Willer and Webster (1970).

of a high rate of mobility are considered together, then much more is known about stratification in the United States than if either angle of vision is ignored.

Yet structural analyses such as those presented in this book appear unscientific to many sociologists because the results seem unmeasurable quantitatively and, hence, imprecise. The assumption that quantitative precision makes an analysis scientific constitutes a frequent mistake by researchers in the so-called soft sciences. In all disciplines, significant questions exist that cannot be measured directly and, as indicated earlier, it becomes necessary to perform a mental experiment. In so doing, however, it is often convenient to think in multivariate statistical terms. Thus, in accounting for the level of impoverishment in the United States, the dependent variable ($Y$ in a regression equation) is the rate of poverty, and the independent variables (the $X$s in a regression equation) comprise a set of structural factors: the reproduction of the class system, macroeconomic policies, and so forth. The advantage of thinking in this way is that each of the variables must be clearly specified and related to one another. The major difference, of course, is that the data are manipulated logically rather than computationally. Now there is no special reason why mathematical values could not be assigned to each of the variables used in explaining the rate of, say, poverty, and numerical results produced. For example, armed with a set of plausible assumptions, one could show that if inflation averages $X$ percent higher and unemployment $X$ percent lower, then the rate of poverty will be reduced by $Y$ percent. Having performed this exercise, however, the result would be neither more precise nor more scientific than before.

A similar judgment could be made about most econometric models, such as forecasts of next year's inflation rate; they constitute mental experiments in quantitative form and the numbers should be translated to mean "a lot" or "a little." So, too, with mental experiments in other disciplines. For example, Sagan calculated that 10,400 thermonuclear explosions with a total yield of 5,000 megatons of which 20 percent explode over cities may produce so much dust and soot in the atmosphere that the average July temperature at mid-latitudes would decline to –9 degrees Fahrenheit within a few weeks.[8] Subsequently, Thompson and Schneider, using a different model of the atmosphere and making somewhat different assumptions, found that the average temperature might decline to between 60 and 70 degrees Fahrenheit.[9] It is important to recognize that in both cases these rather precise numbers are illusions. In reality, Sagan showed that one result of a thermonuclear war might be that the temperature will decline "a lot" as a result of "nuclear winter," while Thompson and Schneider showed that the temperature may decline "a little" due to "nuclear fall." Now this research is imaginative and substantively important; it is good science. It is also a mental experiment, no different in logic from that occurring in many other fields, including those performed in this book. Of course, the effects of one variable on another should be empirically measured whenever possible. But observers should not let either a fetish for measurement or a shortsighted view of what science is get in the way of research. Economists do not. Physicists do not. Neither should sociologists.

[8]Sagan et al. (1984).
[9]Thompson and Schneider (1986).

Nonetheless, both the procedures described here and the structural analyses described in this book often seem alien because they are so unfamiliar, especially in the United States.[10] The emphasis on individuals runs deep. But sociology, Emile Durkheim said, should cause people to see things in a different way than the ordinary, "for the purpose of any science is to make discoveries and all such discoveries more or less upset accepted opinions."[11] A structural approach such as that used in this book is one (but not the only) way of performing this task. The consequences, however, are paradoxical.

## *Paradox in the Study of Stratification*

If sociologists are indeed able to see social life clearly and to understand its dimensions and their interrelationships, the results have implications for people's hopes and fears about the future. Paradox follows. Sociological analyses, including those presented in earlier chapters, often seem to be contradictory; they appear politically radical yet also conservative, liberating for the individual yet also constraining. This paradox, Peter Berger suggested, is inherent to sociological inquiry.[12]

On the one hand, almost any sound analysis of the topics covered in this book can suggest ways in which to improve our society or aspects of it. This fact constitutes people's hope for progress in the future. What happens is that knowledge liberates people by opening up the possibility for change. This is especially true of structural descriptions because they often reveal hidden or nonobvious facets of a phenomenon. As a result, those proposing radical departures from the status quo can point to alienation, exploitation, inequality, and inequity. Yet sociological analyses also show that improvement does not always follow from change, a fact that has conservative implications. Disorder, at least for a short time, often does. This fact makes people fear the future, which constrains them. Thus, most individuals are enmeshed in structures of norms and roles with which they are both familiar and comfortable. Few persons dislike everything about their lives, which means they want to preserve what is good, maintain their traditions, and retain a sense of orderliness and continuity from one generation to another. This orientation militates against radical change.

The result of these contradictory impulses, as Berger commented, is that sociology often produces a paradoxical, but by no means irrational, stance on the part of its practitioners and others exposed to it: that of a person who thinks daringly but acts prudently. Put differently, there are no easy answers to the problems revealed in this book. All solutions carry with them both benefits and liabilities, and it is best to be as clear as possible about each.

---

[10]Much more complex structural orientations exist, as shown by Turner (1984) and by the readings in Blau (1975), Blau and Merton (1981). Unfortunately, most of them are impractical for understanding such real-world issues as social mobility, poverty, political participation, gender inequality, or racial and ethnic inequality.

[11]Durkheim (1895:31).

[12]Berger (1977).

# References

Aaronson, Daniel. 2000. "A Note on the Benefits of Home-ownership." *Journal of Urban Economics* 47:356–69.

Abraham, Katharine G. 1983. "Structural/Frictional vs. Demand Unemployment: Some New Evidence." *American Economic Review* 73:708–24.

Acemoglu, Daron, and James A. Robinson. 2000. "Why Did the West Extend the Franchise? Democracy, Inequality, and Growth in Historical Perspective." *Quarterly Journal of Economics* 115:1167–99.

Acker, Joan. 1973. "Women and Social Stratification: A Case of Intellectual Sexism." *American Journal of Sociology* 78:936–46.

———. 1990. "Hierarchies, Jobs, Bodies: A Theory of Gendered Organizations." *Gender & Society* 4:139–58.

Aguirre, Adalberto, and Jonathan H. Turner. 1993. *American Ethnicity: The Dynamics and Consequences of Discrimination.* New York: McGraw-Hill.

Alexander, Karl L., Bruce K. Eckland, and Larry J. Griffin. 1975. "The Wisconsin Model of Socioeconomic Achievement: A Replication." *American Journal of Sociology* 81:324–42.

Allen, H. W., and K. W. Allen. 1981. "Vote Fraud and Data Validity." Pp. 153–93 in J. M. Chubb, W. H. Flanigan, and N. H. Zingale (eds.), *Analyzing Electoral History.* Beverly Hills, CA: Sage.

Allen, Michael Patrick. 1990. *The Founding Fortunes: A New Anatomy of the Super-Rich Families in America.* New York: E. P. Dutton.

Allport, Gordon W. 1954. *The Nature of Prejudice.* Cambridge, MA: Addison-Wesley.

America's Second Harvest. 2001. *Hunger in America.* Washington, DC: America's Second Harvest.

———. 2003. *The Red Tape Divide State-by-State Review of Food Stamp Applications.* Washington, DC: America's Second Harvest.

Anderson, Eiljah. 1994. "The Code of the Streets." *The Atlantic Monthly* 273(May):80–110.

———. 1999. *The Code of the Street: Decency, Violence, and the Moral Life of the Inner City.* New York: W.W. Norton.

Anker, Richard. 1998. *Gender and Jobs: Sex Segregation of Occupations in the World.* Geneva: International Labour Organization.

Ansolabehere, Stephen, and Shanto Iyengar. 1995. *Going Negative: How Attack Ads Shrink and Polarize the Electorate.* New York: Free Press.

Archer, Melanie, and Judith R. Blau. 1993. "Class Formation in Nineteenth-Century America: The Case of the Middle Class." *Annual Review of Sociology*, Vol 19. New York: Annual Reviews.

Argersinger, Peter H. 1986. "New Perspectives on Election Fraud in the Gilded Age." *Political Science Quarterly* 100:669–89.

Armstrong, T., J. Foulke, C. Bir, et al. 1999. "Muscle Responses to Simulated Torque Reactions of Hand-Held Power Tools." *Ergonomics* 42:146–49.

Arneson, Ben A. 1925. "Non-Voting in a Typical Ohio Community." *American Political Science Review* 19:816–25.

Association of Community Organizations for Reform Now. 1999. *Giving No Credit Where Credit Is Due: An Analysis of Home Purchase Mortgage Lending in Thirty-Five Cities, 1995–1997.* Washington, DC: Association of Community Organizations for Reform Now.

Atkinson, A. B. 1996. "Income Distribution in Europe and the United States." *Oxford Review of Economic Policy* 12:15–28.

Auten, Gerald, and Robert Carroll. 1999. "The Effect of Income Taxes on Household Behavior." *Review of Economics and Statistics* 81:681–93.

Bakke, Edward W. 1940. *The Unemployed Worker.* New Haven, CT: Yale University Press.

Balkovic, Brian. 2002. "High-Income Tax Returns for 1999." *SOI Bulletin* 21(Spring):7–58.

Baltzell, E. Digby. 1958. *Philadelphia Gentlemen: The Making of a National Upper Class.* New York: Free Press.

———. 1964. The Protestant Establishment: Aristocracy and Caste in America. New York: Vintage.

Barlett, Donald L., and James B. Steele. 1994. *America: Who Really Pays the Taxes.* New York: Simon & Schuster.

Barstow, David, and Lowell Bergman. 2003. "At a Texas Foundry, An Indifference to Life." *New York Times,* National Edition. January 8:1, 15.

———. 2003a. "Family's Profits, Wrung from Blood and Sweat." *New York Times,* National Edition. January 9:1, 14.

———. 2003b. "Deaths on the Job, Slaps on the Wrist." *New York Times,* National Edition. January 10:1, 15.

Bassuk, Ellen L. 1991. "Homeless Families." *Scientific American* 265(December):66–74.

Baunach, Dawn Michelle . 2002. "Trends in Occupational Sex Segregation and Inequality." *Social Science Research* 31:77–98.

Beeghley, Leonard. 1983. *Living Poorly in America.* New York: Praeger.

———. 1984. "Illusion and Reality in the Measurement of Poverty." *Social Problems* 31:312–24.

———. 1986. "Social Class and Political Participation: A Review and an Explanation." *Sociological Forum* 1:496–513.

———. 1989. "Individual versus Structural Explanations of Poverty." *Population Research and Policy Review* 8:201–22.

———. 1992. "Social Structure and Voting in the United States: A Historical and Comparative Analysis." *Perspectives on Social Problems* 3:265–87.

———. 1996. *What Does Your Wife Do: Gender and the Transformation of Family Life*. Boulder, CO: Westview.

———. 1999. *Angles of Vision: How to Understand Social Problems*. Boulder, CO: Westview.

———. 2003. *Homicide: A Sociological Explanation*. Boulder, CO: Rowman & Littlefield.

Beeghley, Leonard, E. Wilbur Bock, and John C. Cochran. 1990. "Religious Change and Alcohol Use: An Application of Reference Group Theory." *Sociological Forum* 5:261–78.

Beeghley, Leonard, and John C. Cochran. 1988. "Class Identification and Gender Role Norms among Employed Married Women." *Journal of Marriage and Family* 50:719–29.

Beeghley, Leonard, and Denise Donnelly. 1989. "The Consequences of Family Crowding: A Theoretical Synthesis." *Lifestyles: Family and Economic Issues* 10:83–102.

Beeghley, Leonard, and Jeffrey W. Dwyer. 1989. "Income Transfers and Income Inequality." *Population Research and Policy Review*. 8:119–42.

Beeghley, Leonard, and Debra Van Ausdale. 1990. "The Status of Women Faculty in Graduate Departments of Sociology: 1973 and 1988." *Footnotes* 18(December):3–4.

Beeghley, Leonard, Ellen Van Velsor, and E. Wilbur Bock. 1981. "The Correlates of Religiosity among Black and White Americans." *Sociological Quarterly* 22:403–12.

Bell, Daniel. 1976. *The Coming of Post-Industrial Society*. New York: Basic.

Bendix, Reinhard. 1974. "Inequality and Social Structure: A Comparison of Marx and Weber." *American Sociological Review* 38:149–61.

Berger, Peter M. 1977. "Sociology and Freedom." Pp. x–xix in P. L. Berger, *Facing Up to Modernity*. New York: Basic.

———. 1986. *The Capitalist Revolution*. New York: Basic.

Berlin, Ira. 2003. *Generations of Captivity: A History of American-American Slaves."* Cambridge, MA: Harvard University Press.

Bernstein, Jared. 2001. "Let the War on the Poverty Line Commence." *Working Paper Series*. New York: Foundation for Child Development.

Bernstein, Robert, Anita Chadha, Robert Montjoy. 2001. "Over Reporting Voting: Why It Happens and Why It Matters." *Public Opinion Quarterly* 65:22–44.

Bertrand, Marianne, and Sendhil Mullainathan. 2002. "Are Emily and Brendan More Employable Than Lakisha and Jamal? Field Experiment on Labor Market Discrimination." Unpublished paper. Chicago: School of Business, University of Chicago.

Bianchi, Susanne M., Melissa S. Milkie, Liana C. Sayer, et al. 2000. "Is Anyone Doing the Housework? Trends in the Gender Division of Household Labor." *Social Forces* 79:191–228.

Biblarz, Timothy, Vern L. Bengtson, and Alexander Bucur.

1996. "Social Mobility across Generations." *Journal of Marriage and the Family* 58:188–200.

Bird, Carolyn. 1968. *Born Female: The High Cost of Keeping Women Down*. New York: Van Rees Press.

Birdsall, Nancy, and Carol Graham (eds.). 2000. *Economic and Social Mobility in a Changing World*. Washington, DC: Brookings Institution.

Blank, Rebecca M., and Alan S. Blinder. 1986. "Macroeconomics, Income Distribution, and Poverty." Pp. 180–208 in S. H. Danziger and D. H. Weinberg (eds.), *Fighting Poverty: What Works and What Doesn't*. Cambridge, MA: Harvard University Press.

Blau, Francine D., and Lawrence M. Kahn. 2000. "Gender Differences in Pay." Working Paper 7732. Cambridge, MA: National Bureau of Economic Research.

Blau, Peter M. (ed.). 1975. *Approaches to the Study of Social Structure*. New York: Basic.

Blau, Peter M., and Otis Dudley Duncan. 1967. *The American Occupational Structure*. New York: Wiley.

Blau, Peter M., and Robert K. Merton. 1981. *Continuities in Structural Inquiry*. Beverly Hills, CA: Sage.

Blossfeld, H. P., and G. Rohwer (eds.). 1997. *Between Equalization and Marginalization: Part-Time Working Women in Europe and the United States*. New York: Oxford University Press.

Blumin, Stuart. 1989. *The Emergence of the Middle Class*. New York: Cambridge University Press.

Bobo, Lawrence D. 2001. "Racial Attitudes and Relations at the Close of the Twentieth Century." Pp. 264–301 in Neil Smelser, William Julius Wilson, and Faith Mitchell (eds.), *America Becoming: Racial Trends and Their Consequences*, Volume I. Washington DC: National Academy Press.

Bowler, Mary. 1999. "Women's Earnings: An Overview." *Monthly Labor Review* 130(December):13–21.

Bowles, Samuel, and Herbert Gintis. 1976. *Schooling in Capitalist America*. New York: Basic Books.

Boyd, Richard W. 1981. "Decline of U.S. Voter Turnout: Structural Explanations." *American Politics Quarterly* 9:133–59.

———. 1986. "Election Calendars and Voter Turnout." *American Politics Quarterly* 14:89–104.

———. 1989. "The Effects of Primaries and Statewide Races on Voter Turnout." *Journal of Politics* 51:730–39.

Boyer, Debra, and David Fine. 1992. "Sexual Abuse as a Factor in Adolescent Pregnancy and Child Maltreatment." *Family Planning Perspectives* 24:4–11.

Boyle, Paul, Thomas J. Cooke, Keith Halfacree, et al. 2001. "A Cross-National Comparison of the Impact of Family Migration on Women's Employment Status." *Demography* 38:201–18.

Bradley, Bill. 1997. "Foreward." Pp. ix–xv in Chester Hartman (ed.), *Double Exposure: Poverty and Race in America*. Armonk, NY: M. E. Sharpe.

Brennan, John, and Edward W. Hill. 1999. *Where Are the Jobs?: Cities, Suburbs, and the Competition for Employment*. Washington, DC: Brookings Institution.

Brenner, N. D., P. M. McMahon, C. W. Warren, et al. 1999. "Forced Sexual Intercourse and Associated Health-Risk Behaviors among Female College Students in the United States." *Journal of Consulting and Clinical Psychology* 67:252–59.

Breslin, F. Curtis, and Charles Mustard. 2001. "A Longitudinal Study Examining the Effects of Unemployment on Adults." *American Journal of Epidemiology* 153(Supplement):S235.

Bridges, J. S. 1989. "Sex Differences in Occupational Values." *Sex Roles* 20:205–11.

Brim, Orville G. 1966. "Socialization Through the Life-Cycle." Pp. 1–49 in O. G. Brim and S. Wheeler, *Socialization After Childhood*. New York: Wiley.

Brown, Jeffery D. 2003. "Amputations: A Continuing Workplace Hazard." *Compensation and Working Conditions Online*. Bureau of Labor Statistics: www.bls.gov

Brownlee, W. Elliot. 2000. "Historical Perspectives on U.S. Tax Policy Toward the Rich." Pp. 29–73 in J. Slemrod (ed.), *Does Atlas Shrug? The Economic Consequences of Taxing the Rich*. New York: Russell Sage Foundation.

Bryant, Christopher A. G. 1985. *Positivism in Social Theory and Research*. New York: St. Martin's Press.

Budig, Michelle J., and Paula England. 2001. "The Wage Penalty for Motherhood." *American Sociological Review* 66:204–25.

Bureau of Labor Statistics. 2002. "National Census of Fatal Occupational Injuries in 2001." *News: Bureau of Labor Statistics*. Washington, DC: U.S. Government Printing Office.

———. 2003. "Major Sector Productivity and Cost, Index." www.bls.gov

———. 2003a. "Lost-Worktime Injuries and Illnesses: Characteristics and Resulting Days Away from Work, 2001." *News: Bureau of Labor Statistics*. Washington, DC: U.S. Government Printing Office.

———. 2003b. http://stats.bls.gov/cps

———. 2003c. *Consumer Expenditures in 2001*, Report 966. Washington, DC: U.S. Government Printing Office.

Burnham, Walter Dean. 1980. "The Disappearance of the American Voter." Pp. 35–73 in Richard Rose (ed.), *Electoral Participation*. Beverly Hills, CA: Sage.

Burtless, Gary. 1998. "Can the Labor Market Absorb Three Million Welfare Recipients?" *Focus* 19(Summer/Fall):1–6.

———. 2001. "Has Widening Inequality Promoted or Retarded U.S. Growth?" Washington, DC: Brookings Institution.

Butterfield, Fox. 1996. *All God's Children: The Bosket Family and the American Tradition of Violence*. New York: Avon.

Caltech/MIT. 2001. *Voting: What Is, What Could Be*. Pasadena, CA: California Institute of Technology & Massachusetts Institute of Technology.

Camarillo, Albert M., and Frank Bonilla. 2001. "Hispanics in a Multicultural Society: A New American Dilemma?" Pp. 103–34 in Neil Smelser, William Julius Wilson, and Faith Mitchell (eds.), *America Becoming: Racial Trends and their Consequences*, Volume I. Washington DC: National Academy Press.

Campagna, D., B. Stengel, D. Mergler, et al. 2001. "Blurred Vision and Occupational Toluene Exposure." *American Journal of Epidemiology* 153:125–36.

Campbell, David, and Michael Parisi. 2002. "Individual Income Tax Returns, 2000." *SOI Bulletin* 21(December):7–44.

Carney, Judith A. 2001. *Black Rice: The African Origins of Rice Cultivation in the Americas*. Cambridge, MA: Harvard University Press.

Case, Charles E., Andrew Greeley, and Stephan Fuchs. 1989. "Social Determinants of Racial Prejudice." *Sociological Perspectives* 32:469–83.

Cassel, Carol A. 2003. "Overreporting and Electoral Research." *American Politics Research* 31:81–92.

Catalano, Ralph, Raymond W. Novaco, and William McConnell. 2002. "Layoffs and Violence Revisited." *Aggressive Behavior* 28:233–48.

Catalyst. 1999. "Catalyst Census Posts Solid Gains in Percentage of Women Corporate Officers in Fortune 500 Corporations." Press Release, November 11. www.catalystwomen.org

Cavilli-Sforza, Luca, Paolo Menozzi, and Alberto Piazza. 1995. *The History and Geography of Human Genes*. Princeton, NJ: Princeton University Press.

Center for Community Change. 2002. *Risk or Race? Racial Disparities in the Subprime Refinance Market*. Washington, DC: Center for Community Change.

Center for Responsive Politics. 2003. *Your Guide to the Money in Politics*. www.opensecrets.org

Centers for Disease Control. 2000. Youth Risk Behavior Surveillance—United States, 1999. *Morbidity & Mortality Weekly Report* June 9:1–96.

Centers, Richard. 1949. *The Psychology of Social Classes: A Study of Class Consciousness*. Princeton, NJ: Princeton University Press.

Century Foundation. 1999. *The Basics: Tax Reform*. New York: Century Foundation Press.

Cherlin, Andrew J. 1992. *Marriage, Divorce, and Remarriage*, Revised and Enlarged Edition. Cambridge, MA: Harvard University Press.

Children's Defense Fund. 1998. *New Studies Look at the Status of Former Welfare Recipients*. Washington DC: Children's Defense Fund.

———. 1998a. *Welfare to What: Early Findings on Family Hardship and Well-Being*. Washington, DC: Children's Defense Fund.

Chinhui Juhn, and Kevin M. Murphy. 1997. "Wage Inequality and Family Labor Supply." *Journal of Labor Economics* 15:72–97.

Chirot, Daniel. 1986. *Social Change in the Modern Era*. New York: Harcourt Brace Jovanovich.

Citro, Constance F., and Robert T. Michael (eds.). 1995.

*Measuring Poverty: A New Approach.* Washington, DC: National Academy Press.

Clark, Rodney, Norman B. Anderson, Vernessa R. Clark, et al. 1999. "Racism as a Stressor for African Americans: A Biosocial Model." *American Psychologist* 54:805–16.

Cobb-Clark, Deborah A., and Yvonne Dunlop. 1999. "The Role of Gender in Job Promotions." *Monthly Labor Review* 122(December):32–38.

Cohen, Mark A. 2001. Final Report on Racial Impact of NMAC's Finance Charge Markup Policy. Nashville, TN: Owen Graduate School of Management, Vanderbilt University.

Cohen, Philip N. 1998. "Black Concentration Effects on Black-White and Gender Inequality." *Social Forces.* 77:207–30.

Coleman, James S. 1966. *Equality of Educational Opportunity.* Washington, DC: U.S. Government Printing Office.

Collins, William J., and Melissa A. Thomasson. 2002. "Exploring the Racial Gap in Infant Mortality Rates, 1920–1970." Working Paper 8836. Cambridge, MA: National Bureau of Economic Research.

Commission on Wartime Relocation and Internment of Civilians. 1982. *Personal Justice Denied.* Washington DC:United States Government Printing Office.

Committee on Ways and Means. 2000. *1998 Green Book: Background Material and Data on Programs within the Jurisdiction of the Committee on Ways and Means.* Washington DC: U.S. Government Printing Office.

Conger, Rand, Katherine Conger, and Glen Elder. 1997. "Family Economic Hardship and Adolescent Adjustment: Mediating and Moderating Processes." Pp. 288–310 in G. Duncan and J. Brooks-Gunn (eds.), *Consequences of Growing Up Poor.* New York: Russell Sage.

Converse, Philip E. 1972. "Change in the American Electorate." Pp. 263–338 in Angus Campbell and Philip E. Converse (eds.), *The Human Meaning of Social Change.* New York: Russell Sage.

Conway, M. Margaret. 2000. *Political Participation in the United States,* 3rd edition. Washington, DC: Congressional Quarterly Press.

Corcoran, Mary, Linda Datcher, and Greg J. Duncan. 1980. "Most Workers Find Jobs Through Word of Mouth." *Monthly Labor Review* 103(August):33–36.

Coser, Lewis A. 1956. *The Functions of Social Conflict.* New York: Free Press.

———. 1967. "Some Social Functions of Violence." Pp. 73–92 in his *Continuities in the Study of Social Conflict.* New York: Free Press.

Cott, Nancy. 1987. *The Grounding of Modern Feminism.* New Haven, CT: Yale University Press.

Cottle, Thomas J. 1994. "When You Stop, You Die: The Human Toll of Unemployment." Pp. 75–82 in J. H. Skolnick and E. Currie (eds.), *Crisis in American Institutions,* 9th Edition. New York: HarperCollins.

Council of Economic Advisors. 1969. *Economic Report of the President.* Washington, DC: U.S. Government Printing Office.

Dahl, Robert A. 1967. *Pluralist Democracy in the United States: Conflict and Consent.* Chicago: Rand McNally.

Dahrendorf, Ralf. 1959. *Class and Class Conflict in Industrial Society.* Stanford CA: Stanford University Press.

Dansky, Bonnie. 1997. "The National Women's Study: Relationship of Victimization and Post-traumatic Stress Disorder to Bulimia Nervosa." *International Journal of Eating Disorders* 21:213–28.

Danziger, Sheldon, Robert Haveman, and Robert Plotnick. 1981. "How Income Transfer Programs Affect Work, Savings, and the Income Distribution." *Journal of Economic Literature* 19:975–1026.

Danziger, Sheldon, and Jeffrey Lehman. 1997. "How Will Welfare Recipients Fare in the Labor Markets." *Challenge* 39(March/April):8–15.

Danziger, Sheldon, and Robert Plotnick. 1977. "Demographic Change, Government Transfers, and Income Distribution." *Monthly Labor Review* 100(April):7–11.

Dash, Leon. 1989. *When Children Want Children: The Urban Crisis of Teenage Childbearing.* New York: William Morrow.

Davidson, James D. 1995. "Persistence and Change in the Protestant Establishment, 1930–1992." *Social Forces* 74:159–78.

Davis, Kingsley, and Wilbert Moore. 1945. "Some Principles of Stratification." *American Sociological Review* 7:242–49.

Davis, Nancy J., and Robert V. Robinson. 1998. "Do Wives Matter? Class Identities of Wives in the United States, 1974–1994." *Social Forces* 76:1063–86.

Davis, Theodore J. 1997. "The Occupational Mobility of Black Males Revisited: Does Race Matter?" *Social Science Journal* 32:121–36.

DeFronzo, James. 1973. "Embourgeoisement in Indianapolis?" *Social Problems* 21:269–83.

Degler, Carl N. 1980. *At Odds: Women and the Family in America from the Revolution to the Present.* New York: Oxford University Press.

de la Garza, Rodolfo. 1992. *Latino Voices: Mexican, Puerto Rican, and Cuban Perspectives on American Politics.* Boulder, CO: Westview Press.

Delgado, Richard. 1997. *The Coming Race War? And Other Apocalyptic Tales of America after Affirmative Action and Welfare.* New York: New York University Press.

DeParle, Jason. 1993. "Secretary of Housing's Intentions on Homeless Raise Questions." *New York Times,* National Edition. January 30:1.

DiNatale, Marisa, and Stephanie Boraas. 2002. "The Labor Force Experiences of Women from 'Generation X.'" *Monthly Labor Review* 133(March):3–15.

DiPasquale, Denise, and Edward L. Glaeser. 1999. "Incentives and Social Capital: Are Homeowners Better Citizens?" *Journal of Urban Economics* 45:354–84.

DiPrete, Thomas A., and K. Lynn Nonnemaker. 1997.

"Structural Change, Labor Market Turbulence, and Labor Market Outcomes." *American Sociological Review* 62:386–404.

DiPrete, Thomas A., Paul M. de Graaf, Ruud Luijkx, Michael Tåhlin, et al. 1997. "Collectivist versus Individualist Mobility Regimes? Structural Change and Job Mobility in Four Countries." *American Journal of Sociology* 103:318–58.

Djilas, Milovan. 1965. *The New Class*. New York: Praeger.

Dooley, David, and Joann Prause. 1998. "Underemployment and Alcohol Misuse in the National Longitudinal Survey of Youth." *Journal of Studies on Alcohol*. 59:669–71.

Domhoff, G. William. 1970. *The Higher Circles*. New York: Random House.

———. 1974. *The Bohemian Grove and other Retreats*. New York: Harper.

Dye, Thomas R. 2002. *Who's Running America*, 7th Edition. Englewood Cliffs, NJ: Prentice-Hall.

Duncan, Greg J., W. Jean Yeung, Jeanne Brooks-Gunn, et al. 1998. "How Much Does Childhood Poverty Affect the Life Chances of Children?" *American Sociological Review* 63:406–23.

Durkheim, Emile. 1895. *The Rules of the Sociological Method*. New York: Free Press, 1982.

———. 1897. *Suicide*. New York: Free Press, 1951.

Easton, Barbara. 1976. "Industrialization and Femininity: A Case Study of 19th Century New England." *Social Problems* 23:389–401.

Ehrenreich, Barbara. 1990. *Fear of Falling: The Inner Life of the Middle Class*. New York: Harper Collins.

———. 2001. *Nickel and Dimed: On (Not) Getting by in America*. New York: Henry Holt.

Elder, Glen, Robert Conger, Elizabeth Foster, et al. 1992. "Unemployment and Alcohol Disorder in 1910 and 1990: Drift vs. Social Causation." *Journal of Occupational and Organizational Psychology* 5:277–90.

Elias, Norbert. 1978. *The Civilizing Process: The Development of Manners: Changes in the Code of Conduct and Feeling in Early Modern Times*. New York: Urisen Books.

Engelberg, Stephen, and Deborah Sontag. 1994. "Behind One Agency's Walls: Misbehaving and Moving Up." *New York Times*, National Edition. December 21:A1.

England, Paula. 1982. "The Failure of Human Capital Theory to Explain Occupational Sex Segregation." *Journal of Human Resources* 17:358–70.

———. 1992. *Comparable Worth: Theories and Evidence*. New York: Aldine de Gruyter.

Erikson, Robert, and John H. Goldthorpe. 1993. *The Constant Flux: A Study of Class Mobility in Industrial Societies*. New York: Oxford University Press.

Eshleman, J. Ross. 1994. *The Family: An Introduction*, 7th Edition. Boston: Allyn & Bacon.

Eurostat. 2000. *European Social Statistics: Income, Poverty, and Social Exclusion*. Luxembourg: Eurostat.

Feather, Norman T. 1990. *The Psychological Impact of Unemployment*. Ann Arbor: Edwards Brothers.

———. 1992. "Expectancy-value Theory and Unemployment Effects." *Journal of Occupational and Organizational Psychology* 65:315–30

Featherman, David L., and Robert M. Hauser. 1978. *Opportunity and Change*. New York: Academic Press.

Federal Election Commission. 2001. "Voter Registration and Turnout 2000." www.fec.gov/pages/2000turnout

Federal Reserve Board. 1983. *Survey of Consumer Finances*. Washington, DC: Federal Reserve Board.

———. 1998. *Survey of Consumer Finances*. Washington, DC: Federal Reserve Board.

Feenberg, Daniel, and James M. Poterba. 1993. "Income Inequality and the Incomes of Very High-Income Taxpayers: Evidence from Tax Returns." Pp. 145–77 in J. Poterba (ed), *Tax Policy and the Economy*, Vol. 7. Cambridge, MA: MIT Press.

Felson, Marcus, and David Knoke. 1974. "Social Status and the Married Woman." *Journal of Marriage and Family* 36:63–70.

Ferree, Myru Marx, and Beth B. Hess. 2000. *Controversy and Coalition: The New Feminist Movement*. New York: Routledge.

Fifield, Adam. 2001. "Shopping While Black." *Good Housekeeping Magazine*. November, pp. 128–38.

Financial Markets Center. 2000. "Employee Stock Options." *Background Report: A Publication of the Financial Markets Center*. April. www.fmcenter.org

Firebaugh, Glenn. 1999. "Empirics of World Income Inequality." *American Sociological Review* 104:1597–1630.

———. 2000. "The Trend in Between-Nation Income Inequality." *Annual Review of Sociology* 26:323–39.

Fischer, David Hackett. 1978. *Growing Old in America*. New York: Oxford University Press.

———. 1989. *Albion's Seed: Four British Folkways in America*. New York: Oxford University Press.

———. 1994. *Paul Revere's Ride*. New York: Oxford University Press.

Fisher, Bonnie, John J. Sloan, Francis T. Cullen, et al. 1998. "Crime in the Ivory Tower: The Level and Sources of Student Victimization." *Criminology* 36:671–710.

Fisher, Gordon M. 1997. "Disseminating the Administrative Version and Explaining the Administrative and Statistical Versions of the Federal Poverty Measure." *Clinical Sociology Review* 15:163–82.

———. 1998. "Setting American Standards of Poverty: A Look Back." *Focus* 19(Spring): 47–53.

Fix, Michael, and Raymond J. Struyk. 1993. *Clear and Convincing Evidence: Measurement of Discrimination in America*. Washington, DC: Urban Institute Press.

Foner, Eric. 1988. *Reconstruction, 1863–1877*. New York: Harper & Row.

Forbes, Hugh D. 1997. *Ethnic Conflict: Commerce, Culture, and the Contact Hypothesis*. New Haven, CT: Yale University Press.

Foster, Eugene A., M. A. Jobling, P. G. Taylor, et al. 1998. "Jefferson Fathered Slave's Last Child." *Nature* 396 (November 3):27–28.

Fosu, Augustin Kwasi. 1997. "Occupational Gains of Black Women since the 1964 Civil Rights Act: Long-Term or Episodic?" *American Economic Review* 87:311–15.

Fountain, John W. 2002. "Team Leaves White League in Silence Instead of Cheers." *New York Times*, National Edition, p. A1.

Frank, Erica. 1998. "Prevalence and Correlates of Harassment among U.S. Women Physicians." *Archives of Internal Medicine* 158(February 23):352–58.

Franklin, Benjamin. 1961. *The Autobiography and Other Writings.*New York: New American Library.

Friedan, Betty. 1963. *The Feminine Mystique.* New York: Norton.

Fryer, Bronwyn. 1999. "Executive Privilege: The Perk That Big Shots Don't Want You to Talk About." *Worth Guide To Benefits, Compensation, and Perks* 8(Winter):71–72.

Fussell, Paul. 1983. *Class: A Guide Through the American Status System.* New York: Ballantine.

Gagliani, Giorgio. 1981. "How Many Working Classes?" *American Journal of Sociology* 87:259–85.

Galbraith, John Kenneth. 1992. *The Culture of Contentment.* New York: Houghton Mifflin.

Gallman, Robert E. 1969. "Trends in the Size Distribution of Wealth in the 19th Century." In Lee Soltow (ed.), *Six Papers on the Size Distribution of Wealth and Income.* New York: Columbia University Press.

Gallo, William T., Elizabeth H. Bradley, Michelle Siegel, et al. 2001. "The Impact of Involuntary Job Loss on Subsequent Alcohol Consumption by Older Workers." *The Journals of Gerontology*, Series B 56:S3–10.

Gallup Poll. 1994. *The Gallup Poll: Public Opinion 1993.* Wilmington, DE: Scholarly Resources.

———. 1997. "Black/White Relations in the U.S." http://www.gallup.com

———. 2001. *The Nine Weeks of Election 2000.* Wilmington, DE: Scholarly Resources.

Gamson, William A. 1975. *The Strategy of Protest.* Homewood, IL: Dorsey Press.

Gans, Herbert. 1972. "The Positive Functions of Poverty." *American Journal of Sociology* 78:275–89.

Garner, Thesia I., Kathleen Short, Stephanie Shipp, et al. 1998. "Experimental Poverty Measurement for the 1990s." *Monthly Labor Review* 121(March):39–43.

Garrow, David. 1986. *Bearing the Cross: Martin Luther King, jr., and the Southern Christian Leadership Congress.* New York: William Morrow.

Gelles, Richard. 1990. *Intimate Violence in Families.* Newbury Park, CA: Sage.

General Social Survey. 1996. *Cumulative Codebook.* Chicago: National Opinion Research Corporation.

———. 1998. *Cumulative Codebook.* Chicago: National Opinion Research Corporation.

———. 2000. *Cumulative Codebook.* Chicago: National Opinion Research Corporation.

———. 2003. "Occupational Prestige Studies: Summary." www.icpsr.umich.edu:8080/GSS/homepage.htm

Gerber, Alan S. 1998. "Estimating the Effect of Campaign Spending on Senate Election Outcomes Using Instrumental Variables." *American Political Science Review* 92:401–12.

Gerber, Alan S., and Donald P. Green. 2000. "The Effects of Canvassing, Telephone Calls, and Direct Mail on Voter Turnout: A Field Experiment." *American Political Science Review* 94:653–65.

Glick, Peter. 1995. "Images of Occupations: Components of Gender and Status in Occupational Stereotypes." *Sex Roles* 32:565–83.

Glyptis, Sue. 1989. *Leisure and Unemployment.* Philadelphia: Open University Press.

Goldin, Claudia. 1990. *Understanding the Gender Gap: An Economic History of American Women.* New York: Oxford University Press.

Goldin, Claudia, and Cecilia Rouse. 2000. "Orchestrating Impartiality: The Impact of "Blind" Auditions on Female Musicians." *American Economic Review* 90: 715–42.

Goode, William J. 1973. "Functionalism: The Empty Castle." Pp. 64–96 in W. J. Goode, *Explorations in Social Theory.* New York: Oxford University Press.

Gordon, David M. 1996. *Fat and Mean: The Corporate Squeeze of Working Americans and the Myth of Managerial "Downsizing."* New York: Free Press.

Gordon-Reed, Annette. 1997. *Thomas Jefferson and Sally Hemings: An American Controversy.* Charlottesville, VA: University Press of Virginia.

Gosnell, Harold F. 1927. *Getting Out the Vote: An Experiment in the Stimulation of Voting.* Chicago: University of Chicago Press.

Gottschalk, Peter, Björn Gustafsson, and Edward Palmer. 1997. "What's Behind the Increase in Inequality? Pp. 1–11 in P. Gottschalk, B. Gustafsson, and E. Palmer (eds.), *Changing Patterns in the Distribution of Economic Welfare.* Cambridge: Cambridge University Press.

Graham, Lawrence Otis. 1995. *Member of the Club.* New York: Harper & Row.

Granovetter, Mark. 1995. *Getting a Job: A Study in Contacts and Careers,* 2nd edition. Chicago: University of Chicago Press.

Graybill, Wilson H., Clyde V. Kiser, and Pascal K. Whelpton. 1958. *The Fertility of American Women.* New York: Wiley.

Green, John, Paul Hermson, Lynda Powell, et al. 1998. "Individual Congressional Campaign Contributors: Wealthy, Conservative, and Reform Minded." www.opensecrets.org

Green, Richard K., and Michelle White. 1997. "Measuring the Benefits of Homeownership: The Effects on Children." *Journal of Urban Economics* 41:441–61.

Greven, Philip. 1991. *Spare the Child: The Religious Roots of Punishment and the Psychological Impact of Physical Abuse.* New York: Knopf.

Grieco, Margaret. 1987. *Keeping It in the Family: Social Networks and Employment Chance.* New York: Tavistock Publications.

Grimsrud, Tom K., Steiner R. Berge, Tor Haldorsen, et al. 2002. "Exposure to Different Forms of Nickel and Risk of Lung Cancer." *American Journal of Epidemiology* 156:12–13.

Grossman, James. 1989. *Land of Hope: Chicago, Black Southerners, and the Great Migration.* Chicago: University of Chicago Press.

Grusky, David B., and Jesper B. Sørensen. 1998. "Can Class Analysis be Salvaged?" *American Journal of Sociology* 103:1187–1234.

Grusky, David B., and Kim A. Weeden. 2001. "Decomposition without Death: A Research Agenda for a New Class Analysis." *Acta Sociologica* 44:201–18.

Guest, Avery M., Nancy S. Landale, and James C. McCann. 1989. "Intergenerational Occupational Mobility in the Late 19th Century United States." *Social Forces* 68:351–78.

Hacker, Andrew. 1992. *Two Nations: Black and White, Separate, Hostile, Unequal.* New York: Scribners.

Hagedorn, John. 1998. *The Business of Drug Dealing in Milwaukee.* Titusville, WI: Wisconsin Policy Research Institute.

Hakim, Catherine. 1994. "A Century of Change in Occupational Segregation." *Journal of Historical Sociology* 7:435–54.

Hale, Edward Everett. 1903. "Old Age Pensions." *Cosmopolitan* 35:168–69.

Hamermesh, Daniel S. 1998. "Changing Inequality in Markets for Workplace Amenities." *Working Paper 6515.* Cambridge, MA: National Bureau of Economic Research.

Harms, Robert. 2001. *The Diligent: A Voyage Through the Worlds of the Slave Trade.* New York: Basic Books.

Hartley, William B. 1969. *Estimation of the Incidence of Poverty in the United States, 1870–1914.* Madison, WI: Unpublished Ph.D. Dissertation, Department of Economics, University of Wisconsin.

Hauser, Robert M. 1975. "Structural Changes in Occupational Mobility: Evidence for Men in the United States." *American Sociological Review* 40:585–98.

Haveman, Robert, and Barbara Wolfe. 1995. "The Determinants of Children's Attainments: A Review of Methods and Findings." *Journal of Economic Literature* 33:1829–78.

Heilbroner, Robert L., and Lester C. Thurow. 1982. *Economics Explained.* Englewood Cliffs, NJ: Prentice-Hall.

Heller, Joseph. 1961. *Catch-22: A Novel.* New York: Simon & Schuster.

Henshaw, Stanley K., Susheela Singh, and Taylor Haas. 1999. "Recent Trends in Abortion Rates Worldwide." *International Family Planning Perspectives* 25 (March):44–48.

Herbert, Bob. 1998. "Mounting a War on Bias." *New York Times*, National Edition. January 18:A-21.

Herman, Judith Lewis. 1981. *Father-Daughter Incest.* Cambridge, MA: Harvard University Press.

———. 1989. "Wife Beating." *Harvard Mental Health Newsletter* 5(April):4–6.

———. 1992. *Trauma and Recovery.* New York: Basic.

Hertzberg, Vicki S., Kenneth D. Rosenman, Mary Jo Reilly, et al. 2002. "Effect of Occupational Sillica Exposure on Pulmonary Function." *Chest* 122:721–29.

Hibbs, Douglas A. 1977. "Political Parties and Macroeconomic Policy." *American Political Science Review* 71:1467–87.

Hicks, Alexander M., and Duane H. Swank. 1992. "Politics, Institutions, and Welfare Spending in Industrialized Democracies." *American Political Science Review* 86:658–74.

Highton, Benjamin. 1997. "Easy Registration and Voter Turnout." *Journal of Politics* 59:564–75.

Highton, Benjamin, and Raymond E. Wolfinger. 2001. "The Political Implications of Higher Turnout." *British Journal of Political Science* 31:179–223.

Higley, Stephen Richard. 1995. *Privilege, Power, and Place: The Geography of the American Upper Class.* Lanham, MD: Rowman & Littlefield.

Hiro, Dilip. 1991. *Black British, White British: A History of Race Relations in Britain.* London: Grafton.

Hochschild, Jennifer. 1981. *What's Fair? American Beliefs about Distributive Justice.* Cambridge, MA: Harvard University Press.

Holzer, Harry, and David Neumark. 2000. "Assessing Affirmative Action," *Journal of Economic Literature* 38:483–568.

Horsfield, Margaret. 1998. *Biting the Dust: The Joys of Housework.* New York: St. Martin's Press.

Hout, Michael. 1988. "More Universalism, Less Structural Mobility: The American Occupational Structure in the 1980s." *American Journal of Sociology* 93:1358–1400.

Hout, Michael, and William R. Morgan. 1975. "Race and Sex Variations in the Causes of the Expected Attainments of High School Seniors." *American Journal of Sociology* 81:364–94.

Hyman, Herbert. 1942. "The Psychology of Status." *Archives of Psychology*, No. 269.

Ingham, John. 1978. *The Iron Barons.* Chicago: University of Chicago Press.

Inland Revenue. 2003. "Personal Wealth [in the United Kingdom]." www.inlandrevenue.gov.uk/stats/personal_wealth/dopw_t04

Inniss, Leslie. 1992. "The Black 'Underclass' Ideology in Race Relations Analysis." *Social Justice* 16:13–34.

Institute on Taxation and Economic Policy. 2003. "Who Pays? A Distributional Analysis of the Tax Systems in all 50 States," 2nd edition. www.ctj.org

Internal Revenue Service. 2003. "The 400 Individual Income Tax Returns Reporting the Highest Adjusted Gross Incomes Each Year, 1992–2000." *SOI Bulletin* 25(Spring):7–9.

International Institute for Democracy and Electoral Assistance. 2003. www.idea.int/vt/country_view.cfm

Jackman, Mary R., and Robert W. Jackman. 1983. *Class*

*Awareness in the United States.* Berkeley, CA: University of California Press.

Jacobs, David, and Katherine Wood. 1999. "Interracial Conflict and Interracial Homicide: Do Political and Economic Rivalries Explain White Killings of Blacks or Black Killings of Whites? *American Journal of Sociology* 105:157–90.

Jacobs, Janet Liebman. 1994. *Victimized Daughters: Incest and the Development of the Female Self.* New York: Routledge.

Jacobs, Jerry A. 1990. *Revolving Doors: Sex Segregation and Women's Careers.* Stanford, CA: Stanford University Press.

Jaffe, A. J. 1940. "Differential Fertility in the White Population in Early America." *Journal of Heredity* 31:407–11.

Jaynes, Gerald David, and Robin M. Williams. 1989. *A Common Destiny: Blacks and American Society.* Washington, DC: National Academy Press.

Jefferson, Thomas. 1999. *Notes on the State of Virginia.* New York: Penguin.

Jencks, Christopher S. 1972. *Inequality: A Reassessment of the Effect of Family and Schooling in America.* New York: Basic.

———. 1979. *Who Gets Ahead: The Determinants of Economic Success in America.* New York: Basic.

Jesuit, David, and Timothy Smeeding. 2002. "Poverty Levels in the Developed World." *Luxembourg Income Study Working Paper No. 321.* Syracuse, NY: Maxwell School of Citizenship and Public Affairs.

Johansen, Christoffer, Maria Feychting, Mogens Moller, et al. 2002. "Risk of Severe Cardiac Arrhythmia in Male Utility Workers." *American Journal of Epidemiology* 156:857–62.

Joint Committee on Taxation. 2002. *Estimates of Federal Tax Expenditures for Fiscal Years 2002–2006.* Washington DC: U.S. Government Printing Office.

Kain, John F. 1968. "Housing Segregation, Negro Employment, and Metropolitan Decentralization." *Quarterly Journal of Economics* 82:165–97.

Kanter, Rosabeth Moss. 1978. "Some Effects of Proportion on Group Life: Skewed Sex Ratios and Responses to Token Women." *American Journal of Sociology* 82:965–90.

Kasarda, John. 1990. "Structural Factors Affecting the Location and Timing of Urban Underclass Growth." *Urban Geography* 11:234–64.

———. 1995. "Industrial Restructuring and the Changing Location of Jobs." Pp. 215–65 in Reynolds Farley (ed.), *State of the Union: America in the 1990s.* New York: Russell Sage.

Katt, Peter. 1997. "A Reality Check: Do You Need to Buy Long-term Care Insurance?" *AAII Journal* 19(November):2–4.

Kaufman, Gayle, and Peter Uhlenberg. 2000. "The Influence of Parenthood on the Work Effort of Married Men and Women." *Social Forces* 78:931–51.

Keen, Geraldine. 1971. *Money and Art: A Study Based on the Times-Sotheby Index.* New York: Putnam.

Keister, Lisa A., and Stephanie Moller. 2000. "Wealth Inequality in the United States." *Annual Review of Sociology* 26:63–81.

Kennedy, Stetson. 1995. *After Appomattox: How the South Won the War.* Gainesville, FL: University Press of Florida.

Kennickell, Arthur B. 2003. "A Rolling Tide: Changes in the Distribution of Wealth in the U.S., 1989–2001." Washington, DC: Federal Reserve Board.

Kenworthy, Lane. 1995. "Equality and Efficiency: The Illusory Tradeoff." *European Journal of Political Research* 27:225–54.

Key, V. O. 1949. *Southern Politics in State and Nation.* New York: Vintage Books.

Keyssar, Alexander. 2000. *The Right to Vote: The Contested History of Democracy in the United States.* New York: Basic.

Khan, Shaila, Robert P. Murray, and Gordon E. Barnes. 2002. "A Structural Equation Model of the Effect of Poverty and Unemployment on Alcohol Abuse." *Addictive Behaviors* 27:405–23.

King, Mary C. 1992. "Occupational Segregation by Race and Sex, 1940–88." *Monthly Labor Review* 115 (April):30–36.

Kingston, Paul W. 2000. *The Classless Society.* Stanford, CA: Stanford University Press.

Kitsantas, Panagiora, Anastasia Kitsantas, and H. Richard Travis. 2000. "Occupational Exposures and Associated Health Effects Among Sanitation Landfill Employees." *Journal of Environmental Health* 63:17–23.

Klass, Perry. 1992. "Tackling Problems We Thought We Solved." *New York Times Magazine.* December 12: 54–64.

Kohn, Melvin. 1987. "Cross-National Research as an Analytic Strategy." *American Sociological Review* 52: 713–31.

Kolko, Gabriel. 1962. *Wealth and Power in America.* New York: Praeger.

Komarovsky, Mira. 1940. *The Unemployed Man and His Family.* New York: Octagon Books.

Konner, Melvin. 1991. *Childhood.* Boston: Little Brown.

Koss, Mary P., Christine A. Gidycz, and Nadine Wisniewski. 1987. "The Scope of Rape: Incidence and Prevalence of Sexual Aggression and Victimization in a National Sample of Higher Education Students." *Journal of Consulting and Clinical Psychology* 55: 162–70.

Krymkowski, Daniel H. 1991. "The Process of Status Attainment in Poland, the U.S., and West Germany." *American Sociological Review* 56:46–59.

Krugman, Paul. 1995. "What the Public Doesn't Know Can't Hurt Us." *Washington Monthly* 27(October):8–12.

———. 2003. "Still Blowing Bubbles." *New York Times, National Edition.* June 20:A18.

Kuznets, Simon. 1955. "Economic Growth and Income Inequality." *American Economic Review* 45:1–28.

Laband, David N., and Bernard F. Lentz. 1998. "The Effects of Sexual Harassment on Job Satisfaction, Earnings, and Turnover among Female Lawyers." *Industrial and Labor Relations Review* 51:594–608.

Lareau, Annette. 1989. *Home Advantage: Social Class and Parental Education in Elementary Education.* Philadelphia: Falmer Press.

LeMasters, E. E. 1976. *Blue Collar Aristocrats.* Madison, WI: University of Wisconsin Press.

Lenski, Gerhard. 1984. *Power and Privilege.* Chapel Hill, NC: University of North Carolina Press.

Lenton, Robert L. 1990. "Techniques of Child Discipline and Abuse by Parents." *Canadian Review of Sociology and Anthropology* 27:157–85.

Lester, Will. 2002. "Voter Turnout up from Last Midterm Election." *Gainesville (FL) Sun*, Nov. 7, p. 1.

Levitt, Steven D., and Sudhir Alladi Vankatesh. 2000. "An Economic Analysis of a Drug-selling Gang's Finances." *Quarterly Journal of Economics* 115:755–75.

Levy, Frank, and Richard J. Murnane. 1992. "U.S. Earnings Levels and Earnings Inequality: A Review of Recent Trends and Proposed Explanations." *Journal of Economic Literature* 30:1333–81.

Lewis, Charles. 2000. *The Buying of the President 2000.* New York: Avon Books.

Lewis Mumford Center. 2001. *Ethnic Diversity Grows, Neighborhood Integration Lags Behind.* Albany, NY: Lewis Mumford Center at State University of New York.

Lieberson, Stanley. 1980. *A Piece of the Pie: Blacks and White Immigrants since 1880.* Berkeley, CA: University of California Press.

———. 1992. "Einstein, Renoir, and Greeley: Some Thoughts About Evidence in Sociology." *American Sociological Review* 57:1–15.

Lijphart, Arend. 1997. "Unequal Participation: Democracy's Unresolved Dilemma." *American Political Science Review* 91:1–14.

Liker, Jeffrey K., and Glen H. Elder, Jr. 1983. "Economic Hardship and Marital Relations in the 1930s." *American Sociological Review* 48:343–59.

Lin, Nan. 1999. "Social Networks and Status Attainment." *Annual Review of Sociology* 25:467–87.

Lipset, Seymour Martin. 1963. *The First New Nation: The United States in Historical and Comparative Perspective.* New York: Basic.

———. 1977. "Why No Socialism in the United States?" Pp. 31–149 in S. Bialer and S. Sluzar (eds.), *Sources of Contemporary Radicalism.* New York: Westview Press.

Lloyd, Susan. 1998. "Domestic Violence and Women's Employment." *NU Policy Research: An Electronic Journal of the Institute for Policy Research at Northwestern University.* <http:www.nwu.edu/ipr/publications> 3(Spring):1–10.

Lucas, Samuel R. 2001. "Effectively Maintained Inequality: Educational Transitions, Track Mobility, and Social Background Effects." *American Journal of Sociology* 106:1642–90.

Lueck, Thomas J. 1999. "New York's Cabbies Show How Multi-Colored Racism Can Be." *New York Times,* National Edition. November 7, p. C3.

Luker, Kristin. 1984. *Abortion and the Politics of Motherhood.* Berkeley, CA: University of California Press.

———. 1996. *Dubious Conceptions: The Politics of Teenage Pregnancy.* Cambridge, MA: Harvard University Press.

MacKinnon, Neil J., and Tom Langford. 1994. "The Meaning of Occupational Prestige Scores." *Sociological Quarterly* 35:215–45.

Mahler, Vincent A. 2002. "Exploring the Subnational Dimension of Income Inequality: An Analysis of the Relationship between Inequality and Electoral Turnout in the Developed Countries." *International Studies Quarterly* 46:117–42.

Maier, Pauline. 1997. *American Scripture: Making the Declaration of Independence.* New York: Knopf.

Main, Jackson Turner. 1965. *Social Structure in Revolutionary America.* Princeton, NJ: Princeton University Press.

Mann, Charles C. 2002. "1491." *The Atlantic Monthly.* March:41–53.

Marsiglio, William. 1993. "Adolescent Male's Orientation Toward Paternity and Contraception." *Family Planning Perspectives* 25(January/February):22–31.

Marston, Cicely, and John Cleland. 2003. "Relationships between Contraception and Abortion: A Review of the Evidence." *International Family Planning Perspectives* 29:6–13.

Martinez, Michael D., and David Hill. 1999. "Did Motor Voter Work?" *American Politics Quarterly* 27:296–315.

Marx, Karl. 1843. "Contribution to the Critique of Hegel's Philosophy of Right." Pp. 16–26 in R. C. Tucker (ed.), *The Marx-Engels Reader*, 2nd Edition. New York: W. W. Norton, 1978.

———. 1867. *Capital.* New York: International, 1967.

———. 1875. "Critique of the Gotha Program." Pp. 9–30 in Karl Marx and Friedrich Engels, *Selected Works*, Volume III. Moscow: Progress Publishers, 1956.

Marx, Karl, and Friedrich Engels. 1848. "The Communist Manifesto." Pp. 85–126 in Dirk Struik (ed.), *The Birth of the Communist Manifesto.* New York: International, 1967.

Massey, Douglas S. 1995. "Getting Away with Murder: Segregation and Violent Crime in Urban America." *University of Pennsylvania Law Review* 143:1203–32.

———. 2001. "Residential Segregation and Neighborhood Conditions in U.S. Metropolitan Areas." Pp. 391–434 in Neil Smelser, William Julius Wilson, and Faith Mitchell (eds.), *America Becoming: Racial Trends and Their Consequences,* Volume I. Washington, DC: National Academy Press.

Massey, Douglas S., and Nancy A. Denton. 1993. *American Apartheid: Segregation and the Making of the Underclass.* Cambridge, MA: Harvard University Press.

Massey, Douglas S., and Mary J. Fischer. 2000. "How Segregation Concentrates Poverty." *Ethnic and Racial Studies* 23:670–91.

Maume, David J. 1999. "Occupational Segregation and the Career Mobility of White Men and Women." *Social Forces* 77:1433–1459.

Mayer, Susan E. 1997. *What Money Can't Buy: Family Income and Children's Life Chances.* Cambridge, MA: Harvard University Press.

———. 2001. "How Did the Increase in Economic Inequality between 1970 and 1990 Affect Children's Educational Attainment?" *American Journal of Sociology* 107:1–32.

Mayer, Susan E., and Paul E. Peterson (eds.). 1999. *Earning and Learning: How Schools Matter.* New York: Russell Sage Foundation.

McIntosh, Peggy. 2000. "White Privilege and Male Privilege: A Personal Account of Coming to See Correspondences through Work in Women's Studies." Pp. 30–38 in Anne Minas (ed.), *Gender Basics,* 2nd Ed. Belmont, CA: Wadsworth.

McManus, Patricia A., and Thomas A. DiPrete. 2001. "Losers and Winners: The Financial Consequences of Separation and Divorce for Men." *American Sociological Review* 66:246–68.

McPherson, Michael S., and Morton Owen Schapiro. 1998. *The Student Aid Game: Meeting Need and Rewarding Talent in American Higher Education.* Princeton, NJ: Princeton University Press.

McWhorter, Diane. 2001. *Carry Me Home: Birmingham, Alabama: The Climactic Battle of the Civil Rights Revolution.* New York: Simon & Schuster.

Meeks, Kenneth. 2000. *Driving While Black: Highways, Shopping Malls, Taxicabs, and Sidewalks.* New York: Broadway Books.

Mellon, Andrew W. 1924. *Taxation: The People's Business.* New York: Macmillan.

Mellor, William H. 1996. "No Jobs, No Work: Local Restrictions Block the Exits from Welfare." *New York Times,* National Edition. August 31:A12.

Mencken, F. Carson, and Idee Winfield. 2000. "Job Search and Sex Segregation." *Sex Roles* 31:847–62.

Merrill, L. L., C. E. Newell, J. S. Milner, et al. 1998. "Prevalence of Premilitary Adult Sexual Victimization and Aggression in a Navy Recruit Sample." *Military Medicine* 163:209–12.

Merton, Robert K. 1968. *Social Theory and Social Structure.* New York: Free Press.

Merton, Robert K. 1968a. "Social Structure and Anomie." Pp. 185–214 in R. K. Merton, *Social Theory and Social Structure.* New York: Free Press.

Merton, Robert K., and Alice S. Rossi. 1968. "Contributions to the Theory of Reference Group Behavior." Pp.

279–334 in R. K. Merton, *Social Theory and Social Structure.* New York: Free Press.

Messner, Steven F., and Richard Rosenfeld. 2001. *Crime and the American Dream,* 3rd Edition. Belmont, CA: Wadsworth.

Meyer, D. R., and Maria Cancian. 1996. "The Economic Well-Being of Women and Children Following an Exit from AFDC." *Discussion Paper 1101–96.* Madison, WI: Institute for Research on Poverty.

Mills, C. Wright. 1951. *White Collar.* New York: Oxford University Press.

———. 1959. *The Sociological Imagination.* New York: Oxford University Press.

Minnite, Lori, and David Callahan. 2003. *Securing the Vote: An Analysis of Election Fraud.* New York: Demos—A Network for Ideas and Action.

Mitchell, Alison. 1998. "A New Form of Lobbying Puts Public Face on Private Interest." *New York Times,* National Edition. September 30:1.

Mitchell, Daniel J. B. 1992. "Employers' Welfare Work: A 1913 BLS Report." *Monthly Labor Review* 115(February):52–55.

Mitra, Tapan, and Efe A. Ok. 1996. "Personal Income Taxation and the Principle of Equal Sacrifice Revisited." *International Economic Review* 37:925–48.

Molnar, Beth E., Stephen L. Buka, and Ronald C. Kessler. 2001. "Child Sexual Abuse and Subsequent Psychopathology." *American Journal of Public Health* 91:753–83.

Moore, Barrington. 1966. *The Social Origins of Dictatorship and Democracy.* Boston: Beacon Press.

Morgenson, Gretchen. 2002. "Pipeline to a Point Man: A Friend on Main St., or Wall St.?" *New York Times,* National Edition. November 3, Section 3, p. 1.

Morgan, Philip D. 1998. *Slave Counterpoint: Black Culture in the Eighteenth Century Chesepeake and Lowcountry.* Chapel Hill, NC: University of North Carolina Press.

Morris, Lydia. 1992. "The Social Segregation of the Long-Term Unemployed in Hartlepool." *Sociological Review* 40:344–69.

Mouw, Ted. 2000. "Job Relocation and the Racial Gap in Unemployment in Detroit and Chicago, 1980 to 1990." American Sociological Review 65:730–53.

Murphy, Gregory C., and James A. Athanasou. 1999. "The Effect of Unemployment on Mental Health." *Journal of Occupational and Organizational Psychology* 72:83–85.

Myrdal, Gunnar. 1944. *An American Dilemma.* New York: Harper & Row.

Nakanishi, Don T. 2001. "Political Trends and Electoral Issues of the Asian Pacific American Population." Pp. 170–99 in Neil Smelser, William Julius Wilson, and Faith Mitchell (eds.), *America Becoming: Racial Trends and their Consequences,* Volume I. Washington, DC: National Academy Press.

Nakao, Keiko, and Judith Treas. 1994. "Updating Occupational Prestige and Socioeconomic Scores: How the

New Measures Measure Up." Pp. 1–72 in Peter V. Marsden (ed.), *Sociological Methodology*. Washington, DC: American Sociological Association.

National Advisory Commission on Civil Disorders. 1968. *Report of the National Advisory Commission on Civil Disorders*. New York: Bantam.

National Center for Educational Statistics. 2000. *America's Kindergartners*. Washington, DC: U.S. Government Printing Office.

National Center for Health Statistics. 2001. "Deaths: Leading Causes for 1999." *National Vital Statistics Reports*, 49, Number 11. Hyattsville, MD: Centers for Disease Control.

———. 2002. "Infant Mortality Statistics from the 2000 Period Linked Birth/Infant Death Data Set." *National Vital Statistics Reports*, Vol. 50, Number 12. Hyattsville, MD: Centers for Disease Control.

———. 2002a. *Health United States, 2001*. Washington, DC: U.S. Government Printing Office. Hyattsville, MD: Centers for Disease Control.

———. 2002b. "Births: Final Data for 2000." *National Vital Statistics Reports*, Vol. 50, Number 5.

National Center for Victims of Crime. 1992. *Rape in America: A Report to the Nation*. Washington, DC: National Center for Victims of Crime.

National Coalition for the Homeless. 1999. "The McKinney Act." *NCH Fact Sheet #18*. Washington, DC: National Coalition for the Homeless.

———. 2002. "How Many People Experience Homelessness?" *NCH Fact Sheet #2*. Washington, DC: National Coalition for the Homeless.

———. 2002a. "Who is Homeless?" *NCH Fact Sheet #3*. Washington, DC: National Coalition for the Homeless.

National Institute of Justice. 2000. *Full Report of the Prevalence, Incidence, and Consequences of Violence Against Women: Findings from the National Violence Against Women Survey*. Washington, DC: U.S. Government Printing Office.

———. 2000a. *The Sexual Victimization of College Women*. Washington, DC: U.S. Government Printing Office.

———. 2000b. *Extent, Nature, and Consequences of Intimate Partner Violence*. Washington, DC: U.S. Government Printing Office.

Neibuhr, Gustave. 1998. "Southern Baptists Declare Wife Should 'Submit' to Her Husband." *New York Times*, National Edition. June 10, p. 1.

Neumark, David M., Roy J. Bank, and Kyle D. Van Nort. 1996. "Sex Discrimination in Restaurant Hiring: An Audit Study." *Quarterly Journal of Economics* 111: 915–41.

Nielsen, François, and Arthur S. Alderson. 1997. "The Kuznets Curve and the Great U-Turn: Income Inequality in U.S. Counties, 1970 to 1990." *American Sociological Review* 62:12–33.

Niemi, Richard. 1989. *Trends in Public Opinion: A Compendium of Survey Data*. New York: Greenwood Press.

Nordheimer, Jon. 1996. "One Day's Death Toll on the Job." *New York Times*, National Edition. December 22:31.

Oakes, Jeannie. 1985. *Keeping Track: How Schools Structure Inequality*. New Haven, CT: Yale University Press.

Office for National Statistics. 2002. *Social Trends 32*. London: The Stationary Office.

———. 2002a. *Labour Force Survey* (August). London: The Stationary Office.

Okun, Arthur M. 1975. *Equality and Efficiency: The Big Tradeoff*. Washington, DC: Brookings Institution.

O'Neill, William L. 1972. *Women at Work, Including 'The Long Day: The Story of a New York Working Girl, by Dorothy Richardson.'* Chicago: Quadrangle Books.

Ondich, Jan, Stephen Ross, and John Yinger. 2000. "Now You See It, Now You Don't. Why Do Real Estate Agents Withhold Available Houses from Black Customers?" Syracuse, NY: Center for Policy Research, Syracuse University.

———. 2000a. "How Common is Housing Discrimination? Improving Traditional Measures." *Journal of Urban Economics* 47:470–500.

Organization for Economic Cooperation & Development. 2002. *Employment Prospects*. Paris: OECD.

Ornati, Oscar. 1966. *Poverty Amid Affluence*. New York: Twentieth Century Fund.

Orr, Tamra B. 2000. "Avoiding Job-Related Injuries." *Current Health* 26:28–33.

Orshansky, Mollie. 1965. "Counting the Poor: Another Look at the Poverty Profile." *Social Security Bulletin* 28:3–29.

Oshinsky, David M. 1996. *Worse Than Slavery: Parchman Farm and the Ordeal of Jim Crow Justice*. New York: Free Press.

Ota, Alan K. 2002. "Top-Tier Lobbyists: Ex-Members' Special Access Becomes an Issue." *CQ Weekly* 60 (January 16):455–62.

Pacek, Alexander, and Benjamin Radcliff. 1995. "Turnout and the Vote for Left-of-Center Parties: A Cross-National Analysis." *British Journal of Political Science* 25:137–43.

Padavic, Irene, and Barbara Reskin. 2002. *Women and Men at Work*, 2nd edition. Thousand Oaks, CA: Pine Forge Press.

Page, Benjamin I. 1983. *Who Gets What from Government*. Berkeley, CA: University of California Press.

Palmer, Phyllis M. 1989. *Domesticity and Dirt: Housewives and Domestic Servants in the United States, 1920–1945*. Philadelphia: Temple University Press.

Parsons, Talcott. 1951. *The Social System*. New York: Free Press.

———. 1954. "A Revised Analytical Approach to the Theory of Social Stratification." Pp. 386–439 in T. Parsons, *Essays in Sociological Theory*, Revised Edition. New York: Free Press.

Passell, Peter. 1998. "Benefits Dwindle Along with Wages for the Unskilled." *New York Times*, National Edition. June 14:A-1.

Patterson, James T. 2000. *America's Struggle Against Poverty in the Twentieth Century.* Cambridge, MA: Harvard University Press.

Patterson, Orlando. 1997. *The Ordeal of Integration: Progress and Resentment in America's "Racial" Crisis."* New York: Civitas.

Perrin, Emily. 1904. "On the Contingency between Occupation in the Case of Fathers and Sons." *Biometrika* 3:467–69.

Persell, Caroline Hodges, and Peter W. Cookson, Jr. 1985. "Chartering and Bartering: Elite Education and Social Reproduction." *Social Problems* 33:114–29.

Personick, Martin E., and Laura A. Harthun. 1992. "Job Safety and Health in Soft Drink Manufacturing." *Monthly Labor Review* 15(April):12–18.

Pessen, Edward. 1971. "The Egalitarian Myth and American Social Reality: Wealth, Mobility, and Equality in the 'Era of the Common Man.'" *American Historical Review* 76:989–1034.

———. 1973. *Riches, Class, and Power before the Civil War.* Lexington, MA: D.C. Heath & Co.

Peterson, Richard A. 1996. "A Re-Evaluation of the Economic Consequences of Divorce." *American Sociological Review* 61:528–66.

Phillips, Kevin. 2002. *Wealth and Democracy.* New York: Broadway Books.

Pillay, Anthony L., and Susan Schoubben-Hesk. 2001. "Depression, Anxiety, and Hopelessness in Sexually Abused Adolescent Girls." *Psychological Reports* 88:727–30.

Piven, Frances Fox, and Richard A. Cloward. 1971. *Regulating the Poor.* New York: Vintage Books.

———. 1977. *Poor People's Movements.* New York: Pantheon.

———. 1988. *Why Americans Don't Vote.* New York: Pantheon.

Plotnick, Robert D., Eugene Smolensky, Eirik Evenhouse, et al. 1998. "Inequality and Poverty in the United States: The Twentieth-Century Record." *Focus* 19:7–14.

Portes, Alejandro. 1998. "Social Capital: Its Origins and Applications in Modern Sociology." *Annual Review of Sociology* 24:1–24.

Public Campaign. 2002. "The Evil of Access." *Ouch! A Regular Bulletin on How Money in Politics Hurts You.* #106(October 18): www.publiccampaign.org

———. 2003. "State of the Union: Congress Meets Wall Street." www.publiccampaign.org

Reagan, Leslie. 1997. *When Abortion Was a Crime: Women, Medicine and the Law in the United States.* Berkeley, CA: University of California Press.

Reardon, Jack. 1993. "Injuries and Illnesses among Bituminous and Lignite Coal Miners." *Monthly Labor Review* 115(October):49–55.

Reed, James. 1978. *From Private Vice to Public Virtue: The Birth Control Movement and American Society Since 1830.* New York: Basic.

Reuter, Peter, Robert MacCoun, and Patrick Murphy. 1990. *Money from Crime: A Study of the Economics of Drug Dealing in Washington, D.C.* Santa Monica, CA: Rand Corporation.

Revell, Janice. 2003. "CEO Pensions: The Latest Way to Hide Millions." *Fortune,* April 28: 68–70.

Reynolds, Morgan, and Eugene Smolensky. 1977. *Public Expenditures, Taxes, and the Distribution of Income: The United States, 1950, 1961, 1970.* New York: Academic Press.

Rhoden, William C. 2002. "Oregon Likes Visibility on Broadway." *New York Times,* National Edition. July 25, p. C10.

Ritakallio, Veli-Matti. 2001. "Trends in Poverty and Income Inequality in Cross-National Comparison." Luxembourg Income Study Working Paper No. 272. http://lisweb.ceps.lu/publications/wpapers.htm

Ritter, Kathleen, and Lowell L. Hargens. 1975. "Occupational Positions and Class Identification: A Test of the Asymmetry Hypothesis." *American Journal of Sociology* 80:934–48.

Rodriguez, Ned, Hendrika V. Kemp, Susan W. Ryan, et al. 1997. "Posttraumatic Stress Disorder in Adult Female Survivors of Childhood Sexual Abuse." *Journal of Consulting and Clinical Psychology* 65:53–60.

Rosenstone, Steven, and John Mark Hansen. 1993. *Mobilization, Participation, and Democracy in America.* New York: Macmillan.

Rosenthal, Robert., and Lenore Jacobson. 1968. *Pygmalion in the Classroom: Teacher Expectations and Pupils' Intellectual Development.* New York: Holt, Rinehart, and Winston.

Rothenberg, Paula S. 2002. *White Privilege.* New York: Worth Publishers.

Rothman, Ellen K. 1984. *Hands and Hearts: A History of Courtship in America.* New York: Basic Books.

Rubin, Lillian. 1994. *Families on the Fault Line.* New York: HarperCollins.

Ruggles, Patricia. 1990. *Drawing the Line: Alternative Poverty Measures and Their Implications for Public Policy.* Washington, DC: Urban Institute Press.

Rusk, Jerrold. 1970. "The Effect of the Australian Ballet Reform on Split Ticket Voting: 1876–1908." *American Political Science Review* 72:22–45.

———. 2001. *A Statistical History of the American Electorate.* Washington, DC: CQ Press.

Russell, Diane E. H., and Rebecca M. Bolen. 2000. *The Epidemic of Rape and Child Sexual Abuse in the United States.* Thousand Oaks, CA: Sage.

Ryscavage, Paul. 1999. *Income Inequality in America: An Analysis of Trends.* New York: M. E. Sharpe.

Rytina, Nancy F., and Suzanne M. Bianchi. 1984. "Occupational Reclassification and Distribution by Gender." *Monthly Labor Review* 107(March):11–17.

Rytina, Steven. 2000. "Is Occupational Mobility Declining in the U.S.?" *Social Forces* 78:1227–1276.

Sagan, Carl. 1984. "Nuclear War and Climatic Catastrophe." *Foreign Affairs* 62:257–92.

Sander, William. 1992. "Unemployment and Marital Status in Great Britain." *Social Biology* 39:299–305.

Sanderson, Warren. 1979. "Quantitative Aspects of Marriage, Fertility, and Family Limitation in Nineteenth-Century America." *Demography* 16:339–58.

Sassen-Koob, Saskia. 1989. "New York's Informal Economy." Pp. 60–77 in A. Portes, M. Castells, and L. A. Benton (eds.), T*he Informal Economy: Studies in Advanced and Less Advanced Countries.* Baltimore, MD: Johns Hopkins Press.

Saunders, Benjamin E., Dean G. Kilpatrick, Rochelle F. Hanson, et al. 1999. "Prevalence, Case Characteristics, and Long-Term Psychological Correlates of Child Rape among Women: A National Survey." *Child Maltreatment* 4:187–200.

Sawhill, Isabel V. 2000. "Opportunity in the United States: Myth or Reality?" Pp. 22–35 in N. Birdsall and C. Graham (eds.), *New Markets, New Opportunities?: Economic and Social Mobility in a Changing World.* Washington, DC: Brookings Institution.

Sawinski, Zbigniew, and Henryk Domanski. 1991. "Stability of Prestige Hierarchies in the Face of Social Changes: Poland, 1958–1987." *International Sociology* 6:227–42.

Sayer, Liana C., and Susanne M. Bianchi. 2000. "Women's Economic Independence and the Probability of Divorce." *Journal of Family Issues* 21:906–43.

Scofea, Laura A. 1994. "The Development and Growth of Employer-Provided Health Insurance." *Monthly Labor Review* 117(March):3–10.

Scott, John. 2001. *Power.* New York: Cambridge University Press.

Searles, Patricia, and Ronald J. Berger (eds.). 1995. *Rape and Society.* Boulder, CO: Westview Press.

Sears, David O., Collete van Laar, Mary Carrillo, et al. 1997. "Is It Really Racism? The Origins of White Americans' Opposition to Race-Targeted Policies." *Public Opinion Quarterly* 61:16–53.

Sewell, William H., Archibald O. Haller, and George W. Ohlendorf. 1970. "The Educational and Early Occupational Attainment Process: Replication and Revisions." *American Sociological Review* 35:1014–27.

Sewell, William H., and Vimal P. Shah. 1968a. "Social Class, Parental Encouragement, and Educational Aspirations." *American Journal of Sociology* 73:559–72.

———. 1968b. "Parent's Education and Children's Educational Aspirations and Achievements." *American Sociological Review* 35:1014–27.

Shakespeare, William. 1989. *Romeo and Juliet.* London: Metheun Drama.

———. 1991. *Measure for Measure.* New York: Cambridge University Press.

Shaw, George Bernard. 1957. *Pygmalion.* New York: Penguin.

Shipler, David. 1993. "Jefferson Is America—And America Is Jefferson." *New York Times*, National Edition. April 12, p. A12.

Sibley, Elbridge. 1942. "Some Demographic Clues to Stratification." *American Sociological Review* 7:315–25.

Silverman, Jay G., Anita Raj, Lorelie A. Mucci, et al. 2001. "Dating Violence Against Adolescent Girls and Associated Substance Use, Unhealthy Weight Control, Sexual Risk Behavior, Pregnancy, and Suicidality." *Journal of the American Medical Association* 286: 572–79.

Simmel, Georg. 1908. "Conflict." Pp. 1–20 in G. Simmel, *Conflict and the Web of Group Affiliations.* New York: Free Press, 1954.

Simon, Scott. 2002. *Jackie Robinson and the Integration of Baseball.* New York: John Wiley & Sons.

Sixma, H., and Ultee, W. C. 1984. "An Occupational Scale for the Netherlands in the Eighties." Pp. 101–15 in B. F. Bakker (ed.), *Social Stratification and Mobility in the Netherlands.* Amsterdam: SISWO.

Skellington, Richard. 1992. *"Race" in Britain Today.* London: Sage.

Slemrod, Joel. 2000. "The Economics of Taxing the Rich." Pp. 3–28 in J. Slemrod (ed.), *Does Atlas Shrug? The Economic Consequences of Taxing the Rich.* New York: Russell Sage Foundation.

Slemrod, Joel, and Jon Bakija. 2000. *Taxing Ourselves: A Citizen's Guide to the Great Debate over Tax Reform.* Cambridge, MA: MIT Press.

Smith, J. Owens. 1987. *The Politics of Racial Inequality.* New York: Greenwood Press.

Smock, Pamela J., Wendy D. Manning, and Sanjiv Gupta. 1999. "The Effect of Marriage and Divorce on Women's Economic Well-Being." *American Sociological Review* 64:794–812.

Sniderman, Paul M., and Edward G. Carmines. 1997. *Reaching Beyond Race.* Cambridge, MA: Harvard University Press.

Sobel, Michael E., Mark P. Becker, and Susan M. Minick. 1998. "Origins, Destinations, and Association in Occupational Mobility." *American Journal of Sociology* 104:687–721.

Social Security Administration. 2003. "Tax Rate Table." www.ssa.gov/oact/cola/taxrates.html

———. 2003a. "Annual Statistical Supplement." *Social Security Bulletin* 64:151–205.

Solon, Gary. 1992. "Intergenerational Income Mobility in the United States." *American Economic Review* 82: 393–408.

Soltow, Lee. 1975. "The Wealth, Income, and Social Class of Men in Large Northern Cities in1860." Pp. 233–76 in James D. Smith (ed.), *The Personal Distribution of Income and Wealth.* New York: National Bureau of Economic Research.

Sorokin, Pitirim. 1927. *Social and Cultural Mobility.* New York: Free Press, 1959.

Special Advisor to the Board of Police Commissioners on the Civil Disorders in Los Angeles. 1994. *City in Crisis.* Los Angeles: Special Advisor to the Board of Police Commissioners.

Stanley, Thomas J., and William D. Danko. 1996. *The Millionaire New Door.* New York: Pocket Books.

Staples, Brent. 2003. "Just Walk on By: A Black Man Ponders His Power to Alter Public Space." Pp. 130–33 in Donald M. McQuade and Robert Atwan (eds.), *The Writer's Presence*. Boston: St. Martin's Press.

Starr, Paul. 1982. *The Transformation of American Medicine*. New York: Basic.

Statistics Sweden. 2001. *Statistical Yearbook of Sweden, 2001*. Stockholm: Publications Services.

Stock, Jacqueline L. 1997. "Adolescent Pregnancy and Sexual Risk-Taking Among Sexually Abused Girls." *Family Planning Perspectives* 29:200–203.

Strathlee, S. A., R. Ikeda, N. Shah, et al. 2001. "Childhood Sexual Abuse Independently Predicts Early Initiation of Injection Drug Use." *American Journal of Epidemiology* 153:179–90.

Sullivan, Harry Stack. 1940. *Conceptions of Modern Psychiatry*. Washington, DC: William A. White Foundation.

Swain, Carol M. 2001. "Affirmative Action: Legislative History, Judicial Interpretations, Public Consensus." Pp. 318–47 in Neil Smelser, William Julius Wilson, and Faith Mitchell (eds.), *America Becoming: Racial Trends and their Consequences*, Volume I. Washington, DC: National Academy Press.

Sygnatur, Eric F. 1998. "Logging Is Perilous Work." *Compensation and Working Conditions* 4(Winter):3–7.

Takaki, Ronald. 1989. *Strangers from a Different Shore: A History of Asian Americans*. New York: Penguin Books.

Tax Policy Center. 2003. "Historical Highest Marginal Income Tax Rates." www.taxpolicycenter.org

———. 2003a. "Tax Brackets: 2002 Taxable Income." www.taxpolicycenter.org

Taylor, A. J., G. McGwin, F. Valent, et al. 2002. "Fatal Occupational Electrocutions in the United States." *Injury Prevention* 8:306–13.

Teixeira, Ruy A. 1992. *The Disappearing American Voter*. Washington, DC: Brookings Institution.

Television Bureau of Advertising. 1991. *Trends in Viewing*. New York: Television Bureau of Advertising.

Thernstrom, Stephan, and Abigail Thernstrom. 1997. *America in Black and White: One Nation Indivisible*. New York: Simon & Schuster.

Thompson, Dennis F. 1970. *The Democratic Citizen: Social Science and Democratic Theory in the Twentieth Century*. London: Cambridge University Press.

Thompson, Starley, and Stephen H. Schneider. 1986. "Nuclear Winter Reappraised." *Foreign Affairs* 64:981–1005.

Thornton, Russell. 1987. *American Indian Holocaust and Survival: A Population History since 1492*. Norman, OK: University of Oklahoma Press.

———. 2001. "Trends among American Indians in the United States." Pp. 135–69 in Neil Smelser, William Julius Wilson, and Faith Mitchell (eds.), *America Becoming: Racial Trends and their Consequences*, Volume I. Washington DC: National Academy Press.

Thurow, Lester C. 1975. *Generating Inequality: Mechanisms of Distribution in the U.S. Economy*. New York: Basic Books.

Tobias, Sarah, and David Callahan. 2002. *Expanding the Vote: The Practice and Promise of Election Day Registration*. New York: Demos—A Network for Ideas and Action.

Tocqueville, Alexis de. 1835. *Democracy in America*. New York: New American Library, 1954.

Treiman, Donald J. 1977. *Occupational Prestige in Comparative Perspective*. New York: Academic Press.

———. 2000. "Occupations, Stratification, and Mobility." Pp. 297–313 in Judith R. Blau (ed.), *The Blackwell Companion of Sociology*. Malden, MA: Blackwell Publishers.

Treiman, Donald J., and Harry B. G. Ganzeboom. 1990. "Cross-National Status Attainment Research." *Research in Social Stratification and Mobility* 9:105–130.

Treiman, Donald J., and Kam-Bor Yip. 1989. "Educational and Occupational Attainment in 21 Countries." Pp. 373–94 in M. L. Kohn (ed.), *Cross-National Research in Sociology*. Newbury Park, CA: Sage.

Turner, Frederick Jackson. 1920. *The Significance of the Frontier in American History*. New York: Henry Holt.

Turner, Jonathan H. 1984. *Societal Stratification*. New York: Columbia University Press.

———. 2003. *The Structure of Sociological Theory*, 7th Edition. Belmont, CA: Wadsworth.

Turner, Jonathan H., Leonard Beeghley, and Charles Powers. 2002. *The Emergence of Sociological Theory*, 5th Edition. Belmont, CA: Wadsworth.

Turner, Jonathan H., and David W. Musick. 1985. *American Dilemmas*. New York: Columbia University Press.

United States Bureau of the Census. 1974. *Statistical Abstract of the United States*. Washington, DC: U.S. Government Printing Office.

———. 1975. *Historical Statistics of the United States: Colonial Times to 1970*. Washington, DC: U.S. Government Printing Office.

———. 2000. "Child Support for Custodial Mothers and Fathers." *Current Population Reports*, p60-212. Washington, DC: U.S. Government Printing Office.

———. 2001. *Statistical Abstract of the United States*. Washington, DC: U.S. Government Printing Office.

———. 2001a. "Money Income in the United States: 2000." *Current Population Reports*, p60-213. Washington, DC: U.S. Government Printing Office.

———. 2001b. "The Asian and Pacific Islander Population in the United States." *Current Population Reports*, p20-529. Washington, DC: U.S. Government Printing Office.

———. 2001c. "The Hispanic Population in the United States." *Current Population Reports*, p20-535. Washington, DC: U.S. Government Printing Office.

———. 2001d. "The 65 Years and Over Population: 2000."

*Census 2000 Brief.* Washington, DC: U.S. Government Printing Office.

———. 2001e. "The Hispanic Population in the United States." *Current Population Reports*, p20-535. Washington, DC: U.S. Government Printing Office.

———. 2002. "Money Income in the United States: 2001." *Current Population Reports,* p60-218. Washington, DC: U.S. Government Printing Office.

———. 2002a. "Annual Demographic Survey, March Supplement." http://ferret.bls.census/macro/032002/perinc

———. 2002b. "Voting and Registration in the Election of November 2000." *Current Population Reports*, p20-542. Washington, DC: U.S. Government Printing Office.

———. 2002c. *Statistical Abstract of the United States.* Washington, DC: U.S. Government Printing Office.

———. 2002d. "The Asian Population: 2000." *Census 2000 Brief.* Washington, DC: U.S. Government Printing Office.

———. 2002e. *American Housing Survey: 2001.* Washington, DC: U.S. Government Printing Office.

———. 2002f. "Poverty in the United States, 2001." *Current Population Reports*, p60-219. Washington, DC: U.S. Government Printing Office.

United States Bureau of Labor Statistics. 2002. http://stats.bls.gov/cps

United States Conference of Mayors. 2002. *A Status Report on Hunger and Homelessness in America's Cities: 2002.* Washington, DC: United States Conference of Mayors.

United States Department of Agriculture. 1998. *Agriculture Fact Book.* Washington, DC: U.S. Government Printing Office.

———. 2002. "Household Food Security in the United States, 2001." *Food Assistance and Nutrition Report,* Number 29. Washington, DC: U.S. Government Printing Office.

———. 2003. "Food Stamp Program." www.fns.usda.gov.fsp

———. 2003a. *Characteristics of Food Stamp Households: Fiscal Year 2001.* Washington, DC: U.S. Government Printing Office.

United States Department of Health and Human Services. 1998. "Change in Welfare Caseloads." www.acf.dhhs.gov

———. 2002. *Child Maltreatment 2000.* Washington, DC: U.S. Government Printing Office.

———. 2003. *Temporary Assistance for Needy Families Program,* Fifth Annual Report to Congress. Washington, DC: U.S. Government Printing Office.

United States Department of Labor. 1997. *Employee Benefits in Small Private Establishments, 1994.* Bulletin 2475. Washington, DC: U.S. Government Printing Office.

———. 1998. *Employee Benefits in Medium and Large Private Establishments, 1995,* Bulletin 2496. Washington, DC: U.S. Government Printing Office.

———. 2002. *Employment & Earnings* 49(January). Washington, DC: U.S. Government Printing Office.

———. 2003. *National Compensation Survey: Employee Benefits in Private Industry in the United States, 2000.* Washington, DC: U.S. Government Printing Office.

Useem, Jerry. 2003. "Have They No Shame? Their Performance Stank Last Year, Yet Most CEOs Got Paid More Than Ever. Here's How They're Getting Away with It." *Fortune,* April 28:56–64.

Valian, Virginia. 1998. *Why So Slow? The Advancement of Women.* Cambridge, MA: MIT Press.

van den Berg, Axel. 1993. "Creeping Embourgeoisement? Some Comments on the Marxist Discovery of the New Middle Class." *Research in Stratification* 12:295–328.

van der Lippe, Tanja, and Liset van Dijk. 2002. "Comparative Research on Women's Employment." *Annual Review of Sociology*, Vol. 28. New York: Annual Reviews.

Van Natta, Don, and Richard A. Oppel. 2002. "Parties Create Ways to Avoid Soft Money Ban." *New York Times,* National Edition, p. 1.

Van Velsor, Ellen, and Leonard Beeghley. 1979. "Class Identification Among Employed Married Women." *Journal of Marriage and the Family* 41:771–79.

Vanneman, Reeve, and Fred C. Pampel. 1977. "The American Perception of Class and Status." *American Sociological Review* 42:422–37.

Veblen, Thorstein. 1899. *The Theory of the Leisure Class.* New York: Penguin Books, 1979.

Verba, Sidney. 1996. "The Citizen as Respondent: Sample Surveys and American Democracy." *American Political Science Review* 90:1–7.

Vernon, Amelia Wallace. 1993. *African Americans at Mars Bluff, South Carolina.* Baton Rouge, LA: Louisiana State University Press.

Voslenski, Michael. 1985. *Nomenklatura: The Soviet Ruling Class.* New York: Doubleday.

Wagner, Ellen J. 1992. *Sexual Harassment in the Workplace.* New York: AMACOM.

Wallace, James. 1993. *Hard Drive: Bill Gates and the Making of the Microsoft Empire.* New York: HarperCollins.

Wallace, Michael. 1997. "Revisiting Broom and Cushing's 'Modest Test of an Immodest Theory,'" In *Research in Social Stratification and Mobility* 17:239–54.

Wallerstein, Immanuel. 1974. *The Modern World System.* New York: Academic Press.

Warren, John Robert, Robert M. Hauser, and Jennifer T. Sheridan. 2002. "Occupational Stratification across the Life Course: Evidence from the Wisconsin Longitudinal Study." *American Sociological Review* 67:432–55.

Weber, Max. 1904. " 'Objectivity' in Social Science and Social Policy." Pp. 50–112 in Weber, *The Methodology of the Social Sciences*. New York: Free Press, 1949.

———. 1905. *The Protestant Ethic and the Spirit of Capitalism*. New York: Scribners, 1958.

———. 1913. *Religion of China*. New York: Free Press, 1951.

———. 1917. *Religion of India*. New York: Free Press, 1952.

———. 1920. *Economy and Society*. Totowa, NJ: Bedminster Press, 1968.

———. 1923. *General Economic History*. New York: Collier Books, 1961.

Webster, Timothy. 1999. "Work-Related Injuries, Illnesses, and Fatalities in Manufacturing and Construction." *Compensation and Working Conditions* 5(Fall):34–38.

Weedon, Kim A. 1998. "Revisiting Occupational Sex Segregation in the United States, 1910–1990: Results from a Log-Linear Approach." *Demography* 35:475–87.

Weisbrot, Mark. 1998. *Welfare Reform: The Jobs Aren't There*. Washington, DC: Preamble Center for Public Policy.

Welsh, Sandy. 1999. "Gender and Sexual Harassment." *Annual Review of Sociology*, Vol. 25. New York: Annual Reviews.

Westoff, Charles F. 1988. "Contraceptive Paths Toward a Reduction of Unintended Pregnancy and Abortion." *Family Planning Perspectives* 20:4–13.

Whelpton, Pascal K. 1928. "Industrial Development and Population Growth." *Social Forces* 6:458–67.

Willer, David, and Murray Webster. 1970. "Theoretical Concepts and Observables." *American Sociological Review* 35:748–56.

Williams, Bruce B. 1987. *Black Workers in an Industrial Suburb: The Struggle Against Discrimination*. New Brunswick, NJ: Rutgers University Press.

Williams, Robin. 1977. *Mutual Accommodation: Ethnic Conflict and Cooperation*. Minneapolis, MN: University of Minnesota Press.

Williamson, Jeffrey G., and Peter H. Lindert. 1980. *American Inequality: A Macroeconomic History*. New York: Academic Press.

Wilson, Fiona, and Paul Thompson. 2001. "Sexual Harassment as an Exercise of Power." *Gender, Work, and Organization* 8:61–83.

Wilson, George. 1997. "Pathways to Power: Racial Differences in the Determinants of Job Authority." *Social Problems* 44:38–54.

Wilson, George, Ian Sakura-Lemessy, Jonathan P. West. 1999. "Reaching the Top: Racial Differences in Mobility Paths to Upper-Tier Occupations." *Work and Occupations* 26:165–86.

Wilson, William J. 1996. *When Work Disappears: The World of the New Urban Poor*. New York: Knopf.

Winkler, Anne E. 1998. "Earnings of Husbands and Wives in Dual-Earner Families." *Monthly Labor Review* 121(April):42–48.

Winship, Christopher. 1992. "Race, Poverty, and 'The American Occupational Structure.'" *Contemporary Sociology* 21:639–43.

Wirth, Linda. 2001. *Breaking Through the Glass Ceiling: Women in Management*. Geneva: International Labour Office.

Wolfe, Alan. 1998. "Climbing the Mountain: The Second Volume of Taylor Branch's Study of Martin Luther King Jr. Runs from the March on Washington to Selma." *New York Times Book Review* January 18:12.

Wolfe, Jessica, Erica Sharkansky, Jennifer P. Read, et al. 1998. "Sexual Harassment and Assault as Predictors of PTSD Symptomatology among U.S. Female Persian Gulf War Military Personnel." *Journal of Interpersonal Violence* 13:40–58.

Wolff, Edward N. 2002. *Top Heavy: The Increasing Inequality of Wealth in American and What Can Be Done about It*. New York: The New Press.

Wolfinger, Raymond E., and Jonathan Hoffman. 2001. "Registering and Voting with Motor Voter." *PS: Political Science and Politics* 34:85–93.

Woodward, C. Vann. 1966. *The Strange Career of Jim Crow*. New York: Oxford University Press.

Wordes, Madeline, and Michell Nunez. 2002. *Our Vulnerable Teenagers: Their Victimization, Its Consequences, and Directions for Prevention and Intervention*. Washington, DC: National Center for Victims of Crime.

World Bank. 2003. *World Development Report*. New York: World Bank.

Wright, Erik Olin. 1997. *Classes*. New York: Verso.

Xu, Wu, and Ann Leffler. 1992. "Gender and Race Effects on Occupational Prestige, Segregation, and Earnings." *Gender & Society* 6:376–392.

Yamaguchi, Kazuo, and Yantao Wang. 2002. "Class Identification of Married Employed Women and Men in America." *American Journal of Sociology* 108:440–77.

Yaqub, Reshma Memon. 1999. "Perking Right Along: The Trends in Benefits and Goodies." *Worth Guide to Benefits, Compensation, and Perks* 8(Winter):14–21.

Yinger, John. 1997. "Cash in Your Face: The Cost of Racial and Ethnic Discrimination in Housing." *Journal of Urban Economics* 42:339–65.

Zax, Jeffrey S., and John F. Kain. 1996. "Moving to the Suburbs: Do Relocating Companies Leave Their Black Employees Behind?" *Journal of Labor Economics* 14:472–504.

Zelizer, Viviana A. 1994. *The Social Meaning of Money*. New York: Basic.

Zipp, John F., and Eric Plutzer. 2000. "From Housework to Paid Work: The Implications of Women's Labor Force Experiences on Class Identity." *Social Science Quarterly* 81:538–54.

Zweig, Michael. 2000. *The Working Class Majority: America's Best Kept Secret*. Ithaca, NY: ILR Press.

# *Index*